# THE
# COMPLETE
# ENCYCLOPEDIA
# OF
# STITCHERY

# The Complete Encyclopedia of Stitchery

MILDRED GRAVES RYAN

Illustrated by Marta Cone

Doubleday & Company, Inc.
Garden City, New York

Library of Congress Cataloging in Publication Data

Ryan, Mildred Graves, 1905–
The complete encyclopedia of stitchery.

Bibliography: p.
1. Needlework. I. Title
TT760.R92     746.4
ISBN: 0-385-12385-x
Library of Congress Catalog Card Number 77–16942

# Contents

Assissi · Bargello · Beadwork · Berlin Work · Black Work · Broderie Anglaise · Candlewicking · Canvas Work · Card Embroidery · Composite Stitches · Crewel Work · Cutwork · Drawn-fabric Work · Drawn-thread Work · Florentine Work · Gros Point · Hardanger · Hedebo · Huck Embroidery · Insertion Stitches · Laid Work · Machine Embroidery · Metal Thread Work · Monogramming · Needlepoint · Needleweaving · Net Embroidery · Openwork · Petit Point · Pulled Thread Work · Quick Point · Raised Work · Reticella Work · Richelieu Work · Rick Rack Embroidery · Sampler · Shadow Work · Smocking · Stump Work · Swedish Weaving · Tambour Work · Teneriffe Embroidery · Tufted Wool Embroidery · Tufting · Turkey Work · White Work · Wool Work

## Part III · Knitting

Aran Knitting · Argyle Pattern · Design Knitting · Duplicate Stitch · Fair Isle Knitting · Ribbon Knitting · Scandinavian Knitting · Shetland Knitting · Slip Stitch Patterns · Twist Stitch Patterns · Yarn-over Stitch Patterns

## Part IV · Macramé

## Part V · Rugmaking

## Part VI · Sewing

Appliqué · Patchwork · Quilting—Hand and Machine

## Part VII · Tatting

# Preface

This book is about stitches: what they are, how they are made, where they are used. And it was written for you. I wanted you to enjoy creating an attractive piece of needlework. Perhaps you, like me, have at times found directions perplexing, terms confusing. To avoid such experiences, this material has been compiled with special attention given to ease—information easy to find, meanings easy to understand, directions easy to follow.

There are seven sections in the book—crocheting, embroidering, knitting, macramé, rugmaking, sewing, and tatting. Hundreds of stitches are described, each one playing a part in the production of some type of needlework. In each segment, directions are written in a simple, informal manner. If you are a beginner, there are step-by-step descriptions in pictures and words of the basic processes by which a lovely piece of handwork can be produced; and if you are a more experienced needleperson, there are suggestions for perfecting your skill and ideas for more complicated and artistic work.

To make the book easier to use, each section has been alphabetized. No longer will you have to thumb through an index in a vain effort to find a bit of information. Instead, you can quickly turn to the appropriate page to locate the item you need.

Many drawings have been used to clarify directions. Rather than crowding several procedures into a single drawing, each step is shown separately in progressive fashion. This speeds the work and, in some instances, may allow you to proceed without reading the directions. Also, cross reference is used for some names and terms, making them quicker to locate. For instance, stitches and stitch patterns may be known by several names, some of them unfamiliar; so different names are listed.

Another feature I hope you will like is the elimination of abbreviations in the directions for stitches and stitch patterns. Some abbreviations are easy to remember; others, difficult. Perhaps you have found yourself flipping pages back and forth as you refer to the general list of abbreviations just to be sure that you are doing the process correctly. This is annoying and time-consuming. When the complete word is used, all the instructions you need are found in one place.

In the selection of the material for this book, thought was given to your abilities, activities, and interests. I wanted to offer you a variety of stitches that might be used in each type of handwork. Old favorites are shown, as well as the more contemporary. Fashions in needlework change just as in clothing. It is wise to remember the old but at the same time be attuned to the modern adaptations.

As in all endeavors of this type, one needs the help and encouragement of friends and associates. I am especially indebted to Lonnie Darling and Marcia McEnroe, who made hundreds of the samples used by the artist as a guide for the illustrations. And to the artist herself, Marta Cone, whose interpretation of the needlework is so beautifully done. I am also indebted to the many people who supplied information on various types of needlecraft and to those companies and individuals who provided materials, especially June King of Coats & Clark, Incorporated, and Ellen Yard of William E. Wright Company.

M.G.R.

# THE
# COMPLETE
# ENCYCLOPEDIA
# OF
# STITCHERY

# Part I

# Crocheting

One usually thinks of crocheting as being an old form of needlecraft, although no one seems to know for sure when it began. Apparently its history does not date as far back as that of embroidery and knitting. Historians do mention weaving with one stick, and this might have been an early type of crocheting. There is, however, one thing that is known. The word crochet is derived from the French word crochet, meaning "hook."

During the sixteenth century, a lacy type of crocheting was popular. In fact, at one time crocheting seemed to mean working with a very fine white thread to create delicate, openwork designs. It was even considered a form of American lace.

Since those early days, the popularity of crocheting has fluctuated, but it always seems to survive periods of little interest. Today new threads and yarns, coupled with ingenuity, make it possible to crochet attractive fashions as well as practical household articles. Everything from smart separates to colorful pot holders are feasible crochet projects.

The information that follows treats the basics of crocheting. It can be referred to when a problem develops or when inspiration is needed for crocheting pleasure. Unless otherwise mentioned, the directions are written for the right-handed person. The material is divided into 5 parts, with each arranged in alphabetical order for easy reference. The titles shown here indicate the contents of each section.

1

## ABBREVIATIONS AND TERMS

Crocheting has a language of its own. Directions are written in a series of abbreviations, and these can prove troublesome for the novice. Because of this, one of the first problems to solve when crocheting an article is interpreting the abbreviations that are used. Always study the list of abbreviations accompanying the directions. The meaning of some may change from book to book.

Also, watch carefully for the symbols indicating repetition. Asterisks and parentheses are most frequently used. The directions to be repeated can appear between 2 asterisks, followed by a statement indicating the number of times the step is to be done. For instance, when directions such as these appear— * 2 dc in next stitch, 1 dc in following stitch, repeat from * twice—return to the first asterisk and follow the directions to the second asterisk. Do this 2 times. Actually, the stitch sequence is worked 3 times.

Sometimes parentheses are used to indicate repetition. For example, "(1 dc in next st, ch 1) 8 times" means to make the sequence of stitches 8 times. Sometimes the parentheses are found in directions enclosed in asterisks.

The parentheses are also used to set apart a sequence of stitches that are to be placed in a stitch or space. The directions might read: "(1 dc, ch 1, 1 dc) in turning ch space."

A list of the most widely used abbreviations and terms is given here. It should be noted that in a few instances the meaning changes when the directions have been prepared for the British market.

| Term | American | British |
|---|---|---|
| beginning | beg | |
| block (solid mesh) | bl | |
| chain stitch | ch | |
| cluster | cl | |
| decrease | dec | |
| double crochet | dc | tr |
| double treble crochet | dtr, d tr, or dbl tr | tr tr |
| half double crochet | hdc, h dc, or h.d.c. | h.tr |
| inclusive | incl | |
| increase | inc | |
| loop | lp | |
| pattern | pat | |
| picot | p or P | |
| popcorn stitch | pc st | |
| repeat | * (asterisk)<br>( ) (parentheses) | |
| round | rnd | |
| single crochet | sc | dc |
| skip | sk | |
| slip stitch | sl st or ss | sc |
| space (open mesh) | sp | |
| stitch | st | |
| stitches | sts | |
| together | tog | |
| treble or triple | tr | long or double treble—dbl tr |
| treble or triple treble | tr tr | quad tr |
| yarn over hook | O, yo, or yoh | |

## Other Terms and Procedures

There are also other terms that may cause some confusion in the reading of directions. To avoid such a situation, an explanation in words and pictures follows. The terms are listed alphabetically for easy reference.

## Around Bar

This term is sometimes used to develop a special stitch pattern. The directions suggest a "stitch around bar of stitch in a previous row." To do this, the hook is inserted around the stitch, instead of into the top of the stitch, in the usual manner. If working with the right side toward you, the hook is placed as in A; with the wrong side, as in B.

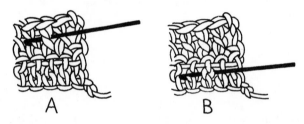

## Attaching New Thread or Yarn

When it is necessary to attach a new thread to a piece of crocheting, try to avoid knotting it. Plan the work so that a stitch can be crocheted up to the last step. Then pick up the new thread and continue the crocheting, completing the last step of the stitch. Keep both ends on the wrong side.

When it is necessary to attach a thread while crocheting, such as a second color, leave an end in the new thread about 4 inches (10 cm) long. Pull up a loop in the stitch where joining is to be made. Then draw end through this loop. Pull tightly to fasten. Draw up another loop in the same stitch. Continue to follow the directions for making the stitch pattern.

## Bind Off

Sometimes, when making a garment, it is necessary to shape a certain area, such as an armhole. The directions will indicate this by using the term **bind off.** Several stitches are left unworked at one end or both ends of a row. When starting to bind off, slip-stitch across the top of the designated number of stitches. Continue to make a row of stitches as instructed, stopping the right number of stitches from the opposite side, depending on the design. Start the next row of stitches from this point.

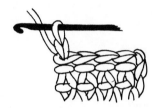

## Blocking

This procedure shapes a crochet article, giving it a more professional look. Smooth the piece. Pin it, wrong side up, to a well-padded board, using rustproof pins. Place the pins at the top and bottom of the piece and then the sides. Gently stretch and shape the article to the required measurements. Put the pins close together to avoid a scalloped edge.

For crocheting worked with smooth yarns in flat rows, use a damp cloth to cover it. Press lightly, allowing the steam to penetrate the article. Do not slide the iron or let it rest on the work. The piece should remain pinned to the board until thoroughly dry.

For crocheting worked with fluffy yarns and in raised pattern stitches, use a steaming technique. Hold the steaming iron close to the article so steam penetrates it. If extra steam is needed, use a wet pressing cloth. Allow the piece to remain in position until thoroughly dry.

Pieces made with synthetic threads or yarns can be dampened and allowed to dry. Pressing with an iron is not necessary.

## Changing Color

When a second color is used and is to continue in the same line and direction as the first color, introduce it at the second step of the last single or double crochet. Insert the hook under the 2 top threads of the stitch from the front. Begin the single or double crochet in the usual manner, picking up the second color. Pull it through the loop or loops on the hook. Drop the first color, allowing it to dangle until it is picked up at the designated point.

If the first color is not to be used again, place it along the top of the previous row. Crochet over it for 3 or 4 stitches to hold it in place. Then cut the yarn.

## Decrease—Afghan Stitch

To make a 1-stitch decrease, insert the hook under 2 vertical bars and pull up 1 loop. When working at the right end, join the first and second stitches by pulling up a loop in the second bar, and then carrying this loop through the first (A).

At the left end of the work, the decrease is made on the return row. Put the yarn over the hook. Draw a loop through 2 loops, instead of the usual 1, making the first stitch (B).

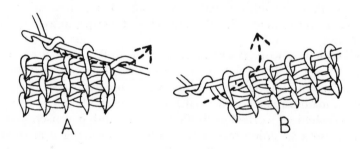

A                                          B

## Decrease—Double Crochet

Work a double crochet to the place where 2 loops remain on the hook. Put yarn over hook and pass the hook through the next stitch. Then put yarn over hook and draw it through the stitch, leaving 4 loops on hook (A).

Put yarn over hook (A). Pull it through 2 loops, leaving 3 loops on hook (B).

Put yarn over hook again (B) and draw it through the 3 loops, leaving 1 loop on hook (C).

Two double crochet stitches have been worked together. This reduces the number of stitches on the row by 1.

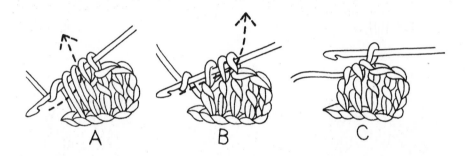

## Decrease—Single Crochet

When working single crochet, work the stitch until 2 loops are left on the hook. (The instructions will indicate where the decrease is to be taken.) Keeping the 2 loops on the hook, insert it in the next stitch. Put yarn over hook. Draw it through the stitch, leaving 3 loops on hook (A).

Put yarn over hook again (A) and pull it through the 3 loops, leaving 1 loop on hook (B).

Two single crochet stitches have been worked together so that there is 1 less stitch in the row.

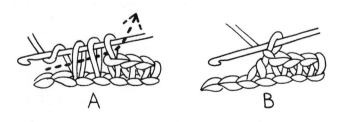

## Decrease—Treble Crochet

In working this decrease, put yarn over hook twice. Insert the hook in the first stitch at the place where the decrease is to be made. Place yarn over hook and draw through a loop. Put yarn over hook and pull a loop through 2 loops (A).

Place the yarn over hook again and draw another loop through 2 loops, leaving 2 loops on hook (B).

Begin the next stitch by putting the yarn twice over the hook. Insert the hook into the second stitch. Draw through a loop. Then put yarn over hook, and pull a loop through 2 loops (C).

Put the yarn over the hook. Draw a loop through 2 loops, leaving 3 loops on the hook (D). Place the yarn over the hook, and draw a loop through the 3 loops on hook (E). This completes the decreasing of 1 treble crochet (F).

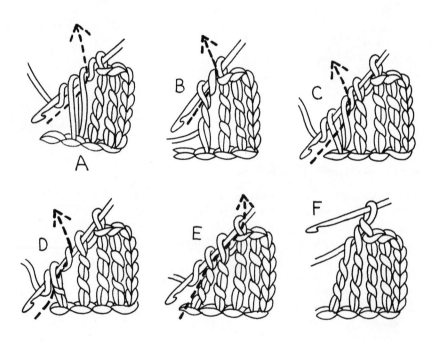

## Draw Through

This term is constantly seen in crocheting directions. It refers to the pulling through the stitch of the yarn or thread that has been placed over the hook. It produces a loop.

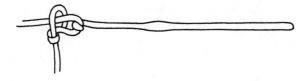

## End Off

This direction is found at the end of the instructions. Clip the yarn about 3 inches (7.5 cm) from the final stitch. Insert hook in last loop. Put yarn over hook and draw end right through loop. Pull the end to tighten the stitch.

To conceal the end of the yarn, thread a needle with it. Slip it in and out through the back of the work.

## Gauge

This term relates to the number of stitches and rows needed to produce a piece of crocheting of a certain size. Usually the gauge is stated at the beginning of the crocheting directions. It is important that the statement be given careful attention if the size of the article is to be correct. Variations in the size of the yarn and the hook and the degree of tightness with which one crochets influence the size of the article.

To be sure that the crocheting is correctly sized, it should be checked. Before beginning to work, crochet a swatch 3 inches by 3 inches (7.5 cm by 7.5 cm), using the required pattern stitch, yarn, and hook. Block the sample and then measure it with a ruler, as shown.

If the stitches and rows are not the same as the stated gauge, then some changes must be made. When the number of stitches is less than the number required, a smaller crochet hook should be used; when the number is more, a larger hook.

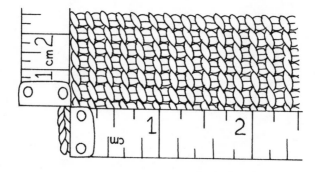

## Holding Hook—Left-handed

Using the left hand, follow the directions given for the right-handed person (see diagram).

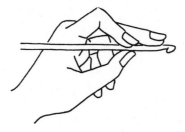

## Holding Hook—Right-handed

Place the crochet hook in the right hand between the thumb and first (index) finger as you would a pencil. Put the middle finger close to the tip of the hook, and the thumb and index finger closer to the center of the hook (see diagram).

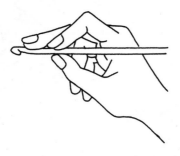

## Holding Yarn—Left-handed

If working with the left hand, hold the yarn in the right hand. Position the yarn in the same way as if working right-handed, as shown in diagrams A, B, and C.

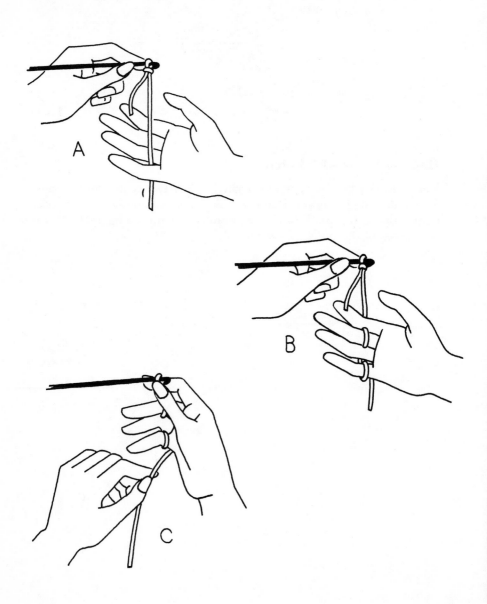

## Holding Yarn—Right-handed

If working with the right hand, hold the yarn between the fingers of the left hand. Place the ball end of the yarn between the little and ring fingers about 4 inches (10 cm) from the loop on the hook (A). Keep palm of hand up. Wrap yarn around the base of the little finger. Carry it under the back of the third (ring) finger, over the middle, and under the first, or index, finger (B).

If the position of the yarn needs to be adjusted, hold the hook and loop between the left thumb and index finger. Gently pull the thread down until it lies firmly but not tightly (C). This allows one to regulate the movement of the yarn.

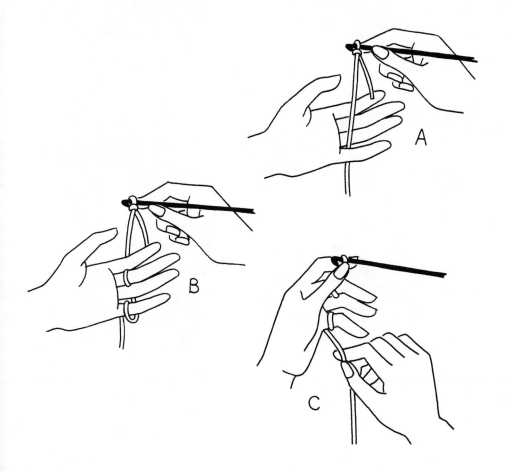

### Increase—Afghan Stitch

When making afghan stitches, increase a stitch by drawing up a loop in the chain stitch between the vertical bars. The increases are always worked in the first row—the one in which loops are made and retained on the hook.

For an increase at the beginning of a row, work a loop in the first vertical bar (A). At the other end, make a loop between the last 2 vertical bars, entering the top part of the chain. Then pick up a loop in the last vertical bar (B).

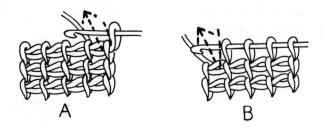

### Increase—One Stitch

Crochet stitches are usually increased in this way: make 2 stitches into 1 stitch instead of the usual 1 (A). Instructions always indicate where it should be done. It can also be done at the end of the row (B).

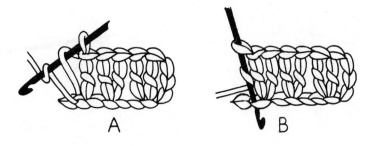

## Joining

A slip stitch is used when the directions indicate that the stitches are to be joined. Insert the hook under 2 top threads of stitch, working from the front. Put yarn over hook. Draw yarn through stitch and loop on hook in a single motion. This procedure leaves 1 loop on hook, allowing work to continue.

## Multiple Of

This is another term often seen when a pattern stitch is being made that requires a definite number of stitches. When the instructions read "multiple of," it indicates that the number of foundation stitches to be made must be divisible by the stated number. For instance, a multiple of 5 would mean that 10, 15, or 20 stitches would be needed.

If the directions read "multiple of 5 plus 3," then 3 would be added to the total number, making it necessary to use 13, 18, or 23 stitches.

## Turn Work

At the end of each row, 1 or more chain stitches are made and the work is turned so that the crocheting proceeds in the same direction. The number of chains varies depending on the type of stitch being used. The following information lists the number of chains to employ:

|         |     |                          |
|---------|-----|--------------------------|
| 1 chain | for | single crochet (sc)      |
| 2 chains| for | half double crochet (hdc)|
| 3 chains| for | double crochet (dc)      |
| 4 chains| for | treble crochet (tr)      |
| 5 chains| for | double treble (dtr)      |
| 6 chains| for | triple treble (tr tr)    |

## Under Two Top Threads

This wording, often found in directions, actually means that the hook
is slipped under the top part of the stitch.

## Work Even

When this direction is given, continue to work the pattern stitch as
before, over the same number of stitches, without increasing or decreasing.

## Yarn Over

In order to create a new loop or stitch, pass the hook under and
over the yarn or thread so that the end of the hook catches the yarn
in preparation for pulling it through the loop or stitch. This procedure
is known as **yarn over** or **yarn over hook.**

If thread is being used, then the term is **thread over.**

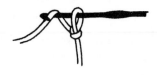

## BASIC STITCHES AND VARIATIONS

Crocheting, like knitting, is an interlocking of loops. However, the loops are formed with only 1 needle, or hook, instead of the 2 needed for knitting. Although there are hundreds of stitch patterns and motifs, they are all made with a few basic stitches. Many strands of yarn may be interlaced through a single loop, producing innumerable variations and patterns. Once the technique for making the basic stitches is mastered, the stitches can be combined in creative ways. To make the directions that follow easier to understand, abbreviations have not been used.

### Chain Stitch

With the hook through a loop, slip the hook under the yarn and over it so that the yarn is wrapped around the hook (A). This process is called **yarn over**.

Catch the yarn with the hook. Draw it through the loop, making the first chain stitch (B).

It is important to keep the stitches the same size. They should be just loose enough for the hook to pass through easily. Always keep the thumb and first, or index, finger of the left hand near the stitch that is being made.

A series of chain stitches is used to form the foundation row for all types of crocheting.

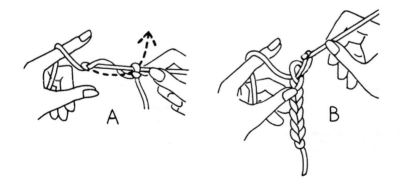

## Double Crochet

Start with a foundation chain using an even number of stitches.

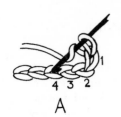

A

For the **first row,** put yarn over hook. Insert it in the fourth chain from the hook by placing it under the 2 top threads (A).

Put yarn over hook and draw it through the chain, leaving 3 loops on the hook (B).

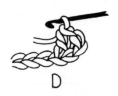

B

Place yarn over hook (B) and draw through 2 loops, leaving 2 loops on the hook (C).

Put yarn over hook once more (C) and draw through 2 loops, leaving 1 loop on hook (D). This completes the first double crochet stitch.

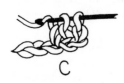

C

To make the second double crochet, put yarn over hook and insert the hook from the front in the next chain stitch, slipping under the 2 top threads. Continue as for the first double crochet.

At the end of the row, chain 3 stitches (E) and turn the work so that the reverse side is toward you.

D

For the **second row,** place yarn over hook. Insert hook in the fifth stitch from the hook (F), passing under the 2 top threads. Proceed in the usual way to complete the stitch.

E

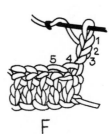

F

## Double Crochet—
### Chain-two Block
*See directions for* Filet crochet, in "Stitch Patterns."

## Double Crochet—
### Chain-one Space
*See directions for* Mesh crochet, in "Stitch Patterns."

## Double Crochet—Crossed

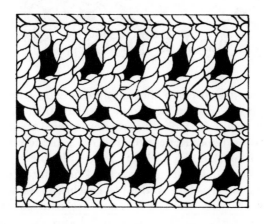

Make a foundation chain the required length. Use a multiple of 2 stitches plus 1 and an additional chain.

For the **first row,** make a double crochet in the fourth chain from the hook, and a double crochet in third chain from hook. Repeat the following procedure to end of row. * Skip 1 chain. Make a double crochet in next chain and also 1 in skipped chain. * At end of chain, make 2 chains and turn.

For the **second row,** skip first 2 stitches. Make 1 double crochet in third stitch and 1 double crochet in second stitch. Repeat the following procedure to end of row. * Skip first stitch. Make a double crochet in next stitch and a double crochet in skipped stitch. * At end of row, chain 2 and turn.

Repeat **second row** until work is completed.

## Double Crochet—Lacy

Start with a foundation chain the required length, using a multiple of 2 stitches plus 1, with an additional 2 chain stitches.

For the **first row,** take 1 double crochet in third chain from hook, leaving 2 loops on hook. Repeat the following procedure to the end of row. * Begin by skipping 1 chain. Take 1 double crochet in next chain to 3 loops on hook. Put yarn over hook and pull through remaining 3 loops. Chain 1. Make 1 double crochet in same stitch to 2 loops on hook. * When the last 2 chains are reached, skip 1 chain. Take 1 double crochet in last chain to 3 loops on hook. Put yarn over hook. Pull through remaining 3 loops. Chain 3 and turn.

For the **second row,** make 1 double crochet in first stitch to 2 loops. Repeat the following procedure to the end of the row. * Begin by skipping 1 chain. Take 1 double crochet in next chain to 3 loops on hook. Put yarn over hook and pull through remaining 3 loops. Chain 1. Make 1 double crochet in same stitch to 2 loops on hook. * At end of row, take last double crochet in top of turning chain. Chain 3 and turn.

Repeat **second row** until work is completed.

## Half Double Crochet

Begin with a chain the required length. Place the yarn over the hook. Insert it in the third chain from the hook, entering from the front of the stitch and passing under the 2 top threads (A).

Pull the yarn through the stitch, leaving 3 loops on the hook (B). This part of the stitch is made exactly like double crochet.

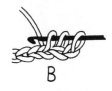

Put yarn over hook. Draw it through all loops on hook (C). This procedure completes the making of a half double crochet. One loop remains on hook (D).

To make the next half double crochet, put yarn over hook. Insert the hook in the next chain, entering from the front under the 2 top threads. Continue as for the first stitch.

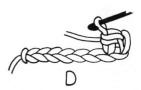

When the row is completed, chain 2 stitches (E) and turn the work. The turning chain-2 does not count as a stitch on the following row.

For the **second row,** put yarn over hook. Insert the hook in the first stitch, which is the last stitch of the previous row. Enter from the front under the 2 top loops. Continue making half double crochet stitches, as for previous row.

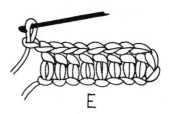

## Loop

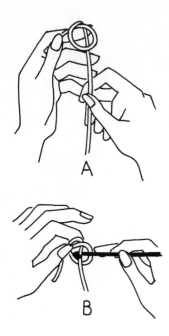

Crocheting begins with a slip knot, or loop. To make the knot, hold the thread or yarn about 2 inches (5 cm) from the end. Form a small circle by bringing the ball end of the thread over the short end (A).

Hold the circle in place between the left thumb and first (index) finger. Insert the hook through the circle, holding it in the right hand as shown (B).

Pick up ball end of thread and draw it through the circle, forming a small loop (C).

So that the loop fits the hook more closely, pull the yarn ends in opposite directions. The loop should be just loose enough to allow the hook to pass through it.

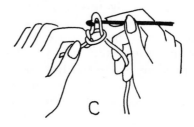

## Single Crochet—Flat

Make a foundation chain the required length. Hold the chain with the right side toward you. Insert the hook in the second stitch from the loop. Do not count loop on hook. Slip the hook from the front of the stitch under the 2 top threads (A).

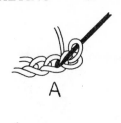

A

Catch the yarn, passing the hook under and over the yarn (B).

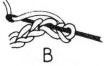

B

Draw the yarn through the chain stitch, leaving 2 loops on the hook (C).

Put the yarn over the hook again. Pull it through the 2 loops on the hook (D).

C

One loop remains on the hook (E). One single crochet has been completed.

To make the second single crochet, insert the hook in the next stitch of the chain. Remember the hook slips under the 2 top threads. Continue this process until a single crochet is made in each of the chain stitches.

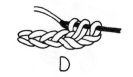

D

At the end of the row, make 1 chain stitch (F). This makes it easier to turn the work.

Turn the work so the reverse side is toward you (G).

For the **second row** of single crochet, insert the hook in the second stitch from the hook. This stitch is the last stitch of the preceding row. Pass the hook, from the front, under the 2 top threads (H). Continue this way until row is completed.

E

H

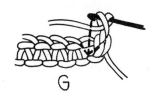

G

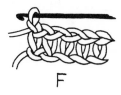

F

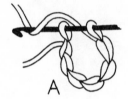

A

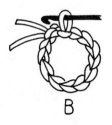

B

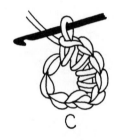

C

D

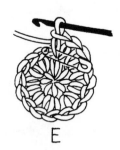

E

## Single Crochet—Round

Make a short foundation chain, perhaps 4 stitches. To form a circle or ring, join the first and fourth stitches with a slip stitch. To do this, put hook **through** the 2 top threads of first chain, working from the front (A).

Place thread over hook. Pull through chain stitch and loop on hook in a single motion, leaving 1 loop on hook (B).

For the **first round**, take 8 single crochet stitches through center of ring (C).

Mark the end of the first round with a safety pin in the last stitch (D). Move the pin to mark the end of each round when it is completed.

For the **second round**, work 2 single crochets into each stitch of the previous round, leaving 16 stitches on the round.

For the **third round**, make a single crochet in the first stitch and 2 single crochets in the next stitch. Continue this procedure so that there is an increase of 1 stitch in every other stitch in the round, leaving 24 stitches on the round (E). Work progresses in the same manner.

## Single Crochet—
### with Chain-one Spaces

Begin with a foundation chain the required number of stitches. Use a multiple of 2 stitches plus 1, with an additional 2 chains.

For the **first row,** take a single crochet in third chain from hook. Repeat the following procedure to end of row. * Chain 1. Skip 1 chain. Make 1 single crochet in next chain. * Finish with 3 chains. Turn.

For the **second row,** skip first 2 stitches. Repeat the following procedure to end of row. * Take a single crochet in next single crochet. Chain 1. * End with 1 single crochet in second stitch of turning chain. Chain 3 and turn.

Repeat the **second row** until work is completed.

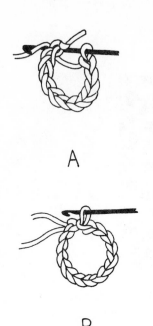

A

B

### Slip Stitch

This stitch can be used in various ways. However, it is most often thought of as a joining or an invisible stitch.

For a joining, insert the hook in the stitch at the end of the chain to be joined (A). Put thread over hook. Draw through stitch and the loop that is on the hook in a single motion. One loop remains on the hook (B).

The same procedure is followed when a slip stitch is needed in a row of stitches. A row of slip stitches can be worked across a row. Insert hook into second stitch from hook. Put yarn over hook (C). Draw a loop through the stitch and the loop on the hook (D).

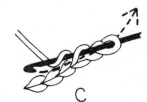

C

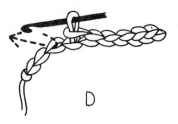

D

## Treble Crochet

Make a foundation chain the required length.

To make the **first treble,** put yarn over hook twice (A). Insert hook in the fifth chain from the hook. Enter from the front under the 2 top threads. Put yarn over hook and draw through the chain stitch. Four loops remain on the hook (B).

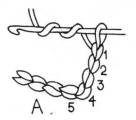

Place yarn over hook again and draw through 2 loops. Three loops remain on the hook (C).

Place yarn over hook again and pull through 2 loops. Two loops remain on the hook (D).

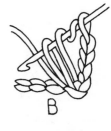

Put yarn over hook again and draw through 2 loops (E). One loop remains on hook. The first treble stitch has been completed (F).

For the **second treble,** put yarn over hook twice. Insert it under the 2 top threads of the next stitch. Continue as for the first treble stitch.

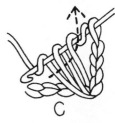

Complete the row by making a treble stitch in each chain. Chain 4 stitches, which will become the first treble on the second row.

For the **second row,** put yarn over hook twice. Insert hook in the sixth stitch from the hook. Enter from the front under the 2 top threads. This stitch falls under the second stitch on the previous row. Continue working as for the first row (G).

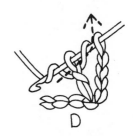

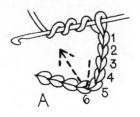

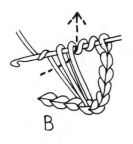

A

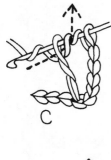

B

## Treble Crochet—Double

Begin with a foundation chain the required length.

Put the thread over the hook 3 times before inserting it in the sixth stitch from the hook (A).

Put the thread over the hook again and draw a loop through the stitch, leaving 5 loops on hook (B).

Put the thread over the hook again (B) and pull through 2 loops, leaving 4 loops on hook. Repeat this procedure (C), leaving 3 loops (D), then 2 loops (E), and finally 1 loop (F) on the hook. At this stage, 1 double treble stitch has been made.

At the end of the row, chain 5 and turn the work. The chain becomes the first double treble stitch on the second row. Continue to make the stitches as for the first row (G).

C

E

G

D

F

## Treble Crochet—Triple

Make a foundation chain the required length.

Put the thread over the hook 4 times (A) before inserting it in the seventh stitch from the hook.

Put the yarn over the hook and draw through a loop. Six loops remain on the hook (B).

Put the yarn over the hook (B) and draw a loop through 2 loops, leaving 5 loops on hook. Repeat this procedure (C), leaving 4 loops (D), then 3 (E), and 2 (F), and finally 1 loop (G). This completes 1 triple treble stitch. Continue in this way to end of row.

At end of row, chain 6 and turn the work. The chain is counted as the first stitch in the second row (H).

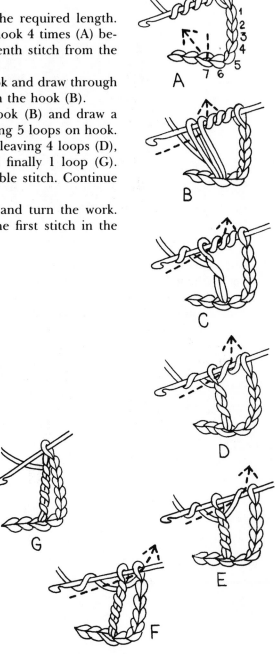

## Treble Pattern—Crossed

Begin with a foundation chain the required length, using a multiple of 2 stitches plus 1, with an additional 2 chains.

For the **first row,** take 1 treble stitch in fifth chain from hook, and another in fourth chain from hook. Repeat the following procedure to the end of the row. * Skip 1 chain. Take 1 treble crochet in next chain and another in skipped chain. * At end of chain, make 3 chains and turn.

For the **second row,** skip first 2 stitches in preceding row. Then make a treble crochet in third stitch and another in second stitch. Repeat the following procedure to end of row. * Skip 1 stitch. Make a treble crochet in next stitch and another in skipped stitch. * At end of row, chain 3 and turn.

Repeat **second row** until work is completed.

## MATERIALS AND TOOLS

The equipment needed for crocheting is simple—a hook and thread or yarn. It is important, however, that the hook and yarn are compatible. Because hooks are available in a wide range of sizes, there is one to use with a particular size and type of thread or yarn.

### Crochet Hooks

Hooks are made of a variety of materials and in a variety of sizes. They range from a very fine steel hook for fine threads to large wooden ones for coarser yarns and jiffy knitting.

There are also special hooks for working the afghan stitch. This type of hook has a straight, even shaft and is made of aluminum or plastic. The hooks are 9 to 14 inches (23 to 35.5 cm) in length and range in size from 1 to 10 and F to J. When the hook is sized by number, the shaft is comparable to a knitting needle of the same size. But when the hook is sized by letter, it is equivalent to a crochet hook sized in the same way.

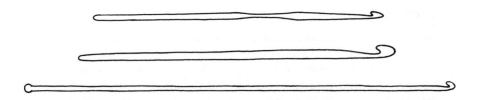

**Aluminum, Bone, and Plastic Hooks.** Aluminum hooks are available in sizes B to K and in a 6-inch (15 cm) length. Bone hooks come in sizes 1 to 6, which are comparable to sizes B to G. Plastic hooks are made in sizes D to J and in a 5½-inch (14 cm) length.

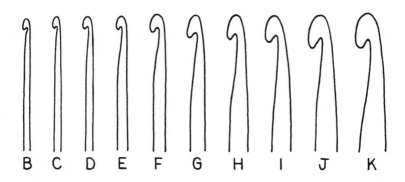

B   C   D   E   F   G   H   I   J   K

**Steel Hooks.** These hooks range in size from a large one, 00, to the very fine, 14. The length is 5 inches (12.5 cm).

**Wooden Hooks.** These hooks are large and long, 9 or 10 inches (23 or 25.5 cm) in length. They are used for quick crocheting.

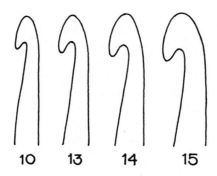

## Thread or Yarn

The beauty of crocheting depends to a great extent on the thread or yarn. The size, the twist, and the finish provide variations in texture that influence the appearance of the work. Always select the material that is especially suited to the stitch and the article. A tightly twisted yarn produces a firm surface finish with long-wearing qualities, whereas a light, airy one gives a fluffy, soft finish. Delicate, lacy designs require fine thread, with heavy yarns being used for bold, coarse effects.

## STITCH PATTERNS

Although a great deal of crocheting can be done by using just the basic stitches, it becomes more interesting when the stitches are combined in various ways. The pages that follow offer many suggestions for doing this. The effects vary in texture from cobwebby fineness to opaque coarseness. Directions are written without abbreviations, eliminating the need to refer to the listing of abbreviations and terms. It seems to make the crocheting process easier and quicker to do, especially if one is unfamiliar with them.

Except for a few old favorites, the naming of crochet stitches is confusing. There does not seem to be a definitive list of names that everyone can use for identification. Instead, the titles seem to describe the combination of stitches used or the effect created as the author sees it. Sometimes the stitch patterns are simply identified by number.

On the following pages, a cross section of crocheting stitch patterns is shown. They suggest an insight into the wide range of possibilities offered the crocheter.

## Afghan Stitch—Basic

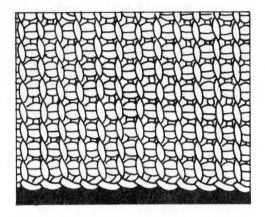

Crocheting made of afghan stitches is sometimes referred to as Tunisian Crochet. The stitches are made on a long hook that resembles a knitting needle. As one proceeds from right to left across a row, each stitch remains on the hook. The stitches are then worked off as the crocheting travels from left to right. Afghan stitches create an attractive, textured effect.

Begin with a row of chain stitches to form a foundation the required length.

For the **first row,** make a series of loops drawn through each stitch of the foundation chain. Leave all loops on the hook. To do this, insert the hook in the second chain from the hook. With yarn over the hook, draw a loop through the chain stitch. Continue the procedure to end of row.

For the **second row,** remove the loops from the hook without turning the work. Do this by placing the yarn over the hook. Draw a loop through first stitch on the hook. Then repeat the following procedure until only 1 chain remains on the hook. * Put the yarn over the hook and draw it through 2 loops. * At the end of the row, make 1 chain.

For the **third row,** leave the loops on the hook as for the first row. Working from right to left, insert the hook under the vertical stitch. Put yarn over hook. Draw through the loop. Continue this way to end of row.

For the **fourth row,** use the directions for the second row.

For the remainder of the work, repeat the **third and fourth rows.**

## Afghan Stitch—Cluster

Make a foundation chain the required length. Use a multiple of 4 stitches plus 1.

For the **first row,** insert hook into second chain from hook. Repeat the following procedure to the end of the row. * Place yarn over hook. Pull it through a loop. Do this in each chain to end of foundation chain, retaining all loops on hook. * Do not turn work.

For the **second row,** repeat the following procedure to end of row. * Chain 3. Put yarn over hook. Pull through 5 loops to make a cluster. Put yarn over hook. Draw through 1 loop. * At end of row, chain 1.

For the **third row,** repeat the following procedure to end of row. * Insert hook through top of cluster. Put yarn over hook. Pull through a loop. Insert hook in each chain stitch and draw through a loop. *

For the **fourth row,** use the directions for the second row.

Repeat the **third and fourth rows** to end of work.

## Afghan Stitch—Crossed Tunisian

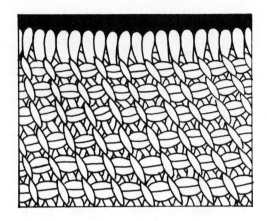

For this afghan stitch, make a foundation chain the required length.

For the **first row,** insert hook in the second chain from hook. Repeat the following procedure to end of row. * Put yarn over hook. Draw through a loop. Insert hook into next stitch. * Leave all loops on the hook. Do not turn work.

For the **second row,** put yarn over hook. Draw through a loop. Repeat the following procedure to end of row. * Put yarn over hook. Draw through 2 loops. *

For the **third row,** insert hook from right to left under the first vertical stitch. Put yarn over hook. Draw through a loop. Repeat the following procedure to end of row. * Insert hook from right to left under the third vertical stitch. Put yarn over hook. Draw through a loop. Repeat through second vertical stitch for crossed stitch. * This completes the first crossed stitch row.

For the **fourth row,** use the directions for second row with this exception: after the first loop, draw through 3 loops instead of 2, to the end of the row.

For the **fifth row,** follow directions for third row, continuing to work 1 stitch farther to the left for each alternating or crossed stitch row. This creates the diagonal or bias direction to the stitches.

Continue to work in this way, alternating the **second and third rows.**

## Afghan Stitch—Framed Squares

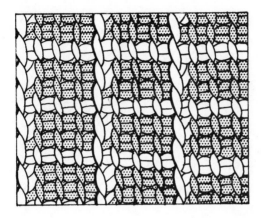

This stitch is made with a multiple of 4 stitches. It is most effective when worked in 2 colors. Begin with a foundation chain the required length.

For the **first row,** insert hook into second chain from hook. Repeat the following procedure to end of row. * Put the yarn over the hook. Pull through a loop. Then do the same thing in the next stitch. * Leave all loops on the hook. Do not turn work.

For the **second row,** put yarn over hook and pull through first loop. Place yarn over hook again and draw through 2 loops. Continue this way to end of row. Chain 1. Attach second color.

For the **third row,** repeat the first row, using second color.

For the **fourth row,** repeat the second row, using second color.

For the **fifth row,** repeat the third row.

For the **sixth row,** repeat the fourth row.

For the **seventh row,** use first color. Repeat the following procedure to end of row. * Pick up 3 loops. Put yarn over hook. Insert hook under vertical loop in second row. Place yarn over hook and pull through loop. Put yarn over hook and draw through 2 loops. *

For the **eighth row,** repeat second row, using first color.

Repeat the **second through seventh rows,** forming squares as described in the seventh row.

## Afghan Stitch—Knitted

For this afghan stitch, use a foundation chain of any number of stitches. The stitches produce a knitted effect.

For the **first row,** insert hook into second chain from hook. Put yarn over hook and pull through loop. Repeat this procedure, working in each chain to end of foundation chain. Keep all loops on hook. Do not turn work.

For the **second row,** put yarn over hook. Draw loop through first stitch on hook. Then place yarn over hook and pull through next 2 loops. Continue drawing the yarn through 2 loops until only 1 is left on hook. Chain 1.

For the **third row,** insert hook between the 2 double vertical stitches from front to back. Put yarn over hook. Pull through a loop. Continue to do this until row is completed.

For the **fourth row,** repeat the second row.

Repeat the **third and fourth rows** until work is completed.

## Afghan Stitch—Mesh

Begin with a foundation chain the required length. Use a multiple of 2 stitches plus 1.

For the **first row,** insert hook in third chain from hook. Put yarn over hook and draw through a loop. Repeat the following procedure to the end of row. * Chain 1. Skip 1 chain. Insert hook in next chain. Place yarn over hook and pull through a loop. * Keep all loops on hook. Do not turn work.

For the **second row,** put yarn over hook. Pull loop through first stitch on hook. Repeat the following procedure to end of row. * Chain 1. Place yarn over hook. Draw it through 2 loops. * At end of row, chain 1.

For the **third row,** insert hook through vertical stitch of previous row. Put yarn over hook and pull through a loop. Chain 1. Continue across row.

For the **fourth row,** use directions for the second row.

Repeat the **third and fourth rows** until work is completed.

## Afghan Stitch—Mock Rice

*See* Bicolor Afghan Stitch (in "Styles and Types of Crocheting," under Multicolor Crochet).

## Afghan Stitch—Plain Tunisian

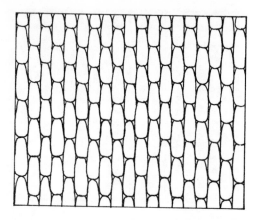

Make a foundation chain of the required number of stitches.

For the **first row,** make a series of loops drawn through each stitch of the foundation chain. Leave all loops on the hook. To do this, insert the hook in the second chain from the hook. With yarn over hook, draw loop through the chain stitch. Continue this procedure to end of row.

For the **second row,** remove the loops from the hook without turning the work. Do this by placing the yarn over the hook. Draw loop through first stitch on the hook. Then repeat the following procedure until only 1 chain remains on the hook. * Put the yarn over the hook and draw it through 2 loops. * At the end of the row, chain 1.

For the **third row,** repeat the following procedure to end of row. * Insert hook under the stitch between the vertical stitches of previous row. Put yarn over hook. Draw it through the loop. *

For the **fourth row,** use directions for the second row.

Repeat the **third and fourth rows** until work is completed.

## Afghan Stitch—Purl

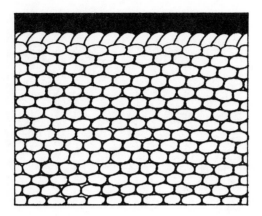

For this afghan stitch, work a foundation chain the required length. Any number of stitches can be used.

For the **first row,** repeat the following sequence of stitches to end of row. * Hold yarn in front of work. Insert hook from back through chain with yarn under hook. Draw through a loop. * Keep all stitches on hook.

For the **second row,** put yarn over hook. Pull loop through first stitch on hook. Repeat the following procedure until 1 loop is left on hook. * Put yarn over hook and draw through 2 loops on hook. * Chain 1.

For the **third row,** repeat the following procedure. * With yarn in front of work, insert hook from right to left through vertical stitch of previous row. Put yarn over hook and draw through loop. * Keep all stitches on hook.

For the **fourth row,** use directions for the second row.

Repeat the **third and fourth rows** to end of work.

## Afghan Stitch—Ribbed

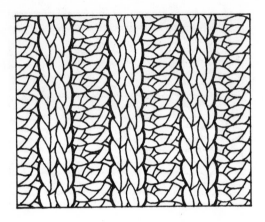

This afghan stitch is started with a foundation chain, using a multiple of 4 stitches. Make a chain the required length. The stitches create a knitted effect.

For the **first row,** insert hook into second chain from hook. Repeat the following procedure to end of row. * Put yarn over hook. Draw through a loop. * Do this in each chain. Keep all loops on hook. Do not turn work to start second row.

For the **second row,** put yarn over hook. Pull loop through first stitch on hook. Repeat the following procedure to end of row. * Put yarn over hook. Draw through next 2 loops on hook. * At end of row, 1 loop remains on hook. Chain 1.

For the **third row,** repeat the following procedure. * Insert hook under vertical stitch from right to left. Put yarn over hook and draw through a loop; repeat. Then, with yarn in front of work, insert hook from right to left through vertical stitch of previous row. Put yarn over hook and draw through a loop. Do this twice. * Repeat the 4 stitches that have just been made to the end of the row.

For the **fourth row,** put yarn over hook and draw loop through first stitch on hook. Repeat the following procedure to end of row. * Put yarn over hook. Draw through next 2 loops. *

Repeat the **third and fourth rows** until work is completed.

## Afghan Stitch—Twill

Begin with a foundation chain the required length. Use an even number of stitches.

For the **first row,** use the plain afghan stitch. Insert the hook into second chain from hook. Repeat the following procedure in each chain to.end of row. * Put yarn over hook. Draw through a loop. * Keep loops on hook. Do not turn work.

For the **second row,** work off the loops by putting yarn over hook and pulling it through the first loop. Repeat the following procedure to end of row. * Put yarn over hook. Pull through next 2 loops. * End with 1 loop on hook. It is considered as the first stitch of the next row.

For the **third row,** skip the first vertical bar. Repeat the following procedure to end of row. * Pull up a loop under next vertical bar, making a plain stitch. Holding yarn with thumb in front and below hook, pull up a loop under next vertical bar, making a purl stitch. * End last stitch by inserting hook under last vertical bar and in loop at back of bar. Pull up 1 loop, making an edge stitch.

For the **fourth bar,** use directions for the second row.

For the **fifth row,** keeping all loops on hook, skip first vertical bar. Repeat the following procedure to end of row. * Make a purl stitch over a plain stitch. Make a plain stitch over a purl stitch. * End with an edge stitch.

Repeat the **fourth and fifth rows,** until work is completed.

## Albanian Stitch

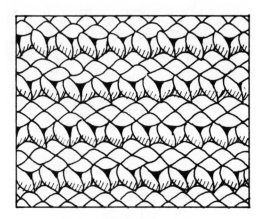

An interesting textural effect results when single crochet stitches are made this way. Begin with a foundation chain the required length. Use an even number of stitches.

For the **first row,** take a single crochet in each chain. Chain 1 and turn.

For the **second row,** make a single crochet in each stitch. Insert hook through front horizontal thread at top of previous row. Chain 1 and turn.

Repeat the **second row** until work is completed.

## Arch Mesh Stitch

By combining a series of chain stitches with single and double crochet, an openwork design with a textural quality is produced. Begin with a row of chain stitches to form a foundation the required length. Use a multiple of 4 stitches plus 3.

For the **first row,** chain 6 stitches. Then repeat the following sequence of stitches to the end. * Make 1 single crochet. Chain 2. Skip 1 stitch. Make 1 double crochet. Chain 2. Skip 1 stitch. * End the row with 1 double crochet. Turn work.

For the **second row,** repeat the following sequence of stitches. * Make 1 single crochet in double crochet of previous row. Then chain 2. Take 1 double crochet in the single crochet of previous row. Chain 2. * The row should end with a single crochet. Turn work.

Repeat the **first and second rows** until work is completed.

## Arch Stitch

This easy-to-make stitch pattern creates a very open effect, with curving lines. Begin with a foundation chain the required length. Use an odd number of stitches.

For the **first row,** take a single crochet in each chain.

For the **second row,** chain 5. Take a double crochet in third stitch of first row. Repeat the following procedure to end of row. * Chain 5. Skip 3 stitches. Take a double crochet in next stitch. * At end of row, chain 5 and turn.

For the **third row,** make a double crochet by inserting hook in center chain of chain-5 of previous row. Repeat the following procedure to end of row. * Chain 5. Take 1 double crochet in next chain-5 space. * Finish row with a double crochet in third stitch of turning chain. Chain 5 and turn.

Repeat the **third row** until work is completed.

## Arrow Pattern

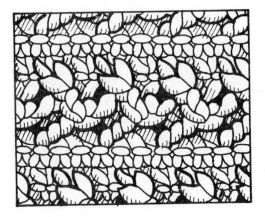

A raised effect, resembling an arrow, dominates this stitch. To determine length of work, use a multiple of 4 stitches plus 1 chain. Make a foundation chain the required length.

For the **first row,** take a single crochet in the second chain from hook. Make 1 single crochet in each chain to end of row. Then chain 1 and turn.

For the **second row,** skip first stitch. Make 1 single crochet in each stitch to end of row. Chain 3 and turn.

For the **third row,** skip first stitch. Make a double crochet in next single crochet. Repeat the following sequence of stitches. * Skip 3 single crochets. Make 1 half double crochet in next single crochet. Working behind the half double crochet, take 1 double crochet in each of the 3 skipped single crochets. * End the row with 1 double crochet in each of the last 2 single crochets. Then chain 3 and turn.

For the **fourth row,** skip first double crochet. Make 1 double crochet in the next double crochet. Repeat the following sequence of stitches. * Skip 3 double crochets. Make 1 half double crochet in the half double crochet. Working in front of the half double crochet, take 1 double crochet in each of the 3 skipped double crochets. * End the row with a double crochet in each of the last 2 stitches. Chain 1 and turn.

For the **fifth row,** skip first double crochet. Make 1 single crochet in each remaining double crochet. Chain 1 and turn.

Repeat the **second through fifth rows** until work is completed.

## Bobble Stitch

Rows of puffy mounds add interest to this openwork stitch pattern. Start with a row of chain stitches to form a foundation the required length. Use a multiple of 2 stitches plus 1 and 1 extra chain stitch.

For the **first row,** make a single crochet in the second chain from the hook. Take a single crochet in each chain to end of row. Then chain 2 and turn.

For the **second row,** skip first stitch. Make a double crochet in next stitch up to where there are 2 loops on the hook. (This is sometimes called a *post.*) Place the yarn over the hook and pull up a loop around the post 3 times. Put the yarn over the hook again and draw through all 8 loops to form a bobble. Repeat the following procedure. * Chain 1. Skip 1 stitch. Make bobble in next stitch. * At end of row, make 1 double crochet in last stitch. Then chain 1 and turn.

For the **third row,** skip first stitch. Make 1 single crochet in each bobble and in each chain 1. End with a single crochet in top of turning chain. Then chain 2 and turn.

For the **fourth row,** skip first stitch. Make bobble in next stitch. Repeat the following sequence of stitches to end of row. * Chain 1. Skip 1 stitch. Make bobble in next stitch. * Then make a double crochet in last stitch. Chain 1 and turn.

Repeat the **third and fourth rows** until work is completed.

## Bow Pattern

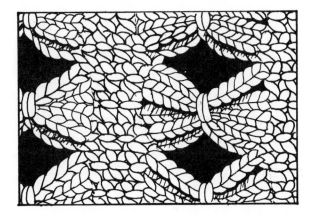

A combination of chain and single crochet stitches produces this design. Rows of chain stitches are bound together, creating the bow effect. Begin with a foundation chain the required length. Use a multiple of 10 stitches plus 4.

For the **first row,** take a single crochet in each stitch to end of row. Then chain 2 and turn.

For the **second row,** skip 1 stitch. Make 1 single crochet in next 3 stitches. Repeat the following sequence of stitches to end. * Chain 10. Take a single crochet in next 4 stitches. * End with 4 single crochets. Chain 2 and turn.

For the **third, fourth, and fifth rows,** use directions for second row.

For the **sixth row,** skip 1 stitch. Take a single crochet in next 3 stitches. Repeat the following sequence of stitches to end of row. * Chain 5. Make a single crochet going below 4 previously chained rows. Chain 4. Make a single crochet in 4 stitches. * End with 4 single crochets. Chain 2 and turn.

Repeat the **second through sixth rows** until work is completed.

## Brick Loop Pattern

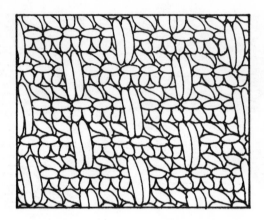

By using extended loops in an alternating design, it is possible to create the effect of laid bricks. To determine length of a row, use a multiple of 4 stitches plus 1 chain. Make a foundation chain the required length.

For the **first row,** make a single crochet in the second chain from hook. Then take a single crochet in each chain to the end. Chain 1 and turn.

For the **second row,** skip first stitch. Take 1 single crochet in each stitch of previous row, ending with 1 single crochet in turning chain. Chain 1 and turn.

For the **third row,** skip first stitch. Repeat the following procedure to end of row. * Make 1 single crochet in each of the next 3 stitches. Insert hook in first row. Chain directly below next stitch. Draw up a loop to make next stitch. * At the end of the row, chain 1 and turn.

For the **fourth row,** skip first stitch. Make 1 single crochet in each stitch to end of row. Chain 1 and turn.

For the **fifth row,** skip first stitch. Make a single crochet in next stitch. Repeat the following procedure. * Insert hook in stitch 2 rows below next stitch. Draw up a long loop. Take a single crochet in each of the next 3 stitches. End the last repeat with 1 single crochet in each of last 2 stitches. * Then chain 1 and turn.

For the **sixth row,** repeat the fourth row.

Repeat the **fourth through sixth rows** until work is completed.

## Broomstick Lace

Jiffy lace is another name given this lacy stitch pattern. Use a multiple of 5 stitches to make a foundation chain the required length.

For the **first row,** pull up last loop. Put it on a large knitting needle, size 50, which is held in left hand. Insert hook in each chain. Pull yarn through and place on needle (A).

For the **second row,** repeat the following procedure the length of the foundation chain. * Insert hook in center of first 5 loops (B). Hold the loops together as 1 loop. Put yarn over hook and pull loops off the needle. Make 1 chain stitch. Follow with 5 single crochets in the same set of 5 loops. * Do not turn work at end of row.

For the **third row,** put the last stitch on knitting needle. Work in back loop. With crochet hook, pull yarn through each single crochet of previous row and place on knitting needle.

Repeat the **second and third rows** until work is completed.

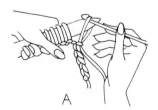

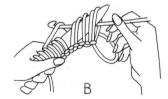

A          B

## Butterfly Pattern

A miniature butterfly motif dots this lacy design. Begin with a foundation chain of the required number of stitches. Use a multiple of 16 stitches plus 6.

For the **first row,** chain 3 stitches. Make 3 double crochets in fourth stitch from hook. Repeat the following procedure. * Skip 5 stitches. Make 4 double crochets in next stitch. Chain 5. Skip 4 stitches. Make 1 single crochet in next stitch. Chain 5. Skip 4 stitches. Take 4 double crochets in next stitch. * End with skip 4 stitches and 1 double crochet in last stitch. Turn.

For the **second row,** chain 3. Make 4 double crochets in last double crochet of previous row. Skip 6 stitches. Take 4 double crochets in next stitch. Repeat the following sequence of stitches. * Chain 5. Make single crochet in single crochet of previous row. Chain 5. Make 4 double crochets in next double crochet of previous row. Skip 6 stitches. Make 4 double crochets in next double crochet of previous row. * End with 4 crochets in last double crochet. Turn.

For the **third row,** chain 3. Make 3 double crochets in first double crochet. Repeat the following procedure. * Skip 6 double crochets. Take 4 double crochets in next double crochet. Chain 5. Take 1 single crochet in the single crochet. Chain 5. * Make 4 double crochets in first double crochet. End with 1 double crochet in last stitch. Turn.

For the **fourth row,** chain 1. Take 1 single crochet in last stitch of previous row. Repeat the following procedure to end of row. * Chain 5. Skip 3 stitches. Take single crochet in next stitch. Chain 5. Make 4 double crochets in next stitch. Skip 6 stitches. Take 4 double crochets in next stitch. * End with chain 5. Take 1 double crochet at edge and turn.

For the **fifth row,** chain 6. Repeat the following procedure to end of row. * Make a single crochet in the double crochet. Chain 5. Skip 5 stitches. Take 4 double crochets in next stitch. Skip 6 stitches. Make 4 double crochets in next stitch. Chain 5. * End with a single crochet. Turn.

For the **sixth row,** chain 1. Make a double crochet in first stitch. Repeat the following procedure to end of row. * Chain 5. Take 1 single crochet in the single crochet. Chain 5. Make 4 double crochets in next stitch. Skip 6 stitches. Make 4 double crochets in next stitch. End with chain 5. * Make 1 double crochet in last stitch.

Repeat the **first through sixth rows** until work is completed.


## Cable Pattern

A look similar to that of cable knitting is produced by following this sequence of crochet stitches. Begin with a foundation chain the required length. Use a multiple of 10 stitches plus 1.

For the **first row,** insert afghan crochet hook into second chain from hook. Put yarn over hook and draw through a loop. Then pull through a loop in each chain to end of row. Leave all loops on hook.

For the **second row,** work loops off hook by putting yarn over hook and drawing it through first loop. Repeat the following procedure to end of row. * Put yarn over hook. Pull it through next 2 loops. * End with 1 loop remaining on hook. This loop becomes first stitch of next row.

For the **third row,** pull up a loop under vertical bar of next stitch, holding yarn with thumb in front and below hook. This makes a purl stitch. Repeat the preceding procedure twice. Still keeping all loops on hook, and by holding yarn in back, insert hook from front to back through center of next loop between vertical bar and strand behind it. Put yarn over hook and pull up a loop, making a knit stitch. Repeat this procedure in next 3 stitches. In the last 3 stitches, make 3 purl stitches.

For the **fourth or cable row,** put yarn over hook. Draw yarn through first loop. Put yarn over hook again and draw through next 2 loops. Do this twice. Slip next 2 stitches onto a double-pointed needle and hold in front of work. Put yarn over hook and pull through loop, working off the next 2 loops twice. Slip loops from double-pointed needle back to hook and work off, making a cable. Work off the 3 purl stitches also.

For the **fifth row,** repeat the third row.

For the **sixth row,** repeat the second row.

For the **seventh row,** repeat the third row.

For the **eighth row,** repeat the fourth row.

Repeat the **first through eighth rows** until work is completed.

## Checkerboard Pattern

This stitch pattern can be used for soft, airy shawls. The lacy design forms a checkerboard of diamonds. Begin with a foundation chain the required length. Use a multiple of 10 stitches plus 1.

For the **first row,** chain 2 stitches. Make a double crochet in first stitch. Repeat the following procedure to end of row. * Chain 4. Skip 4 stitches. Take a single crochet in next stitch. To make 1 petal design, chain 7, take single crochet in same stitch. Repeat the preceding sequence of stitches twice. After making the petal design, chain 4. Skip 4 stitches. Take a double crochet in next stitch. * Turn.

For the **second row,** chain 1. Make a single crochet in double crochet of previous row. Repeat the following procedure to end of row. * Chain 1. Take a single crochet in first petal. Chain 3. Make a single crochet in second petal. Chain 3. Take a single crochet in third petal. Chain 1. Take a single crochet in double crochet of previous row. * Turn.

For the **third row,** chain 7. Take a single crochet in first stitch. Chain 7. Single crochet in same stitch. Chain 7. Single crochet in same stitch. Chain 4. Double crochet in single crochet of second petal. Repeat the following procedure. * Chain 4. Take single crochet in single crochet above double crochet. To make 3 petals, repeat this sequence of stitches 3 times: chain 7 and take a single crochet in the same stitch. * End with chain 7, a single crochet, chain 3, and a double crochet taken in the last stitch. Turn.

For the **fourth row,** chain 1. Make 1 double crochet in chain-3 space. Chain 3. Make double crochet in next petal. Repeat following sequence across row. * Chain 1. Single crochet in double crochet of previous row. Chain 1. Take single crochet in first petal. Chain 3. Make single crochet in second petal. Chain 3. Single crochet in third petal. * End row with chain 3 and single crochet in second petal. Turn.

For the **fifth row,** chain 2. Double crochet in first stitch. Repeat the following procedure. * Chain 4. Take 1 single crochet in single crochet above double crochet. To make petals, repeat this sequence of stitches 3 times: chain 7 and take a single crochet in same stitch. * End with chain 4 and a double crochet in single crochet above second petal of previous row.

Repeat the **second through fifth rows** until work is completed.

## Clam Stitch

Tiny eyelets defining a small motif add interest to this textured stitch. Begin with a foundation chain the required length. Use a multiple of 16 stitches plus 11.

For the **first row,** take a double crochet in second chain. Repeat across row. At the end, turn.

For the **second row,** chain 3 stitches which take the place of the first double crochet. Make a double crochet in the next 10 stitches. Repeat the following procedure. * Skip 2 stitches. In the next stitch, take 1 double crochet, 1 chain, 1 double crochet, 1 chain, and 1 double crochet. Then skip 2 stitches. Double crochet in next 11 stitches. * Turn.

For the **third row,** chain 3. Work a double crochet in each stitch to end of row. Turn.

For the **fourth row,** chain 3. Double crochet in 3 stitches. Repeat the following procedure. * Skip 2 stitches. In next stitch, make 1 double crochet, 1 chain, 1 double crochet, 1 chain, and 1 double crochet. Skip 2 stitches. Double crochet in next 10 stitches. * End row by skipping 2 stitches. In next stitch, take 1 double crochet, 1 chain, 1 double crochet, 1 chain, and 1 double crochet. Then skip 2 stitches. Make a double crochet in the last 4 stitches. Turn.

For the **fifth row,** chain 3. Take a double crochet in each stitch to end of row.

Repeat the **second through fifth rows** until work is completed.

## Cluster Stitch

When several stitches are grouped together, an openwork block effect results. Begin with a foundation chain the required length. Use a multiple of 2 stitches plus 1 and then add 1 extra chain.

For the **first row,** make 1 single crochet in second chain from hook. Continue with 1 single crochet in each chain to end of chain. Finish with 2 chains. Turn.

For the **second row,** skip the first stitch. Put yarn over hook. Pull up a loop 4 times in next stitch. Now there should be 9 loops on hook. Place yarn over hook and draw through the 9 loops. This forms a cluster. Repeat the following procedure to the last stitch. * Make 1 chain stitch. Skip 1 stitch. Make cluster in next stitch. * When last stitch is reached, take 1 double crochet in last stitch. Chain 2 and turn.

For the **third row,** skip first stitch. Make cluster in top of first cluster. Repeat the following procedure to end of row. * Chain 1. Make cluster in next cluster. * At the end of the row, make a double crochet in top of turning chain. Turn.

Repeat the **third row** until work is completed.

## Crescent Pattern

By changing the placement of the hook in making alternating single crochet stitches, an interesting textured effect results. Begin with a foundation chain the required length, using an even number of stitches.

For the **first row,** chain 1. Make single crochet stitches to end of row. Turn.

For the **second row,** chain 1. Make a single crochet in first stitch. Follow with a single crochet, inserting hook into the base of next single crochet of previous row. Alternate these 2 stitches to end of row.

Repeat the **second row** until work is completed.

## Cross Stitch

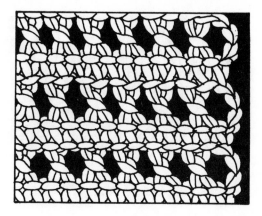

A raised effect is created by rows of crossed stitches. Begin with a foundation stitch the required length, using a multiple of 2 stitches plus 1, with an additional chain stitch.

For the **first row,** make a single crochet in each chain stitch.

For the **second row,** repeat the following procedure. * Skip 1 single crochet. Make 1 double crochet in next single crochet. For the cross stitch, take 1 double crochet in skipped single crochet. * End the row with a double crochet in last stitch. Chain 1 and turn.

For the **third row,** take a single crochet in each stitch across the row. Make a single crochet in top of turning chain. Chain 3 and turn.

Repeat the **second and third rows** until work is completed.

## Fan Cluster Pattern

Wavy rows of fanlike clusters add special design interest to this lacy stitch pattern. Start with a foundation chain the required length, using a multiple of 8 stitches plus 1, with an additional chain stitch.

For the **first row,** make a single crochet in second chain from hook. Then repeat the following procedure to end of row. * Start by making 3 chain stitches. Then skip 3 chains. In next chain, take 1 double crochet, 3 chains, and 1 double crochet. Follow with 3 chains. Skip 3 chains. Make 1 single crochet in next chain. * At the end of the row, chain 1 and turn.

For the **second row,** work with right side toward you. Make a single crochet in first single crochet. Repeat the following procedure to end of row. * Take 3 single crochets in chain loop. Then make 1 single crochet in next double crochet. Make 5 single crochets in next chain loop. Continue with 1 single crochet in next double crochet, 3 single crochets in next chain loop, and 1 single crochet in next single crochet. * At end of row, chain 3 and turn.

For the **third row,** skip 5 single crochets. Repeat the following procedure to the end of row. * Put yarn over hook. Insert hook in next stitch. Pull up a loop about ½ inch (1.3 cm) long. Do this 3 times. Put yarn over hook. Draw through first 6 loops. Place yarn over hook again and pull through remaining 2 loops to make a cluster. Follow with 3 chain stitches and a cluster in next single crochet. Do this until 5 clusters have been made. Then skip 4 single crochets. Make a treble crochet in next single crochet. Skip 4 single crochets. * End row with 1 treble crochet in last stitch. Chain 1 and turn.

For the **fourth row,** begin with 1 single crochet in first treble crochet. Repeat the following procedure to end of row. * Chain 4. Skip next chain loop. Make 1 single crochet in next chain loop. Chain 3. Take 1 single crochet in following chain loop. Skip next chain loop. Chain 4. Make 1 single crochet in next treble crochet. * At end of row, take 1 single crochet in top of turning chain. Then chain 1 and turn.

For the **fifth row,** make a single crochet in first single crochet. Repeat the following procedure to end of row. * Chain 3. Skip the chain-4 loop. In next chain-3 loop, make 1 double crochet, 3 chains, and 1 double crochet. Then chain 3. Skip next chain-4 loop. Take 1 single crochet in next single crochet. * At end of row, chain 1 and turn.

Repeat the **second through fifth rows** until work is completed.

## Forget-me-not Stitch

This shell-like pattern creates a scalloped effect with a dainty floral design. Begin with a foundation chain the required length. Use a multiple of 3 stitches plus 1.

For the **first row,** chain 3. Then, in first stitch, take 1 double crochet, 2 chains, and 1 single crochet. Repeat the following procedure to end of row. * Start by skipping 2 stitches. Then, in next stitch, make 2 double crochets, 2 chains, and 1 single crochet. * At the row's end, turn.

For the **second row,** chain 2. Then, in chain-2 space, make 1 double crochet, 2 chains, and 1 single crochet. Repeat the following procedure to end of row. * Take 2 double crochets, 2 chains, and 1 single crochet in chain-2 space. * At end of row, turn.

Repeat the **second row** until work is completed.

## Frieze Pattern

The arrangement of stitches for this design produces a border effect with openwork details. Begin with a foundation chain the required length. Use a multiple of 3 stitches plus 1.

For the **first row,** chain 1. Make 1 half double crochet in each stitch to end of row. Turn.

For the **second row,** chain 1. Then repeat this procedure to end of row. * Start with 1 single crochet and 3 chains. Then skip 2 stitches. * End the row with a single crochet. Turn.

For the **third row,** repeat the following procedure to end of row. * Chain 3. Make 1 single crochet in chain-3 space. * End the row with 2 chains and 1 single crochet. Turn.

For the **fourth row,** repeat the following procedure to end of row. * Begin by chaining 2. Then take 1 half double crochet in first space. Make 3 half double crochets in following spaces. * End with 2 half double crochets in last space.

Repeat the **second through fourth rows** until work is completed.

## Granny Square

This square medallion can be made with yarns in different colors. It provides a good way of using bits of leftover yarn. One way of combining the colors is shown here. However, other color designs can be created, such as crossed diagonals, with the stitch pattern remaining the same. Begin by working 5 chain stitches. Make ring by joining stitches with a slip stitch.

For the **first round,** chain 3. Make 2 double crochets in ring. Chain 1. Follow with 3 double crochets in ring, repeating this step 3 times. End with 1 chain. Join with a slip stitch in third turning chain. If different colors are being used, fasten off first color.

For the **second round,** attach second color in any chain-1 space. Chain 3. Make 2 double crochets in same space. Repeat the following procedure 3 times. * To make corner, take 3 double crochets, 1 chain, and 3 double crochets in next chain-1 space. * Ending with 3 double crochets, make 1 chain in beginning chain-1 space. Join with a slip stitch to top of chain-3. Fasten off second color.

For the **third round,** attach third color in any chain-1 space. Chain 3. Make 2 double crochets in same space. Repeat the following procedure 3 times. * Start with 3 double crochets in space between the next 2 groups of 3 double crochets. Take 3 double crochets in next chain-1 space. Chain 1. To make corner, make 3 double crochets in same space. * End round with 3 double crochets in space between next 2 groups of 3 double crochets. Chain 1 in beginning chain-1 space. Join round with a slip stitch to top of chain-3. Fasten off third color.

As each round is worked, continue to change colors. Three more rounds complete the design. In corners, work 3 double crochets, 1 chain, and another 3 double crochets. Take 3 double crochets between each 3-double-crochet group on the sides.

## Knot Stitch

This stitch is also known as the Lover's Knot Stitch. It creates a dainty, gauzy effect. Begin with a foundation chain the required length.

For the **first row,** make a single crochet in the second chain from hook. Repeat the following procedure to end of row. * Begin by drawing up a ¾-inch (2 cm) loop (A). Put yarn over hook and draw a loop through the longer loop. Make a single crochet in single strand of long loop. This procedure produces a knot stitch. Make another knot stitch. Skip 4 chains. Single crochet in next chain. * At the end of the row, turn.

For the **second row,** repeat the following procedure to the end of the row. * Make 3 knot stitches. Then take a single crochet in first long loop of next double knot stitch to the right of knot. Take a single crochet in second loop of the same knot stitch to the left of the same knot. Make a double knot stitch. *

Repeat the **second row** until work is completed.

## Lacy Diamond Pattern

This stitch produces a geometric design with openwork spaces defining the lines. Begin with a foundation chain the required length. Use a multiple of 3 stitches plus 1, with an additional 1 chain.

For the **first row,** make a single crochet in second chain from hook. Take a single crochet in each chain to end of foundation chain. Chain 5 and turn.

For the **second row,** start with a treble crochet in first stitch, leaving 2 loops on hook. Skip 2 stitches. Make a treble crochet in next stitch, leaving 3 loops on hook. Put yarn over hook and draw through the 3 loops on hook. Chain 2. Repeat the following procedure to end of row. * Make 1 treble crochet in same stitch as last treble crochet, leaving 2 loops on hook. Skip 2 stitches. Take a treble crochet, leaving 3 loops on hook. Put yarn over hook and draw through 3 loops on hook. Chain 2. End with 1 treble crochet in last stitch, which was used for the last treble crochet. * Chain 3 and turn.

For the **third row,** skip first 3 stitches. Take 1 treble stitch in next stitch. Chain 2. Repeat the directions in second row from asterisk (*). Make last treble stitch in third stitch of turning chain. Chain 5 and turn.

Repeat the **second and third rows** until work is completed.

## Lattice Pattern

A series of triangular shapes provide a latticelike look to this stitch pattern. Make a foundation chain the required length. Use a multiple of 3 stitches plus 1, with an additional 4 chains.

For the **first row,** make lattice in fifth chain from hook with 1 treble crochet, 1 chain, and 1 treble crochet. Repeat the following procedure to end of row. * Skip 2 chains. Make lattice in next chain. * At the last 3 chains, skip 2 chains and make 1 treble crochet in last chain. Chain 4 and turn.

For the **second row,** make lattice in each chain-1 space to end of row. Make a treble crochet in top of turning chain. Chain 4 and turn.

Repeat the **second row** until work is completed.

## Loop Stitch

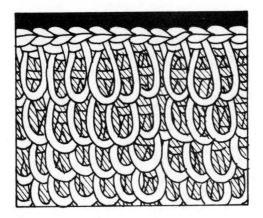

As its name implies, a series of loops is used to create a shaggy look. Begin with foundation chain the required length, using any number of stitches plus 1 chain.

For the **first row,** make a single crochet in second chain from hook. Continue to place a single crochet in each chain to end of row. Chain 1 and turn.

For the **second row,** skip first stitch. Repeat the following procedure to end of row. * Insert hook in next stitch. To determine length of loop, place yarn around middle finger of left hand. Draw yarn through stitch. Put yarn over hook and pull through 2 loops. Slip long loop off finger. Continue, keeping loops the same size. * Chain 1 and turn.

For the **third row,** skip first stitch. Make 1 single crochet in each stitch to end of row. Chain 1 and turn.

Repeat the **second and third rows** until work is completed.

## Looped Chevron Stitch

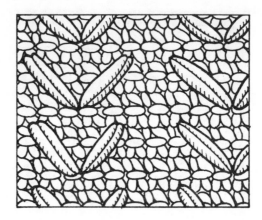

The design for this stitch pattern is developed by placing long loops diagonally on the surface of the crochet background. Make a foundation chain the required length. Use a multiple of 6 stitches plus 1 chain.

For the **first row,** make a single crochet in second chain from hook. Take a single crochet in each chain to end of foundation chain. Then chain 1 and turn.

For the **second row,** skip first stitch. Take 1 single crochet in each stitch of previous row. Chain 1 and turn.

For the **third and fourth rows,** repeat the second row.

For the **fifth row,** skip first stitch. Make 1 single crochet in next stitch. Then place yarn over hook and draw up a loop ½ inch (1.3 cm) long around first stitch in second row. The loop may be worked as a double crochet. Repeat the following procedure. * Skip the next 4 stitches in the second row. Make loop in next stitch. Skip next 2 stitches in fourth row. Take 1 single crochet in each of the next 4 stitches. Next make a loop in stitch in second row adjacent to last loop. * When the last 4 stitches are reached, make a loop in last stitch crocheted in second row. Skip next 2 stitches in fourth row. Make 1 single crochet in each of last 2 stitches. Chain 1 and turn.

Repeat the **second through fifth rows** until work is completed.

## Looped Cross Stitch

The rows of zigzag loops seem to produce a cross stitch effect on the surface of this stitch pattern. Start with a foundation chain the required length. Use a multiple of 6 stitches plus 1 chain.

For the **first row,** make a single crochet in second chain from hook. Then take a single crochet in each chain to end of foundation chain. Chain 1 and turn.

For the **second row,** skip first stitch. Make a single crochet in each stitch of previous row. Chain 1 and turn.

For the **third and fourth rows,** use directions for second row.

For the **fifth row,** skip first stitch. Make a single crochet in next stitch. To make a long loop, put yarn over hook. Pull up a loop, ½ inch (1.3 cm) long, around first stitch in second row. Work this loop as a double crochet, creating a long double crochet. Repeat the following procedure to the last 4 stitches at end of row. * Skip next 4 stitches in second row. Make another long double crochet in next stitch. Skip next 2 stitches in fourth row. Take a single crochet in each of the next 4 stitches. Make another long double crochet in stitch in second row next to the last long double crochet. * When the last 4 stitches are reached, take a long double crochet in last stitch. Skip next 2 stitches in fourth row. Make a single crochet in each of last 2 stitches. Chain 1 and turn.

For the **sixth and seventh rows,** use directions for second row.

For the **eighth row,** use directions for second row with this exception: omit chain 1 at end of eighth row.

For the **ninth row,** make a long double crochet in fourth stitch in sixth row. Skip first stitch in eighth row. Take a single crochet in each of the next 4 stitches. Make a long double crochet in stitch in sixth row next to last long double crochet. Repeat the following procedure. * Skip next 4 stitches in sixth row. Make a long double crochet in next stitch. Skip next 2 stitches in eighth row. Take 1 single crochet in each of next 4 stitches. * Make another long double crochet in stitch adjacent to last long double crochet in sixth row. Take a single crochet in last stitch. Chain 1 and turn.

Repeat the **second through ninth rows** until work is completed.

## Looped Zigzag Pattern

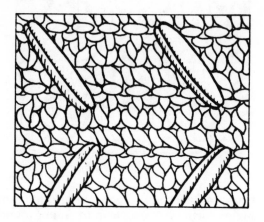

By alternating the direction of long loops, a zigzag design is created. Begin with a foundation chain the required length. Use a multiple of 5 stitches plus 1 chain.

For the **first row,** make a single crochet in second chain from hook. Take a single crochet in each chain to end of chain. Chain 3 and turn.

For the **second row,** skip first stitch. Take 1 double crochet in each stitch to end of row. Chain 1 and turn.

For the **third row,** skip first stitch. Take 1 single crochet in each stitch to end of row. Chain 3 and turn.

For the **fourth row,** use directions for second row.

For the **fifth row,** draw a loop, ½ inch (1.3 cm) long, between fifth and sixth double crochet of second row. Work this long loop as a single crochet. Skip first stitch on fourth row. Repeat the following procedure. * Take 1 single crochet in each of next 4 stitches. Skip 4 stitches in second row. Make a long loop between next 2 stitches. Skip 1 stitch in fourth row. * At last 4 stitches in fourth row, take a single crochet in each of the last 4 stitches. Chain 3 and turn.

For the **sixth, seventh, and eighth rows,** follow directions for second, third, and fourth rows.

For the **ninth row,** skip 2 stitches. Take a single crochet in each of next 3 stitches. Make a long loop between first and second stitches of sixth row. Repeat the following procedure to end of row. * Skip 1 stitch in eighth row. Take 1 single crochet in each of next 4 stitches. Skip 4 stitches in sixth row. Make a long loop between next 2 stitches.* At end of row, chain 3 and turn.

Repeat the **second through ninth rows** until work is completed.

## Lover's Knot Stitch

*See* Knot Stitch.

## Meadow Stitch

An interesting arrangement of chain and double crochet produces an allover effect of cluster blocks and triangular spaces. Begin with a foundation chain the required number of stitches.

For the **first row,** chain 5. Take 1 double crochet in sixth chain from hook. Chain 2. Double crochet in same stitch. Repeat the following procedure to end of row. * Skip 2 stitches. Take a double crochet in next stitch. Chain 2. Make a double crochet in the same stitch in which the previous double crochet was taken. * Turn.

For the **second row,** chain 3. Make 3 double crochets in chain-2 space. Repeat the following procedure to end of row. * Make 4 double crochets in each chain-2 space across row. * End with a double crochet in top of starting chain of previous row. Turn.

For the **third row,** chain 4. Repeat the following procedure to end of row. * Between the groups of 4 double crochets, work 1 double crochet, 2 chains, and 1 double crochet. * End with 1 double crochet in the chain-3 space at the beginning of the previous row. Turn.

For the **fourth row,** chain 3. Work 4 double crochets into each chain-2 space. End with 1 double crochet in last stitch. Turn.

Repeat the **third and fourth rows** until work is completed.

## Mesh Crochet

An open, allover design can be created by combining basic and chain stitches. The spaces vary in size depending on the type of basic stitch used. For instance, the mesh will be larger with treble crochet stitches than with double crochet stitches. Directions for mesh crochet in various degrees of openness are given here. Select the one that produces the desired effect.

## Mesh—Double Crochet
### with Chain-one Spaces

Make a foundation chain the required length. Use multiple of 2 stitches plus 1, with an additional 2 chains.

For the **first row,** make a double crochet in fifth chain from hook. Repeat the following procedure to end of row. * Chain 1. Skip 1 chain. Make a double crochet in next chain. * At end of foundation, chain 4 and turn.

For the **second row,** skip first 2 stitches. Repeat the following procedure to end of row. * Take 1 double crochet in next double crochet. Chain 1. * End row with a double crochet in third stitch of turning chain. Chain 4 and turn.

Repeat the **second row** until work is completed.

## Mesh—Double Crochet
### with Chain-two Spaces

Start with a foundation chain the required length. Use a multiple of 3 stitches plus 1, with an additional 2 chains.

For the **first row,** make 1 double crochet in sixth chain from hook. Repeat the following procedure to end of row. * Chain 2. Skip 2 chains. Take a double crochet in next chain. * At end of row, chain 5 and turn.

For the **second row,** skip first 3 stitches. Repeat the following procedure to end of row. * Take 1 double crochet in next double crochet. Chain 2. * At end of row, take a double crochet in third stitch of turning chain. Chain 5 and turn.

Repeat the **second row** until work is completed.


## Mesh—Half Double Crochet
### with Chain-one Spaces

Begin with a foundation chain the required length. Use a multiple of 2 stitches plus 1, with an additional 3 chains.

For the **first row,** make a half double crochet in fourth chain from hook. Repeat the following procedure to end of row. * Chain 1. Skip 1 chain. Make a half double crochet in next chain. * At end of row, chain 3 and turn.

For the **second row,** skip first 2 stitches. Repeat the following procedure to end of row. * Make a half double crochet in next half double crochet. Chain 1. * End with 1 half double crochet in second stitch of turning chain. Chain 3 and turn.

Repeat the **second row** until work is completed.

## Mesh—Treble Crochet
### with Chain-one Spaces

Begin with a foundation chain the required length. Use a multiple of 2 stitches plus 1, with an additional 1 chain.

For the **first row,** make 1 treble crochet in sixth chain from hook. Repeat the following procedure to end of row. * Chain 1. Skip 1 chain. Make 1 treble crochet in next chain. * Finish with 5 chains. Turn.

For the **second row,** skip first 2 stitches. Repeat the following procedure to end of row. * Make 1 treble crochet in next treble crochet. Chain 1. * End with 1 treble crochet in fourth stitch of turning chain. Chain 5 and turn.

Repeat the **second row** until work is completed.


## Mesh—Treble Crochet
### with Chain-two Spaces

Commence with a foundation chain the required length. Use a multiple of 3 stitches plus 1 with an additional 3 chains.

For the **first row,** take 1 treble crochet in the seventh chain from hook. Repeat the following procedure to end of row. * Chain 2. Skip 2 chains. Take 1 treble crochet in next chain. * Finish with 6 chains. Turn.

For the **second row,** skip first 3 stitches. Repeat the following sequence of stitches to end of row. * Take 1 treble crochet in next treble crochet. Chain 2. * End with 1 double crochet in third stitch of turning chain. Chain 6 and turn.

Repeat the **second row** until work is completed.

## Mesh Diamonds—Chain Five

Commence with a foundation chain the required length. Use a multiple of 6 stitches plus 1, with an additional 6 chains.

For the **first row,** make a single crochet in seventh chain from hook. Repeat the following procedure to end of row. * Chain 5. Skip 5 chains. Take a single crochet in next chain. * At the end, chain 5 and turn.

For the **second row,** take a single crochet in first chain space. Repeat the following procedure to the end of the row. * Chain 5. Make a single crochet in next chain space. * End with a single crochet in last chain space. Then chain 5 and turn.

Repeat the **second row** until work is completed.

## Mesh Diamonds—Chain Four

Make a foundation chain the required length. Use a multiple of 5 stitches plus 1, with an additional 5 chains.

For the **first row,** take 1 single crochet in the sixth chain from hook. Repeat the following procedure to end of row. * Chain 4. Skip 4 chains. Take a single crochet in next chain. * At the end, chain 4 and turn.

For the **second row,** make a single crochet in first chain space. Repeat the following procedure to end of row. * Chain 4. Make a single crochet in next chain space. * End the row with a single crochet in last chain space. Then chain 4 and turn.

Repeat the **second row** until work is completed.

### Mesh Diamonds—Chain Three

Begin with a foundation chain the required length. Use a multiple of 4 stitches plus 1, with an additional 4 chains.

For the **first row,** make a single crochet in the fifth chain from hook. Repeat the following procedure to end of row. * Chain 3. Skip 3 chains. Make a single crochet in next chain. * At end of row, chain 3 and turn.

For the **second row,** take a single crochet in first chain space. Repeat the following procedure to end of row. * Chain 3. Make a single crochet in next chain space. * End the row with a single crochet in last chain space. Then chain 3 and turn.

Repeat the **second row** until the work is completed.

### Mesh Diamonds—Chain Two

Make a foundation chain the required length. Use a multiple of 3 stitches plus 1, with an additional 3 chains.

For the **first row,** make a single crochet in the fourth chain from hook. Repeat the following procedure to end of row. * Chain 2. Skip 2 chains. Then take a single crochet in the next chain stitch. * At end of row, chain 2 and turn.

For the **second row,** take a single crochet in first chain space. Repeat the following procedure to end of row. * Chain 2. Take 1 single crochet in next chain space. End with a single crochet in last chain space. * Chain 2 and turn.

Repeat the **second row** until work is completed.

### Mock Rice Stitch

*See* Bicolor Afghan Stitch (in "Styles and Types of Crocheting," under Multicolor Crochet).

## Moss Stitch

This stitch produces a solid effect with an interesting textural quality. Begin with a foundation chain the required length. Use a multiple of 2 stitches plus 1, with an additional chain stitch.

For the **first row,** start by taking 1 single crochet and 1 double crochet in the second chain from hook. Repeat the following procedure to end of row. * Skip 1 chain. Then, in the next stitch, make 1 single crochet and 1 double crochet. * At the end, chain 1 and turn.

For the **second row,** skip first 2 stitches. Then take 1 single crochet and 1 double crochet in each double crochet across row. At the end, chain 1 and turn.

Repeat the **second row** until the work is completed.

## Open Cluster Ribs

Clusters of stitches are grouped in vertical rows, giving a ribbed effect to this lacy pattern. Begin with a foundation chain the required length. Use a multiple of 8 stitches plus 1 and an additional chain.

For the **first row,** make a single crochet in second chain from hook. Repeat the following procedure to end of row. * Chain 2. Skip 3 chains. In the next chain, make 1 double crochet, 3 chains, and 1 double crochet. Chain 2, skip 3 chains. Make 1 single crochet in next chain. * At end of row, chain 6 and turn.

For the **second row,** make a single crochet in chain-3 space. Repeat the following procedure to end of row. * Chain 3. In the next single crochet, do this 3 times: put yarn over hook, insert hook, and pull through a loop about ½ inch (1.3 cm) long. Then place yarn over hook and draw through 7 loops. Chain 1, forming cluster. Chain 3. Make 1 single crochet in chain-3 space. * End row with 1 double crochet in last stitch. Chain 1 and turn.

For the **third row,** make a single crochet in the double crochet. Repeat the following procedure to end of row. * Chain 2. Make 1 double crochet, 3 chains, and 1 double crochet in single crochet. Chain 2. Take 1 single crochet in cluster. * End row with a single crochet in third stitch of chain stitch of chain-6. Chain 6 and turn.

Repeat the **second and third rows** until work is completed.

## Open Squares

An interesting arrangement of stitches creates a series of squares, outlined with open spaces and moving in a diagonal direction. Begin with a foundation chain the required length. Use a multiple of 4 stitches plus 3.

For the **first row,** chain 3. In the fourth chain from the hook, take 3 double crochets, 3 chains, and 1 single crochet. Skip 1 stitch. Repeat the following sequence of stitches to end of row. * Make 3 double crochets, 3 chains, and 1 single crochet in next stitch. Skip 1 stitch. * End with 3 double crochets and turn.

For the **second row,** chain 2. Then place 3 double crochets, 3 chains, and 1 single crochet in chain-3 space of each motif. End with 1 double crochet in last chain.

Repeat the **second row** to the end of work.

## Open Stripes

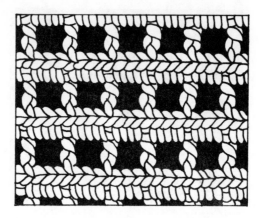

Rows of open squares create an allover eyelet effect in a striped design. Ribbon can be run through a row of eyelets as if it were an insertion. Begin with a foundation chain the required length. Use an even number of stitches.

For the **first row,** make a double crochet in fourth chain from hook. Repeat the following procedure to end of row. * Chain 1. Skip 1 stitch. Make a double crochet in next stitch. * Turn.

For the **second row,** chain 2. Make a half double crochet in each space and in each double crochet of previous row until row is completed. Turn.

For the **third row,** chain 3. Skip 1 stitch. Double crochet in next stitch. Repeat the following procedure to end of row. * Chain 1. Skip 1 stitch. Double crochet in next stitch. * At end of row, turn.

Repeat the **second and third rows** until work is completed.

## Overlay Stripe Pattern

A series of graduated loops added to a background of single crochet creates an effective design, especially when worked in stripes of different colors. Begin with a foundation chain the required length. Use a multiple of 5 stitches plus 1. Crochet with yarn in 4 different colors: A, B, C, and D.

For the **first row,** work on the right side. Using yarn A, make a single crochet in second chain from hook. Repeat in each remaining chain. Chain 1 and turn.

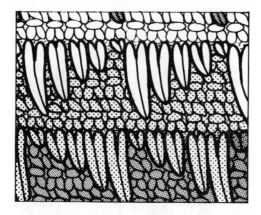

For the **second through sixth rows,** single crochet in each single crochet to end of row.

For the **seventh row,** use yarn B. Repeat following procedure to end of row. * Single crochet in next crochet. Then, to make overlay stitches, take a long single crochet in next single crochet in second row below. Follow with 1 in the next stitch in third row below; next stitch, fourth row below; next stitch, fifth row below. * End row with a single crochet in last single crochet.

For the **eighth through twelfth rows,** continue to use yarn B. Make a single crochet in each single crochet to end of row.

For the **thirteenth row,** change to yarn C. Repeat the following procedure to end of row. * Begin with a long stitch in next single crochet in fifth row below. Follow with 1 in the next stitch, fourth row below; next stitch, third row below; next stitch, second row below. Single crochet in next single crochet. * End with a single crochet in last stitch.

For the **fourteenth through eighteenth rows,** continue to use yarn C. Single crochet in each single crochet to end of row.

For the **nineteenth through twenty-fourth rows,** follow the directions for the seventh through twelfth rows, using yarn D.

For the **twenty-fifth row,** repeat the thirteenth row, using yarn A.

For the remainder of the work, repeat the **second through twenty-fifth rows.**

## Pineapple Stitch

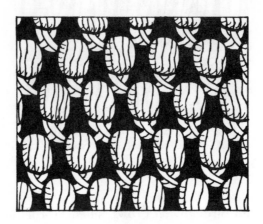

An arrangement of cluster blocks in rows produces a puffy, textural effect. Make a foundation chain the required length, using an even number of stitches.

For the **first row,** chain 2. Repeat the following sequence of stitches to end of row. * Begin by repeating this procedure 4 times: put yarn over hook, insert hook in fourth chain, place yarn over hook again, and draw through loop. When there are 9 loops on hook, put yarn over hook and draw through 8 loops. Then put yarn over hook again and draw through last 2 loops on hook. Chain 1. Skip 1 chain. *

For the **second row,** repeat pattern in each chain-1 space of previous row.

Repeat the **second row** until work is completed.

## Picot Mesh Pattern

This mesh design is given a special decorative effect through the use of picots. Begin with a foundation chain the required length. Use a multiple of 4 stitches.

For the **first row,** repeat the following sequence of stitches. * Chain 5. Skip 3 stitches. In next stitch, take 1 single crochet, 3 chains, and 1 single crochet. * End with 5 chains. Skip 3 stitches. Make 1 single crochet, and turn.

For the **second row,** repeat the following sequence of stitches to end of row. * Chain 5. In the third stitch of the chain-5, make 1 single crochet, 3 chains, and 1 single crochet. * End with chain 5. Make 1 single crochet.

Repeat the **second row** to end of work.

## Point Stitch

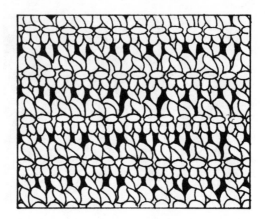

A sequence of loops and single crochets form this unusual design pattern with a repeating 1-line detail. Begin with a foundation chain the required length. Use a multiple of 2 stitches plus 1 chain.

For the **first row,** skip 2 chains. Repeat the following sequence to end of row. * Bring a loop through each of the next 2 chains, leaving 3 loops on hook. Put yarn over hook and draw through first 2 loops. Put yarn over hook again and draw through last 2 loops. Chain 1. * Turn.

For the **second row,** skip first stitch. Take 1 single crochet in each stitch to end of row. Make 1 single crochet in turning chain. Chain 2 and turn.

For the **third row,** skip first stitch. Repeat the following sequence of stitches to end of row. * Bring a loop through each of the next 2 stitches. Put yarn over hook and draw through first 2 loops. Put yarn over hook again and draw through last 2 loops. Chain 1. * Turn.

Repeat the **second and third rows** until work is completed.

## Popcorn Stitch

This stitch has been popular for a long time. A puffy effect is created on the surface. It can be worked with or without the bars or posts between each cluster of stitches. Begin with a foundation chain using the required number of stitches.

For the **first row,** make 5 double crochets in the sixth chain from hook. Remove hook from loop. Insert the hook in top of the first double crochet that was made in this grouping and also in the dropped loop. Draw the loop through the double crochet stitch. Make 1 chain to secure the stitch, making the popcorn motif. Repeat the following sequence of stitches to end of row. * Chain 1. Skip next stitch. Make a double crochet in next stitch. Chain 2. Skip next stitch. Make a popcorn in next stitch. * At end of row, chain 3 and turn.

For the **second row,** repeat the following sequence of stitches to end of row. * Make 1 double crochet in popcorn. Take another double crochet in next chain-2 space, also 1 in next double crochet. Follow with a double crochet in chain-2 space. * End with 1 double crochet in popcorn. Make a double crochet in turning chain. Chain 4 and turn.

Repeat the **first and second rows** until work is completed.

## Puff Stitch

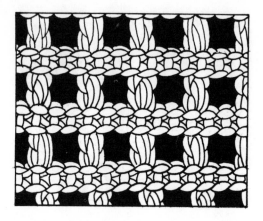

Cluster blocks, alternating with open spaces, produce this puffy design. Begin with a foundation chain of an even number of stitches.

For the **first row,** take a single crochet stitch in each of the foundation chain stitches. Chain 6 and turn.

For the **second row,** put yarn over hook. Skip 1 single crochet. To make the puff stitch, insert hook in next single crochet. Draw through a ½-inch (1.3 cm) loop. Repeat this procedure twice, leaving 7 loops on hook, all made in same stitch. Place yarn over hook and pull through the 7 loops. Chain 1. Then repeat the following sequence of stitches to end of row. * Chain 2. Skip 2 single crochets. Make puff stitch in next stitch. * Chain 1 and turn.

For the **third row,** make a single crochet in each chain stitch and in each puff stitch to end of row. Chain 4 and turn.

Repeat the **second and third rows** until work is completed.

## Raised Diagonal Pattern

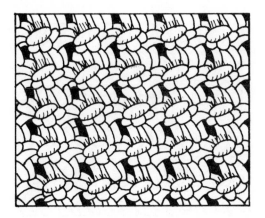

This stitch pattern creates a textural quality by combining slip and half double crochet stitches. Start with a foundation chain using an even number of stitches.

For the **first row,** chain 1. Make a slip stitch in the next stitch and a half double crochet in the next. Then repeat the following sequence of stitches to the end of the row. * Chain 1. Slip stitch in next stitch. Half double crochet in next stitch. * At the end of row, turn.

For the **second row,** repeat the following procedure across the row. * Chain 1. Slip stitch in half double crochet. Then take half double crochet in slip stitch. *

Repeat the **second row** until work is completed.

## Raised Stripe Pattern—
## Alternating Rows of Double and Half Double Crochet

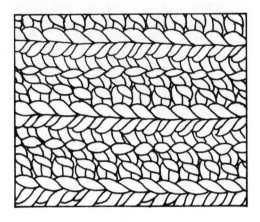

Begin with a foundation chain the required length. Any number of stitches can be used, with the addition of 2 chains.

For the **first row,** make a double crochet in fourth chain from hook. Take 1 double crochet in each chain to end of foundation chain. Then chain 2 and turn.

For the **second row,** skip first stitch. Make 1 half double crochet in each stitch of previous row, ending with 1 half double crochet in top of turning chain. Chain 3 and turn.

For the **third row,** work only into the back loop of each stitch. Skip first stitch. Take 1 double crochet in each stitch of previous row, ending with 1 double crochet in top of turning chain. Chain 2.

Alternate the **second and third rows** until work is completed.

## Raised Stripe Pattern—
### Alternating Rows of Double and Single Crochet

Make a foundation chain the required length, using any number of stitches plus 2 chains.

For the **first row,** make 1 double crochet in fourth chain from hook. Take 1 double crochet in each chain to end of foundation chain. Then chain 1 and turn.

For the **second row,** skip first stitch. Make a single crochet in each double crochet, finishing with a single crochet in turning chain. Chain 3 and turn.

For the **third row,** skip first stitch. Make 1 double crochet in each stitch of previous row. End with 1 double crochet in turning chain. Chain 1 and turn.

Repeat the **second and third rows** until work is completed.

## Raised Stripe Pattern—
### Alternating Rows of Treble and Half Double Crochet

Begin with a foundation chain the required length. Use any multiple of stitches plus 3 chains.

For the **first row,** take 1 treble crochet in fifth chain from hook. Then take 1 treble crochet in each chain to end of foundation chain. Chain 2 and turn.

For the **second row,** skip first stitch. Make 1 half double crochet in each stitch in the previous row. End with 1 half double crochet in top of turning chain. Chain 4 and turn.

For the **third row,** skip first stitch. Take 1 treble crochet in each stitch in previous use. End with 1 treble crochet in top of turning chain. Chain 2 and turn.

Alternate the **second and third rows** until work is completed.

## Roll Stitch

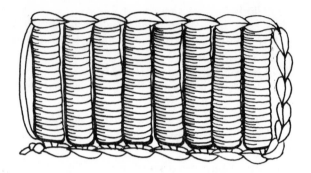

This is an old stitch pattern often found in early-nineteenth-century crochet designs. Yarn is wrapped around the hook to create the raised effect. Begin with a foundation chain the required length. Wrap yarn 16 times around shank part of hook. Do this evenly and loosely. Insert hook in sixth chain from hook. Draw loop through this chain. Put yarn over hook. Hold the wrapped stitches with left hand. Keep the hook pointed downward and carefully draw loop through wrapped stitches. Chain 1 stitch to secure the roll. Work another roll in the next stitch. Continue this way until work is completed.

**Russian Stitch**

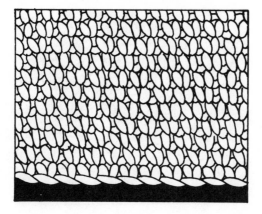

This stitch is worked only on the right side. If it is to be used flat, the yarn is to be joined at beginning of each row and cut at the end.

Start with a foundation chain the required length. Work each row in single crochet, inserting hook under both horizontal loops of each stitch of the previous row. Continue this way until work is completed.

## Scallop Pattern

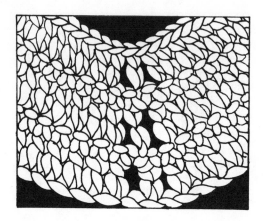

Begin this wavy design with a foundation chain the required length. Use a multiple of 14 stitches plus 13, with an additional 1 chain.

For the **first row,** make a double crochet in fourth chain from hook. Follow with a double crochet in each of next 3 chains. Repeat the following sequence of stitches. * Make 3 double crochets in next chain and 1 double crochet in each of next 5 chains. Skip 1 chain. Take 1 double crochet in next chain. Skip 1 chain. Make 1 double crochet in each of next 5 chains. * At last 6 chains, take 3 double crochets in next chain. Then 1 double crochet in each of last 5 chains. Turn.

For the **second row,** chain 1. Skip first 2 stitches. Take 1 single crochet in each of next 4 stitches. Repeat the following sequence of stitches. * Make 3 single crochets in next stitch and 1 single crochet in each of next 5 stitches. Skip one stitch. Take a single crochet in next stitch. Skip 1 stitch. Make a single crochet in each of next 5 stitches. * At the last 7 stitches, make 3 single crochets in next stitch. Then take 1 single crochet in each of next 4 stitches. Skip 1 stitch. Make 1 single crochet in top of turning chain. Turn.

For the **third row,** chain 3. Skip first 2 stitches. Take 1 double crochet in each of next 4 stitches. Repeat the following sequence of stitches. * Make 3 double crochets in next stitch and 1 double crochet in each of next 5 stitches. Skip 1 stitch. Take 1 double crochet in next stitch. Skip 1 stitch. Make 1 double crochet in each of next 5 stitches. * At the last 7 stitches, take 3 double crochets in next stitch. Make 1 double crochet in each of next 4 stitches. Skip 1 stitch. Take 1 double crochet in top of turning chain. Turn.

Repeat the **second and third rows** until work is completed.

**Shawl Cluster Pattern**

Dainty clusters amid a network of chains give a lacy look to this stitch pattern. Begin with a foundation chain the required length. Use a multiple of 6 stitches plus 1.

For the **first row,** chain 3. Make a cluster in next stitch. To make the cluster, repeat the following procedure 4 times. * Put yarn over hook, draw through a loop. Put yarn over hook again and draw through first 2 loops on hook. Then put yarn over hook and draw through the 4 loops on hook. To secure, chain 1. * Then repeat the following sequence. * Skip 2 stitches. In next stitch, take 1 double crochet, chain 2, and take 1 double crochet. Skip 2 stitches, make one cluster in next stitch. Chain 1. * End with skip 2 stitches. In next stitch, make 1 double crochet, 2 chain stitches, and 1 double crochet. In the last stitch, 1 double crochet. Chain 3 and turn.

For the **second row,** repeat the following sequence of stitches to end of row. * Make cluster in chain-2 spaces between 2 double crochets. Then make 1 double crochet, 2 chains, and 1 double crochet under the 2 threads, securing the cluster of the previous row. * Finish with 1 double crochet in chain-3 space of previous row.

Repeat the **first and second rows** until work is completed.

## Shell and Bar Pattern— Double Crochet

Begin with a foundation chain the required length. Use a multiple of 6 stitches plus 1, with an additional 2 chains.

For the **first row**, take 1 double crochet in third chain from hook. Repeat the following procedure to the last 6 stitches. * Skip 2 chains. Take 1 double crochet in next chain. Skip 2 chains. Make 5 double crochets for shell in next chain. * At the last 6 chains, skip 2 chains. Take 1 double crochet in next chain. Skip 2 chains. Then make 3 double crochets in last chain. Chain 3 and turn.

For the **second row**, make 2 double crochets in first stitch. Skip 2 double crochets. Repeat the following procedure to end of row. * Make 1 double crochet in next double crochet. Make a shell of 5 double crochets in the center double crochet of next shell. * End with 2 double crochets in top of turning chain. Chain 3 and turn.

For the **third row**, take 1 double crochet in first stitch. Skip 1 double crochet. Repeat the following procedure to end of row. * Take 1 double crochet in next double crochet. Make a shell of 5 double crochets in center stitch of next shell. * End with 1 double crochet in last double crochet. Then take 3 double crochets in top of turning chain. Chain 3 and turn.

Repeat the **second and third rows** until work is completed.

## Shell and Bar Pattern—
### Treble Crochet

Start with a foundation chain the required length. Use a multiple of 6 stitches plus 1, with an additional 3 chains.

For the **first row,** make 1 treble crochet in fifth chain from hook. Repeat the following procedure. * Skip 2 chains. Take 1 treble crochet in next chain. Skip 2 chains. To make shell in next chain, take 5 treble crochets. * At the last 6 chains, skip 2 chains. Make 1 treble crochet in next chain. Skip 2 chains. Make 3 treble crochets in last chain. Chain 4 and turn.

For the **second row,** make 2 treble crochets in first stitch. Skip 2 treble crochets. Repeat the following procedure. * Take 1 treble crochet in next treble crochet. Make a shell of 5 treble crochets in center stitch of next shell. * End with 1 treble crochet in last treble crochet. Take 2 treble crochets in top of turning chain. Chain 4 and turn.

For the **third row,** make 1 treble crochet in first stitch. Skip 1 treble crochet. Repeat the following procedure to end of row. * Take 1 treble crochet in next treble crochet. Make shell of 5 treble crochets in center stitch of next shell. * End with 1 treble crochet in last treble crochet. Take 3 treble crochets in top of turning chain. Chain 4 and turn.

Repeat the **second and third rows** until work is completed.

## Shell Pattern—
### Alternating Double Crochet

This is a popular pattern and is often spoken of as a fancy stitch. The shells can be made in various sizes, depending on the basic crochet stitch used, and placed in different ways for a wide variety of effects. Start with a foundation chain the required length. Use a multiple of 6 stitches plus 1, with an additional 3 chains.

For the **first row,** take 2 double crochets in fourth chain from hook. Repeat the following procedure. * Skip 2 chains. Take 1 single crochet in next chain. Skip 2 chains. For shell, make 5 double crochets in next chain. * At last 6 chains, skip 2 chains. Take 1 single crochet in next chain. Skip 2 chains. Make 3 double crochets in last chain. Chain 3 and turn.

For the **second row,** skip 3 double crochets. Repeat the following sequence of stitches. * Make 1 single crochet in next single crochet. Chain 2. Take 1 single crochet in third double crochet of shell. Chain 2. * At last 6 stitches, take 1 single crochet in next single crochet. Chain 2. Skip 2 double crochets. Take 1 single crochet in top of turning chain and turn.

For the **third row,** take a single crochet in first stitch. Repeat the following procedure to end of row. * Make shell in next stitch. Take 1 single crochet in next single crochet. * End with 1 single crochet in bottom of turning chain. Chain 3 and turn.

For the **fourth row,** take 1 single crochet in third double crochet of first shell. Repeat the following procedure to end of row. * Chain 2. Take a single crochet in next single crochet. Chain 2. Make a single crochet in third double crochet of next shell. * End with a single crochet in last stitch. Chain 3 and turn.

For the **fifth row,** make 2 double crochets in first single crochet. Repeat the following sequence of stitches to end of row. * Take 1 single crochet in next single crochet. Make shell in next single crochet. * End with 3 double crochets in bottom of turning chain. Chain 3 and turn.

Repeat the **second through fifth rows** until work is completed.

## Shell Pattern—
### Alternating Treble Crochet

Begin with a foundation chain the required length. Use a multiple of 6 stitches plus 1, with an additional 4 chains.

For the **first row,** take 2 treble crochets in fifth chain from hook. Repeat the following procedure. * Skip 2 chains. Take 1 single crochet in next chain. Skip 2 chains. To make shell, take 5 treble crochets in next chain. * At the last 6 chains, skip 2 chains. Make 1 single crochet in next chain. Skip 2 chains and then take 3 treble crochets in last chain. Chain 4 and turn.

For the **second row,** skip 3 treble crochets. Repeat the following procedure. * Take 1 double crochet in next single crochet. Chain 2. Follow with 1 single crochet in third treble crochet of shell. Chain 2. * At the last 6 stitches, take 1 double crochet in next single crochet. Chain 2. Skip 2 treble crochets. Make 1 single crochet in top of turning chain and turn.

For the **third row,** take 1 single crochet in first stitch. Repeat the following procedure to end of row. * Make shell of 5 treble crochets in next double crochet. Take 1 single crochet in next single crochet. * End with 1 single crochet in bottom of turning chain. Chain 4 and turn.

For the **fourth row,** make 1 single crochet in third treble of first shell. Repeat the following procedure to end of row. * Chain two. Make 1 double crochet in next single crochet. Chain two. Take 1 single crochet in third treble crochet of next shell. * End with 2 chains. Take 1 single crochet in last stitch. Chain 4 and turn.

For the **fifth row,** make 2 treble crochets in first single crochet. Repeat the following procedure to end of row. * Take 1 single crochet in next single crochet. Make shell of 5 treble crochets in next double crochet. * End with 3 treble crochets in bottom of turning chain. Chain 4 and turn.

Repeat the **second through fifth rows** until work is completed.

## Shell Pattern—
### Basic Double Crochet

Begin with a foundation chain the required length. Use a multiple of 5 stitches plus 1, with an additional 2 chains.

For the **first row,** make 1 double crochet in third chain from hook. Skip 4 chains. Repeat the following procedure to end of row. * For shell, take 5 double crochets in next chain. Skip 4 chains. * At last chain, take 3 double crochets. Chain 3 and turn.

For the **second row,** take 2 double crochets in first stitch. Repeat the making of shell in third double crochet of each shell. End with 2 double crochets in top of turning chain. Chain 3 and turn.

For the **third row,** make 1 double crochet in first stitch. Repeat the making of a shell in third double crochet of each shell. End with 3 double crochets in top of turning chain. Chain 3 and turn.

Repeat the **second and third rows** until work is completed.

## Shell Pattern—
### Basic Treble Crochet

Start with a foundation chain the required length. Use a multiple of 5 stitches plus 1, with an additional 3 chains.

For the **first row,** make 1 treble crochet in fourth chain from hook. Skip 4 chains. Repeat the following procedure to end of row. * To make a shell, take 5 treble crochets in next chain. Skip 4 chains. * In last chain, take 3 treble crochets. Chain 4 and turn.

For the **second row,** take 2 treble crochets in first stitch. Make shell, taking 5 treble crochets in third treble crochet of each shell to end of row. Finish with 2 treble crochets in top of turning chain. Chain 4 and turn.

For the **third row,** take 1 treble crochet in first stitch. Make shell, taking 5 treble crochets in third crochet of each shell to end of row. Finish with 3 treble crochets in top of turning chain. Chain 4 and turn.

Repeat the **second and third rows** until work is completed.

## Shell-Pattern—
## Double Crochet with Single Crochet Row

Commence with a foundation chain the required length. Use a multiple of 5 stitches plus 1, with additional 1 chain.

For the **first row,** take 1 single crochet in second chain from hook. Make 1 single crochet in each chain to end of foundation chain. Chain 3 and turn.

For the **second row,** take 1 double crochet in first stitch. Skip 4 stitches. Repeat the following procedure to end of row. * To make shell, take 5 double crochets in next stitch. Skip 4 stitches. * In last stitch, take 3 double crochets. Chain 1 and turn.

For the **third row,** skip first stitch. Make 1 single crochet in each stitch of previous row. End with 2 single crochets in top of turning chain. Chain 3 and turn.

Repeat the **second and third rows** until work is completed.


## Shell Pattern—
## Fish Scale Design

This is a variation of the shell stitch. Begin with a foundation chain the required number of stitches.

For the **first row,** place in fourth chain 1 double crochet, 3 chains, and 1 double crochet. Repeat the following procedure to end of row. * Chain 3. Skip 3 stitches. Make 1 single crochet in each of next 3 stitches. Chain 3. Skip 3 stitches. In next stitch, take 1 double crochet, 3 chains, and 1 double crochet. * At end of row, turn.

For the **second row,** chain 3. Repeat the following procedure to end of row. * Make 7 double crochets in the chain-3 space between double crochets of previous row. Make 3 chains. Take 1 single crochet in second single crochet. Chain 3. * End with 7 double crochets in last chain-3 space. Turn.

For the **third row,** repeat the following sequence of stitches to end of row. * Take 1 single crochet in each of double crochets of shell. Chain 5. * At end of row, turn.

For the **fourth row,** chain 5. Repeat the following sequence of stitches to end of row. * Make 3 single crochets in 3 middle single stitches of shell. Chain 3. In third stitch of chain-5 space, make 1 double crochet, 3 chains, and 1 double crochet. Chain 3. * End with 3 single crochets in middle of shell. Turn.

For the **fifth row,** chain 5. Repeat the following procedure. * Take 1 single crochet in second single crochet. Chain 3. Make 7 double crochets in chain-3 space between double crochets in previous row. Chain 3. * End with one single crochet, 3 chains, and one single crochet in chain-5 loop. Turn.

For the **sixth row,** chain 5. Repeat the following procedure to end of row. * Take 7 single crochets in double crochet stitches. Chain 5. * End with 1 single crochet in middle stitch of turning chain. Turn.

For the **seventh row,** chain 3. Repeat the following procedure to end of row. * In third stitch of chain-5 space, make 1 double crochet, 3 chains, and 1 double crochet. Chain 3. Take 3 single crochets in middle stitches of shell. Chain 3. * In last stitch, make 1 double crochet, 3 chains, and 1 double crochet.

Repeat the **second through seventh rows** until work is completed.

## Shell Pattern— Graduated

Begin with a foundation chain the required length. Use a multiple of 5 stitches plus 1, with an additional 2 chains.

For the **first row,** take 1 double crochet in fourth chain from hook. Skip 4 chains. Repeat the following procedure to end of row. * Make shell in next chain by taking 2 double crochets, 1 chain, and 2 double crochets. Skip 4 chains. * Take 2 double crochets in last chain. Then chain 3 and turn.

For the **second row,** make 2 double crochets in first stitch. Then, in each chain-1 space, take 3 double crochets, 1 chain, and 3 double crochets. End with 3 double crochets in top of turning chain. Chain 5 and turn.

For the **third row,** make 2 treble crochets in first stitch. Then, in each chain-1 space, take 3 treble crochets, 1 chain, and 3 treble crochets. End with 3 treble crochets in top of turning chain. Then chain 5 and turn.

For the **fourth row,** make 3 treble crochets in first stitch. Then, in each chain-1 space, take 4 treble crochets, 2 chains, and 4 treble crochets. End with 4 treble crochets in top of turning chain. Then chain 5 and turn.

For the **fifth row,** start with 4 treble crochets in first stitch. Then, in each chain-2 space, take 5 treble crochets, 2 chains, and 5 treble crochets. End with 5 treble crochets in top of turning chain. Chain 6 and turn.

For the **sixth row,** crochet in first stitch 3 times: 1 treble crochet and 1 chain. Also take another treble crochet in same stitch. In each chain-2 space, repeat the following procedure 5 times: 1 treble crochet and 1 chain. Follow with 1 treble crochet and 1 chain repeated 4 times and add 1 treble crochet. End with the following stitches in top of turning chain: repeat 4 times 1 treble crochet and 1 chain. In same stitch, take 1 treble crochet. Chain 6 and turn.

For the **seventh row,** repeat this procedure 4 times in the first stitch: 1 treble crochet and 1 chain. Also in the first stitch, take 1 treble crochet. In each of chain-2 spaces, repeat this sequence of stitches 6 times: 1 treble crochet and 1 chain. Chain 1. Then do this 5 times: 1 treble crochet and 1 chain; add 1 treble crochet. End with 1 treble crochet and 1 chain taken 5 times in top of turning chain. Also add 1 treble crochet in the same turning chain.

This procedure for increasing the size of the shells can be continued until work is completed.

## Shell Pattern—
### Lacy Alternating

Begin with a foundation chain the required length. Use a multiple of 8 stitches plus 2, with an additional chain stitch.

For the **first row,** make a single crochet in second chain from hook. Then take another 1 single crochet in the next chain. Repeat the following procedure to end of row. * Chain 2. Skip 2 chains. Then in next chain make a double crochet, 3 chains, and 1 double crochet. Chain 2. Skip 2 chains. Make a single crochet in each of the next 3 chains. * End with single crochet in each of the last 2 chains. Chain 1 and turn.

For the **second row,** take 1 single crochet in first single crochet. Repeat the following procedure to end of row. * Chain 2. Make 7 double crochets in chain-3 space. Chain 2. Make 1 single crochet in second single crochet of 3- single-crochet group. * End with chain 2. Then make a single crochet in last single crochet. Chain 1 and turn.

For the **third row,** make a single crochet in first single crochet. Chain 2. Repeat the following procedure to end of row. * Take 1 single crochet in each of next 7 double crochets. Chain 5. * End with chain 2. Then take a single crochet in last single crochet. Chain 5 and turn.

For the **fourth row,** take 1 double crochet in first single crochet. Repeat the following procedure to end of row. * Start with chain 2. Take a single crochet in each of third, fourth, and fifth single crochets of 7-single-crochet group. Chain 2. In third chain of chain-5 space, make 1 double crochet, 3 chains, and 1 double crochet. * End with 1 double crochet, 3 chains, and 1 double crochet in last single crochet. Chain 3 and turn.

For the **fifth row,** make 3 double crochets in first chain-3 space. Repeat the following procedure to end of row. * Chain 2. Make 1 single crochet in second single crochet of 3-single-crochet group. Chain 2. Take 7 double crochets in chain-3 space. * End with 4 double crochets in turning chain loop. Chain 1 and turn.

For the **sixth row,** take a single crochet in each of first 4 double crochets. Repeat the following procedure to end of row. * Chain 5. Make a single crochet in each of next 7 double crochets. * End with chain 5. Take a single crochet in each of last 3 single crochets. Make a single crochet in top of turning chain. Chain 1 and turn.

For the **seventh row,** take a single crochet in each of first 2 single crochets. Repeat the following procedure to end of row. * Chain 2. In third chain of chain-5 loop, make 1 double crochet, 3 chains, and 1 double crochet. Chain 2. Take a single crochet in each of the third, fourth, and fifth single crochets of the 7-single-crochet group. * End with chain 2. Make 1 single crochet in each of last 2 single crochets. Chain 1 and turn.

Repeat the **second through seventh rows** until work is completed.

## Shell Pattern—
### Lacy Double Crochet

Begin with a foundation chain the required length. Use a multiple of 5 stitches plus 1, with an additional 3 chains.

For the **first row,** make 1 double crochet in fourth chain from hook. Repeat the following procedure to end of row. * Skip 4 chains. Make a shell in the chain by repeating 3 times: 1 double crochet and 1 chain. Then add 1 double crochet. * End with 1 double crochet, 1 chain, and 1 double crochet in last chain. Chain 4 and turn.

For the **second row,** take 1 double crochet in first chain-1 space. Make a shell in second chain-1 space of each shell. End with 1 double crochet, 1 chain, and 1 double crochet in the last chain-1 space. Chain 4 and turn.

Repeat the **second row** until work is completed.

## Shell Pattern—
### Lacy Treble Crochet

Start with a foundation chain the required length. Use a multiple of 6 stitches plus 1, with an additional 4 chains.

For the **first row,** take 1 treble crochet in fifth chain from hook. Repeat the following procedure to end of row. * Skip 5 chains. Make shell in next chain by repeating 3 times: 1 treble crochet and 1 chain. Then add 1 treble crochet. * End with 1 treble crochet, 1 chain, and 1 treble crochet in last chain. Chain 5 and turn.

For the **second row,** take 1 treble crochet in first chain-1 space. Make shell in second chain-1 space of each shell. End with 1 treble crochet, 1 chain, and 1 treble crochet in last chain-1 space. Chain 5 and turn.

Repeat the **second row** until work is completed.

## Shell Pattern—
### Split Double Crochet

Start with a foundation chain the required length. Use a multiple of 5 stitches plus 1, with an additional 2 chains.

For the **first row,** take 1 double crochet in third chain from hook. Skip 4 chains. Repeat the following procedure to end of row. * To make shell in next chain, take 2 double crochets, 1 chain, and 2 double crochets. Skip 4 chains. * In last chain, take 2 double crochets. Chain 3 and turn.

For the **second row,** take 1 double crochet in first stitch. Make shell in chain-1 space of each shell. End with 2 double crochets in top of turning chain. Chain 3 and turn.

Repeat the **second row** until work is completed.

## Shell Pattern—
### Split Treble Crochet

Commence with foundation chain the required length. Use a multiple of 5 stitches plus 1, with an additional 3 chains.

For the **first row,** take 2 treble crochet in fourth chain from hook. Skip 4 chains. Repeat the following procedure to end of row. * To make shell in next chain, take 3 treble crochets, 1 chain, and 3 treble crochets. Skip 4 chains. * In last chain, take 3 treble crochets. Chain 4 and turn.

For the **second row,** make 2 treble crochets in first stitch. Make shell—3 treble crochets, 1 chain, and 3 treble crochets—in chain-1 space of each shell. End with 3 treble crochets in top of turning chain. Chain 4 and turn.

Repeat the **second row** until work is completed.


## Shell Pattern—
### Treble Crochet with Half Double Crochet Row

Start with a foundation chain the required length. Use a multiple of 6 stitches plus 1, with an additional 2 chains.

For the **first row,** take 1 half double crochet in third chain from hook. Then make 1 half double crochet in each chain until row is completed. Chain 5 and turn.

For the **second row,** make 1 treble crochet in first stitch. Skip 5 stitches. * Make shell in next stitch by repeating 4 times: 1 treble crochet and 1 chain. Then add 1 treble crochet. Skip 4 stitches. * End with 1 treble crochet and 1 chain made twice. Take 1 treble crochet in turning chain. Chain 2 and turn.

For the **third row,** skip first stitch. Take 1 half double crochet in each stitch of previous row. End with 1 half double crochet in each of 2 top stitches of turning chain. Chain 5 and turn.

For the **fourth row,** take 1 treble crochet in first stitch. Skip 6 stitches. Repeat the following procedure. * Make shell in next stitch. Skip 8 stitches. * End with 1 treble crochet and 1 chain made twice. Take 1 treble crochet in turning chain. Chain 2 and turn.

Repeat the **third and fourth rows** until work is completed.

## Shell Pattern—
### Treble Crochet with Open Half Double Crochet Row

Begin with a foundation chain the required length. Use a multiple of 8 stitches plus 1, with an additional 3 chains.

For the **first row,** take 1 half double crochet in fourth chain from hook. Repeat the following procedure to end of row. * Chain 1. Skip 1 chain. Make 1 half double crochet in next chain. * At the end of chain, chain 4 and turn.

For the **second row,** take 3 treble crochets in first chain-1 space. Chain 1. Skip 3 chain-1 spaces. Repeat the following procedure to end of row. * To make shell, place 7 treble crochets in next chain-1 space. Chain 1. Skip 3 chain-1 spaces. * End with 4 treble crochets in last space. Chain 3 and turn.

For the **third row,** skip first stitch. Repeat the following procedure to end of row. * Take 1 half double crochet in next stitch. Chain 1. Skip 1 stitch. * End with a half double crochet in top of turning chain. Chain 4 and turn.

Repeat the **second and third rows** until work is completed.

## Shell Pattern—
### Treble Crochet with Single Crochet Row

Begin with a foundation chain the required length. Use a multiple of 5 stitches plus 1, with an additional 1 chain.

For the **first row,** make a single crochet in second chain from hook. Take 1 single crochet in each chain to end of chain. Chain 4 and turn.

For the **second row,** take 1 treble crochet in first stitch. Skip 4 stitches. Repeat the following procedure to end of row. * To make the shell, take 5 treble crochets in next stitch. Skip 4 stitches. * End with 3 treble crochets in turning chain. Chain 1 and turn.

For the **third row,** skip first stitch. Make 1 single crochet in each stitch of previous row. End with 2 single crochets in top of turning chain. Chain 4 and turn.

Repeat the **second and third rows** until work is completed.

## Star Stitch

This is another of the frequently used stitches. Threads seem to radiate from a center point to create the effect of a tiny star. Begin with a foundation chain the required length.

For the **first row,** insert hook in second chain from hook and pull through loop. Continue to do this in the next 3 chains. Put yarn over hook and pull through the 5 loops on hook. To make eye or small circle, chain 1. This completes the first star stitch. Repeat the following procedure to end of row. * Draw a loop through the eye. Pull another loop through the same chain that was last used for previous star stitch and in each of the next 2 chains. Put yarn over hook and pull through the 5 loops on hook. Chain 1 to make the eye, completing the second star stitch. * At end of row, chain 2 and turn.

For the **second row,** count the chain-2 as 1 half double crochet. Make a half double crochet in first eye. Repeat the following procedure to end of row. Make 2 half double crochets in each eye. End with 1 half double crochet in top of turning chain. Chain 3 and turn.

For the **third row,** draw a loop through the second and third chains from hook. Skip first half double crochet. Draw a loop through each of the next 2 half double crochets. Put yarn over hook and pull it through 5 loops on hook. Chain 1 for eye, completing first star stitch. Repeat the following procedure to end of row. * Draw a loop through the eye just made. Also draw a loop through the same half double crochet last worked and in the next 2 half double crochets. Put yarn over hook and pull yarn through 5 loops on hook. Make 1 chain for eye. * End with last half double crochet of the last star stitch in top of turning chain. Chain 2 and turn.

Repeat the **second and third rows** until work is completed.

## Twisted Russian Stitch

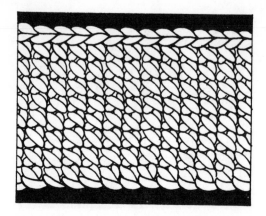

This stitch is worked only on the right side of the piece. If, instead of crocheting round and round, it is made flat, the yarn is joined at beginning of each row and cut at the end. Start with a foundation chain the required length.

For the **first row,** insert hook into second chain from hook. Put hook over yarn and draw through loop. Notice that the hook is passed over the yarn rather than the yarn over the hook. Then put the yarn over hook and pull through 2 loops. Continue to end of row. Fasten thread and clip.

For the **second row,** attach yarn at right-hand end of work. Insert hook under both horizontal loops of each stitch of previous row and pull through a loop as before. Continue as for the first row.

Repeat the **second row** until work is completed.

## Urchin Stitch

Rows of tiny spoked motifs create an interesting raised textural effect. Begin with a foundation chain the required length, using an even number of stitches.

For the **first row,** chain 1. Repeat the following procedure to end of row. * Skip 1 stitch. In next stitch, take 1 single crochet, 2 chains, and one single crochet. *

For the **second row,** follow directions for first row, inserting hook in chain-2 space of previous row for pattern stitches.

Repeat the **second row** until work is completed.

## V Stitch

This is another of the popular fancy stitches. It produces a lovely openwork effect. Begin with a foundation chain the required length. Use a multiple of 4.

For the **first row,** make a V stitch by placing in the fifth chain from hook 1 double crochet, 3 chains, and 1 double crochet. Repeat the following procedure to end of row. * Skip 3 chains. For the second V, put 1 double crochet, 3 chains, and 1 double crochet in next chain. * At end of row, skip 2 chains. Make double crochet in last chain. Chain 3 and turn.

For the **second row,** repeat the following procedure in V stitch space to end of row. * Make 1 double crochet, 3 chains, and 1 double crochet in the chain-3 space of next V stitch. This places 1 V stitch over V stitch made. * At the end of row, take a double crochet in top of turning chain. Chain 3 and turn.

Repeat the **second row** until work is completed.

## Veil Stitch

Motifs with an open circular feeling alternate to give this stitch pattern an airy look. For this lacy stitch, make a foundation chain the required number of stitches.

For the **first row,** take a single crochet in first stitch. Chain 1. Skip 2 stitches. Repeat the following sequence of stitches to end of row. * Make 3 single crochets. Chain 3. Skip 2 stitches. Take 3 single crochets, chain 3, skip 2 stitches. * End with 1 single crochet. Turn.

For the **second row,** chain 3. Skip 1 single crochet. Take 1 double crochet in next single crochet. Skip 1 single crochet. Chain 3. Repeat

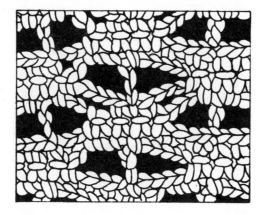

the following procedure to end of row. * Take 1 single crochet before the 3 single crochets of previous row, 1 single crochet in each single crochet, and 1 single crochet after the 3 single crochets. Chain 3. Take 1 double crochet in center of the next 3 single crochets. Chain 3. * End with chain 3 and 1 single crochet in last stitch. Turn.

For the **third row,** take 1 single crochet in first stitch. Chain 3. Repeat the following procedure to end of row. * Take 1 single crochet before the double crochet, 1 single crochet in the double crochet, and 1 single crochet after the double crochet. Chain 3. Skip 1 single crochet. Work single crochet in next 3 stitches. Skip next single crochet. Chain 3. * End with 1 single crochet before last stitch and 1 single crochet in last stitch. Turn.

For the **fourth row,** take 1 single crochet in first 2 stitches and another 1 in chain-3 space. Repeat the following procedure to end of row. * Chain 3. Skip 1 single crochet. Take double crochet in next stitch. Skip next single crochet. Chain 3. Make a single crochet before next 3 single crochets and then in all 3 stitches, and 1 single crochet after making them. * End with chain 3 and 1 double crochet in last stitch. Turn.

For the **fifth row,** take 1 single crochet in first stitch. Chain 3. Repeat the following procedure to end of row. * Skip 1 single crochet. Work single crochets in next 3 stitches. Skip 1 single crochet. Chain 3. Work 1 single crochet before the double crochet, 1 in the double crochet, and 1 after it. Chain 3. * End with single crochet in last 2 stitches.

Repeat the **second through fifth rows** until work is completed.

## Viaduct Stitch

This stitch is frequently used for making a shawl. Begin with a foundation chain the required length.

For the **first row,** chain 1. Take 3 single crochets. Repeat the following procedure to end of row. * Chain 5. Skip 3 stitches. Take 5 single crochets. * End by making 5 chains and 3 single crochets. Turn.

For the **second row,** chain 2. Skip 2 single crochets. Make 1 single crochet in next stitch. Repeat the following procedure. * Make 9 treble crochets in chain-5 space. Take 1 single crochet in the first of the next 5 single crochets. Chain 2. Skip 3 stitches. Take 1 single crochet in the fifth single crochet. * End with 9 treble crochets in chain-5 space. Take 1 single crochet, 1 chain, and 1 single crochet in last single crochet. Turn.

For the **third row,** chain 6. Repeat the following procedure to end of row. * Make 3 single crochets in the 3 center treble crochets of motif in previous row. Chain 3. Take 1 treble crochet in chain-2 space of previous row. Chain 3. * End row with 3 chains and 1 treble crochet in turning chain of previous row. Turn.

For the **fourth row,** chain 3. Repeat the following procedure. * Take 1 single crochet in chain-3 space, before the first motif in the previous row. Make 1 single crochet in each of next 3 single crochets, and 1 single crochet in space following motif. This results in 5 single crochets. Then chain 5. Skip the treble crochet in the previous row. * End with 1 single crochet before the motif. Take 3 single crochets in motif. Chain 3. Make 1 single crochet in top of turning chain of previous row. Turn.

For the **fifth row,** chain 3. Make 4 treble crochets in first chain-3 space. Repeat the following sequence of stitches to end of row. * Take 1 single crochet in first of the 5 single crochets of previous row. Chain 2. Take 1 single crochet in the fifth single crochet and 9 treble crochets in next chain-5 space. * End with 1 single crochet, 2 chains, and 5 treble crochets in turning chain of previous row. Turn.

For the **sixth row,** chain 1. Make 1. Make 2 double crochets in the first 2 treble crochets. Repeat the following procedure. * Chain 3. Take 1 treble crochet in chain-2 space. Chain 3. Make 3 single crochets in the three center treble crochets of motif. * End with chain 3, 1 treble crochet, chain 3, and 2 single crochets in the last 2 treble crochets of previous row. Turn.

For the **seventh row,** follow directions for fourth row.

Repeat the **second through seventh rows** until work is completed.

## Waffle Stitch

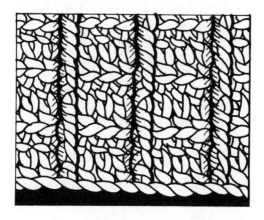

This is one of the popular stitch patterns that creates a raised ridge on the right side, adding textural interest. Begin with a foundation chain the required length. Use a multiple of 4 plus 1.

For the **first row,** make a double crochet in fourth chain from hook. Continue to make a double crochet in each chain to end of row. Chain 1 and turn.

For the **second row,** make a single crochet in first 3 double crochets, picking up only the front loop of each stitch. Repeat the following procedure to end of row. * Chain 1. Skip next stitch. Make a single crochet in next 3 double crochets. * End with chain 1. Skip next stitch. Make a single crochet in last 2 double crochets and in top of turning chain. This makes a horizontal ridge on the right side. Chain 3 and turn.

For the **third row,** work through both loops of each stitch. Skip first single crochet. Make a double crochet in next 2 single crochets. Repeat the following procedure to end of row. * Make a treble crochet around fourth double crochet of first row by inserting hook from right to left under the stitch. Skip the chain-1 space. Make a double crochet in next 3 single crochets. * At end of row, chain 1.

Repeat the **second and third rows** until work is completed.

## Web Pattern

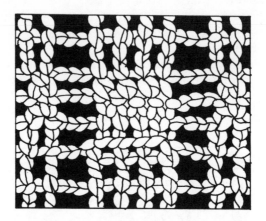

Rows of open motifs that seem to resemble a spider web produce a lacy effect. Start with a foundation chain the required length. Use a multiple of 11 stitches plus 1, with an additional 2 chains.

For the **first row,** take 1 double crochet in fourth chain from hook. Repeat the following procedure to end of row. * Begin by repeating this sequence of stitches 5 times: skip 1 chain, chain 2, and take 1 double crochet. Follow with a double crochet in next chain. * At end of foundation chain, chain 3 and turn.

For the **second row,** which is the right side of the work, skip first stitch. Repeat the following procedure to end of row. * Take 1 double crochet in next double crochet. Chain 4. Make 1 single crochet in each of next 4 double crochets. Chain 4. Take 1 double crochet in next double crochet. * End with 1 double crochet in top of turning chain. Chain 3 and turn.

For the **third row,** skip first stitch. Repeat the following procedure to end of row. * Make 1 double crochet in next double crochet. Chain 4. Take 1 single crochet in each of next 4 single crochets. Chain 4. Take 1 double crochet in next double crochet. * End with 1 double crochet in top of turning chain. Chain 3 and turn.

For the **fourth row,** skip first stitch. Repeat the following procedure to end of row. * Make 1 double crochet in next double crochet. Chain 4. Take 1 single crochet in each of next 4 single crochets. Chain 4. Make 1 double crochet in next double crochet. * End with 1 double crochet in top of turning chain. Chain 3 and turn.

For the **fifth row,** repeat directions for the fourth row.

For the **sixth row,** skip first stitch. Repeat the following procedure to end of row. * Take 1 double crochet in next double crochet. In next 4 single crochets, repeat this sequence of stitches; 2 chains and 1 double crochet in next double crochet. Then chain 2. Take 1 double crochet in next double crochet. * End with 1 double crochet in top of turning chain. Chain 3 and turn.

Repeat the **second through sixth rows** until work is completed.

## Window Pattern

Two types of openwork squares alternate to give this stitch pattern an interesting lacy look. Each pattern requires 20 stitches. Multiply the number of squares by 20 stitches and then add 1 stitch. Make a foundation chain the required length.

For the **first row,** make a double crochet in first 10 stitches. Chain 10. Skip 10 stitches. Take 1 double crochet in last stitch. Chain 2. Continue across row. Turn.

For the **second row,** chain 10. Skip 10 stitches. Take a double crochet in next 2 stitches. Chain 2. Skip 2. Take a double crochet in next 2 stitches. Chain 2. Double crochet in last 2 stitches. Chain 2 and turn.

For the **third row,** take a double crochet in second stitch and 2 double crochets in chain-2 space. Chain 2. Take 2 double crochets in next chain-2 space, and a double crochet in next 2 stitches. Chain 10. Skip 10 stitches. Make double crochet in next stitch. Chain 2. Turn.

For the **fourth row,** chain 4. Take 1 single crochet in linking together the 3 rows of chain-10 stitches. Chain 5. Make double crochet in next 2 stitches. Chain 2. Skip 2 stitches. Take 2 double crochets in chain-2 space. Chain 2. Take 2 double crochets in last 2 stitches. Chain 2 and turn.

For the **fifth row,** use directions for first row. However, the sequence of stitches should be arranged so that the second group of 10 stitches is made first. This creates the checkerboard effect.

For the **sixth, seventh, and eighth rows,** repeat the second, third, and fourth rows. The eight rows complete the design pattern.

Repeat the **first through eighth rows** until work is completed.

## Zigzag Mesh

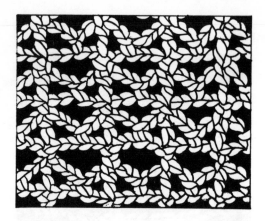

An interesting arrangement of chain stitches produces a dainty open-work design. Begin with a foundation chain the required length. Use a multiple of 4 stitches plus 3.

For the **first row,** chain 6. Repeat the following procedure to end of row. * Take 1 single crochet. Chain 2. Skip 1 stitch. Make 1 double crochet. Chain 2. Skip 1 stitch. * End with 1 double crochet. Turn.

For the **second row,** repeat the following procedure to end of row. * Make 1 single crochet in double crochet. Chain 3. * End with single crochet in third chain of starting chain-6. Turn.

For the **third row,** chain 5. Repeat the following procedure to end of row. * Make a single crochet in second chain. Chain 2. Take 1 double crochet in single crochet. Chain 2. * End with 1 double crochet.

Repeat the **second and third rows** until work is completed.

## Zigzag Stripes

This lacy design forms rows of stitches in a zigzag pattern to produce a striped effect. Begin with a foundation chain the required length. Use a multiple of 4 stitches plus 1, with an additional 1 chain.

For the **first row,** take 1 single crochet in second chain from hook. Then make a single crochet in each chain to end of chain. Chain 7 and turn.

For the **second row,** skip 3 stitches. Take a single crochet in next stitch. Repeat the following procedure to end of row. * Chain 7. Skip 3 stitches. Take 1 single crochet in next stitch. * At the last 3 stitches, chain 3. Make 1 treble crochet in turning chain. Chain 1 and turn.

For the **third row,** take 1 single crochet in first stitch. Chain 3. Make 1 single crochet in fourth stitch of the first chain-7. Repeat the following procedure. * Chain 3. Make 1 single crochet in fourth stitch of next chain-7. * At the last chain-7, chain 3. Make a single crochet in fourth and fifth stitches of last chain. Chain 1 and turn.

For the **fourth row,** take a single crochet in second single crochet. Repeat the following procedure to end of row. * Make 3 single crochets in chain-3 space. Take 1 single crochet in next single crochet. * End with 1 single crochet in last single crochet. Make 1 single crochet in top of turning chain. Crochet 7 and turn.

Repeat the **second through fourth rows** until work is completed.

## STYLES AND TYPES OF CROCHETING

Although crocheting is generally worked in allover stitch patterns, it is possible to crochet for a specific purpose, shape, or design. Trimmings, lacy or tailored; medallions, round or square; designs, imaginative or realistic: all are creative possibilities. Some suggestions for producing attractive effects are shown on the following pages.

### Edging—Cluster

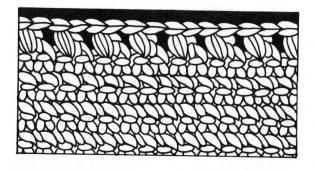

A row of cluster stitches provides a decorative but tailored trim to an edge. Work with the right side toward you. Join yarn at side edge. Crochet along edge to be trimmed by beginning with 3 chain stitches. Repeat the following procedure to end of edge. * Start by putting yarn over hook and drawing a loop through the next stitch. Do this 4 times. Then put yarn over hook and draw it through the 9 loops. Place yarn over hook and draw through last loop to form a cluster. Skip 1 stitch. * End row with a cluster in last stitch.

**Edging—Fan**

An edge can be given a dainty scalloped trim when this edging is used. Make 1 double crochet. Chain 3. Follow with a slip stitch in third chain from hook for picot. Do this 3 times. Then make a single crochet in next stitch. Skip 2 stitches. Make 1 single crochet in next stitch.

**Edging—Picot**

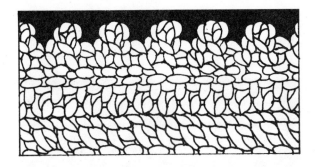

This is a popular edge finish. The distance between the picots can be made for any desired spacing. However, in planning the spacing, the placement of the last picot should duplicate the first. Start this edging with the wrong side facing you. Join yarn at side edge.

For the **first row,** work 1 row of single crochet and then turn.

For the **second row,** chain 3. Make 1 single crochet in third chain from hook to form picot. Take a single crochet in each of next 2 stitches.

Repeat until work is completed.

### Edging—Pineapple Stitch

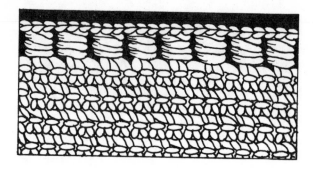

Many crochet stitches can be used for a decorative trim. This is one that gives a puffy effect along the edge. Attach the yarn at the right-hand edge with the right side of material facing you. Chain 2. Repeat the following procedure to the end of row. * Make 1 half double crochet. Then put yarn over hook, insert hook behind half double crochet, place yarn over hook again, and draw through a loop. Do this step 3 times. After this process has been completed, put yarn over hook. Draw through the 7 loops on hook. Chain 1 and skip 1 stitch. * After repeating these directions to end of work, finish with 1 half double crochet.

### Edging—Popcorn Stitch

The popular popcorn stitch creates a pleasing ball-like trim. Before beginning the edging, make 1 foundation row of single crochet along edge. Then, with right side of work toward you, attach yarn at the point where foundation row begins. Take a single crochet in first 5

single crochets in foundation row. Repeat the following procedure to end of edge to be trimmed. * Chain 3. Take 5 double crochets in third chain of the just worked chain-3. Remove hook from loop. Insert it into the top of the first double crochet stitch. Pick up dropped loop and draw it through stitch. Chain 1 stitch to fasten the popcorn. Then chain 3. At the base of the popcorn, make a slip stitch in the top of the single crochet. Take a single crochet in the next 5 stitches. * Repeat until the edge is trimmed.

## Edging—Ruffle

This attractive edging is started with the wrong side facing you. Attach the yarn at the side edge. Crochet along edge to be trimmed.

For the **first row,** chain 4. Repeat the following procedure to end of edge. * Skip 2 stitches. Take 1 double crochet in next stitch. Chain 2. * End with 1 double crochet in last stitch. Turn.

For the **second row,** work this way to construct the ruffle. Use the length of the stitch instead of the usual top of each stitch. It is known as a post. Work 5 double crochets around first post, working downward. Repeat the following sequence of stitches to end of row. * Chain 1. Work 5 double crochets down each post. * Fasten yarn and clip.

In case a wider ruffle is needed, use treble crochet in first row instead of double crochet and work 7 double crochets down each post.

### Edging—Shell

This stitch is worked with a multiple of 5 stitches. Start with the wrong side of work toward you. Attach the yarn at side edge.

For the **first row,** work a foundation row of single crochet. Chain 4 and turn.

For the **second row,** begin with a double crochet in the first stitch. Repeat the following procedure. * Start by skipping 4 stitches. Then make a shell by taking 1 double crochet and 1 chain 3 times, following with a double crochet in same stitch. * When the last 5 stitches are reached, skip 4 stitches. Then in the last stitch, take 1 double crochet, 1 chain, and 1 double crochet.

### Edging—Tailored

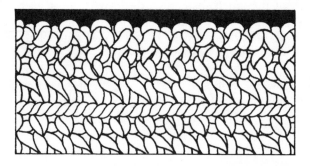

To give an edge a corded finish, work 1 row of single crochet with right side of work facing the crocheter. Without turning, make the second row, crocheting from left to right. Note that this reverses the usual direction for working. Chain 1. Take 1 single crochet in each stitch of previous row.

## Filet Crochet

Filet is a type of crochet that is made of a series of solid blocks and spaces. They can be arranged in a single checkerboard pattern or with an arrangement of solid blocks forming a design pattern. The size of the blocks and spaces can be varied to produce a particular effect. In crocheting a design, follow a chart worked in squares. Using such a guide, allows a design to be adapted for crocheting. Some suggestions for filet crochet are shown on the following pages.

## Filet Crochet—
   Checkerboard

This stitch pattern is made by combining double crochet with chain-2 blocks. Begin by making a foundation chain the required length, using a multiple of 4 stitches plus 2, with 2 additional chains.

For the **first row,** make 1 double crochet in fourth chain from hook. Repeat the following procedure to end of row. * Chain 2. Skip 2 chains. Take a double crochet in each of the next 2 chains. * At end of row, chain 4 and turn.

For the **second row,** skip first 2 double crochets. Make a double crochet in each chain stitch. Repeat the following procedure. * Chain 2. Skip 2 double crochets. Take 1 double crochet in each chain stitch. At last 2 double crochet, chain 2. Skip 1 double crochet. Take a double crochet in top of turning chain. Chain 3 and turn. *

For the **third row,** skip first stitch. Take 1 double crochet in next chain stitch. Repeat the following procedure. * Chain 2. Skip 2 double crochets. Take 1 double crochet in each chain stitch. * At the last 2 double crochets, chain 2. Skip 2 double crochets. Make 1 double crochet in top of turning chain. Then take 1 double crochet in next stitch of turning chain. Chain 4 and turn.

Repeat the **second and third rows** until work is completed.

## Filet Crochet—
### Checkerboard, Large

Treble crochet with chain-3 blocks is used for this larger version of the checkerboard design. Start with a foundation chain the required length. Use a multiple of 6 stitches plus 3, with an additional 3 chains.

For the **first row,** take 1 treble crochet in fifth chain from hook. Make another treble crochet in next chain. Repeat the following procedure to end of row. * Chain 3. Skip 3 chains. Take 1 treble crochet in each of next 3 chains. * Finish with 7 chains. Turn.

For the **second row,** repeat the following procedure to end of row. * Skip first 3 stitches. Take 1 treble crochet in each chain stitch. * At the last 3 stitches, chain 3. Skip 2 stitches. Make 1 treble crochet in top of turning chain. Chain 4 and turn.

For the **third row,** skip first stitch. Take 1 treble crochet in each of next 2 chains. Repeat the following procedure to end of row. * Chain 3. Skip 3 stitches. Take 1 treble crochet in each chain stitch. * End with 1 treble crochet in each of first 3 chains of turning chain. Chain 7 and turn.

Repeat the **second and third rows** until work is completed.

## Filet Crochet—Design

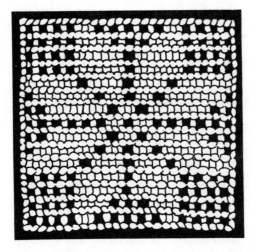

This type of crochet uses a double crochet with a chain-1 space. Designs are created by filling a space with a double crochet. Placing the design on graph paper makes the work easier to follow. Begin with a foundation chain the required length. Use an even number of stitches.

For the **first row,** make a double crochet in each chain stitch or every other chain.

The **following rows** require 4 chain stitches for turning; a double crochet in a double crochet of the previous row where an open mesh is needed; and a double crochet in a space where the design is needed. Each row is finished with a double crochet in the third chain of the chain-4 stitch at the beginning of the previous row.

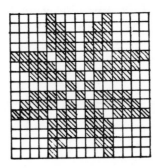

## Filet Crochet in Squares

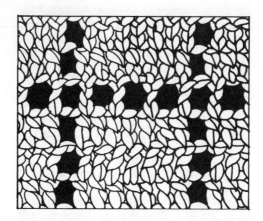

This pattern is worked so that spaces outline solid blocks of crochet. Begin with a foundation chain the required length. Use a multiple of 8 stitches plus 3 with an additional 2 chains.

For the **first row,** take 1 double crochet in fourth chain from hook. Then make a double crochet in each chain to end of foundation chain. At end of row, chain 4 and turn.

For the **second row,** skip first 2 stitches. Take a double crochet in next stitch. Repeat the following procedure to end of row. * Chain 1. Skip 1 stitch. Take 1 double crochet in next stitch. * End row with 1 double crochet in top of turning chain. Chain 4 and turn.

For the **third row,** skip first double crochet and 1 chain. Repeat the following procedure to end of row. * Take 1 double crochet in each of next 7 stitches. Chain 1. Skip 1 stitch. * Skip first stitch of turning chain. Make 1 double crochet in second stitch of turning chain. Chain 4 and turn.

For the **fourth and fifth rows,** repeat the third row.

Repeat the **second through fifth rows** until work is completed.

## Fringe—Chain

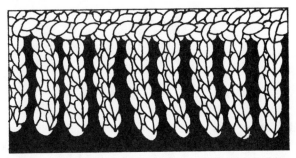

This method for making fringe produces a series of sturdy cords along the edge. To prepare edge for fringe, work with wrong side toward you. Attach yarn at side edge.

For the **first row,** work a row of single crochet along edge. Chain 1 and turn.

For the **second row,** slip stitch in first stitch. Repeat the following procedure to end of row. * Start by chaining 12 stitches. Turn. Crochet back along chain, working 1 slip stitch in each chain stitch. Slip stitch in next stitch. *

The length of the fringe can be changed by varying the number of chain stitches.

## Fringe—Looped

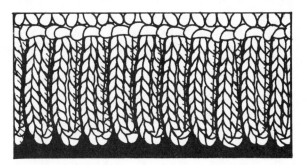

Crocheted chains are looped to form this decorative trim. Attach yarn at side edge with the wrong side facing you.

For the **first row,** work a row of single crochet along edge to be trimmed. Chain 1 and turn.

For the **second row,** make a single crochet in first stitch. Repeat the following procedure to end of row. * Begin by making 18 chain stitches. Take 1 single crochet in next stitch. *

The length of the fringe can be changed by varying the number of stitches in chain.

## Hairpin Lace

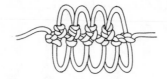

This is a distinctive type of crochet. The lacy loops are made with a special fork, loom, or staple. The size can vary, depending on type of yarn or thread being used. The fork is held in the left hand with the left prong between the thumb and first (index) finger. The removable portion should be at the bottom so the lace can be removed. It is thought that hairpin lace was first made on a hairpin, which would explain its name.

Begin with a slip knot at end of yarn. Chain 1 stitch. Put the chain loop on the left-hand prong. Keep yarn in front of the work. Replace the bottom piece (A).

Return hook to slip-knot loop, drawing the loop to a center point between the 2 prongs. Wrap working yarn around right-hand prong. Hold yarn in back.

With the hook in the slip-stitch loop, insert it into the front of the loop on the left prong. Catch the working thread and make 1 single crochet (B).

Raise hook to a vertical position with hook end pointed downward. Turn the fork once, using a clockwise motion (C).

Bring hook into position in front of work. Insert it into the front loop to the left of the center. Put yarn over hook and make 1 single crochet (D).

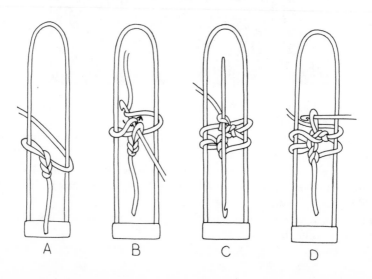

A          B          C          D

Continue to work in this way. Always keep yarn in back of lace.

The lace can be varied by replacing the single crochet stitches with double ones. Cluster and shell stitches can also be used. The important thing to remember is to keep the working thread in back of the work and the hook in a vertical position between the prongs so that it can be brought to the correct side of the lace after each turn.

When the fork is filled, remove lace except for the last 4 loops. Continue as before until required length is reached.

## Hairpin Lace—Linked

By joining 2 strips of hairpin lace, a decorative border trim with looped edges can be made. Be sure the 2 strips have the same number of loops, and that each can be divided evenly by number of loops to be used in the joining. For example, if the joining is to utilize 3 loops, then be sure that the number of loops can be divided by 3 in order to give an even appearance.

Arrange the 2 lace strips on a table with the beginning points of the strips opposite each other. Decide whether twisted loops or untwisted loops are to be used. Only one type should be employed. Care should also be taken to pick up each loop. Check the reverse side at regular intervals for missing ones. In case one has been skipped, rip work and correct mistake. Work upward.

To join the loops, place hook, pointing upward, through 3 loops on left-hand strip. Then put the hook through 3 loops on the right-hand strip. Keep the hook in the same position. Pull the second group of 3 loops through the first group. Pick up next 3 loops on the left-hand strip and pull these loops through the 3 loops on the hook. Continue working from side to side until the top of the strips is reached. This procedure creates a braided effect. After all the loops have been joined, fasten the last loops to the center with needle and yarn.

## Hairpin Scalloped Edging

A strip of hairpin lace can be converted into an edging or insertion. The loops are joined, giving a scalloped effect to the trim. They can be twisted or untwisted, depending on the effect desired.

For the **lower edge** of this edging, attach yarn by passing it through the first 3 twisted loops. Make a single crochet in the same 3 loops. Repeat the following procedure across edge. Chain 3. Then make 1 single crochet in the next 3 loops. End with a single crochet.

## Irish Crochet

A rose dominates an Irish crochet design. It creates a lovely 3-dimensional effect with a dainty, lacy background. This distinctive type of crochet can be used for a medallion or an allover pattern.

For this medallion, begin at the center of the rose by chaining 8 stitches. Join with a slip stitch to form ring.

For the **first round,** chain 1. Make 18 single crochets in ring. Join with a slip stitch to first single crochet.

For the **second round,** make a single crochet in same place as last slip stitch. Repeat the following procedure to end of round. * Chain 5. Skip 2 single crochets. Single crochet in next single crochet. Mark this point with pin. * Six loops will have been made.

For the **third round,** take a slip stitch in first loop. In each of the 6 loops, make 1 single crochet, 1 half double crochet, 5 double crochets, 1 half double crochet, and 1 single crochet. This procedure creates 6 petals. Make a slip stitch in next stitch.

For the **fourth round,** repeat the following procedure to end of round. * Make 6 chains. Then make a single crochet in back of work in the next single crochet, which was marked with a pin in the second round. * This step makes 6 loops across the back of the petals.

For the **fifth round,** make a slip stitch in first loop. Then in each loop, make 1 single crochet, 1 half double crochet, 6 double crochets, 1 half double crochet, 1 single crochet. This procedure creates 6 petals behind the first layer of petals. Make a slip stitch in next stitch.

For the **sixth round,** repeat the following procedure to end of round. Chain 7. Make a single crochet in back of work in next single crochet of fourth round. This sequence of stitches makes 6 loops across back of petals.

For the **seventh round,** make a slip stitch in the first loop. Then work 1 single crochet, 1 half double crochet, 7 double crochets, 1 half double crochet, 1 single crochet in each loop. This procedure completes the rose motif, placing 6 petals behind the second layer of petals.

For the **eighth round,** make a slip stitch in each of the first 3 stitches of next petal. Then chain 1 and make a single crochet in same place as last slip stitch. Repeat the following procedure to end of round. * To make a picot, chain 5, and work a single crochet in fourth chain from hook. Then chain 7 and make a picot in fourth chain from hook. Follow with chain 1, skip 5 double crochets, make a single crochet in next double crochet, chain 5. Then make another picot and chain 7. Work another picot, chain 1, and make a single crochet in first double crochet of next petal. * This procedure creates 12 loops.

For the **ninth round,** make a slip stitch in each stitch, except picots, to the center of next loop. Then chain 3, make a double crochet in same place as last slip stitch, and chain 5. Make a picot, chain 7, and make another picot and chain 1. Holding back the last loop of each double crochet on hook, work 2 double crochets in same place where last double crochet was made. Put yarn over hook and draw through all 3 loops on hook. This completes a 2-double-crochet cluster and first corner loop. Repeat the following procedure. * Chain 5, make picot, chain 7, make picot, chain 1, make single crochet in center of next loop, chain 5, make single crochet in center of next loop, chain 5, make picot, chain 7, make picot, chain 1. Then work cluster in center of next loop, chain 5, make a picot, chain 7, make picot, chain 1. Work cluster in same place as last cluster, making a corner loop. * The preceding procedure is repeated 3 more times. End last repeat by joining last loop with slip stitch to top of first chain-3.

For the **tenth round,** begin with a slip stitch in each stitch to center of next loop at corner. Then chain 3. Make a double crochet in same place as last slip stitch. Chain 5. Make a picot. Chain 7. Make a picot. Chain 1. Work cluster in same place as last double crochet, placing a corner loop over corner loop. The following procedure is repeated 3 more times. * Chain 5. Make a picot. Chain 7. Make a picot. Chain 1. Make single crochet in center of next loop. Chain 3 in next chain-5 loop. Work this sequence of stitches 3 times: 3 double-crochet clusters, 4 chains, and 1 picot. Follow with a 3-double-crochet cluster. Four clusters and 3 picots have been made over the loop. Then chain 3. Make a single crochet in center of next loop. Chain 5. Make a picot. Chain 7. Make a picot. Chain 1. Work a 2-double-crochet cluster in center of next loop. Chain 5. Make a picot. Chain 7. Make a picot. Chain 1. Again placing corner loop over corner loop, work a 2-double-crochet cluster in same place as last cluster. * After the preceding procedure has been repeated 3 times, end last repeat by joining last loop with a slip stitch to top of first chain-3.

## Medallion

A favorite type of crocheting is done in medallion form. These small pieces of crocheting can be made in various shapes and sizes, utilizing many of the popular stitch patterns. They are frequently joined, creating a colorful afghan or an item for household or personal wear. A few of the many design possibilities are shown here to illustrate how versatile the crocheting of medallions can be. Sometimes the medallions are called motifs. No matter which shape is being made, the work is done in the round.

**Medallion—Cross**

A cross of open spaces is the design pattern for this square medallion. Begin with a chain of 6 stitches. Join with a slip stitch to form circle.

For the **first round,** chain 3. Take 15 double crochets in circle. Slip stitch in top of chain 3.

For the **second round,** chain 3. Work two double crochets in same stitch. Repeat the following procedure twice. * Chain 2. Skip 1 double crochet. Make 1 double crochet in next double crochet. Chain 2. Skip 1 double crochet. Take 3 double crochets in next double crochet. * After this has been done, chain 2. Skip 1 double crochet. Make 1 double crochet in next double crochet. Chain 2. Slip stitch in top of chain 3.

For the **third round,** begin with chain 3. Repeat the following procedure 3 times. * Make 5 double crochets in next double crochet and 1 double crochet in next double crochet. Then chain 2 and take 1 double crochet in next double crochet. The preceding step should be repeated. * End last repeat with 1 double crochet and 2 chains. Slip stitch in top of chain 3.

For the **fourth round,** chain 3. Take 1 double crochet in each of next 2 double crochets. Repeat the following procedure 3 times. * Make 5 double crochets in next double crochet. Take 1 double crochet in each of next 3 double crochets. Chain 2. Make 1 double crochet in next double crochet. Chain 2. Make 1 double crochet in each of next 3 double crochets. * End last repeat with 1 double crochet. Chain 2. Slip stitch in top of chain 3.

For the **fifth round,** chain 3. Make 1 double crochet in first 4 double crochets. Repeat the following procedure 3 times. * Make 5 double crochets in the next double crochet. Take 1 double crochet in each of next 5 double crochets. * End with 2 chains. Slip stitch in top of chain 3. Fasten yarn and clip.

## Medallion—Granny

*See* Granny Square (in "Stitch Patterns" section).

## Medallion—Octagonal

Begin with 6 chain stitches. Form a circle by joining stitches with a slip stitch.

For the **first round,** chain 2. Take 23 double crochets in circle. Slip stitch in top of chain-2.

For the **second round,** chain 4. Take 1 double crochet in same stitch. Chain 1. Repeat the following sequence of stitches 7 times. * Skip 2 stitches. Make 1 double crochet, 2 chains, and 1 double crochet in next stitch. Chain 1. * Slip-stitch in second stitch of chain-4.

For the **third round,** chain 2. In the first chain-2 space, make 1 double crochet, 2 chains, and 2 double crochets. Repeat the following sequence of stitches 7 times. * Take 1 double crochet in chain-1 space. In next chain-2 space, make 2 double crochets, 2 chains, and 2 double crochets. * End with 1 double crochet in last chain-1 space. Slip stitch in top of chain-2.

For the **fourth round,** take 1 single crochet in each stitch and 2 single crochets in each chain-2 space. Do this to end of round. Slip stitch in first single crochet. Fasten yarn and clip.

## Medallion—Pinwheel

Begin by making 4 chain stitches. To form a ring, join with a slip stitch.

For the **first round,** take 12 single crochets in center of ring.

For the **second round,** make a single crochet in first single crochet. Repeat the following sequence of stitches 6 times. * Chain 3. Skip next single crochet. Make a single crochet in next single crochet. * This procedure creates 6 spaces, each chain-3.

For the **third round,** make a single crochet in chain-3 space. Repeat the following sequence of stitches 5 times. * Chain 3. Single crochet in next single crochet. Follow with a single crochet in chain-3 space. * Chain 3. Skip next single crochet. Then single crochet in next single crochet.

For the **fourth round,** take 2 single crochets in chain-3 space. Repeat the following sequence of stitches 5 times. * Chain 3. Skip next single crochet. Take single crochet in next single crochet and then 2 single crochets in chain-3 space. * Chain 3. Skip next single crochet. Then make a single crochet in each of next 2 single crochets.

For the **fifth round,** make 2 single crochets in chain-3 space. Repeat the following sequence of stitches 5 times. * Chain 3. Skip next single crochet. Make single crochet in each of next 2 single crochets and 2 single crochets in chain-3 space. * Chain 3. Skip next single crochet. Make single crochet in each of next 3 single crochets.

For the **sixth round,** make 2 single crochet in chain-3 space. Repeat the following sequence of stitches 5 times. * Chain 3. Skip next single crochet. Single crochet in each of next 3 single crochets. Make 2 single crochets in chain-3 space. * Chain 3. Skip next single crochet. Single crochet in each of next 4 single crochets.

Continue in this way until the medallion is the desired size. Fasten yarn and clip.

## Medallion—Popcorn

Begin with 5 chain stitches. Use a slip stitch to join, forming a circle.

For the **first round,** chain 3. Make 2 double crochets in circle. Repeat the following sequence of stitches 3 times. * Chain 3. Take 3 double crochets in circle. * Follow with 3 chain stitches. Join round with a slip stitch in third stitch of the chain-3 made at the beginning of the round.

For the **second round,** chain 3. Take a double crochet in next 2 double crochets. Pick up only back loop. Do this throughout work. Then take 2 double crochets in space. Repeat the following sequence of stitches to end of round. * Chain 3. Make 2 double crochets in space. Then take a double crochet in each of the next 3 double crochets. Make 2 double crochets in next space. * End with 3 chain stitches. Make 2 double crochets in space. Join round with a slip stitch in third stitch of the chain-3 made at the beginning of the round.

For the **third round,** chain 3. Take 5 double crochets in next double crochet. Remove loop from hook. Insert hook through the top of the first double crochet and the dropped loop. Pull the dropped loop through the stitch. Chain 1 to secure the popcorn motif. Then make a double crochet in each of the next 3 double crochets and 2 double crochets in next space. Repeat the following sequence of stitches to end of round. * Chain 3. Make 2 double crochets in same space. Take double crochet in each of next 3 double crochets. Make a popcorn in next double crochet. Take double crochet in each of next 3 double crochets and 2 double crochets in next space. * End with double crochet in each of next 2 double crochets. Join round with a slip stitch in the third stitch of the chain-3 made at the beginning of the round.

For the **fourth round,** chain 3. Repeat the following sequence of stitches to end of round. * Make a double crochet in next popcorn. Take another double crochet in next double crochet. Make a popcorn in next double crochet. Then make a double crochet in each of next 3 double crochets and 2 double crochets in space. Chain 3. Make 2 double crochets in same space. Then take 1 double crochet in each of next 3 double crochets. Make popcorn in next double crochet. Take 1 double crochet in next double crochet. * Join round with a slip stitch in third stitch of the chain-3 made at the beginning of the round.

For the **fifth round,** chain 3. Repeat the following sequence of stitches to end of round. * Make 1 popcorn in next double crochet. Take a double crochet in each of next 3 double crochets. Make popcorn in next double crochet. Take a double crochet in each of next 3 double crochets and 2 double crochets in space. Chain 3. Take 2 double crochets in same space and a double crochet in each of next 3 double crochets. Make a popcorn in next double crochet. Make double crochet in each of next 3 double crochets. * Join round with a slip stitch in third stitch of the chain-3 made at the beginning of the round.

For the **sixth and seventh rounds,** continue to work in same way. Add corner stitches but place only 2 popcorn stitches in each section.

For the **eighth round,** continue as before, adding corner stitches but placing only 1 popcorn stitch in each section.

For the **ninth round,** continue to work around medallion in double crochet. Increase at each corner as before, but do not use any popcorn stitches.

The medallion can be made larger by using increased stitches in the corners and increasing the number of popcorns. A reverse crochet stitch can be used to finish the medallion.

## Medallion—Shell Octagon

Begin by making a foundation chain of 6 stitches. Join with a slip stitch to form circle.

For the **first round,** chain 2. Then take 23 double crochets in circle. Make a slip stitch in top of chain-2.

For the **second round,** chain 4. Take 1 double crochet in same stitch. Chain 1. Repeat the following sequence of stitches 7 times. * Skip 2 stitches. In next stitch, take 1 double crochet, 2 chains, and 1 double crochet. Chain 1. * Slip stitch in top of chain-2.

For the **third round,** chain 2. In first chain-2 space, take 1 double crochet, 2 chains, and 2 double crochet. Repeat the following procedure 7 times. * Chain 1. In next chain-2 space, make 2 double crochets, 2 chains, and 2 double crochets. * Chain 1. Slip stitch in top of chain-2.

For the **fourth round,** repeat the following procedure 8 times. * Make 7 double crochets in chain-2 space for shell. Then 1 single crochet in chain-1 space. * Slip stitch in first stitch. Fasten yarn and clip.

## Medallion—Shell Square

Begin by chaining 6 stitches. Join with a slip stitch to form circle.

For the **first round,** chain 2. Take 1 double crochet in circle. Repeat the following 4 times in circle: chain 1 and 4 double crochets. Chain 1. Take 2 double crochets in circle.

For the **second round,** take slip stitch in first chain-1 space. In first chain-1 space, chain 2, make 2 double crochets, chain 2, and make 3 double crochets. In each of the next 3 chain-1 spaces, make 3 double crochets, 2 chains, and 3 double crochets. Take a slip stitch in top of chain-2.

For the **third round,** make slip stitch in first chain-2 space. In the first chain-2 space, chain 3, make 3 treble crochets, chain 3, and finally take 4 treble crochets. In each of the next 3 chain-2 spaces, make 4 treble crochets, 3 chains, and 4 treble crochets. Take slip stitch in top of chain-2.

For the **fourth round,** take 1 single crochet in each stitch and 4 single crochets in each chain-3 space to end of round. Make slip stitch in first single crochet. Fasten yarn and clip.

## Multicolor Crochet

By working a stitch pattern in different colors, new and interesting effects can be created. Several suggestions, using 2 or 3 colors, are given here.

**Bicolor Afghan Stitch.** This use of yarns in 2 colors creates a tweedy look. Sometimes the stitch is referred as Mock Rice. Begin this afghan stitch with a foundation chain the required length. Any number of stitches can be used. It should be remembered that the stitch can be made in 1 color.

For the **first row,** insert hook into the second chain from hook. Repeat the following procedure to end of row. * Put yarn over hook. Draw through a loop. Insert hook into next stitch and pull through another loop. * Leave all loops on hook. Do not turn work.

For the **second row,** put yarn over hook and draw through a loop. Repeat the following procedure to end of row. * Put yarn over hook. Draw through 2 loops. * At end of row, chain 1.

For the **third row,** change to a second color. Repeat the following procedure to end of row. * Insert hook from right to left of first vertical loop. Draw through a loop. Insert hook through vertical loop from left to right. Draw through a loop. With yarn in front, insert hook from right to left. Put yarn over hook and draw through a loop. With yarn in front, insert hook from left to right. Put yarn over hook and draw through a loop. *

For the **fourth row,** follow directions for the second row.

For the **fifth row,** follow directions for the first row.

For the **sixth row,** change back to first color. Follow directions for the second row.

Repeat from **third row,** displacing pattern by 2 loops for each repeat.

**Tricolor Stripes.** Begin with a foundation chain the required length. Use a multiple of 4 stitches plus 1, with an additonal 1 chain. Work with 3 colors—dark (A), medium (B), light (C), using each for alternating 2-row bands.

For the **first row,** use the dark color (A). Take 1 single crochet in second chain from hook. Make another single crochet in each chain to end of row. Turn.

For the **second row,** continue with the same color. Begin by making 3 chains. Take 1 double crochet in first stitch. Repeat the following procedure to end of row. * Skip 3 stitches. Take 3 double crochets in next stitch. * At the last 4 stitches, skip 3 stitches. Take 2 double crochets in last stitch. Turn.

For the **third row,** attach medium color (B). Chain 2. Repeat the following procedure to end of row. * Make 3 double crochets in center of 3 stitches skipped in previous row. * End with 1 half double crochet in center of chain-3. Turn.

For the **fourth row,** continue with the same color. Chain 3. Take 1 double crochet in space between half double crochet and next group of double crochets. Insert hook in center of double-crochet group 2 rows below. Make 3 double crochets between each double-crochet group. End with 2 double crochets in space between last group and chain. Turn.

For the **fifth row,** attach light color (C). Chain 2. Take 3 double crochets in center of double-crochet group 2 rows below. End with 1 half double crochet in center of chain 3. Turn.

For the **sixth row,** follow directions for the fourth row, continuing to use the light color (C).

For the **seventh row,** follow directions for the fifth row, using dark color (A).

For the **eighth row,** follow directions for the fourth row, using the dark color (A).

For the **ninth row,** return to the medium color (B), using the directions for the fifth row.

Repeat the **fourth through ninth rows** until work is completed, retaining the same sequence of colors.

**Tricolor Zigzag Pattern.** The ripple pattern is most effective when worked in 3 colors. After deciding on color scheme, make a foundation chain the required length with 1 color (A). Use a multiple of 14 stitches plus 13, with an additional 1 chain.

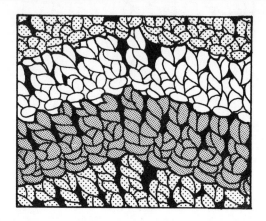

For the **first row,** continue with color (A). Make 1 double crochet in fourth chain from hook. The make 1 double crochet in each of next 3 chains. Repeat the following sequence of stitches. * Take 3 double crochets in next chain and 1 double crochet in each of next 5 chains. Skip 1 chain. Make 1 double crochet in next chain. Skip 1 chain. Take 1 double crochet in each of next 5 chains. * At the last 6 chains, take 3 double crochets in next chain and 1 double crochet in each of last 5 chains. Turn.

For the **second row,** continue with same color (A). Chain 1. Skip 2 stitches. Take one single crochet in each of next 4 stitches. Repeat the following sequence of stitches. * Take 3 single crochets in next stitch. Make 1 single crochet in each of next 5 stitches. Skip 1 stitch. Make 1 single crochet in next stitch. Skip 1 stitch. Take 1 single crochet in each of next 5 stitches. * At last 7 stitches, take 3 single crochets in next stitch and 1 single crochet in each of next 4 stitches. Skip 1 stitch. Take 1 single crochet in top of turning chain. Chain 3. Turn.

For the **third and fourth rows,** change to second color (B). Use directions for first and second rows.

For the **fifth and sixth rows,** change to first color (A). Use directions for first and second rows.

For the **seventh and eighth rows,** change to third color (C). Use directions for first and second rows.

For the **ninth and tenth rows,** change to color (A). Use directions for first and second rows.

Continue in this way until work is completed. The width of the stripes can be adjusted to create different effects.

## Ring Trim

This easy-to-make trim can be made in varying sizes depending on how the yarn is wound. For a small size, wrap yarn around top of left thumb 3 times. This becomes the foundation for the ring. Then make single crochet stitches into center of ring until one half is covered. Remove ring from thumb so that the second ring can be started. Do not break yarn. Make the second and remaining rings in the same way. When the required length is reached, crochet completely around last ring. Continue to crochet around unfinished half of each ring until starting point is reached. Take a slip stitch in first single crochet. Fasten yarn and clip.

### Rings—Covered

Plastic rings can be covered for a decorative effect. A single ring or a series of rings can be used. Holding the yarn in back of the ring, pull the yarn through the ring, forming a loop. Work single crochet stitches over the ring. As the stitches are made, also cover the end of the yarn.

For **one ring,** continue until ring is completely covered. Slip stitch in first single crochet. Fasten yarn and clip.

For a **series of rings,** cover half of the first ring. Do not fasten yarn. Instead continue single crochet around one half of the ring and as many other rings as required. On the last ring, continue completely around, covering it. Then work over the uncovered half of each ring. When all rings are covered, make a slip stitch in the first single crochet that was made over first ring.

### Tunisian Crochet
*See* Afghan Stitch—Basic (in "Stitch Patterns").

## Woven Crochet

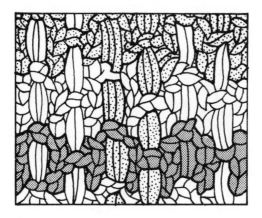

By interlacing yarn through a crochet mesh, a woven effect is created. It may be varied using different colors, size of mesh and width of stripes. A mesh made of double crochet stitches and chain-1 space is suggested. Begin with a foundation chain the required length. Use a multiple of 2 stitches plus 1, with an additional 2 chains.

For the **first row,** make 1 double crochet in fifth chain from hook. Repeat the following procedure to end of row. * Chain 1. Skip 1 chain. Make 1 double crochet in next chain. * Chain 4 and turn.

For the **second row,** skip 2 stitches. Repeat the following procedure to end of row. * Make 1 double crochet in next double crochet. Chain 1. * End with 1 double crochet in third stitch of turning chain. Chain 4 and turn.

Repeat **second row** until mesh is completed.

If a striped effect is required, introduce a different color at the beginning of an appropriate row.

For the weaving, use 3 strands of yarn. Weave over and under the chain bars, alternating from row to row. Use a blunt needle.

# Part II

# Embroidering

Embroidery is one of our oldest and most beautiful arts. It has been part of the cultural growth of every nation. As far back as the days of Abraham, it was considered a distinguished art. Descriptions of early Egyptian costumes mention the lovely embroidered borders decorating the simple sheaths. Examples of the exquisite work done in the seventeenth and eighteenth centuries by English and French needlewomen are inspiring. It is difficult to believe that a needle and thread could produce such beautiful effects. But they could—and can. To become an artist with thread requires only a love of beauty, a feeling for perfection, and a creative spirit.

Fashions in needlework change, just like fashions in clothing. At one period in history, one style is more "in" than another. The pages that follow provide information on various phases of the embroidery process. Use them as a guide in developing this artistic skill, adapting it to contemporary forms.

# DESIGN DETAILS

Embroidering falls into two categories, and both can produce beautiful results. For some people, commercially prepared material satisfies a creative need. For others, the freedom to use imagination and skill to produce an original, in the manner of the artist, is more fulfilling. Knowing how and where to use a stitch is most important. Because of the wide range of available stitches, this may not be as easy as it seems. Some stitches seem to interpret one design detail or area better than another. Because of this, it is wise to experiment before beginning the actual embroidery. Suggestions for utilizing various stitches are given here. Of course, there are many others that could be used. And remember that the type of the thread or yarn will influence the effect.

## Band and Border Stitches

One of the favorite embroidery forms is the band or border. Stitches are used to define an area for a decorative trim. Usually the band consists of stitches worked solidly in a continuous line. Some of the most effective band and border stitches are shown below.

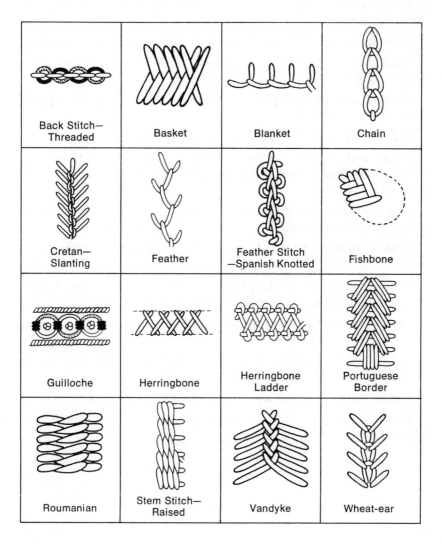

| | | | |
|---|---|---|---|
| Back Stitch—Threaded | Basket | Blanket | Chain |
| Cretan—Slanting | Feather | Feather Stitch—Spanish Knotted | Fishbone |
| Guilloche | Herringbone | Herringbone Ladder | Portuguese Border |
| Roumanian | Stem Stitch—Raised | Vandyke | Wheat-ear |

## Design Stitches

Certain stitches seem more appropriate for one type of design than another. It is wise to experiment before beginning the actual embroidery. Try some of these stitch suggestions (see facing chart) for creating certain design details. Of course, there are many others that you could use.

**Animals:** Chain, French Knot, Long and Short, Outline, Satin, Split, Stem, Turkey Work.

**Baskets:** Blanket, Burden, Buttonhole, Chain, Outline, Split, Stem.

**Birds:** Blanket, Bullion Knot, Buttonhole, Fishbone, Herringbone—Close, Laid Work, Satin, Turkey Work.

**Centers and Circles:** Blanket, Bullion Knot, Buttonhole, French Knot, Satin, Spider Web.

**Faces:** Backstitch, French Knot, Satin, Split, Stem.

**Fruits and Vegetables:** Brick, Burden, Chain, Coral, Fishbone, French Knot, Herringbone—Close, Laid Work, Long and Short, Spider Web, Split, Stem.

**Houses:** Backstitch, Brick, Burden, Chain, Couching, Laid Work, Satin, Split, Stem—Raised.

**Leaves:** Burden, Chain, Cretan, Fern, Fishbone, Herringbone—Close, Leaf, Long and Short, Seed, Stem.

**Petals:** Buttonhole, Cretan, Fishbone, Herringbone—Closed, Laid Work, Long and Short, Needleweaving, Satin, Seed, Trellis.

**Sea:** Burden, Chevron, Couching, French Knot, Split, Stem, Straight.

**Sky:** Cloud Filling, Laid Work, Long and Short, Running, Seed, Straight.

**Stems:** Back, Chain, Coral, Herringbone, Pekinese, Rope, Stem.

**Trees:** Burden, Cretan, Fishbone, French Knot, Herringbone—Close, Laid Work, Satin, Seed.

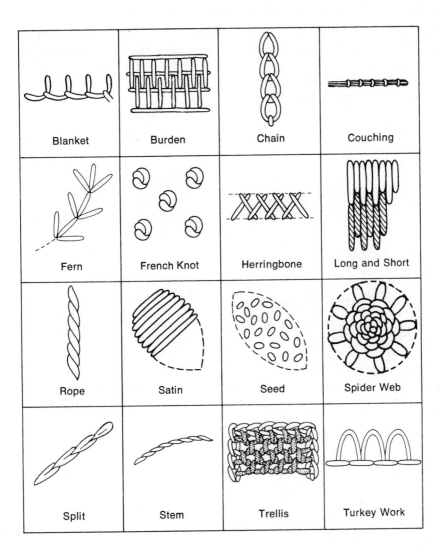

| | | | |
|---|---|---|---|
| Blanket | Burden | Chain | Couching |
| Fern | French Knot | Herringbone | Long and Short |
| Rope | Satin | Seed | Spider Web |
| Split | Stem | Trellis | Turkey Work |

## Cut-and-Drawn Thread Stitches

For an openwork effect, fabric threads can be removed by cutting or drawing out. This procedure requires that the edges and threads remaining be carefully secured. Certain embroidery stitches fulfill this requirement nicely and, at the same time, produce a beautiful effect. Some of these stitches are shown below.

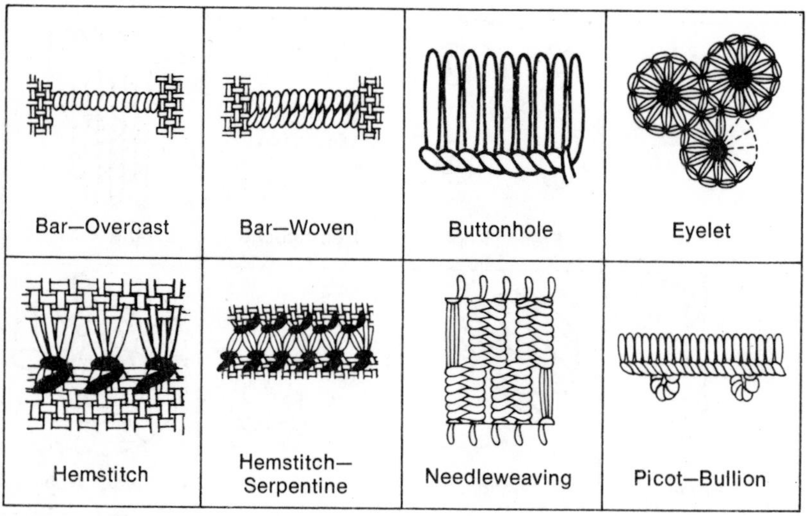

| | | | |
|---|---|---|---|
| Bar—Overcast | Bar—Woven | Buttonhole | Eyelet |
| Hemstitch | Hemstitch—Serpentine | Needleweaving | Picot—Bullion |

## Edge Stitches

Sometimes embroidery stitches are used to finish an edge or to hold two edges together, creating an insertion. The stitches are functional as well as decorative. When the stitches are placed over cut edges, they are made close together. Some of the stitches that provide the finishing touch along an edge are shown below.

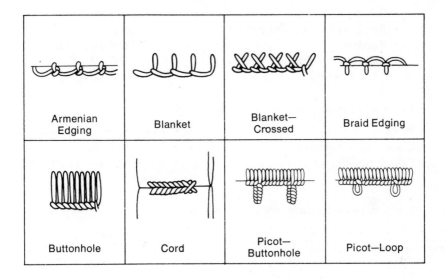

| | | | |
|---|---|---|---|
| Armenian Edging | Blanket | Blanket—Crossed | Braid Edging |
| Buttonhole | Cord | Picot—Buttonhole | Picot—Loop |

## Filling Stitches

To add interest to motifs, the fabric within the design boundaries is sometimes decorated, producing a textured look. By the selection of the correct stitch, an open or solid effect can be produced. Detached stitches can be scattered within the design outline. Some examples of filling stitches are shown on the facing page.

For an open filling, try these stitches:

- Arrowhead
- Brick and Cross Filling
- Burden
- Chessboard Filling
- Cloud Filling

- Ermine
- Seed
- Tête-de-boeuf
- Trellis
- Wave—Open

For a solid filling, try these stitches:

- Brick
- Couching—Bokhara
- Couching—Roumanian
- Cross

- Darning Stitch—Double
- Long and Short
- Satin Stitch—Whipped
- Stem

For a detached filling, try these stitches:

- Blanket—Knotted
- Buttonhole Filling
- Ceylon
- Hollie

- Honeycomb
- Lattice Stitch—Twisted
- Maltese Cross Filling
- Trellis

Solid filling stitches can be used for shading.

Color variations in a design pattern can be most effective. When the color changes are subtle, the results can be lovely.

The stitches listed here can be used for this purpose.

- Brick
- Buttonhole
- Long and Short

- Satin—Encroaching
- Stem

OPEN EFFECT

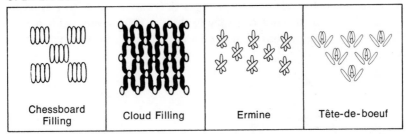

| Chessboard Filling | Cloud Filling | Ermine | Tête-de-boeuf |

SOLID EFFECT

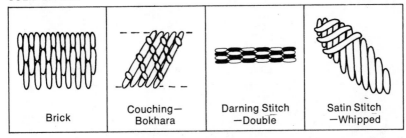

| Brick | Couching— Bokhara | Darning Stitch —Double | Satin Stitch —Whipped |

DETACHED EFFECT

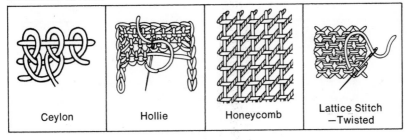

| Ceylon | Hollie | Honeycomb | Lattice Stitch —Twisted |

## Outline Stitches

A motif is usually defined by using a decorative stitch to cover the design line. The stitches can vary in degree of heaviness and design detail. Always select one that seems appropriate. Some suggestions are shown below.

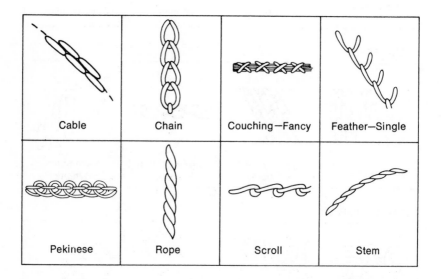

| Cable | Chain | Couching—Fancy | Feather—Single |
|-------|-------|----------------|----------------|
| Pekinese | Rope | Scroll | Stem |

## Pulled or Drawn Stitches

Lovely lace effects can be created by placing this type of stitch on evenly woven fabric so that the threads can be easily counted. In order that the threads can be pulled together to create the design, there should be a certain openness to the plain weave. Some of the stitches that can produce this openwork effect are shown below.

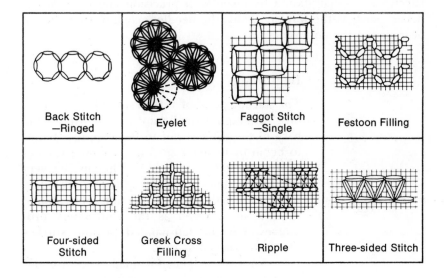

| Back Stitch —Ringed | Eyelet | Faggot Stitch —Single | Festoon Filling |
| Four-sided Stitch | Greek Cross Filling | Ripple | Three-sided Stitch |

# GENERAL DIRECTIONS

The wide variety of embroidery stitches is due to the placement of the needle and of the thread. The needle may enter the material at various angles. The thread may be brought in front of the needle, held to one side of it, or wrapped around it. Sometimes the thread is looped or twisted to give the desired effect. But each small change produces a new result that can be interesting. To create the right effect, each stitch should be taken with precision and care. Minor details, such as the way one holds the needle, may influence the appearance of the embroidery.

## Beginning

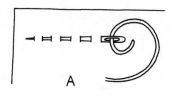

The starting point of a stitch should not be obvious. Although a small knot can be used if the back of the work is not to be seen, it is better to begin by taking 2 or 3 tiny running stitches toward the starting point (A). Then make a very small backstitch (B). Follow with an embroidery stitch taken in the correct direction. The running stitches are covered as the embroidery progresses. For the left-handed person, stitches should be started as in C.

If a knot is used, keep it small. Tuck it under a stitch so that the end is covered.

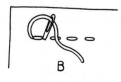

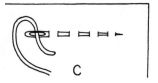

## Direction

Generally, embroidery stitches are made from left to right. (Of course, the left-handed person will proceed in the opposite direction, right to left.) Certain stitches, such as the running stitch, are made from right to left, as in sewing.

## Ending

The thread should be fastened on the wrong side of the work under the last 2 or 3 stitches. Or a tiny backstitch can be taken over the last stitch before the needle is run in and out through the embroidery. Another way allows 2 tiny backstitches to be taken over and under the last stitches and the thread clipped close.

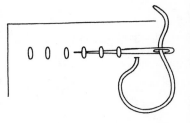

## Holding the Needle

Hold the needle between the thumb and the index (first) finger. Let the needle touch the side of the thimble near the top.

The thimble is a "must" when the stitches are made in sewing fashion, in and out through the fabric. When the needle moves up and down in a separate motion, in stabbing fashion, the thimble is not quite as necessary.

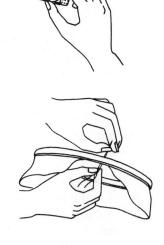

## Increasing or Decreasing Size

The size of a design can be changed in this way. Make a tracing of the design to be used. Mark the tracing with a series of vertical and horizontal lines, forming squares. The size of the squares can vary from ⅛ inch (3 mm) for a small design to 1 inch (2.5 cm) for a larger one.

On another piece of tracing paper, duplicate the same number of lines and squares but in a larger size, if the design is to be enlarged. For instance, if the design is to be increased to twice the original size, then the squares should be drawn twice as large. With the squared paper prepared, copy the design outline from the smaller squares to the corresponding larger ones.

To decrease the size, reverse the procedure, making the squares smaller instead of larger.

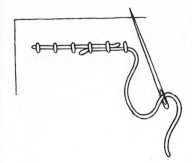

## Introducing a New Thread

Care should be taken that there is no joining mark when a new thread must be started in a row of stitches. Pass the new thread through several stitches on the wrong side. Then bring it through to the right side at the point where the next stitch should be made. Do not carry the thread from one design to another because it produces an untidy look on the wrong side.

## Pressing

Pressing improves the appearance of many types of embroidery. Place the completed work right side down on a thickly padded board. This allows the raised surface of the embroidery to sink into the soft padding, and thus the iron is kept from flattening the design.

If the embroidery has been worked on cotton, linen, or wool fabric, cover it with a slightly damp cloth. Press lightly with a moderately hot iron. Remove the moist cloth. Continue to press until fabric is dry.

If the material is made of silk or synthetic fibers, put a piece of tissue paper between the fabric and the damp cloth before pressing.

If the embroidery has been flattened during the working process and pressing will not correct the condition, try this. Mount the embroidered piece on a frame. Then place a wet cloth over an upright hot iron. Hold the embroidery above the steaming iron so that the steam passes through the work from the wrong side to the right side.

## Stretching and Blocking

Some types of embroidery are pulled out of shape as the stitches are worked. When this happens, it is necessary to restore the embroidery to its original shape.

For crewel work, moisten it in cold water. Place it dripping wet on a covered board with the right side up. Using rustproof pins, tack the embroidery to the board. Keep the fabric taut and the threads at right angles to each other as the work is pulled into shape. Let it dry thoroughly before removing it from the board.

For needlepoint, place the dry material right side down on a covered board. Tack it to the board with rustproof pins, starting in the corners. Be careful not to place pins in the stitches. Keep the canvas threads at right angles. Pull them taut. Dab the needlepoint with a wet cloth to soak it. Let the piece dry thoroughly.

## Threading a Needle

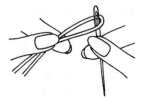 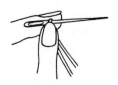 

A thread about 18 inches (46 cm) long is convenient to use. A longer thread often becomes fuzzy, untwisted, or tangled before the end is reached. Cut the thread from the spool or skein. Place the cut end though the eye of the needle. Be careful to avoid snarls when separating 6-strand floss.

When using heavier yarns and threads, it is difficult to place the end through the eye without fraying. To avoid this, place the yarn around the needle. Hold it firmly, close to the needle. Pull the needle away. Squeeze thread tightly to flatten it. Bring the eye of the needle down over the folded yarn a short distance. Then pull yarn through the eye.

## Transferring a Design

Embroidery designs can be purchased ready to be transferred to material, or they can be adapted or created and then transferred. The commercial form is, of course, easier to use.

**Commercial Transfers.** Some commercial transfers can be used only once; others, several times. The number usually depends on the type of fabric when using multiprint transfers. Generally you can obtain the most impressions on fine fabrics, and fewer on heavier materials. Some transfers require the use of an iron.

Read carefully the directions that accompany this type of transfer. Be sure to cut away the lettering and any part of the design that is not needed.

Because the temperature of the iron is important, test it with a bit of the discarded lettering. When the test is satisfactory, put the transfer design face down on the material in the correct position. Anchor the transfer with pins. Apply the iron for a few seconds. Do not shove the iron around. Moving the fabric or transfer will leave a smudged double impression.

To be sure that the transferring of the design is correct, check before removing the design. Lift just a corner of the transfer paper. Reapply the iron if the impression needs to be clearer.

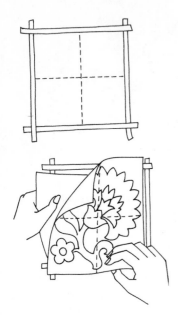

**Tracing Method.** There are several ways to draw a design on the foundation material. One simple method is to use dressmaker's carbon paper.

To guarantee the correct positioning, start by folding the material in half and then in half again. This establishes the guidelines for the placement of the design.

Place the material on a flat, hard surface, such as a board. Fasten it to the board with masking tape.

Then fold the design paper into 4 parts. Open it and match the folds with those of the fabric. When they are in position, slip the carbon paper, face downward, between the material and design paper. Hold the 3 thicknesses in place with weights.

Trace the design with a pencil, pressing firmly so that a clear design appears on the material.

On fine fabrics, the design can be placed under the material and traced directly on it. Use a soft pencil or water-color paint.

**Basting Method.** The pile of rough or textured material makes it difficult to trace a design. In this case, duplicate the design on tracing paper or transparent material such as batiste, chiffon, organdy, or tissue paper. Pin the design to the wrong side. Transfer the design with small running stitches through all thicknesses, using a thread in a contrasting color. Remove the paper or material gently and embroider over the running stitches.

**Canvas Method.** Using canvas is an easy way to embroider a cross stitch or geometric design on the material without marking the fabric beforehand. Baste the canvas to the material. Place in a frame. Make the stitches even by counting the canvas threads. When the design is completed, the canvas threads are pulled out.

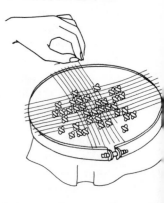

## MATERIALS AND TOOLS

The beauty of embroidery depends in part on the use of the correct materials and equipment. Co-ordinating the fabric, thread, and needle in order to interpret a stitch and design effectively is most important.

### Canvas

This open-mesh material forms the foundation of needlepoint. It is available in two basic types: single-thread, or mono, and double-thread, or Penelope. Both are made in a variety of sizes and of various fibers—acrylic, cotton, and linen. There is also a plastic canvas.

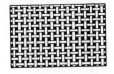

Threads can be easily counted in the single-thread canvas, making it excellent for interpreting geometric designs. Stitches worked on this type of canvas seem to melt into one another. This makes it easier to work curved and shaded areas.

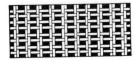

The double-thread canvas is firmer, partly because of the interlocking of the threads.

### Fabric

As fashions in embroidery change, so do the fabrics. Dainty stitches seem more effective on fine fabric; bold stitches, on coarse textures. Fabrics can vary from transparent materials such as organdy, lawn, and batiste, to monk's cloth and homespun, to denim, ticking, and twill. The favorite fabric, however, has always been linen, from very fine to coarse. It allows threads to be quickly counted and easily pierced by the needle. Whichever fabric is selected, be sure that it is woven on grain. In this way, the stitches can be kept in perfect alignment.

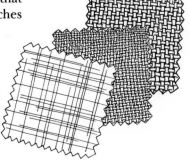

## Frames and Hoops

This piece of equipment is a must. It keeps the fabric flat and smooth, the stitches even. Frames and hoops are available in a variety of sizes, shapes, and types—small and large, round and rectangular, to hold in the hand or stand on the floor. Always select the one that is best for the embroidery being done and that is convenient to use.

Small hoops or rings are used for small pieces of embroidery. A hoop consists of 2 wooden or metal rings. Some have a small screw or spring on the larger ring. It allows the ring to be adjusted to accommodate the thickness of the fabric, in order to keep the material taut.

Place the fabric over the smaller ring. Press the other ring over it. Be sure the fabric is taut and that the lengthwise and crosswise threads are straight when the rings are in place.

Rectangular frames are usually employed for larger pieces of embroidery. Generally they consist of 4 pieces, 2 rollers for top and bottom and 2 side pieces that fit into holes or slots in the rollers. The rollers have pieces of tape or fabric attached to which the embroidery is fastened.

When the fabric is in place, it is laced to the sides of the frame to hold it taut. Directions for mounting the material accompany the frame. Read them carefully before starting the mounting procedure.

Large oval rug or quilting hoops, square frames, and artist's stretcher frames offer other possibilities. Standing frames leave the hands free. This is often thought to increase one's skill and to speed up the embroidery process.

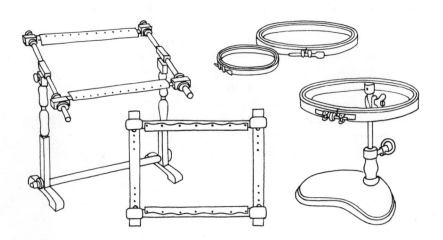

## Needles

Different types of embroidery require different types of needles. When working on fabric, use one that has a sharp point, such as a crewel or chenille. For needlepoint, huck embroidery, and other counted-thread embroidery, work with a blunt or tapestry needle.

The crewel needle is the most commonly used. It is short, about 1¾ inches (4.5 cm) in length, and has a long, slender eye. Since the needle separates the threads of the cloth so that the embroidery thread may pass through easily, it is important to use one slightly thicker at the eye end than the thread. Crewel needles are numbered 1 to 12 to denote size. The higher the number is, the finer the needle. Chenille and tapestry needles are also available in a variety of sizes.

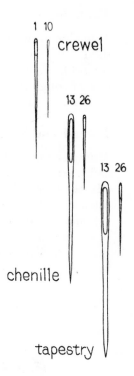

## Scissors

Two pairs of scissors make embroidery easier to do—a small pair, about 3 inches (7.5 cm) in length, for snipping fine thread, and a larger one, about 4 or 5 inches (10 or 12.5 cm) long, to cut fabric and coarser threads. Both types should have very sharp points and narrow blades.

## Special Equipment

Certain types of embroidery require special equipment. A stiletto is helpful for making eyelets, heavy paper for fagoting, and dressmaker's carbon paper for transferring designs. Embroidery materials and tools should be kept in a special container, not in the one used for your general sewing.

## Thimble

A thimble protects the middle finger when pushing the needle through the fabric. This makes it possible to embroider with greater skill. It should be light in weight, fit the middle finger comfortably, and be free of rough spots that might snag the fabric or thread.

## Thread and Yarn

The selection of thread and yarn depends on the type of embroidery and where it is to be placed. The same stitch can produce different effects when different types of thread are employed. Sometimes unusual embroidery materials such as twine can be used effectively.

Some of the commonly used threads are 6-strand cotton floss and pearl cotton. Yarns vary from the very fine French wool to heavy rug wool. Always correlate thread and needles to the type of embroidery.

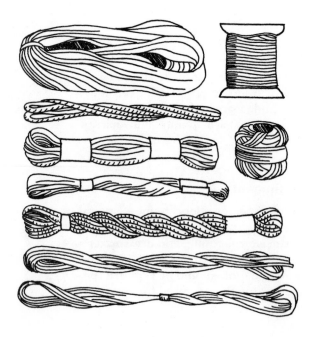

## STITCHES

Although there are hundreds of embroidery stitches, they are in reality variations of four basic types of stitches: flat, knotted, linked or chain, and looped or blanket. Some of these are worked by counting threads; others, by following a design marked on the material.

Flat stitches are those that lie on the surface of the fabric, such as the Cross, Running, and Satin stitches. Knotted stitches, such as the French Knot, create a raised or studded look. Linked include the Chain Stitch, in which 2 stitches are interlocked. Looped stitches are flat ones made with the thread held by the thumb to form a loop under the needle, as in the Blanket and Feather stitches.

There is also a group of stitches called composite stitches. These are made by combining two or more stitches. Composite stitches are produced in two ways. A basic stitch may be interlaced with another, as in the Pekinese Stitch, or several stitches may be combined with an interlacing thread, as in the Guilloche Stitch.

In studying information about embroidery, one finds that a single stitch may have several names. For this reason, stitches are cross-referenced in the following pages for easier identification.

### Algerian Eye Stitch

Eight straight stitches radiate from a central point to create a star effect in this drawn-fabric stitch. Sometimes the stitch is called Star Eyelet. The stitches are evenly spaced and arranged in a square.

Use a stiletto to push the threads apart to form a tiny hole at the center point. Be careful not to break the threads.

Bring the needle through the fabric at A, inserting it in the hole. Continue in this way until the 8 stitches are made.

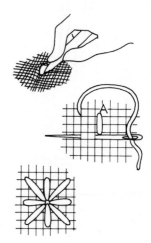

### Algerian Eyelet

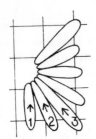

This is a filled-in version of the Algerian Eye Stitch. Straight stitches radiate from a central point and form a square or diamond outline.

Work the stitches over the same number of threads of canvas vertically and horizontally. Place the stitches close together but not overlapping. Move the needle around in the hole as each stitch is taken to keep it open. The beauty of the effect depends on the openness of the eyelet and flat regularity of the stitches.

### Algerian Stitch

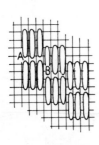

This is a filling stitch, sometimes referred to as Algerian Filling Stitch. It belongs to the pulled-thread or drawn-fabric group, in which the stitches are pulled tight for an open effect.

Begin at point A. Take 3 satin stitches over 4 threads, forming a square. Start the second group of stitches (B) 2 threads above or below the first group.

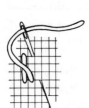

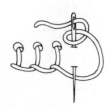

### Antique Stitch
      *See* Roumanian Stitch.

### Antwerp Edging Stitch
      *See* Blanket Stitch—Knotted.

## Armenian Edging Stitch

A small knot gives a decorative touch to this edging. It is especially effective when worked in a heavy thread.

Bring the thread to the right side (A) on the finished edge. Working from left to right, insert the needle again from the underside as at B. Before pulling the thread completely through, twist the thread into a loop (C). Slip the needle through the loop, pulling the thread tight. Repeat procedure for the next stitch.

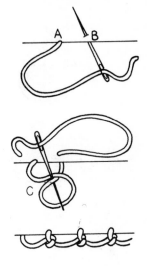

## Arrowhead Stitch

This is a filling or line stitch made by 2 straight stitches placed at right angles to each other, forming a small V. A row of stitches produces a zigzag effect. The evenness of the stitches is important. Working over guidelines or counted threads makes this easier to achieve.

Bring the needle to the right side of the fabric at A. Insert it below and to the right at B, forming a short diagonal stitch. Come up again at C, to the right and above. Return the needle to point B so that the V or arrowhead is formed. Continue this procedure, working vertically or horizontally.

For a vertical row of stitches, bring the needle up at D and continue to E, F, and E. The stitch should be directly under the one above.

For a horizontal row of stitches, come up at C and proceed to D, E, and D.

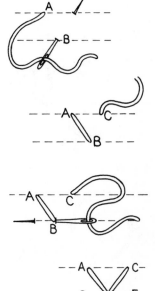

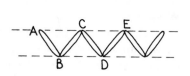

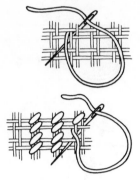

## Aubusson Stitch

This stitch is also known as Rep Stitch. It is worked on double-thread canvas to produce a solid effect. Be sure to choose a yarn that will create the effect.

Make 2 small diagonal stitches over the intersection of the canvas threads. Place the top stitch over the upper horizontal thread, the bottom one over the lower thread.

## Backstitch

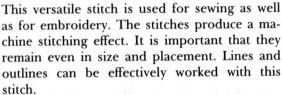

This versatile stitch is used for sewing as well as for embroidery. The stitches produce a machine stitching effect. It is important that they remain even in size and placement. Lines and outlines can be effectively worked with this stitch.

Begin at the right end of the line to be covered. Bring the needle to the right side of the fabric, a stitch length from the end (A). Insert the needle at the end (B). Pick up twice the amount of material as covered by the first stitch, coming up at C.

For the second stitch, carry needle back to A and insert it. Continue this procedure.

## Backstitch—Crossed or Double

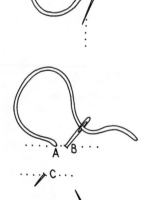

The stitches appear as 2 rows of backstitching on the right side and as a crossed or Close Herringbone stitch on the wrong side. The smaller the backstitches are, the closer the crossed stitches will be. This is also used for Shadow Work.

Work between 2 guidelines. Make a backstitch on the upper line (A–B). Slip the needle under the material so that it can emerge in the lower line (C), 1 stitch length to the left of A.

Insert the needle at D, directly below A, for the second stitch. Return the needle to the upper

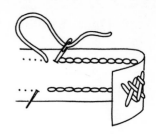

line, crossing under the fabric and emerging at E, directly above C. The thread stitch is taken between E and A. Continue to alternate the placement of the stitches.

## Backstitch—Ringed

Ring and half-ring designs can be created by this stitch. When half rings are used, the stitch is called Festoon Filling Stitch. It is most effective as a drawn-fabric filling when the stitches are pulled tightly.

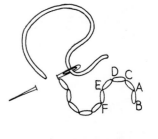

Make the first backstitch by bringing the needle up at A; down at B, 3 threads below; and up at C, 6 threads up and 3 threads to the left.

For the second stitch, insert the needle at A and bring it up at D, 3 threads up and 6 threads to the left of A.

For the third stitch, enter the fabric at C and come up at E, 3 threads down and 6 threads to the left.

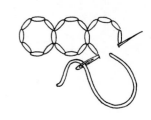

For the fourth stitch, insert the needle at D, emerging at F, 6 threads down and 3 threads to the left.

After making a row of half rings, turn the fabric around and continue filling in the rings.

## Backstitch—Threaded

Lacing contrasting threads through a row of backstitches makes an attractive border. The threads produce a looped effect.

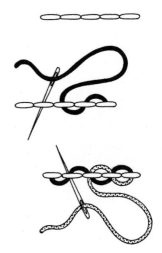

After working a foundation row of backstitches, bring the first lacing thread through the fabric, under the first backstitch. This is the only time the needle enters the material until the work is completed.

Carry the thread under the second stitch. Continue this procedure, alternating the stitches above and below the row of backstitches.

If a second thread is used, it is interlaced in the same way, filling in the vacant spaces with loops.

### Bar—Buttonholed

Bars are used for a lacy effect in various types of embroidery. Usually 3 or more threads form a foundation. For drawn-thread work, the bar threads remain after required threads have been removed. For cutwork, the threads are added and bars made before the fabric is cut away. The threads are held together here with a buttonhole stitch.

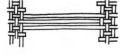

**For drawn-thread work,** withdraw the desired number of threads, leaving the foundation threads for the bars. Working from left to right, bring up the working thread beside the lower thread. Hold the working thread down with the left thumb.

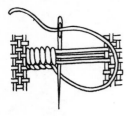

Slip the needle over and under the bar threads, emerging close to the spot where it first appeared. Draw the needle through the loop that has been formed, making a buttonhole stitch.

Place the second stitch close to the first one. Continue in this way until the foundation threads are covered and the bar made.

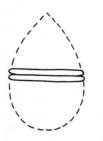

**For cutwork,** add the foundation threads after preparing the design. Cover the threads with buttonhole stitches, as described above, without picking up any of the fabric beneath.

Another way to make the bars is to use a double buttonhole stitch. Put a row of stitches along the upper edge, leaving a space between each stitch. Follow this with another row of stitches along the lower edge, filling in the spaces.

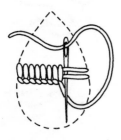

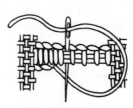

## Bar—Overcast

This type of bar is also known as Corded or Twisted Bar.

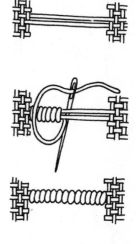

Withdraw the necessary number of threads, leaving a group of threads that may be made into a bar. Hold the threads together by wrapping with closely placed overcasting stitches. Begin at the left end of the bar. Place the stitches so that a firm, smooth bar results.

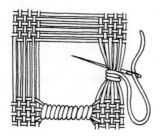

## Bar—Woven

This type of bar is used in Italian cutwork and Hardanger embroidery. The working thread creates a woven effect, producing a strong, flat bar. Use an even number of threads to make the bar.

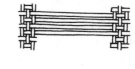

Starting at the left, pass the needle over and under the upper half of the stitches. Pull the thread tight, binding the bar threads together. Follow this with a stitch around the lower half of the threads.

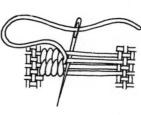

Alternate the stitches in this way until the bar is completed. Keep the stitches close together.

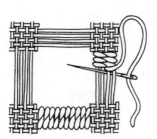

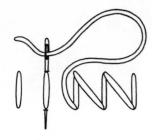

## Barrier Stitch

This filling stitch is also called Fence Stitch. It resembles a row of letter **N's**.

Begin with a row of vertical stitches, working from left to right. Connect these with a diagonal stitch, forming an **N**. Always point the needle downward as it moves under the fabric.

## Basket Stitch—Open or Closed

Although this stitch resembles a Herringbone Stitch, its effect can be varied by placing the stitches apart or close together. It makes an attractive border or a solid line.

For the **Open Basket Stitch,** follow the accompanying diagram, beginning at A. Insert the needle at B above A and to the right, making a diagonal stitch. Bring up the needle below B at C, in a line with A. Then take another slanting stitch from C to D, which is above A and in a line with B.

Start the second stitch at E, a point to the left of C. Continue to F, G, H, and I, ready to start the third stitch.

The stitches appear as vertical stitches crossed by diagonals on the back of the work.

For the **Closed Basket Stitch,** follow the same procedure, keeping the stitches close together. On the wrong side, the work appears as pairs of straight stitches.

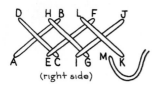

(right side)

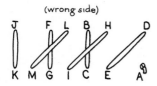

(wrong side)

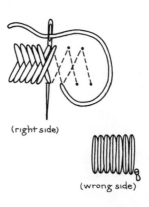

(right side)

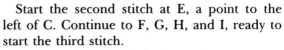

(wrong side)

## Basket Weave Stitch

When tent stitches are worked diagonally, a basket weave design appears on the back of the canvas, producing a solid effect.

The needle is pointed down when working downward, horizontal when working upward. This allows the canvas to be held in the same position whether working downward or upward.

Check the directions for Tent Stitch for more detailed instructions.

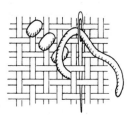 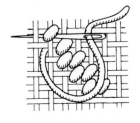 

## Basque Stitch

This looped stitch gives the effect of chain stitches worked horizontally, with an extra twist. As its name implies, it is often found in embroideries originating in the Basque country.

Working from left to right, bring the needle to the right side at A. Arrange the thread in a question mark design before inserting the needle at B, to the right of A and below the top loop. Let the needle emerge at C, directly below B. Draw the thread through the loop.

Hold the loop in place by a small vertical stitch placed over the loop, at D. Bring up the needle at B. Begin the second stitch by inserting the needle at E. Then continue in the same way.

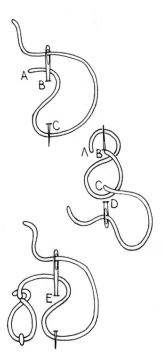

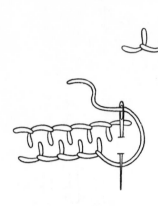

## Blanket Stitch

Although the method for making the Blanket and Buttonhole stitches is the same, it should be remembered that the Blanket Stitch is made with space between the stitches. It is a stitch that lends itself to variations. By varying the length and direction of the stitches, as well as the spaces between, you can create interesting effects for lines and outlines. Some of the variations are shown here.

It is important that a regularity to the stitches be maintained. Working between 2 guidelines is helpful.

Work from left to right. Bring the needle to the right side of the fabric on the lower line. Hold the thread down with the left thumb. Insert the needle at the upper line a short distance to the right, letting it emerge directly below on the lower line. Draw the thread through the loop that has been formed, ready to make the next stitch.

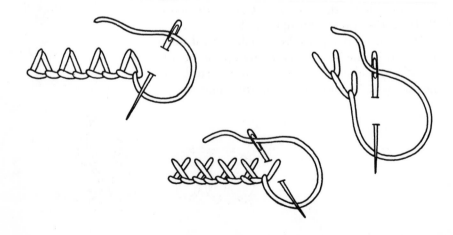

## Blanket Stitch—Knotted

The small knot made at the end of each blanket stitch provides an interesting variation. The stitch is most effective when made of heavy thread.

Twist the thread exactly as shown in the accompanying diagram. This is important because unless the loop is made this way there will not be a knot.

Hold the loop in place as the needle is slipped through it and the fabric, completing the stitch.

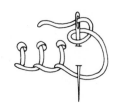

## Blanket Stitch—Knotted Edging

This pretty edging is most effective when made of heavy thread. It is used to decorate a finished edge.

Start with a blanket stitch. However, before completing the stitch, slip the needle under the working thread as it passes through the loop. The knot is formed when the thread is pulled tight. Guide the placement of the knot so the stitches will remain even.

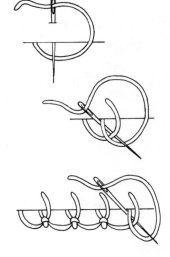

## Blanket Stitch Insertion—Whipped

This stitch is used to hold 2 finished edges together, as in fagoting.

Make a row of blanket stitches along the edges to be joined. Be sure that the stitches are spaced evenly and placed to lie opposite each other. Then hold the work together with a diagonal whipping stitch, slipping the needle through opposite loops in 2 sets of blanket stitches.

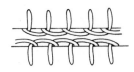

### Braid Edging Stitch

This stitch creates a scalloped effect on a finished edge. Although it appears simple to make, it requires some practice in order to keep the loops even. Use a guideline to regulate the depth of the stitches.

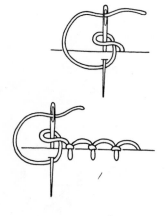

Working from right to left, bring the needle through the fabric at the folded edge. Loop the thread as shown in the accompanying diagram. With the needle entering the fabric from the back, slip it through first the loop and then the fabric, a short distance from the folded edge. The needle passes over the working thread as it is pulled through the material.

Before the thread is drawn through completely, check the evenness of the loops. There is still time to make an adjustment with the needle.

Reverse the direction of the working thread, pulling it away. This allows a firm knot to be made against the edge.

### Braid Stitch
*See* Chain Stitch—Heavy.

## Brick and Cross Filling

This simple filling stitch is most effective when worked in contrasting colors. Groups of 3 or 4 satin stitches alternate with cross stitches, producing a checkerboard pattern. It is important to maintain an evenness in placement and size of the stitches.

## Brick Stitch

This is a good filling stitch that may be used effectively when shading is required. Straight stitches are arranged to simulate "laid bricks." They may be worked close together for a solid effect or with small spaces between. A regularity to the placement of stitches is important.

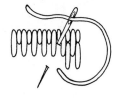

Work the first row of stitches in alternating long and short stitches. Make the subsequent rows of identical stitches in the longer length.

Proceed from left to right for the first row, right to left for the second. Be sure to bring up the needle in the hole of the stitch above.

## Bullion Knot or Stitch

Floral motifs are often created by using this stitch. It requires practice for perfection. The tiny coils of thread are difficult to keep in place. A short thread and a rather thick needle with a narrow eye make the process easier.

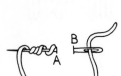

Bring the needle to the right side of the fabric (A). Insert it to the right (B) the required length of the stitch, emerging again at A.

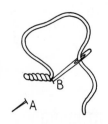

Before pulling the needle through the fabric, twist the thread around the needle close to the place where it emerged. The number of twists depends on the length of the stitch; 6 or 7 coils are an average number.

After the thread has been coiled around the needle, place the left thumb on the coils to hold them in place. Gently pull the needle and the thread through the coils. As this is done, reverse the position of the thread so that the coils lie between A and B. Pull the working thread to tighten the coils. Insert the needle at B and pull the thread to the wrong side.

## Burden Stitch

This is a good filling stitch that can be used to cover large background spaces. The stitches can be placed close together or apart.

One version of this stitch is composed of darning stitches placed to give a "laid brick" effect. The stitches are longer than the usual ones, with a long stitch used on the right side, a short one on the wrong side. The stitches and spaces should be placed to maintain a regular pattern.

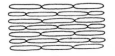

Another version gives a woven appearance. Straight stitches are placed over and between a series of parallel lines.

Make 3 long stitches or horizontal lines about ¼ inch (6 mm) apart. Start at A, continuing to B, C, D, E, and F, in that order.

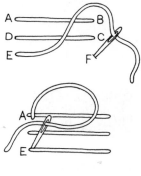

Begin the first vertical stitch just below A, bringing the needle through at this point. Insert it again just above E. Continue in this way to complete the row, placing the stitches a short distance apart and at right angles to the laid threads.

Before beginning the second row of vertical stitches, lay another horizontal stitch between H and G. Make the first stitch from the second horizontal line, D–C, to the fourth one, H–G. Continue filling in the open spaces left by the first row of stitches.

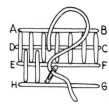

When the rows are completed, fill in the first row with a series of short stitches to create a solid surface.

## Buttonhole Filling Stitch—Open

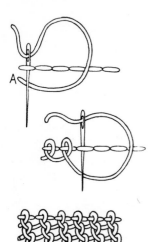

When the Blanket or Buttonhole Stitch is used in this manner, a lacy effect is created. Only the outline or border stitches are worked through the fabric. Sometimes a back- or chain stitch forms the attaching stitch; sometimes the buttonhole stitches are attached to the outline of the design. This is referred to as a detached filling stitch.

If backstitches are used, begin with a row of them. Start the first buttonhole stitch by bringing the needle up at A. Make a buttonhole stitch through the first backstitch, leaving a small loop. Be careful not to pick up the fabric when making this stitch. Continue to the end of the row.

The next row of stitches can be taken from right to left, or in the same direction as the first—left to right; however, the effect will be different. Make the first and last stitch of each row through the fabric. Be careful to keep the tension between the stitches even.

## Buttonhole Stitch

This stitch makes an excellent edging. A row of closely placed loops keeps the fabric from fraying. The stitch can also be used for bars, floral motifs, and scallops. The technique for working Buttonhole Stitch is the same as for Blanket Stitch. However, buttonhole stitches are placed close together, forming a solid design, whereas blanket stitches are set apart to give an open effect. To keep the length of the stitches even, work between 2 guidelines.

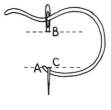

Bring up the needle at the left-hand end of the lower line (A). Hold the thread down with the left thumb. Insert the needle on the upper line (B), letting it emerge on the lower line close to the spot where it first appeared (C). Draw the needle through the loop that has been formed. Work the next stitch close to the first one.

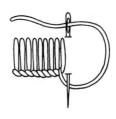

If the buttonhole stitch is used for an edging on material that frays easily, do the embroidery before cutting the fabric. If the cloth does not ravel, however, the design may be cut out and the stitches worked over the raw edge. In either case, a running stitch should be placed close to the edge so that the buttonhole stitch may be worked over it.

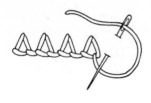

## Buttonhole Stitch—Closed

This is a simple variation of the Blanket or Buttonhole Stitch. Work from left to right. Take the stitches in a diagonal direction, rather than straight, with the first slanting to the left; the second, to the right. They meet, forming a closed point. Uniformity of the stitches is important.

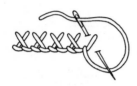

## Buttonhole Stitch—Crossed

This is another variation of the Blanket or Buttonhole Stitch. Work the stitches in pairs with the stitches slanting so they cross each other. Keep the stitches even in size and spacing.

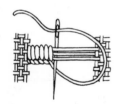

## Buttonhole Stitch—Detached
### *See* Bar—Buttonholed.

The effect is similar, although here blanket or buttonhole stitches are placed over 2 long stitches that have been made across the space to be filled. The stitches do not enter the fabric except at the ends of these long stitches.

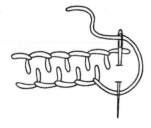

## Buttonhole—Double
### *See* Blanket Stitch.

This stitch is a variation of the Blanket Stitch.

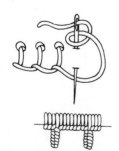

## Buttonhole Stitch—Knotted
### *See* Blanket Stitch—Knotted.

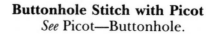

## Buttonhole Stitch with Picot
### *See* Picot—Buttonhole.

## Buttonhole Stitch—Raised

This stitch gives a pleasing three-dimensional effect. Rows of blanket stitches are placed on a series of straight stitches, forming bars.

Begin by making several horizontal stitches, an equal distance apart. Then, starting at the top, bring the needle through the fabric at A. Make a blanket stitch over the first bar. Pull the thread until the loop is snug.

Work the next stitch over the second bar. Continue until a stitch has been made on the lowest bar. Fasten the final loop by inserting the needle in the fabric at B. Be sure to keep the size and tension of each blanket stitch the same so that the horizontal bars remain in their original position.

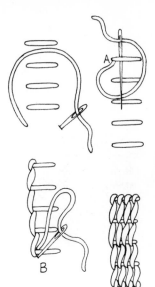

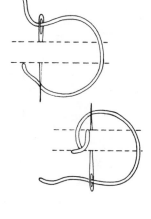

## Buttonhole Stitch—Up and Down

This variation of the Blanket or Buttonhole Stitch makes a good border stitch. The stitches seem to be placed back-to-back in pairs.

Start with a regular blanket stitch. Pull the thread through the fabric.

To make the second part of the stitch, insert the needle close to the point where the working thread emerged. Point the needle upward, letting it reappear next to the end of the first stitch. Be sure the working thread is under the point of the needle.

Pull the thread through the fabric first in an upward movement and then downward. As the position of the thread is changed and it is pulled snug, a loop falls into place at the lower edge, holding both stitches in place.

## Byzantine Stitch

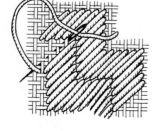

This easy-to-make stitch is used to cover large areas in canvas work. Satin stitches are worked diagonally, and groups of them are placed in step formation.

Begin with 5 stitches, worked diagonally upward over 4 vertical and 4 horizontal threads. Work in a vertical direction.

Then work 5 stitches in a horizontal direction. Continue in this way for the required length.

The subsequent rows follow this procedure, with adjoining stitches using the same holes in the canvas.

## Cable Chain Stitch

A series of chain stitches held together with links characterizes this stitch. It can be used for lines and borders, following a straight or zigzag direction. A fairly heavy twisted thread produces an interesting effect.

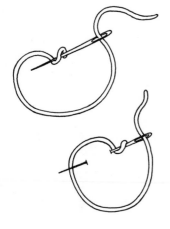

Working from right to left, bring the needle through the fabric at the end of the line to be covered. Before inserting the needle, twist the thread over and under the needle. Keeping the thumb firmly on the thread, take a stitch, inserting the needle a short distance from the emerging working thread. This allows a short link stitch to be made, as well as the chain.

The second and subsequent stitches are made in the same way. Be sure to keep the links between the chain stitches the same length.

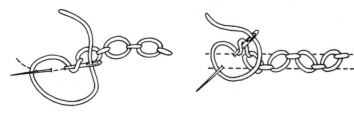

## Cable Chain Stitch—Knotted

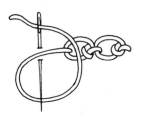

Added interest is given to the Cable Chain Stitch by the introduction of a knotted link.

Working from right to left, bring up the needle at A. Take a small stitch to the left with the needle pointed downward and the thread forming a loop under the needle. When the thread has been pulled through tautly, part of the knot is formed. To complete the knot, pass the needle under the stitch between A and B.

To make the chain stitch, insert the needle close to the knot. Loop the thread under the needle as it is pulled through the fabric. Continue to make a knot followed by a chain stitch.

## Cable Stitch

This stitch is sometimes called Side-to-side Stem Stitch. It is used for outlining a design.

Working from left to right, bring the needle through the fabric at the design line (A). Insert it again a short distance to the right (B), letting it emerge to the left (C), midway between A and B. Keep the thread below the needle.

The next stitch is made in the same way. However, the thread is now above the needle. Continue in this way, alternating the position of the thread.

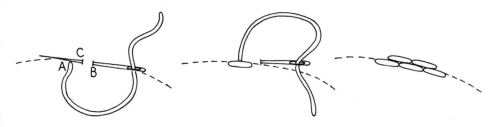

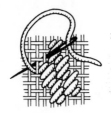

## Cashmere Stitch

This canvas-work stitch creates an interesting textural effect. It is made of a series of 3 stitch units, moving diagonally.

Begin with a short stitch made over 1 intersection of the mesh. Follow with 2 diagonal stitches worked over 2 vertical and horizontal threads of the canvas. This allows the lower ends of the 3 stitches to fall directly under each other.

The second stitch unit is made in the same way. However, it is moved 1 thread to the left, creating the diagonal effect.

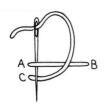

## Caterpillar Stitch
   *See* Bullion Knot or Stitch.

## Ceylon Stitch

This filling stitch can create a knitted effect if the stitches are placed close together. Stitches are looped over horizontal bars.

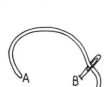

Begin at the upper left-hand corner of the area to be covered by making the first bar or foundation stitch. Come up at A, down at B.

To start the stitches, bring up the needle just below A, at C. Loop the thread over the foundation bar as for blanket stitches. Be careful not to let the needle enter the fabric. The loops should be kept even. At the end of the row, insert the needle in the fabric and let it emerge below C. Start the second stitch at D. Slip the needle under each loop in the previous row, as at E.

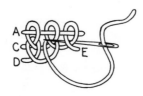

## Chain Stitch

This is a versatile link stitch. It can be used to define design lines or borders and as a filling and padding when a raised effect is needed.

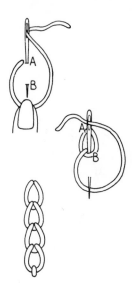

Begin the stitch by bringing the needle to the right side of the material (A). Hold the thread with the left thumb so a loop can be formed as the needle is returned to point A. Insert the needle and bring it up at B, a short distance below. Draw the thread through the loop. Do not pull it tight.

Repeat the stitch by inserting the needle inside the loop at the place where the thread emerges (B). Be sure to keep the stitches equal in size. Chain stitches appear as backstitches on the underside.

## Chain Stitch—Backstitched

This stitch is very effective when worked in two colors. It is a combination of a Chain and Backstitch.

Make a row of regular but rather loose chain stitches. Place a line of backstitches through the center of the stitches, working in each loop.

To do this, bring up the needle in the center of the second chain stitch (A). Insert it again in the center of the first stitch (B). Let the needle emerge again in the third stitch (C).

For the next stitch, the needle returns to point A.

## Chain Stitch—Checkered
 *See* Chain Stitch—Magic.

### Chain Stitch—Crested

This stitch combines Chain and Coral stitches for a ladder effect. It is generally used for wide borders.

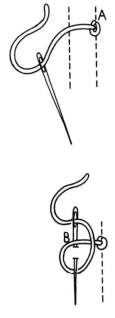

In order to keep the stitches even, establish 2 guidelines, the required distance apart. Then make a small chain stitch at the end of the right-hand line, as at A. Carry the thread diagonally across to the left-hand line, to a point slightly below the first stitch (B).

Hold the thread down with the left thumb. Pass the needle under and over the working thread, making a small loop stitch. When the thread is pulled through the fabric a coral stitch is formed (C).

To get the working thread in a position to make the next stitch, slip the needle downward under the diagonal stitch (D). Make a slightly larger chain stitch beneath the first one. To do this, insert the needle in the first chain, bringing it out at E. Notice that the needle passes over the working thread, as it is pulled through the loop. The second Crested Chain Stitch can now be made.

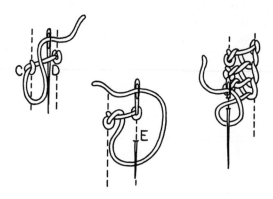

## Chain Stitch—Detached

This stitch is often called Lazy Daisy Stitch. It is used to create floral motifs and as a filling. The stitches can be grouped or scattered for a decorative effect.

Make a single stitch by bringing the needle to the right side of the material. Hold down the thread with the left thumb so that a loop can be formed. Insert the needle at the spot where the thread emerged (A). Bring it up a short distance from this point. When the thread is drawn through, reinsert the needle, making a small stitch over the end of the loop. It holds the chain stitch in place.

## Chain Stitch—Double

This border stitch resembles the Closed Feather Stitch. By alternating the position of the stitches, an effective border design is created. It is most important that the stitches remain even in size and direction.

Working between 2 guidelines, bring up the needle near the end of the left-hand line (A). Hold the thread down with the left thumb. Insert the needle at the end of the right-hand line (B). Let it emerge below B, at C. Pull the thread through the loop.

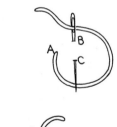

Then carry the thread to the left-hand side in order to form a loop on that side. Put the needle in the fabric at A and come up below this spot, at D.

Continue this way, alternating the stitches from left to right. Take the next stitch from C to E and the following one from D to F.

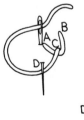

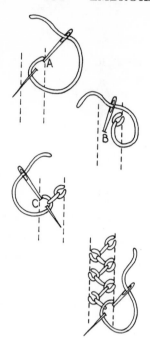

## Chain Stitch—Feathered

Small chain stitches at the end of straight stitches, placed for a zigzag effect, distinguish this border stitch. To keep the width even, work between 2 parallel guidelines. Carefully gauge the placement of each stitch so that the slant and size of the stitches are uniform.

Starting at the end of the right-hand line, make a small diagonal chain stitch (A). Anchor it with a straight stitch placed below and to the left (B). Insert the needle, letting it reappear on the left-hand line and slightly above (C). Take another small chain stitch between points B and C. Continue in this way, alternating from side to side, with all stitches following a diagonal direction.

## Chain Stitch—Heavy

A change in the position of the stitches creates a new look for the Chain Stitch. The textural quality of the stitch makes it useful when embroidering designs such as ears of corn and cattails, and when a heavy treatment is needed for lines.

Bring the needle to the right side of the fabric at the top of the line to be worked. Make a small vertical stitch (A). Come up again about $\frac{1}{16}$ inch (1.5 mm) below this stitch (B). Slip the needle through the vertical stitch without piercing the material. Put it back into the material at B and bring it to the surface $\frac{1}{16}$ (1.5 mm) below, at C. Slide the needle under the vertical stitch for a second time, inserting it at C.

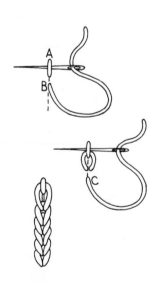

There are now 2 chain loops, held in place with the same vertical stitch. They are close together, with one inside the other.

The next loop is made by passing the needle under the 2 preceding loops, instead of the vertical stitch. This process is repeated, always slipping the needle under 2 stitches.

## Chain Stitch—Magic

This simple-to-make stitch is made of threads in contrasting colors. It is given special interest because one of the colors seems to disappear, producing stitches in alternating colors.

To begin the stitch, thread the needle with 2 threads of contrasting color. Start as for a chain stitch by bringing the threads to the right side. Hold threads down with thumb. Make a loop by inserting needle at A, letting it emerge at B.

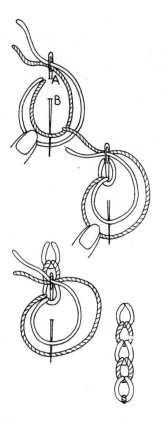

Do not pull the needle over both threads. Instead place one of the threads, perhaps the lighter, above the needle, leaving the darker one below. This allows the stitch to be made with only 1 thread. When the threads are pulled through the loop, the one above the needle seems to disappear.

The second stitch is made like the first but with the darker thread now above the needle, so the stitch will be made with the lighter thread. Continue this way, alternating the colors as the stitches are made.

Be sure that the thread that is not used to make the stitch is carefully pulled to the wrong side.

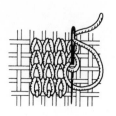

### Chain Stitch—on Canvas

When working on canvas, make the stitches in the same way as for embroidery on fabric. Always begin at the top and proceed downward, taking a stitch over 1 horizontal thread. Be sure the thread is thick enough to cover the canvas completely.

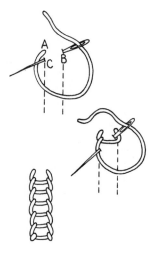

### Chain Stitch—Open

This variation of the Chain Stitch creates a ladder effect. By changing the slant of the needle, its appearance can vary. The stitch is effective when used for broad lines, borders, and casing.

Use 2 parallel guidelines to keep the stitches even. Bring up the needle at the end of the left-hand line (A). Hold the thread down with the left thumb. Insert the needle at the end of the right-hand line (B). Sliding it diagonally under the fabric, let it emerge again at C, below A.

Keep the loop loose so that the needle can be placed in it at a point below B to make the second stitch. Insert the needle, bringing it up on the left-hand side, below C.

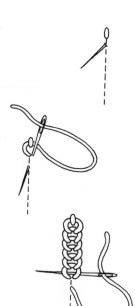

### Chain Stitch—Reverse

This stitch resembles the Heavy Chain Stitch. However, it is easier to do. Work with a stiff thread to obtain the broad effect of these loosely made stitches.

Bring the needle to the right side at the top of the line to be covered. Take a small vertical stitch. Let the needle emerge again at a point below the stitch. The distance depends on the required size of the stitch.

To form the chain loop, slip the needle through the stitch without picking up any of the fabric. Insert the needle at the spot where the thread emerged. Bring up the needle a short distance below.

Make the second stitch by slipping the needle through the first chain stitch. Continue in this way, keeping the loops uniform in size and the distance between stitches even.

## Chain Stitch—Rosette

In order to keep the stitches even, establish 2 parallel guidelines. Small and closely placed stitches create effective lines, borders, and edgings.

Working from right to left, bring up the needle at the end of the upper line (A). Hold the thread down with the left thumb. Insert the needle above the thread at a point (B) to the left and a little below A. Notice that the threads cross at the top of the loop. Let the needle emerge inside the loop (C).

After pulling the thread through, slip the needle under the stitch at A without piercing the fabric. Begin the second stitch by carrying the thread to the left.

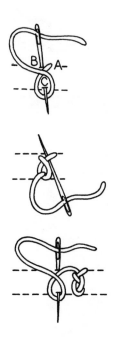

## Chain Stitch—Singalese

This stitch is made in the same way as the Open Chain Stitch. However, 2 threads of a contrasting color are added. The stitch is worked over the contrasting threads, producing a twisted effect.

In order to keep the width of the stitches even, establish 2 parallel guidelines. Bring up a contrasting thread at the end of each line (A, B). Let them lie loosely on the fabric along the guidelines.

Draw the working thread through the fabric just below A. Keep it inside the contrasting thread, as at C. In taking the stitch, the working thread passes over and under the contrasting threads. Insert the needle in the right-hand line, just below B and inside the contrasting thread. Let it emerge in the left-hand line the required distance below C, at D. Make the second stitch after pulling the thread through the loop.

When the work is completed, pull the contrasting threads taut. Fasten them on the wrong side.

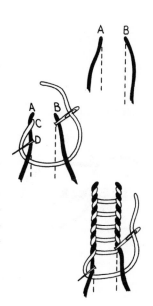

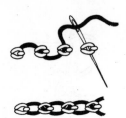

### Chain Stitch—Threaded

A series of detached chain stitches are linked together with a contrasting thread. After making the required number of stitches, slip a thread under each stitch. Be careful not to pierce the fabric as this is done.

A second thread can be used. It fills in the empty spaces.

### Chain Stitch—Twisted

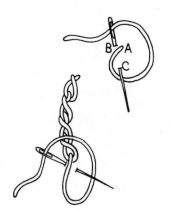

By changing the position of the needle, the Chain Stitch can be given a twisted effect. It can be effectively used for lines.

Work the stitch downward. Begin at the top of the line to be covered (A). Hold the thread down along the design line. Insert the needle to the left of A, so that a cross is formed at the end of the loop (B). Slide the needle diagonally under the line, appearing at C.

When the thread is pulled through the loop, the second stitch can be made. Place it close to the first one.

### Chain Stitch—Whipped

This is a simple way to vary the chain stitch. Pass a thread in a contrasting color over and under the stitches.

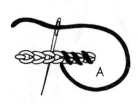

After working a row of chain stitches, bring up the whipping thread at A. Carry the thread over the first stitch and under the second by sliding the needle diagonally under the stitch. Be careful that the needle does not enter the fabric. Leave the thread slightly loose so that it falls between each pair of stitches.

## Chain Stitch—Zigzag

As the name implies, the stitches do not follow a straight line. Each chain loop is worked at an angle to the preceding one. Be sure the stitches remain even in size and direction.

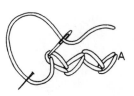

To keep the line of stitches even, work between two parallel guidelines. Bring up the needle at A. Hold the thread down with the left thumb. With the needle moving diagonally, take a stitch.

Follow this with a second stitch, made at right angles to the first. Be sure that the needle enters the end of the loop. This procedure holds the loop flat.

## Chain Stitch Band—Raised

The combination of straight and chain-like stitches produces a pleasing border design. Variations in color make the effect more interesting.

Begin by making the desired number of horizontal stitches about $\frac{1}{16}$ inch (1.5 mm) apart.

Start the chain stitches at the top by bringing the needle through the material just above the top horizontal stitch (A). Pass the needle over and under it, forming a small straight stitch in the center of the bar (B).

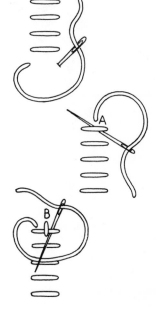

Hold down the working thread as for a blanket stitch. Slip the needle under the bar on the right-hand side, making a loop. Pass the needle through the loop. Secure it with a short, straight stitch, sliding the needle upward as at A. This stitch does not enter the fabric.

Continue to work this way, being careful to keep the tension of the stitches even. The beauty of the stitch depends on uniformity.

### Chequer Stitch

This is a canvas stitch worked to form 2 types of squares, moving in a diagonal direction. A square of identical small stitches alternates with one made of stitches of varying lengths.

Each square is worked over the same number of canvas stitches. If the design requires 4 vertical and 4 horizontal threads, one square will be composed of 16 small diagonal stitches; the other, of 7 stitches of varying lengths.

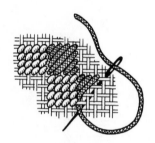

Begin with a square of 16 small stitches. To obtain a diagonal effect, start the next square 1 thread below and 1 to the right.

After making a diagonal row of squares, work an alternate row of squares, commencing at the top. The first stitch is made over 1 thread; the next over 2 threads, followed by 3, 4, 3, 2, and 1 threads in that sequence.

### Chessboard Filling Stitch

An easy-to-do filling stitch is made by grouping 4 satin stitches together and arranging them in a checkerboard pattern. Place a large cross stitch over each group. To hold this stitch in place, add a small vertical stitch at the crossing.

## Chevron Stitch

Lines and borders are given added interest when this stitch is used. Its construction is similar to that of the Herringbone Stitch.

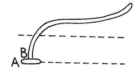

Working from left to right between 2 parallel guidelines, bring up the needle on the lower line, at A. Take a small stitch to the right with the needle reappearing above the stitch, exactly in the center (B).

Carry the thread diagonally to the upper line, inserting the needle at C, which will be the center of the next stitch. Let the needle emerge to the left at point D, which is above the end of the first stitch.

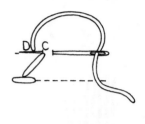

Take a horizontal stitch to the right with the needle returning to center point (C). The thread should emerge below the stitch.

Bring the thread diagonally to the lower line. Insert the needle at the center of the stitch, emerging to the left at a point below the second stitch.

Continue in this way, creating a zigzag effect.

## Chevron Stitch—Raised

An effect similar to a regular Chevron Stitch is produced by interlacing a thread through a foundation of V's. The size of and spaces between the V's should be even. Although the position of alternating V's changes, the point remains in perfect alignment.

Work along a guideline. Bring up the needle on the line at A. Insert it again at B, coming up at C, down at A, to complete the first V.

Make the next V by letting the needle emerge at D, proceeding to points E, F, and D. Note that point E is above C.

When the foundation of V's is completed, interlace a thread through them to create the chevron effect. Be careful not to pierce the fabric.

Begin at the left. Slip the needle under each stitch, moving the needle from right to left so that the thread forms a loop over each V. Keep the loop above the interlacing threads on an upper V; under, on a lower V.

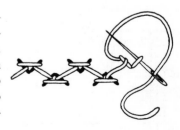

### Chinese Stitch

*See* Pekinese Stitch.

### Cloud Filling Stitch

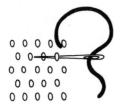

Small stitches form the foundation for this filling stitch. Variations in spacing create different effects. The stitches can be placed close together or far apart. Contrasting threads also produce interesting looks.

To make the foundation, work a series of small vertical stitches. Keep the rows even. Stagger the position of the stitches in alternating rows.

Interlace a thread through these stitches, being careful not to pierce the fabric. Begin by slipping the needle under an upper stitch and then a lower one.

### Cobbler Filling Stitch

This drawn-fabric stitch is worked in horizontal rows, using vertical stitches to form small squares. The threads should be counted carefully and the stitches pulled tightly to create the open effect.

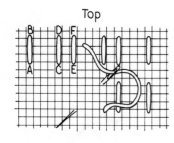

Begin by bringing up the needle at A. Insert it at B, 4 threads up, for the first vertical stitch. For the second stitch, let the needle emerge 4 threads down and 4 to the right (C). Insert it again 4 threads above (D). These 2 stitches will form the sides of the first square.

To start the next square, place the stitch 2 threads to the right, E to F. Continue in this manner, spacing vertical stitches 4 threads apart for a square, and leaving 2 threads between the squares.

Work the second row from right to left. Place the stitches 2 threads below the first row and directly under those above.

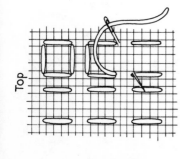

When the area is covered, turn the work so that the process can be continued. The squares are completed with stitches made in a vertical position.

## Coil Stitch
*See* Bullion Knot or Stitch.

## Colcha Stitch
*See* Roumanian Stitch.

## Continental Stitch
*See* Tent Stitch.

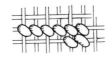

## Coral Knot Stitch
*See* Coral Stitch.

## Coral Stitch

Outlines and fillings are given added interest when this knot stitch is used. By changing the angle of the needle, the appearance of the knot can be varied. Spacing also contributes to variety.

Start at the right end (A) of the line to be covered. Hold the thread down with the left thumb, keeping the thread on the design line.

Place the needle at an angle to the line a short distance to the left. Pick up a small amount of material under the thread. Pull the needle through the loop, over the working thread, until a knot is formed.

Make the next stitch in the same way, the required distance to the left.

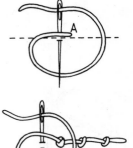

## Coral Stitch—Spanish
*See* Chain Stitch—Crested.

### Coral Stitch—Zigzag

Placing coral stitches in a zigzag design creates a pleasing variation. To keep the stitches even, work between 2 parallel guidelines.

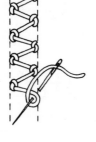

The left-hand stitches require the same placement of needle and thread as does the Coral Stitch. However, for the right-hand stitches, the stitches are changed.

After a left-hand stitch is made, carry the thread to the right. Hold it down with the thumb. It is at this point that the direction of the thread and needle changes, as shown in the accompanying diagram. Carry the thread to the left, forming a loop.

### Cord Stitch

This stitch creates a braided effect when holding 2 finished edges together. The work can be opened up when the stitches are completed. The edges are completely covered.

Turn in the raw edges of the fabric. If necessary, baste the 2 folded edges together. Fasten the threads between the 2 layers.

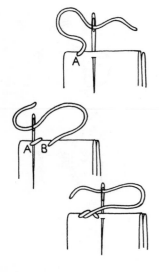

Working from left to right, bring up the needle below the folded edge (A). Take a diagonal stitch to the right, over the edges, keeping the needle at right angles to the edge (B).

The next stitch is taken to the left, with the needle emerging to the right of the first stitch (A).

Continue to make stitches in this way, first to the right and then to the left. To be able to open the fabric, do not pull the stitches tight.

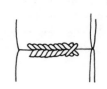

## Cordonnet Stitch

*See* Running Stitch—Whipped.

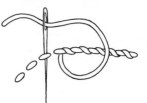

## Couched Filling Stitch

An attractive filling stitch can be made by placing a series of long stitches in a lattice design and tying down the corners with a cross stitch.

Fill the area with horizontal stitches, made from side to side and at regular intervals. Cross these with vertical stitches taken at right angles to the horizontal threads.

Hold these loose threads in place with a cross stitch at each intersection. Sometimes the cross stitch is replaced with a half cross stitch or a single vertical one.

## Couching

A series of tiny stitches is used to hold 1 or more threads in position. Couching gives interest to lines and borders, as well as to appliqué work.

Bring the thread or threads through the material at the right-hand end of the line to be covered. Place them along the line.

Then let the couching thread emerge near the end of the line (A), and close to the laid threads. Hold the laid threads in place with the left thumb.

Take a small vertical upward stitch over the threads, with the needle reappearing a short distance to the left, ready to take the next stitch.

Hold the loose threads firmly so they do not pucker. Pull the small stitches taut.

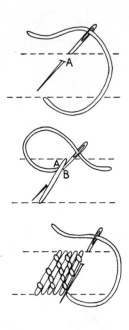

## Couching—Bokhara

In this type of couching, a continuous thread produces the couching effect. It makes a decorative filling for designs, such as leaves.

Start by bringing up the needle on the left-hand side of the design. Carry the thread diagonally across to the right-hand side. Insert the needle, letting it emerge a short distance to the left (A). Keep the long stitch slightly loose.

Keep the working thread below the needle. Take a small securing stitch over the longer one, A to B. Continue to make small holding stitches until the needle reaches the left-hand side of the design. These stitches should be quite close together and taut.

Continue in this way, making each long stitch close to the previous one. Place the small ones to give a woven or diagonal effect.

## Couching—Fancy

Sometimes a decorative stitch, such as Blanket, Open Chain, Chevron, Cross, or Feather, is used to hold down the laid thread. The stitches should be evenly spaced for the most pleasing effect.

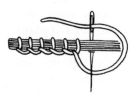

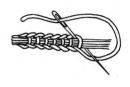

## Couching—Jacobean

*See* Couched Filling Stitch.

## Couching—Roumanian

This type of couching provides a good filling for large areas where an indefinite, flat background is needed. Although the motions for making the stitch are similar to those used for Bokhara Couching, the effect is different.

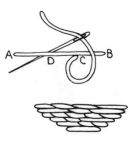

Begin with the needle emerging on the left-hand side of the shape (A). Carry the thread to the right-hand side, taking a short stitch, B to C.

To hold down the long stitch, make a long diagonal stitch over it (D). If necessary, more than 1 long slanting stitch can be used. As the work continues, the stitches should slant enough so that they seem to blend into the background. Do not pull them taut.

## Couching—Satin

This is another type of couching, in which the laid threads are covered with closely placed satin stitches. The stitches can be worked straight or slanting as the threads move in various directions. It resembles a close overcasting stitch with a firm, raised line.

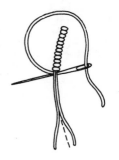

Bring the foundation threads to the right side at the end of the line to be covered. Let the working thread emerge at the same point.

Place small satin stitches over the foundation threads. Keep the stitches close together as the needle passes through the fabric. Guide the position of the foundation threads with the left thumb.

## Couching—Trellis

*See* Couched Filling Stitch.

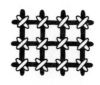

## Cretan Stitch

This stitch can be worked to create a variety of looks. Stitches may be placed close together or apart. The position of the needle and the amount of material picked up by the needle produce great differences in the appearance of the finished work.

Bring the needle to the right side of the fabric at the top of the line or design to be covered (A). Hold the thread down with the left thumb. Insert the needle below and to the right (B). With the needle pointing toward the center, pick up a small amount of fabric (C). Pull the needle through the loop, over the working thread.

Carry the thread to the left-hand side, making a similar stitch, D to E. Continue this process, alternating from side to side. Regulate the length of the stitches so that the center of the design forms a tightly braided effect. Place the stitches close together. To do this, hold the needle in a diagonal direction.

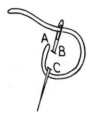

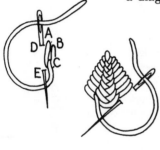

## Cretan Stitch—Open

A variation of the Cretan Stitch is produced by holding the needle in a horizontal position and leaving a space between the stitches.

In order to keep the stitches even, use 2 parallel guidelines. Bring up the needle at the end of the left-hand line. Hold down the thread with the left thumb. Take a stitch with the needle at right angles to the guideline, as at A. Continue in this way, alternating the stitches from right to left.

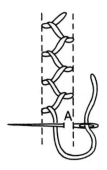

## Cretan Stitch—Slanting

Another version of the Open Cretan Stitch allows the stitches to form a distinctive center line.

Work between 2 parallel guidelines to keep the arms of the stitch even. Bring up the thread at the end of the area to be covered, between the guidelines (A). Hold the thread down with the left thumb. Take a stitch with the needle slanting from the guideline to the center (B–C). Draw the thread through the loop.

Carry the thread to the left-hand side. Make a similar stitch slightly below the first one. Continue in this way, alternating the stitches from right to left.

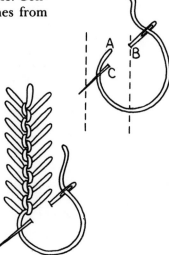

## Cross Stitch

This stitch may be worked directly on material or over canvas. Although the stitch is simple to make, its beauty depends on the regularity of the stitches. Be sure the length and slant of the stitches are even.

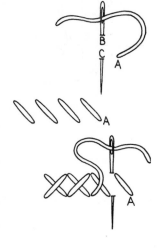

Over material, Cross Stitch is easier to do when the design has been stamped on the fabric. However, the stitches can be made by counting threads or working on gingham.

Make 2 separate rows of single diagonal stitches. Do this by bringing up the needle at the lower right-hand corner of the line to be covered (A). Insert the needle at B, coming up at C. The size of the stitch is determined by this process. Keep the needle in a vertical position. Continue until the row of single slanting stitches is completed.

Then, working from left to right, make a second row of diagonal stitches, crossing those in the first row. Insert the needle at the ends of the stitches in the first row.

## Cross Stitch—Double

A straight cross is imposed over a regular cross stitch. Begin by making a stitch following this sequence: A, B, C, D. Then the straight cross is made by bringing up the needle at E, inserting it at F, up again at G, down at H, returning the needle to point C to begin the next stitch.

The Double Cross Stitch can be used on fabric or as a needlepoint stitch on canvas.

## Cross Stitch—Half

This canvas stitch is worked over double-mesh canvas. Begin the stitches in the upper left-hand corner of the design (A). Take a diagonal stitch upward and to the right over 1 intersection of the canvas (B). Make a straight vertical stitch on the wrong side as the needle emerges 1 mesh below, ready to begin the next stitch.

Repeat this stitch to the end of the row. Then turn the canvas upside down and work another row of identical stitches. Insert the needle into the holes used by the previous row.

## Cross Stitch—Long-armed or Long-legged

As the name of the stitch implies, one of the stitches is longer than the other. Actually it is worked over twice as many threads as the shorter one. The stitch can be worked on fabric as well as on canvas.

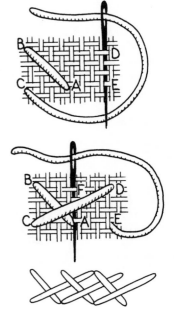

Work from left to right. Complete each stitch before proceeding to the next.

Begin at the bottom of the shorter stitch (A). Insert the needle 4 threads to the left and 4 threads above (B). Bring it up again at C, 4 threads below B.

To make the longer stitch, count over 8 threads from B and insert the needle (D). Come up 4 threads below D, at E.

To start the second stitch, insert the needle 4 threads above A, at F. Let it emerge at A, ready to make the next long stitch. Repeat this procedure.

### Cross Stitch—Montenegrin

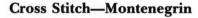
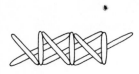

Although the appearance of this stitch is similar to that of the Long-armed Cross Stitch, there is a difference. A vertical stitch has been added at regular intervals. It can be worked on canvas and fabric.

Begin by making the longer stitch, over 8 threads to the right and 4 upward (A–B). Follow this by working the shorter stitch, from C to D.

Return the needle to C ready to make the vertical stitch. Insert the needle 4 threads above, at E.

Bring up the needle at C, ready to begin the second long stitch. Continue in this way. It is interesting to note that this stitch appears equally attractive on the wrong side.

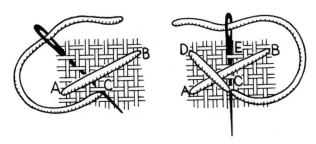

### Cross Stitch—Oblong

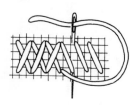

By making a cross stitch over a different number of vertical and horizontal threads, a variation of the regular Cross Stitch is produced. An oblong effect is obtained by working over 2 vertical threads and 4 horizontal ones.

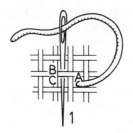

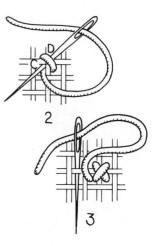

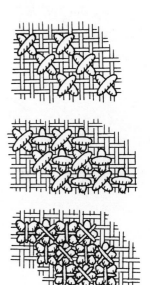

## Cross Stitch over Canvas

For fine cross stitching or when copying a small design, make the stitches over Penelope, or cross stitch, canvas. Although the stitch appears the same as when worked directly on material, the procedure is different. Instead of making rows of slanting stitches, each stitch is completed before passing on to the next one.

After pinning or basting a piece of canvas to the fabric to be embroidered, begin at A and proceed to B and C for the first stitch. Then go from C to D for the second stitch, with the needle emerging at C ready to start the next stitch.

After the design is completed, the threads of the canvas are pulled out. It is easier to remove the threads if the stitches have not been pulled taut.

## Cross Stitch—Reversed

Two layers of regular and straight cross stitches form this canvas stitch. A straight cross stitch is placed over a regular one; a crossed one, over a straight cross stitch. The upper layer is worked in a finer thread than the lower one.

Work the rows in a diagonal direction. Alternate the type of stitch used in each row. This allows a straight cross to fall below a regular one, resulting in a checkerboard design.

After the foundation cross stitches have been made, add the second layer of stitches.

### Cross Stitch—Russian
*See* Herringbone Stitch.

### Cross Stitch—Smyrna
*See* Cross Stitch—Double.

### Cross Stitch—Two-sided

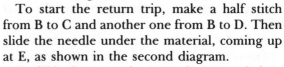

If both sides of the embroidery must appear the same, this is the stitch to use. Instead of 2 trips to make a row of stitches, 4 are needed. Also, 1 or 2 half or extra stitches are required in the turning at the right-hand end. This stitch can be used on both fabric and canvas.

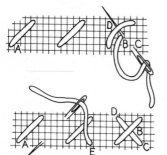

Begin at the left-hand end of the row (A). Work from left to right, making a series of diagonal stitches an equal distance apart, as shown in the first diagram.

To start the return trip, make a half stitch from B to C and another one from B to D. Then slide the needle under the material, coming up at E, as shown in the second diagram.

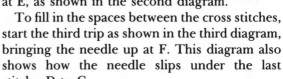

To fill in the spaces between the cross stitches, start the third trip as shown in the third diagram, bringing the needle up at F. This diagram also shows how the needle slips under the last stitch—D to C.

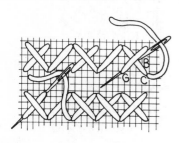

To complete this series of stitches, start the return trip by taking a half stitch between C and B, coming up at G, as shown in the fourth diagram.

## Cross Stitch—Two-sided Italian

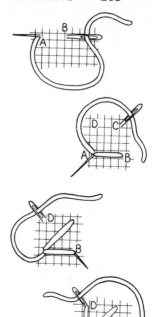

Another variation of the Cross Stitch is this one in which the cross is enclosed in a square. It can be worked on canvas as well as fabric. If the fabric is loosely woven, the stitches can be pulled taut so that an openwork effect is produced.

The stitch is worked in rows, starting with the bottom one. To complete the square effect, the adjoining stitches are needed. Work each row from left to right.

Begin by bringing the needle to the surface at A. Take a horizontal stitch to the right (B), with the needle returning to A.

Make a second stitch from A to C, a point diagonally above B. Return the needle again to A.

Insert the needle at D, forming the left side of the square. Bring it up at B.

Complete the cross with a stitch from B to D.

Return the needle to B ready to start the next sequence of stitches. Finish each row with a vertical stitch.

## Crossed Fly Stitch
*See* Fly Stitch.

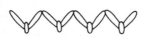

**Daisy Stitch**
    *See* Chain Stitch—Detached.

## Darning on Net

A variety of effects may be created by darning on a net background. Select a good quality so that the meshes will not break as the thread is woven through it.

    To determine the design, count the meshes or tack a design guide to the back of the net. Outlining the design with running stitches often makes the work easier.

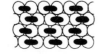

    Use a blunt needle. The ends of the thread should not be visible. Using running stitches to darn in the ends is a good way to do this.

## Darning Stitch

Do not confuse this stitch with the one used for mending. This darning stitch resembles a long running stitch on the surface with a tiny space, usually 1 thread, between the stitches.

    Keep the stitches and spaces even in length. Arrange them to create a design, such as the simple brick pattern shown here. It is easier to do this when the fabric threads are easy to count.

    To produce the brick effect, the position of the stitches changes for alternating rows. Make the first row of long stitches, perhaps over 5 threads, with a 1-thread space between.

    Begin and end the second row with a short stitch, made over 3 threads. Between these 2 stitches place a row of the longer stitches.

## Darning Stitch—Double

This stitch is similar to a double running stitch. Work a row of stitches. Keep the length of the stitches and the spaces between them the same size.

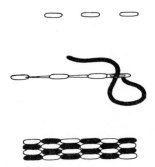

Fill in the spaces with another row of stitches. Take care that, when this row of stitches is made, the needle enters and leaves the fabric in the same holes as the previous stitches. The stitches appear the same on both sides of the work.

## Darning Stitch—Japanese

Diagonal stitches are added to darning stitches to form Japanese Darning. It is used as a filling.

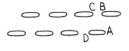

Make a row of darning stitches. Place a second row the required distance from the first. Arrange the stitches in a brick pattern.

Connect the 2 rows with diagonal stitches, creating a triangular effect.

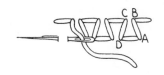

Begin at the end of the second row (A). Insert the needle at B in the first row. Pick up the fabric between the first 2 stitches (B–C). Return the needle to the second row (D). Continue this procedure.

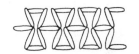

## Diagonal Stitch

This canvas stitch is used to fill large areas when a textured diagonal effect is required. The stitches vary in length, but are arranged so they fit together. The shortest stitches of one row fall diagonally below the longest in the row above.

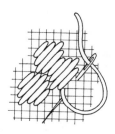

Make a block of 5 diagonal stitches. Start with a stitch taken over 2 horizontal and 2 vertical threads. Follow with stitches made over 3 and 3 threads, 4 and 4 threads, 3 and 3 threads, 2 and 2 threads.

Begin the next block of stitches with one over 3 and 3 threads.

### Diamond Filling Stitch

This stitch requires precision in the making. Each loop and knot must be carefully planned and placed. It is sometimes easier to obtain the necessary regularity if the stitch is anchored to the fabric when the knot is made.

Begin at the upper right-hand corner by bringing up the needle at A. Carry the thread to the left-hand corner (B), making a long stitch. Insert the needle, coming up just below this point.

Hold the thread down with the left thumb. Pass the needle under the long stitch and through the loop, making a coral knot.

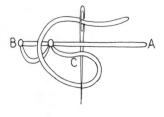

Determine the placement of the next knot. Loop the working thread as shown at C. Pass the needle under the long stitch and through the loop. Pull the thread tight to form a knot and, at the same time, to leave a loop of thread between the first and second knots. Continue in this way to point A. Keep the depth and size of the loops even.

Insert the needle, letting it emerge below, in line with the lower edge of the loops.

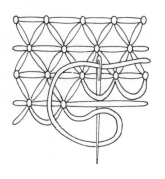

Take another long stitch to the left-hand side. Bring the needle up directly under the left-hand end of the line, the same distance away as between the first and second long stitches. Repeat the knotting and looping procedure as for the first row. In making the knot, pass the needle through the upper loop, under the long stitch, and through the loop made by the working thread. The knot holds down the loop, forming the point of each diamond.

## Diamond Stitch

A series of horizontal stitches and knots creates a diamond effect that makes an interesting border design. Work downward between 2 parallel guidelines. Space the stitches and knots evenly, keeping the threads slightly slack in order to create the diamond effect.

Start at the end of the left-hand line (A). Insert the needle in the right-hand line (B) exactly opposite A.

Make a knot at this point by bringing up the thread just below B. Hold the thread down with the left thumb. Pass the needle under the 2 threads, pulling the thread through the loop to form the knot. Be careful that the needle does not enter the fabric.

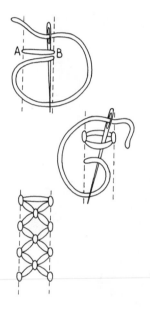

Carry the thread to the left-hand side as if making a horizontal stitch. Before inserting the needle, make another knot at A. Put the needle in the fabric below the knot, letting it emerge a short distance below ready to make the next horizontal stitch.

Before inserting the needle in the right-hand line, make a knot over the horizontal stitch above. Center the knot.

Then take a small stitch under the right-hand line and follow with a knot. Continue this sequence of stitches and knots.

## Dot Stitch

This stitch is used as a powdered filling or seeding. It is frequently seen in leaf embroidery. Two small stitches are grouped together.

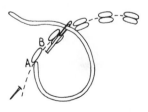

Bring the needle up at A, down at B, for the first stitch. Make the second stitch just below, sliding the needle forward ready to begin the second group of stitches. Notice how the needle slants in order to make the upper stitch.

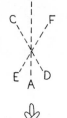

## Ermine Stitch

In making this stitch, 2 diagonal stitches cross a vertical one. Groups of stitches, scattered in rows over an area, make a pleasing filling. It is important that the spacing be kept even.

Follow the accompanying diagram for working each of the stitches. Begin at A. Insert the needle at B, come up at C, and go down at D. Slip the needle under the fabric, emerging at E. Complete the stitch by inserting the needle at F.

## Eye Stitch—Algerian
*See* Algerian Eyelet.

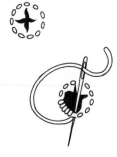

## Eyelet Hole

If the design requires a small opening, this is the stitch to use. It is frequently seen in broderie anglaise work.

For a tiny hole, pierce the fabric with a sewing stiletto or knitting needle. Do it gently so the threads will not be broken. When this treatment cannot be used, the fabric can be cut, as shown in the accompanying diagram.

Begin by outlining the hole with tiny running stitches. Then cut or pierce the fabric. Put closely placed overcasting stitches over the edge. If the hole was made with a stiletto, pull the stitches tightly in order to open up the fabric. If the material was cut, fold back the cut points before making the stitches. Trim away any raveling edges on the back of the work.

## Eyelet Stitch

This stitch resembles a drawn-fabric stitch because of the open effect created by the eyelets. Small circles are worked close together, producing an embroidered background. Each circle is divided into segments of equal size so there is a regularity to the size and placement of the stitches. Trace the design on the fabric.

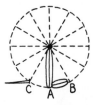

Bring the needle up on the circumference, at the end of one of the radiating lines (A). Insert the needle to the right, at the end of the next line (B). Make 2 backstitches between A and B, returning the needle to A. Use the same holes, pulling the stitches tight.

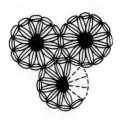

From A, put the needle into the center of the design, returning it to A. Take another stitch into the center, but this time bring the needle up to the left on the circumference at the end of a radiating line (C).

Make 2 backstitches from C to A, and then 2 stitches from C to the center.

Continue this way around the circle, using the same holes and pulling the stitches tight. This procedure produces the eyelets between the stitches.

## Eyelet Stitch—Star
*See* Algerian Eye Stitch.

### Faggot Filling Stitch
   *See* Sheaf Filling Stitch.

### Faggot Stitch—Single

This stitch is used for drawn-fabric work. The stitches are made in step formation, using the same holes. This produces an openwork effect when the stitches are pulled taut.

   Begin by bringing the needle up at A. Insert it 4 threads to the right, forming a horizontal stitch (B).

   Let the needle emerge 4 threads below A, at C. Reinsert the needle at A, making a vertical stitch.

   Slide the needle diagonally under the fabric, bringing it up 4 threads to the left of C, at D. Return the needle to C, making another horizontal stitch.

   Continue this way until row is completed. Then turn the work upside down to make the second row of stitches. Insert the needle in the holes made by the first row of stitches.

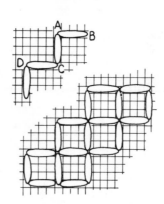

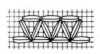

### Faggoting—Bermuda
   *See* Three-sided Stitch.

## Feather Stitch

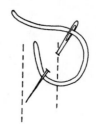

This is a blanket stitch worked at an angle, giving a zigzag effect. It is used for lines and borders, decorating a wide variety of items. The lines can be straight or curved.

Bring up the needle at the top of the line to be covered. Hold down the needle with the left thumb. Take a diagonal stitch to the right and a little below the point where the needle emerged. Point the needle toward the design line, pulling it through the loop, over the working thread.

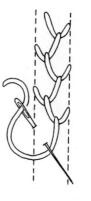

To make the second stitch, carry the thread to the left-hand side of the line. With the needle pointed toward the design, make a similar diagonal stitch.

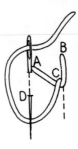

Continue to alternate the stitches from right to left. Keep the stitches uniform in size and an equal distance from the line to be covered. This is easier to do if the stitch is taken between 2 parallel guidelines.

## Feather Stitch—Closed

It is easier to work this stitch if 2 parallel guidelines are used. The method for making the stitch is similar to that used for the Feather Stitch. However, the needle is held in a vertical direction instead of in a diagonal position. The stitch is used for lines and borders.

Begin by bringing up the thread at the top of the left-hand line (A). Hold the thread down with the left thumb. Insert the needle in the fabric on the right-hand line (B), slightly above A. Let it emerge below this point at C. Pull the thread through the loop.

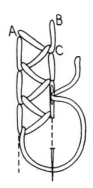

Carry the thread to the left side and, again holding it down, take a stitch from A to D.

Make the next stitch on the right-hand side so close to the preceding one that an almost unbroken line is formed by the outer edge of the stitch.

Continue in this manner, alternating the placement of the stitches from right to left.

### Feather Stitch—Double

This is a popular variation of the Feather Stitch. Instead of making a single stitch on the right-hand side and then one on the left, work 2, 3, or more stitches on one side, and then an equal number on the other side.

### Feather Stitch—Long-armed
*See* Cretan Stitch—Slanting.

### Feather Stitch—Single

This stitch is similar to Blanket Stitch. However, the needle is held in a diagonal position instead of the vertical direction needed for Blanket Stitch. It can be used for lines and also as a decorative feature of smocking.

Let the needle emerge at the top of the line to be covered. Hold the thread down with the left thumb. Make a blanket-type stitch to the right and a little below this point. Insert the needle in a slanting position, letting it emerge on the line to be covered. Pull the thread through the loop, over the working thread.

Repeat this procedure for the remaining stitches.

## Feather Stitch—Spanish Knotted

A diagonal motif dominates this line stitch. Variations in thread direction create this unusual arrangement of stitches, which provides a heavy effect. Careful attention should be given to the placement of the stitches and the making of the loops. Working between 2 parallel guidelines will be helpful.

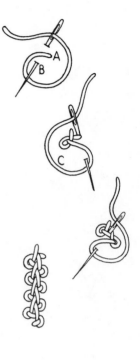

Begin at the top of the line to be covered and work downward. Bring up the needle on the right-hand side (A). Carry the thread to the left-hand side, looping it downward. Insert the needle above the working thread, halfway between the points where the thread emerged and where the needle will appear at the end of this stitch (B). Pull the needle through the loop.

Move the thread to the right-hand side. Make a reverse loop, as shown at C. Hold it in position. Insert the needle above the horizontal stitch, close to the vertical one. Slip it under the fabric, bringing it up diagonally below. Pull it through the loop.

Carry the thread to the left-hand side for the next stitch. Remember to insert the needle above the last horizontal stitch. Continue to alternate the stitches from left to right.

## Fence Stitch

    *See* Barrier Stitch.

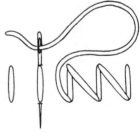

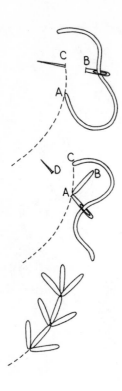

### Fern Stitch

This stitch creates an impression of leaves and fern fronds. Three straight stitches radiate from a central point. It is simple to make and effective to use.

Work along a central line. Bring the needle to the surface a short distance from the end of the line (A). Make a diagonal stitch to the right of the line by inserting the needle at B. Let the needle emerge in the center line at C.

Make another straight stitch by returning the needle to A. For the third stitch, slip the needle diagonally upward, letting it emerge at D, a point in line with B and the same distance from the center line. Return the needle to A.

Repeat this procedure in making the next group of stitches.

### Festoon Filling Stitch

Backstitches are used to create this filling stitch, which is used for drawn-fabric work. It resembles the Ringed Backstitch.

Start at A. Insert the needle 2 threads to the right (B), making a backstitch. Bring it up 2 threads below A at C.

Take the second stitch between C and A, letting the needle emerge 2 threads to the left and 2 threads below C, at D, ready to make the third backstitch from D to C.

Continue this stitch pattern to create the festoon design. Place the next row of stitches 6 threads below the first one. Pull the stitches tight for an openwork effect.

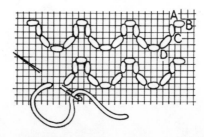

## Figure Stitch
    *See* Couching—Roumanian.

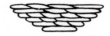

## Fishbone Stitch

This stitch is usually shown as a filling for a leaf or petal design that is too wide for a satin stitch. However, it can be used for other small areas and borders. Use a center line as a guide.

    Begin the work at the tip with a small vertical stitch on the center line (A). Bring the needle up close to the first stitch on the right-hand side of the design (B). Insert it at the base of the first stitch, crossing just to the left-hand side of the center line, making a diagonal stitch.

    Bring up the needle close to the first stitch on the left-hand side of the design (C). Let it re-enter the fabric at the base of second stitch, just to the right of the center line.

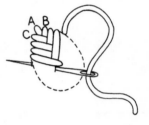

    Each stitch crosses the preceding one at the center line. Repeat this procedure until the design is covered. Keep the stitches close together.

### Fishbone Stitch—Open

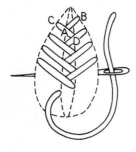

This variation of the fishbone stitch is worked to create an open effect. Work with 2 guidelines placed 1 each side of the center. These mark the ends of the stitches and keep the correct length.

Bring the needle to the surface in the left-hand guideline, a short distance from the tip (A). Insert it on the right-hand outer edge of the design above the point where it emerged, making a diagonal stitch (B).

Slide the needle under the fabric, letting it reappear on the left-hand side of the design (C), slightly below B. It is important that the thread always crosses from right to left on the back of the embroidery.

Carry the thread across the base of the first stitch, inserting the needle in the right-hand guideline below the preceding stitch (D). Let the needle emerge in the left-hand guideline below the stitch that has just been made, leaving a space between stitches.

The needle returns to the right-hand side of the outline, leaving a space below the previous stitch. The distance between the stitches should be kept even.

## Fishbone Stitch—Raised

This stitch is used when a self-padded design is needed. The stitches appear raised, with a braided effect at the center. It is important that they be placed close together.

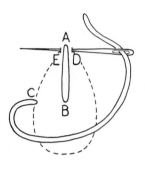

Bring up the needle at the tip of the design (A). Insert the needle halfway down the center line (B), making a vertical stitch. Let the needle emerge directly opposite this point on the left-hand of the design, at C.

Carry the thread across the vertical stitch and insert the needle just below the tip on the right-hand side (D). Pass the needle under the work and let it emerge directly opposite on the left-hand side (E).

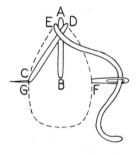

To make the second diagonal stitch, insert the needle on the right-hand side opposite C, at F. Slide the needle under the fabric, letting it reappear just below the first diagonal stitch, at G.

Continue this sequence of stitches until the area is filled.

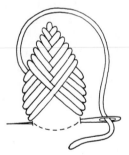

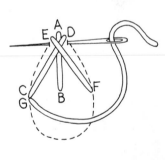

## Flame Stitch

*See* Florentine Stitch.

## Flat Stitch

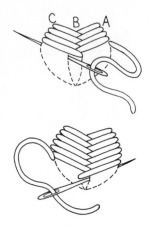

This stitch resembles the Fishbone Stitch except that the stitches are placed in a more horizontal direction. A guideline placed on both sides of a center line will keep the length of the stitches regulated, creating a braided effect in the center of the design.

Bring up the needle on the right-hand side of the design (A). Insert it in the left-hand guideline (B), a little below A. Let it emerge on the left-hand outer edge (C).

Carry the thread across the design, inserting the needle in the right-hand guideline just below the first stitch, making the second stitch.

Return the needle to the outer right-hand side by sliding it under the fabric, coming up just below A. Keep the stitches close together, overlapping at the center of the design.

## Florentine Stitch

A canvas stitch used for creating zigzag patterns, found in Florentine or bargello work. Variations can be created by making the stitches longer or shorter, and by allowing them to go up or down more steeply or more gradually.

For a simple pattern, place straight vertical stitches over 4 horizontal threads of canvas. Let each stitch rise or fall 2 threads above or below the last one.

All rows follow this design pattern, with stitches sharing the meshes of the stitches in adjoining rows.

## Fly Stitch

Although related to an open Detached Chain Stitch, its appearance is changed to resemble a V. A loop is held in place by a vertical stitch that may vary in length. When it is short, the stitch is known as Fly Stitch; when long, Y Stitch. The stitches can be made in rows, scattered in an open design, or as a filling by alternating the position of stitches for a trellis effect. It is then known as Crossed Fly Stitch.

Bring up the needle at a point (A) that will be the top of the left arm of the V. Hold down the thread with the thumb. Insert the needle at the top of the right arm (B). Slide the needle diagonally under the fabric, letting it reappear at a center point (C), which will be the base of the V.

Pull the needle through the loop. Pass it over the thread, letting it re-enter the fabric just below this point, making a straight stitch to hold down the loop.

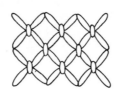

## Four-sided Stitch

This drawn-fabric stitch creates a series of squares that can be used for a single-line border. Straight stitches are worked from right to left to form the design. On the back, the stitches appear as cross stitches.

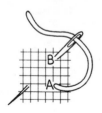

Begin with the needle surfacing at A. Put it in the fabric at B, 4 threads above. Slip it under the fabric 4 threads to the left, bringing it out at C, on a line with A.

Return the needle to A, letting it emerge 4 threads to the left on a line with B.

Take a horizontal stitch from D to B. Slide the needle diagonally under the fabric, coming up at C.

To complete the square, insert the needle at D. Bring it out 4 squares to the left, on a line with C, at E, ready to make the second square.

Pull the stitches taut so that tiny holes appear at the end of each stitch.

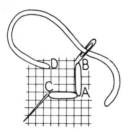

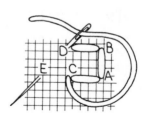

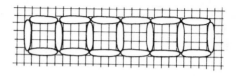

## French Knot

These small knots appear like beads when correctly made. They can be used as a filling for a small area, such as the center of a flower. A single knot also can be employed as a accent when a dot is needed.

The size of the knot varies depending on the weight of the thread and the number of times the thread is twisted around the needle. Some persons prefer only 1 twist. Although these variations may be employed, the beauty of the knot depends on the tautness of the thread around the needle. Be sure to use a needle that allows the working thread to be pulled easily through the coil and at the same time maintain the tightness.

Bring the needle to the right side of the material at the point where the knot is to be made (A). Hold the thread firmly between the left thumb and the first (index) finger quite close to the fabric. Twist the thread around the needle, pulling it taut.

Turn the needle in the opposite direction and insert it close to the point where the thread emerged. Pull the needle through the coils of thread to the wrong side of the work.

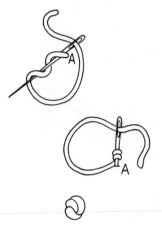

## Gobelin Stitch

This is a diagonal canvas stitch, worked over more horizontal than vertical threads. Because of this, it is sometimes called Oblique Gobelin Stitch. The first row is worked from left to right with the needle moving upward on the wrong side; the second, from right to left with the needle moving downward.

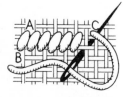

Begin at the left-hand side of the work, bringing up the needle at the top of the first stitch (A). Insert the needle 2 threads below and 1 thread to the left (B). Continue this way until the row is completed.

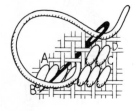

At the end of the row, slip the needle upward, letting it emerge at C, 1 thread to the left of the top of the last stitch. Make the first stitch of the next row from C to D, 1 thread to the right and 2 above. Continue to work to the left.

It is important to follow these line and stitch directions in order to maintain tension on the stitches.

## Gobelin Stitch—Encroaching

This stitch is a longer, less diagonal version of the Gobelin Stitch. The rows are closely worked, with each row overlapping the previous one by 1 thread.

Make a row of stitches with each stitch made over 5 horizontal threads and 1 vertical. Begin the second row 4 threads below the first row. The stitches are, however, still taken over 5 stitches. This allows one row of stitches to intrude into another, creating a blending effect that is good for shading.

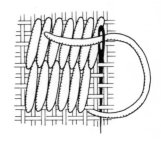

## Gobelin Stitch—Straight

This variation of the Gobelin Stitch is made by placing straight vertical stitches over 4 horizontal ,threads. Place the stitches side by side.

In order to cover the canvas, do not pull the stitches taut. This stitch uses more yarn than diagonal stitches do.

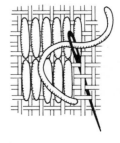

## Gobelin Stitch—Wide

This stitch is worked in the same manner as the Gobelin Stitch. However, the stitches are longer and more diagonal. Work over 3 horizontal threads and 2 vertical ones.

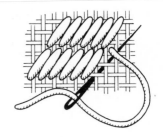

## Greek Cross Filling Stitch

Although this drawn-fabric design seems to emphasize an allover effect of squares, the stitches are taken in a cross formation. Each cross is made of 4 stitches, radiating from a center point.

Start with a blanket-type stitch, bringing up the needle at A. Hold down the thread and insert the needle 3 threads to the right and 3 threads above (B). Let it emerge 3 threads below (C), on a line with A. Draw the needle over the working thread as for a blanket stitch. Pull the thread until it lies flat on the fabric, forming 2 arms of the cross. For the next stitch, insert the needle 3 threads to the right (D). Return it to the center (C). Proceed to E, 3 threads below. Instead of returning to C, slip the needle under the fabric, 6 threads to the left (F), ready to make the next cross.

Adjoining stitches are made with the needle entering the same holes. The thread should be pulled taut so that the openwork effect is produced.

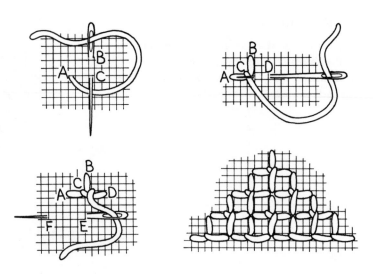

## Greek Stitch

This canvas stitch resembles a Long-armed Cross Stitch worked in a Herringbone technique. Although the stitches are worked in parallel rows, the crossing stitches form a stitch pattern that is reversed in alternating rows. This allows the stitches in each row to lie at an angle to those above and below. The first row is made from left to right, the second, right to left.

Begin at the lower left-hand corner of the first stitch (A). Insert the needle 2 threads to the right and 2 above (B). Let it emerge 2 threads to the left (C). It re-enters the canvas 2 threads below and 4 threads to the right of C, at D, on a line with A, completing the first stitch.

The second stitch begins 2 threads to the left (E). Continue this procedure until the row is completed.

To begin the second row, come up 2 threads below (F), at a point that corresponds to D in the first stitch. Proceed to G, 2 threads above and 2 to the left; H, 2 threads to the right; I, 2 threads below and 4 to the left. Notice how the crossing and position of the stitches are reversed, creating a lovely textured effect.

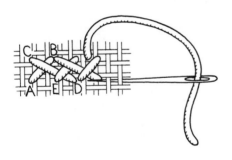 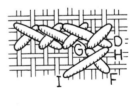

## Guilloche Stitch

Stem, Satin and French Knot stitches make up this wavy design, inspired by an architectural ornament. When this composite stitch is worked in several colors, the effect is most pleasing. It makes an interesting border.

Begin by embroidering 2 parallel lines in stem stitches.

Place blocks of 3 satin stitches at regular intervals between the 2 lines. Lace a thread through the satin stitches with the needle passing upward in the first group, downward in the second. Insert the blunt end of the needle first so that it will not pierce the fabric or the stitches. Keep the interlacing threads loose in order to create the rounded effect.

To complete the circle design, make a return trip with the thread, filling in the gaps. Place a French knot in the center of each circle.

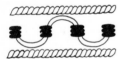

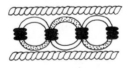

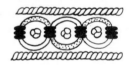

## Half Stitch

*See* Cross Stitch—Half.

## Hemstitch

Hemstitching creates a decorative way to make an insertion or finish a hem. It can be used only on fabric from which threads can be withdrawn. It produces an openwork effect.

Begin by removing the desired number of threads. The number will depend on the size of the threads. If the hemstitching is to be placed above a hem, fold the fabric so that the edge of the hem comes to the edge of the drawn area. Baste the hem carefully in place.

Work the stitches from left to right on the right side of the material. Insert the needle at the edge of the hem, bringing it to the right side. Slip the needle under the first 3 or 4 threads, passing it from right to left.

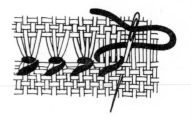

Let the needle re-enter the hem, just to the right of the encircled threads. Pull it through the hem, emerging on the right side. Draw the working thread taut, bringing the threads together at the hemline ready to begin the next stitch. The stitch that holds the hem and binds the threads should be almost invisible.

## Hemstitch—Antique

This type of hemstitching is worked in a manner similar to regular hemstitching, except that the work is done on the wrong side of the material and the needle passes between the layers of fabric.

## Hemstitch—Double

*See* Hemstitch—Italian.

## Hemstitch—Interlaced

Ladder Hemstitch forms the foundation for this hemstitching variation. A lacing thread changes the position of the stitches.

After making the ladder hemstitching, attach a lacing thread to the right-hand side of the work. To overlap one group of stitches over the preceding one, the needle passes over the right-hand group and under the left-hand group so that the thread passes over both groups.

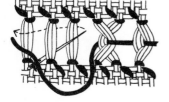

As the left-hand group crosses the right-hand group, the needle is slipped under both groups of threads, coming to the upper side of the work ready to begin the next interlacing procedure, as shown in the accompanying diagram. Keep the working thread taut enough to allow the interlaced threads to lie flat.

## Hemstitch—Italian

This type of hemstitching requires 2 rows of drawn threads and is sometimes called Double Hemstitch. It is often found on lovely linens.

Italian Hemstitch begins with a row of hemstitches, placed just above the hem. Before commencing the second row of stitches, remove another group of threads. Leave a strip of fabric, the required width, between the 2 drawn-thread areas. Draw out the same number of threads that were removed for the first row.

Work the second row of hemstitches from right to left. They will be made over the strip of fabric that separates the 2 rows of drawn threads, as the working thread encircles the threads in the lower part of the upper row and the upper part of the lower row.

Let the needle emerge at A. Pass the thread around the first group of threads, returning it to the starting point. Carry the thread diagonally over the fabric to the upper edge of the first row of drawn threads (B). Slip the needle under this group of threads. Then slide it diagonally under the fabric to the lower edge of the upper row of drawn threads. Pull taut the working thread so that the threads in the encircled group are held together.

Notice that each group of threads falls directly below one another.

The second row of drawn threads is finished with regular hemstitches.

## Hemstitch—Ladder

This is a popular variation of the regular hemstitch. A row of stitches is made in the usual manner along the lower edge of the drawn-thread strip. A second row of stitches is placed along the upper edge of the area. Arrange the stitches so that the same group of threads is bound together as those on the lower edge. It is easier to make the second row of stitches if the work is turned so the upper edge becomes the lower one.

## Hemstitch—Roumanian
   *See* Hemstitch—Italian.

## Hemstitch—Serpentine

This variation of regular hemstitching creates an interesting zigzag effect. An equal number of threads must be included in each group.

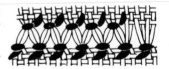

After completing the stitches along the lower edge, work the upper row, dividing evenly each group of threads. For instance, if the group includes 4 threads, divide it so that 2 threads of one group and 2 of the next one can be encircled.

## Hemstitch—Split
   *See* Hemstitch—Serpentine.

## Hemstitch—Zigzag
   *See* Hemstitch—Serpentine.

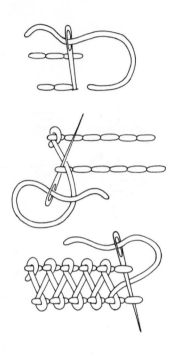

### Herringbone Ladder Stitch

This stitch gives the effect of a Herringbone Stitch but is made in a different way. Start with a foundation of backstitches worked in parallel rows. Be sure the stitches are not placed exactly opposite each other, but, rather, as shown in the accompanying diagram.

After the foundation is completed, bring up the needle at the left-hand end of the upper line. Hold down the working thread. Slip the needle under the stitch and through the loop that has been formed.

Carry the thread to the lower line. Pass the needle upward under the first stitch of the lower row and over the working thread. The interlacing thread seems to create a figure-8 design.

Continue in this way, always pointing the needle from the outer edge of the band toward the center of the design. Remember it passes over the working thread when each diagonal stitch is made.

### Herringbone Stitch

This stitch is called Catch Stitch in sewing. It may be varied by changing the length and direction of the stitches. Although it is simple to make, care should be taken to keep the stitches even. Its beauty depends on regularity.

Work from left to right between 2 guidelines. Bring the needle to the surface at the lower end of the first stitch (A). Carry the thread diagonally to the upper line, inserting the needle a short distance to the right (B).

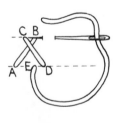

Slip the needle horizontally under the fabric, bringing it up a short distance to the left (C). Pass the thread over the first stitch, making a diagonal stitch of the same length. Insert the needle in the lower line (D), coming up to the left (E), ready to begin the next stitch.

Keep the stitches even in length, with points B and C on the upper line centered between points A and D on the lower line. Continue in this way.

## Herringbone Stitch—Close

*See* Backstitch—Crossed or Double.

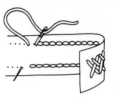

For Close Herringbone Stitch, the crossed stitches are on the wrong side and the back-stitches on the right side.

## Herringbone Stitch—Closed

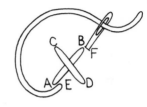

The stitches for this stitch pattern follow the same procedure as for regular herringbone stitches, except that they are placed close together. The crossed points touch each other, as shown in the accompanying diagram. Bring the thread up at A. Insert the needle at B, coming up at C, above A. Return the needle to the fabric at D, below B, letting it emerge (E) close to A. Notice that a cross stitch has been made.

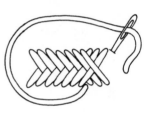

To make the next stitch, insert the needle close to B (F), coming up just to the right of C and re-entering the fabric to the right of D. The stitches overlap each other.

## Herringbone Stitch—Couched

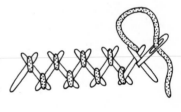

Make a row of herringbone stitches. Hold down the crossed points with a small vertical stitch. Use a thread in a contrasting color for a pleasing effect.

### Herringbone Stitch—Double

There are two ways of making this stitch. The first is quite simple, utilizing regular herringbone stitches for a decorative border. The second method requires more precision in the construction because it is used as a foundation for other interlacing stitches.

For the **first method,** make a row of regular herringbone stitches, leaving a space wide enough between stitches to insert another stitch. Use a thread in a contrasting color for a pleasing effect. The interlacing takes place where the threads cross each other. Be sure the stitches follow a regular direction and sequence at crossing points.

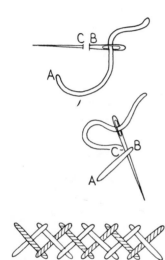

For the **second method,** start the stitch in the usual manner, from A to B to C. However, instead of bringing the thread over the stitch, slip it **under** the stitch before inserting the needle in the lower line. This variation in technique applies only to the upper stitches. Continue in this way, placing the stitches far enough apart for another stitch to be inserted.

Make the second line of stitches in the same way. Use a thread in a contrasting color. Weave the thread over the left-hand arm of the stitch, under the right-hand one. Be sure to follow this sequence.

### Herringbone Stitch—Indian
*See* Herringbone Stitch—Double.

### Herringbone Stitch—Interlaced
*See* Herringbone Stitch—Threaded.

### Herringbone Stitch—Laced

Although the herringbone stitches resemble the regular one, they are made in a slightly different way. Slip the needle under the first stitch (A–B) when making the second stitch (C–D). When starting the next stitch (E–F), also pass the needle under the stitch instead of over it. This change in position is necessary in preparing the foundation for the lacing thread.

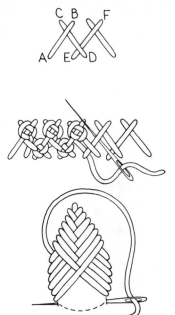

After the row of foundation stitches has been made, use a second thread to encircle the crossed part of the stitches. Let the thread make 2 complete circles around each upper stitch and 1½ circles around each lower one. Weave the thread under and over the foundation stitches and also under and over itself.

## Herringbone Stitch—Overlapping
*See* Fishbone Stitch—Raised.

## Herringbone Stitch—Threaded

Two methods can be used for making this stitch. In the first, an interlacing thread passes over the crossing point of each stitch with the thread alternating from top to bottom.

In the second version, the thread completes the interlacing process along the upper ends before doing the lower ones. This thread slips under one of the crossed ends of each stitch.

For the **first method,** work a row of herringbone stitches. Over this foundation, interlace a contrasting thread. Slip the needle under the diagonal stitches so the thread is placed over the crossed ends. To do this, the needle sometimes moves upward and sometimes downward, but never into the fabric.

The **second version** of the Threaded Herringbone is made by slipping the interlacing thread under the end of the right-hand arm of each cross stitch in the upper row, and also the right-hand arm in the lower row. Notice that this is always the under thread of the cross. Complete weaving the thread along the upper edge before beginning to do the lower one.

### Herringbone Stitch—Tied

A coral stitch gives a new look to this herringbone stitch. Make a foundation row of herringbone stitches. With a contrasting thread, tie the crossed stitches with a knot.

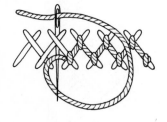

Bring up the needle at the right-hand end of the lower edge. Loop the thread, holding it down with the left thumb. Slip the needle under the lower right-hand end of the stitch and through the loop. Pull the thread taut, forming a knot.

Carry the thread to the upper edge and make another knot. Always point the needle toward the center of the stitch as the knot is made. Do not let the needle pierce the fabric. Notice that the interlacing thread seems to cover the foundation stitch.

### Holbein Stitch

This running stitch is given new interest by the addition of a second group of stitches. It can be used for lines and to outline geometric designs, and it is often found in cross stitch embroideries.

Begin with a row of running stitches. Keep the length of the stitches and the spaces between the stitches even. At the end of the row, turn the work and fill in the spaces between the stitches with a second group of running stitches. When carefully made, this stitch appears the same on both sides of the work.

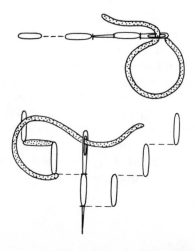

## Hollie Stitch

A lacy effect is given this stitch through the use
of detached stitches, knots, and loops. Although
the stitch may seem difficult to make, it really
isn't.

Begin by outlining the design with small chain
stitches.

To start the first row of detached stitches,
bring up the needle in the center of the top
chain stitch on the right-hand side (A) and carry
the thread across the design to the left-hand side.
Insert the needle in the corresponding chain
stitch (B), making a long foundation stitch. Let
the needle re-enter the fabric in the center of
the chain stitch below (C).

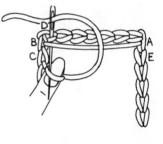

To start the loop stitches, place the left thumb
over the working thread. Wind it around the
thumb from right to left. Slip the needle through
the first chain stitch at the top (D), under the
foundation thread (A–B), and under the working
thread looped around the thumb. Pull the thread
through the loop, making a small knot.

Continue in this way until the row is completed. Be sure to keep the loops even. Slip the
needle into the chain stitch on the right-hand
side (E) and come up in the chain stitch below
E. Carry the thread across to the left-hand side.
Slip the needle through the chain stitch below
C, ready to begin the second row of looped
stitches. Remember, they are taken through the
loop in the preceding row, under the foundation
thread, and through the working thread wound
around the thumb.

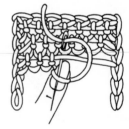

## Holy Point or Holy Stitch
*See* Hollie Stitch.

### Honeycomb Filling Stitch

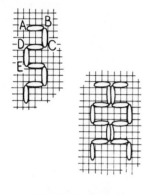

A geometric feeling dominates this filling stitch, used for drawn-fabric work. The stitches are made over the same number of threads, perhaps 3 or 4.

Begin by letting the needle emerge at A, re-entering the fabric at B, 3 threads to the right. For the second stitch, bring the needle up at C, 3 threads below B. Return it to B, and let it re-enter the fabric at C.

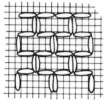

For the third stitch, insert the needle at D, 3 threads to the left of C, and let it emerge 3 threads below, at E.

To begin the fourth stitch, insert the needle at D, bringing it out at E, ready to begin the next group of stitches. Follow the same procedure. Be sure to pull each stitch tightly to create an open effect.

Turn the work around when starting the next row of stitches. Repeat this at the beginning of each of the remaining rows. The design allows the use of double vertical stitches worked in the same holes.

### Honeycomb Filling Stitch—Raised

Vertical and horizontal stitches form a foundation for this filling. They cover the design area, crossing each other at right angles, to create a trellis effect. Anchor the threads only at the outer edges.

After the foundation is made, overcast the stitches. Begin with the vertical ones and then do the horizontal ones.

The next step is made by winding each vertical stitch upward and then downward. This process creates a crossed effect at each intersection. Horizontal stitches are also wound in this manner.

Another winding thread can be used. The resulting effect is somewhat bumpy and knotty.

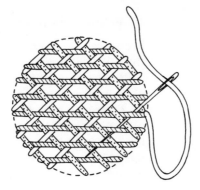

## Honeycomb Stitch

This is a filling stitch that requires 3 steps to make. A hoop should be used to keep an even tension on the stitches.

Begin by placing horizontal stitches across the area to be covered. Keep the spaces between the stitches the same.

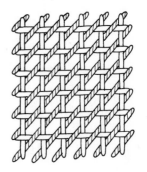

Cover these stitches with a series of evenly spaced diagonal ones. Work from the lower left-hand side to the upper right-hand side. Be sure to plan the degree of slant carefully, so the desired effect is obtained.

In order to hold these two sets of stitches together, a thread is woven diagonally across them. It moves at right angles to the other diagonal stitches, passing under the horizontal and over the diagonal ones.

A simpler version of this filling can be made by using a foundation of horizontal and vertical stitches. The interlacing thread moves in a diagonal direction.

## Hungarian Stitch

Stitches form a diamond-shaped motif for this canvas work design. They can be worked effectively in contrasting colors. The motif consists of a group of 3 vertical stitches, 1 longer than the other 2. The stitches are worked over 2, 4, and 2 horizontal threads of canvas.

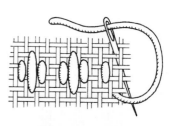

A space of 2 vertical threads, or 1 mesh, is left between each group. This makes it possible to dovetail the rows, filling all spaces, as shown in the accompanying diagram.

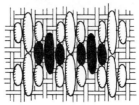

### Insertion Stitch—Buttonhole

Seams can be given a decorative finish by using this stitch. It links 2 pieces of material together.

Prepare the fabric by turning the raw edges of both pieces and pressing. To keep the parts an even distance apart, baste them to a piece of firm paper. Groups of buttonhole stitches are used to hold 2 finished edges together for an open effect. The number of stitches and the size of the spaces between can create a variety of effects. Shown here is an insertion made of 4 stitches on one edge alternating with 4 on the opposite one, to produce a zigzag design.

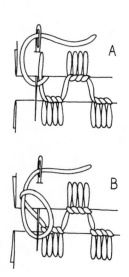

The stitches can be made in 2 ways: simple-to-make Blanket or Buttonhole stitches used in embroidery (A), or Buttonhole stitch used in sewing, sometime called Tailor's Buttonhole Stitch (B). The latter method produces a firmer, knotted edge. Be sure to keep the tension on the stitches even. Remove the paper when the stitches are completed.

### Insertion Stitch—Knotted

This stitch is similar to the Scroll Stitch and the Knotted Blanket Stitch, except that the stitches are used to join 2 pieces of fabric. They move from side to side in alternating fashion.

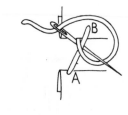

Begin by folding and pressing under the fabric edges and basting them to a firm paper strip. Bring the needle through the fabric on the lower edge at the left-hand side (A). Insert the needle for a blanket or buttonhole stitch on the upper edge, a little to the right (B).

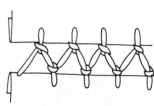

Before completing the stitch, slip the needle under the stitch and the working thread before drawing it through the loop that has been made. This makes a second blanket stitch. When the thread is pulled through, a knot is produced close to the upper edge.

Repeat the process on the lower edge. Continue in this way, alternating the stitches between the upper and lower edges.

## Insertion Stitch—Laced

In this stitch, the edges are decorated with a
Braid Edging Stitch before being formed. The
loops are then laced together with a diagonally
placed thread. Try to plan the placement of the
loops so they can be in an alternating position.

After folding under the edges, make the braid
edging stitches. Bring the needle through the
folded edge (A). Insert it again a short distance
to the left and below the folded edge, after looping the thread as shown in the accompanying
diagram. The needle passes through the loop
as it re-enters the fabric at the back of the work.
Draw the thread through the loop, leaving it
slightly loose to form the scalloped effect. Care
should be taken that the loops remain even. To
tighten the knot, pull the thread away from the
work. Continue in this way until the stitches have
been placed along both edges.

After the embroidering has been completed,
baste the pieces to stiff paper to keep them an
even distance apart. Remember to alternate the
position of the stitches when basting the stitches
to the paper.

Lace the stitches together, moving the thread
over and under the loops to create a diagonal
effect. Using a thread in a contrasting color can
be pleasing.

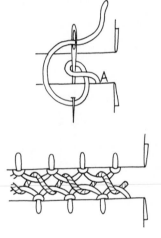

## Insertion Stitch—One-sided

An unusual name has been given to this stitch. Instead of being inserted between 2 pieces of material, it is placed on the fabric. It consists of a series of cross stitches that overlap. It is best to work this stitch on fabric in which the threads can be easily counted. Evenness is important.

The method of working is shown in 4 steps. Begin by making a cross over an equal number of threads, such as 3 vertical and 3 horizontal. Let the needle emerge again at the lower left-hand corner of the cross, ready to begin the second stitch.

Insert the needle 3 threads above the right-hand corner (A). Bring it out 3 threads to the left. Notice that a long slanting stitch has been made. To finish this cross stitch, insert the needle at the upper right-hand corner of the first cross stitch (B). Bring it out 6 threads to the left (C).

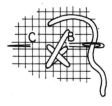

Make the third cross stitch beside the first one, and the same size. Finish by bringing up the needle at the upper left-hand corner (D), ready to begin the fourth cross stitch, placed below the third one.

Insert the needle 6 threads below and 3 to the right (E), forming another long diagonal stitch. Bring it up 3 threads to the left (F), re-entering the fabric at the lower right-hand corner of the second small cross stitch (G). Let the needle emerge 6 threads to the left (H), ready to begin another small cross stitch.

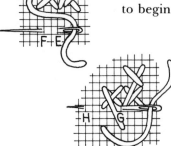

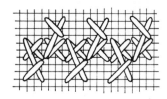

## Insertion Stitch—Plaited

The beauty of this stitch depends on precision. Regularity in size, placement, and the direction of each one is important to the braided or woven effect. For the best results, use a firm, thick thread. Leave about ¾ inch (2 cm) space between the 2 sections of fabric to be joined.

Begin by folding under the edges of 2 pieces of material. Baste them to a firm piece of paper, leaving the required space between.

Bring up the needle at the left-hand side below the edge of the lower section (A). Insert it in the upper piece, an equal distance from the edge and to the right, making a diagonal stitch (B). The length of the stitch is slightly longer than the space left between the fabric sections.

Slide the needle under the fabric, over the working thread. Let the needle re-enter the lower piece to the right, creating a zigzag effect (C). Keep the length and slant of the stitch the same as for the first one.

Carry the needle to the upper section, slipping it under the first stitch (A–B). Pass it through the fabric (D), to the left of B.

As the needle returns to the lower section, it passes over the first stitch. This is the beginning of the woven effect.

As the next group of stitches starts, pass the needle through the fabric to the left of C (E). On its way to the upper section, it weaves over, under, and over the 3 diagonal threads.

Insert the needle in the upper section (F) maintaining the same spacing. Return the needle to the lower section, interlacing the threads. Insert the needle at G.

Continue in this way, repeating the stitches from the beginning.

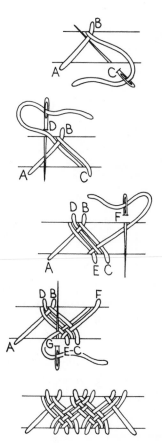

### Insertion Stitch—Twisted

A simple maneuver of the needle creates the twisted effect. As in other insertion stitches, regularity is important.

After basting the 2 folded edges to paper, use a diagonal stitch to join them. Be sure the space between the sections is even. Begin at the lower left-hand end of the work. Bring the needle up from the underside. The needle must always enter the fabric in this direction.

Carry the thread to the upper section. Insert the needle in the underside, passing it through the fabric to the surface.

Take the next stitch in the lower edge. Before the needle enters the material, twist it under and over the thread of the preceding stitch.

Make the third stitch in the upper edge, remembering to pass the needle under and over the stitch that has just been made. Notice that the stitches create a zigzag pattern. Be sure to keep the tension between the stitches even.

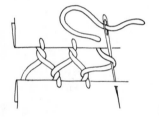

### Interlaced Band Stitch
*See* Herringbone Ladder Stitch.

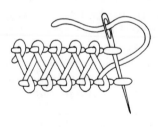

## Interlacing Band Stitch

This stitch creates a pleasing effect when worked in contrasting threads. It requires careful planning so that the stitches cross each other in the correct direction. Unless this is done, the interlacing will not be uniform. The foundation should be made with some slack in the stitches, since the interlacing thread has a tendency to pull the stitches together. Also, the weight of the threads should be considered, so the interlacing thread covers the foundation.

Begin with a series of herringbone stitches, spaced so that a second row of stitches may be placed in between. Keep the weight of the thread in mind when planning the size and spacing of the stitches. The crossed ends of the second row of stitches should be aligned with the first. For more detailed instructions, check the directions for Herringbone Stitch—Double.

In making these stitches, notice that for the top cross the needle passes under the working thread, instead of over it as in the making of a regular herringbone stitch. Also watch the crossing of the threads in making the second row. Notice that it alternates from stitch to stitch.

When the foundation of double herringbone stitches is completed, bring the interlacing thread to the surface (A). Work along the upper half of the foundation. Follow the accompanying diagram for the direction the thread takes.

At the end of the line, lace the thread around the center cross, and begin the return trip along the lower half of the herringbone stitches.

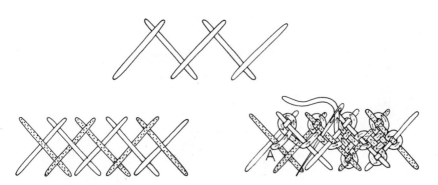

## Interlacing Stitch—German
*See* Herringbone Stitch—Laced.

## Interlacing Stitch—Maltese Cross

The Maltese cross motif dominates this stitch pattern. Straight stitches arranged in a herringbone formation produce the foundation for an interlacing thread. The design can be used to decorate a variety of articles.

It will be easier if the design is transferred to the fabric. Then follow the arrangement of stitches shown in the first diagram.

Bring the needle out at A. Insert it at B. Make a long stitch from C to D, letting needle emerge at E and re-enter fabric at F.

Continue to follow the letters shown on the accompanying diagram to complete the Maltese cross foundation. Return the needle into the fabric at X, completing the crossed stitch begun at A. Be careful to interweave the threads correctly, each crossing over and under in the right direction.

Begin the interlacing thread at the center of the cross (Z), as shown in the second diagram. Follow the direction of the thread as it is interlaced over and under the foundation. Complete each arm of the cross, returning to the center of the design before beginning the next one.

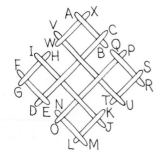

## Irish Stitch
*See* Florentine Stitch.

## Italian Stitch—Two-sided
*See* Cross Stitch—Two-sided Italian.

## Jacobean Couching
*See* Couched Filling Stitch.

## Jacquard Stitch

Diagonal stitches in 2 sizes, worked in steplike formation, create this effective canvas work stitch. It provides an interesting textured quality.

Use 1 row of diagonal stitches made over 2 vertical and 2 horizontal canvas threads. For the next row, use a shorter stitch worked over 1 intersection of the canvas. Alternate the rows to cover the design area.

In making the design, work 4 stitches vertically, 4 horizontally.

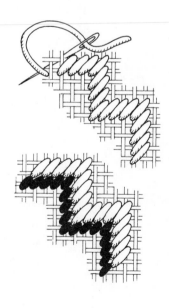

### Japanese Stitch

Horizontal satin stitches are worked in a diagonal direction to create a pleasing effect. Place the stitches close together, moving from left to right. Keep the length of the stitches even, moving each to the right the same amount.

### Kensington Stitch
*See* Split Stitch.

### Knitting Stitch

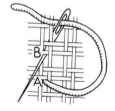

This is an unusual canvas work stitch. Its appearance camouflages its construction. Although the stitch resembles the Chain Stitch, it isn't. Instead, a stem-type stitch is used. The stitch is worked in 2 trips—first upward and then downward, using double-mesh canvas.

To make the stitch, bring the needle up at A in the center of a double mesh. Take a diagonal stitch over 1 vertical and 2 horizontal threads, returning the needle to the center of the mesh above (B). Continue in this way to finish the row.

Complete the knitted effect by repeating the first row of stitches, reversing the direction of the needle. Begin at the top of the row.

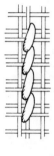
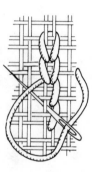
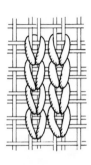

## Knot Stitch
*See* Blanket Stitch—Knotted.

## Knot Stitch—Double

The effect of this stitch seems to be similar to that of Coral Stitch, but somewhat more raised and bumpy. Lines and borders are given added interest when this stitch is used. It is important that the knots be spaced evenly and close together.

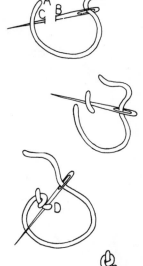

Working from left to right, bring up the needle at the end of the line to be covered (A). Insert the needle a short distance below and to the right (B). Come up to the left (C), making a small horizontal stitch on the underside of the fabric. The appearance of the stitch can be changed if the needle moves in a slanting direction or a wider stitch is taken.

After pulling the thread to the right side, slip the needle through the bar stitch without entering the fabric.

Hold the thread down with the left thumb. Slip the needle through the bar again just below the last stitch. As the needle is pulled through, it passes over the working thread, as in making a blanket stitch (D). A knot falls into place when the thread is completely drawn to the surface.

Start the next stitch below the first, with about the width of one knot between them.

## Knot Stitch—German
*See* Coral Stitch.

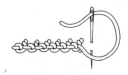

### Knot Stitch—Knotted
*See* Chain Stitch—Detached.

### Knot Stitch—Old English
*See* Knot Stitch—Double.

### Knot Stitch—Simple
*See* Dot Stitch.

### Knot Stitch—Twist
*See* French Knot.

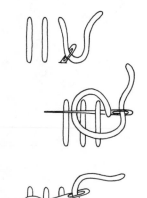

### Knotted Ground Stitch

Long stitches interlaced with knots create an effective filling stitch. It can be worked in contrasting colors.

Begin by laying a series of vertical stitches across the space to be covered. Keep the stitches parallel to each other.

For the first knot, start by bringing up the needle on the right-hand side. Let the working thread form a loop as the needle slides under the stitch and over the working thread. Notice that the working thread is above the point where it emerged. Pull the needle through the loop, drawing it upward to form a knot.

Slip the needle under the next vertical stitch, making another knot. Continue in this way until row is completed. Other rows are worked in the same manner.

## Knotted Pearl Stitch

An interlacing of blanket-type stitches creates a raised knotted effect that is attractive for narrow bands. It is important that the knots fall in the center of the band.

Working between 2 parallel guidelines, bring up the needle at the right-hand end between the 2 lines (A). Insert the needle in the line directly above (B), letting it emerge in the lower line (C).

Hold down the working thread so a loop can be made above the needle as it slips through the stitch from right to left. It forms a blanket-type stitch. Be sure that the needle does not pierce the fabric.

Make a second blanket stitch in the same way, passing the needle under the first stitch. Keep the working thread rather loose. Arrange the stitches so the knot falls in the center of the band.

For the second knot, insert the needle in the upper guideline (D). Bring it up directly below in the lower guideline (E). Space this stitch so the knots will be close together.

Slip the needle under the last stitch, making a blanket stitch. Follow this with another. Repeat this procedure until the row of stitches is completed.

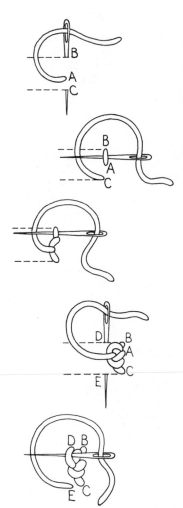

### Knotted Stitch

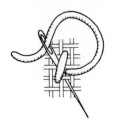

This canvas stitch is worked to produce a solid background, using a long stitch crossed by a short one. The rows overlap each other by 1 horizontal canvas thread.

Begin by taking 1 diagonal stitch over 1 vertical and 3 horizontal threads. Bring up the needle 2 horizontal threads below. Carry the working thread across the stitch, inserting the needle 1 vertical and 1 horizontal thread above. This short stitch holds the longer one in place.

To start the next stitch, bring up the needle 1 thread below and 1 thread to the right.

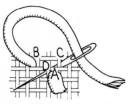

Commence the second row of stitches 2 horizontal threads below the first stitch. This allows the stitch to be placed between 2 stitches in the previous row.

### Knotted Stitch—Single

This stitch resembles the pile of a carpet when the stitches are worked closely together on canvas. Using wool or heavy strands of thread, insert the needle in the canvas (A), coming up 1 thread above and 2 threads to the left (B). Pull the yarn through the canvas, leaving an end of the yarn above the surface.

Insert the needle 3 vertical threads to the right (C), coming up at D, 2 threads to the left and 1 below. Draw the yarn completely through the canvas, pulling it tight to form the knot. Cut the yarn the desired distance from the knot.

After the work is completed, trim the yarn ends so that the pile is the same depth.

## Ladder Stitch

An effect of small braids is a distinguishing characteristic of this band stitch. Straight stitches link the tiny braided stitches. It is important that the spacing be kept even. Working between 2 parallel guidelines will be helpful.

Begin by bringing up the needle on the left-hand side (A). Carry the thread to the right-hand side, inserting the needle in the guideline (B) exactly opposite A. Let it reappear just to the left of this point and above the stitch (C). Make a small diagonal stitch over the first stitch, inserting the needle below B on the right-hand line (D). Slide the needle under the fabric, coming up below A on the left-hand line (E).

Slip the needle under the first long stitch and over the working thread. Pull the thread firmly, forming a knot-type stitch.

Carry the thread to the right-hand side. Slide the needle upward under the crossed ends made by the first 2 stitches.

Insert the needle just below D on the right-hand side (F), bringing it up on the left-hand side (G) just below E.

Slip the needle under the crossed stitches above this point. Pull the thread tight before taking it to the right-hand side, where the needle is passed under the crossed stitches.

Continue this procedure, alternating between left and right.

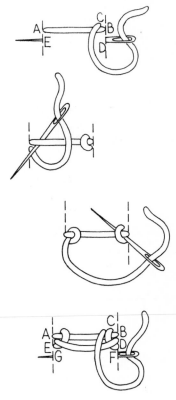

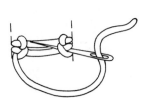

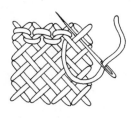

## Lattice Band—Raised

Several stitches create this stitch pattern—Straight, Satin, and Herringbone. By layering the stitches, a raised effect is produced. It makes an attractive decorative band.

Begin with a series of long horizontal stitches placed close together. They form a padding. Sometimes several extra horizontal stitches are placed over these in the center of the space to create a rounded effect.

Cover the foundation with satin stitches worked vertically. Place them close together in order to cover the padding.

For the decoration, use herringbone stitches. Construct them so that the needle enters the fabric above and below the band.

Another thread can be used for interlacing the herringbone stitches. Constrasting threads make the work more interesting.

## Lattice Stitch—Twisted

This filling stitch can be used to cover a surface design or to fill in a cut-out area. It creates a lacy effect in a trellis-like design.

Begin by laying a series of stitches for the square or diamond-shaped foundation. They should follow a diagonal direction, crossing each other at right angles. Weave the second group of stitches into place.

After completing the foundation, start the interlacing. It follows the procedure used for a Threaded Herringbone Stitch. Work horizontally, placing a stitch over each intersection of the foundation stitches. The stitches seem to move in a zigzag fashion, as the thread passes from one intersection to the next, but the result is that of a horizontal stitch. Notice that the thread is above the needle as it points downward, but is below as it slants upward.

A second interlacing thread can be used. The stitches should coincide at each intersection. To do this, be sure that, where the thread was above on the preceding line, it must now be below.

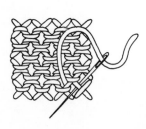

## Lazy Daisy Stitch

*See* Chain Stitch—Detached.

## Leaf Stitch

As its name implies, this filling stitch is often used to give interest to a leaf design.

In order that the crossing of the stitches follows a definite pattern, establish 2 guidelines through the center of the design. They can be straight or curving in direction. When moving in a curved line, the stitches create more of a three-dimensional effect.

Bring up the needle at the lower end of the left-hand guideline (A). Insert it on the outer right-hand edge of the design (B), making a slanting stitch. Let it emerge in the lower end of the right-hand guideline (C).

Carry the thread to the left, inserting the needle on the edge of the design (D), making another diagonal stitch. Notice that this stitch crosses the first one.

Return the needle to the left-hand guideline (E). Bring it up just below the second stitch. Make the third stitch from E to F. Be sure that each stitch crosses the last one.

Continue to work from side to side, with the stitches spaced evenly the required distance apart.

The outline of the design can be defined with chain or stem stitches.

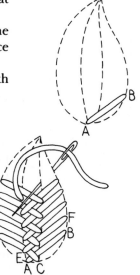

**Leviathan Stitch**
> *See* Cross Stitch—Double.

**Line Stitch**
> *See* Holbein Stitch.

**Line Stitch—Diagonal**
> *See* Faggot Stitch—Single.

**Link Powdering Filling Stitch**
> *See* Chain Stitch—Detached.

## Long and Short Stitch

The Satin Stitch is used for this one. Although the over-all effect is of alternating long and short stitches, they actually are used only for the first row of stitches. The remaining stitches are all of the long length. In spite of the fact that the stitches are simple to make, their placement requires careful attention in order to create a perfect blending in the shading. The stitches can be employed for tapestry shading or the more rounded design.

The stitches are placed in horizontal rows for tapestry shading. Sometimes a row of split stitches is worked first to form an outline and give the edge a rounded effect. When they are used, the long and short stitches cover them.

Begin with a row of long and short stitches. Place the stitches close together. Bring the needle to the surface at A and re-enter the fabric at B, making a long stitch. Put a short stitch, about ¾ as long, to the right. Continue to alternate the stitches until the row is completed.

The stitches for the remaining rows are of the same length except where variation is required to fill a space. The stitches may be fitted between those on the first row (1) or placed through the stitch, splitting it above the lower end (2). If this method is used, work the stitches downward instead of upward as for the first row.

Deciding on the colors to use is important. It is usually best to shade the work gradually from light to dark or dark to light. Sometimes an interesting effect can be produced by varying the intensity of the color, dull to bright.

If the stitches are to be used to fill in a rounded design, the principle for working is the same. However it will be easier if guidelines, radiating from the base, are established. They will regulate the placement of the stitches.

In order to develop the necessary evenness, begin the stitches at the center or high point of the design with a stitch in a vertical position. The other stitches will fan out from this point. Keep the direction constant so that the stitches seem to flow into one another. Continue in this way until design is filled.

Sometimes it is difficult to make a stitch between the stitches of the previous row. When this happens, skip a stitch. Be sure, however, that the effect is of a smooth arrangement of long and short stitches.

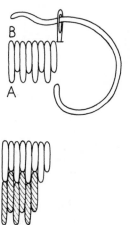

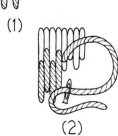

(1)

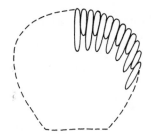

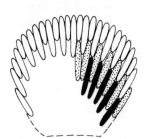

(2)

## Loop Stitch

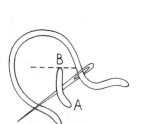

Although this stitch is used to give interest to a line, it can also be employed as a filling. The length of the stitches can be graduated, adapting to the space to be covered. The distance between the stitches should remain the same.

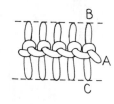

When covering a line, work between 2 parallel guidelines. Begin at the right-hand end of the line to be covered (A). Bring the needle up at this point and insert it in the upper line slightly to the left (B). Let it emerge below B in the lower line (C).

Holding the working thread down with the left thumb, slip the needle under the first stitch and over the working thread. Pull the thread through the loop as for a blanket stitch. Arrange the loop in the center of the guidelines before inserting the needle in the upper line to the left of B.

Continue in this way, keeping the stitches and loops evenly spaced.

## Loop Stitch—Open
*See* Fly Stitch.

## Loop Stitch—Tied
*See* Chain Stitch—Detached.

## Looped Filling Stitch
*See* Buttonhole Filling Stitch—Open.

## Magic Stitch
*See* Chain Stitch—Magic.

## Maltese Cross Filling Stitch

This filling stitch creates a Maltese cross design by interlacing a thread over a basic foundation. It is easier to make than the one produced by the Maltese Cross Interlacing Stitch (see under Interlacing Stitch—Maltese Cross).

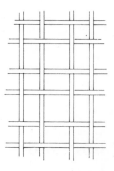

A series of long stitches, woven at right angles to each other, forms the foundation. Circling each corner of a square creates the cross motif; do not let the needle enter the fabric in this step.

In laying the foundation threads, arrange them in groups of 2, leaving a larger space between each group. In filling the design area, the threads may follow a horizontal and vertical direction or be placed diagonally, as for a diamond. Be sure to weave the threads together. To form the Maltese cross design, work a thread across the corners of a square twice before proceeding to the next square.

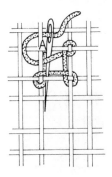

Bring the thread up at A, inside one of the squares. Pass the needle over and under the foundation and working threads as it moves around the inside of the square. Repeat this process. Be sure to go over and under the same threads as in the first trip, interlacing the threads so they lie flat.

At the completion of one square, insert the needle in the fabric. Bring it out in another square, ready to repeat the procedure.

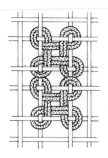

### Maltese Filling Stitch

This is a drawn-fabric stitch in which the working thread is pulled tightly to produce an openwork effect. Several different types of stitches are employed—Satin, Four-sided, and Cross stitches. The stitches are placed to form an openwork square. A series of the squares can be used to cover an area.

Begin by working 1 or 2 rows of vertical satin stitches. Make the stitches over 2 fabric threads. Pull each stitch tightly.

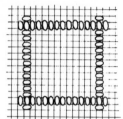

Repeat this procedure, leaving 8 threads between this row and the preceding horizontal row.

Follow with 2 vertical rows of satin stitches made in the same way. Pass the needle under the horizontal rows when crossing them. This results in the creation of a square bound by rows of satin stitches.

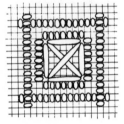

The inside of the square is filled with a Mosaic Filling Stitch. Work a block of fine satin stitches over 2 fabric threads. Pull the thread tightly. Make another block at right angles to the first and touching at the inside corner. Continue until 4 blocks have been made. Notice that these stitches join those in the outer square.

Finish the interior of the square with a Four-sided Stitch and Cross Stitch. Check the directions for these stitches for more detailed instructions.

### Maltese Stitch
*See* Knotted Stitch—Single.

## Mexican Stitch

This filling stitch is made by interlacing a thread through a series of small vertical stitches. The stitches are placed in horizontal rows parallel to each other. Although the stitches must be placed at regular intervals, the spacing can vary, depending on the effect desired. Working with threads in contrasting colors creates a pleasing look.

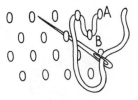

In making the foundation stitches, alternate their position, as shown in the accompanying diagram. Begin the interlacing at the stitch in the upper right-hand corner (A). Pass the needle under the stitch diagonally below in the second row of stitches (B). Continue in this way until the first row is laced. Remember the interlacing thread enters the fabric only at the ends of a row.

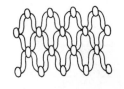

In making the second row, the interlacing thread passes under the stitches so that the loops meet.

## Montenegrin Stitch
    *See* Cross Stitch—Montenegrin.

### Mosaic Filling Stitch

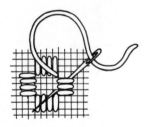

This drawn-fabric stitch is a combination of Satin, Four-sided, and Cross stitches. The cross-like motif can be spaced in alternate rows or placed close together.

Begin by making a block of 4 satin stitches. Take each stitch over 4 threads. Draw each stitch tightly.

Make a second block, placing it at right angles to the first. They should touch at the inner corner. Continue until 4 blocks have been made, forming a square motif.

To outline the inner square, make a four-sided stitch. Begin at the lower right-hand corner (A). Then follow the sequence for the remaining stitches—A to B to C, C to A to D, D to B to C, C to D.

After completing the fourth side of the square, let the needle emerge at the lower right-hand corner (A) ready to make the cross stitch. Do this with a stitch from A to D and then one from C to B.

### Mosaic Stitch
*See* Hungarian Stitch.

When Hungarian Stitch is worked in a diagonal direction, it is known as Mosaic Stitch.

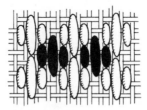

### Mossoul Stitch
*See* Herringbone Stitch.

## Mountmellick Stitch

This stitch is most pleasing when made with a heavy thread. It creates a bold, raised look that adds interest to a line. The stitches are worked vertically.

Begin by bringing up the needle at the end of the line to be covered (A). Take a stitch below this point with the needle entering the fabric slightly to the right (B) and reappearing to the left (C) directly below A.

Slip the needle downward under this diagonal stitch. Be sure that the needle does not enter the fabric.

Hold the working thread down with the left thumb, and insert the needle at A, letting it emerge at C. Be sure to use the holes that were previously made by the stitches. Pull the thread through the loop.

Repeat this process for the next stitch. Insert the needle below B, at D, coming up at E. Slide the needle under the diagonal stitch made between C and D. Insert the needle at C, inside the previous loop. Bring it up at E. Pull the thread through the loop.

Continue in this way until the line is covered.

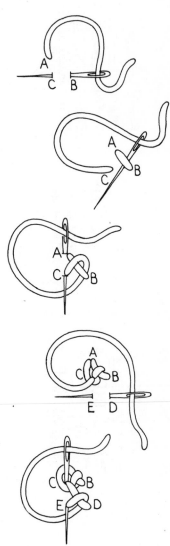

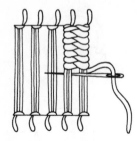

## Needleweaving

This stitch is often thought of as a type of hem-stitching. Threads are drawn from the fabric to form a band or border. The threads are then replaced by weaving a design over the remaining threads. A variety of designs can be made. Often the weaving is done with a thread in a contrasting color.

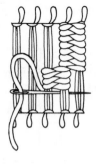

The weaving will be easier to do if the edges of the drawn band are hemstitched. The hem-stitching holds groups of 3, 4, or 5 threads together.

For the weaving, use a blunt needle. Work on the right side of the fabric.

Bring up the needle on the right-hand side of the work. Pass it over the first group of threads and under the second. Then turn the needle and pass it over the second, under the first. Continue in this way until the weaving covers half the depth of the drawn band.

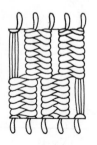

To develop the design, begin to work with the lower half of the second and third group of threads. When starting to work with a new group of threads, pass the needle under the threads.

Continue to make similar woven blocks, alternating up and down, until the band is filled and the original threads are covered. The stitches should be pulled tightly so that spaces develop between the blocks.

## Net Passing Stitch
*See* Honeycomb Filling Stitch.

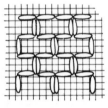

## Oblique Filling Stitch

A 6-pointed star dominates this drawn-fabric stitch. The stars are arranged in horizontal rows with the positions changing in alternating rows to produce an oblique feeling in the design.

The concentration of the stitches in the center of the design produces a large eyelet. Smaller ones appear at the points of the star. Two stitches are required for each stitch; they should be pulled tightly.

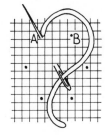

Mark the ends and center of each star on the fabric before beginning the work. Start by bringing the needle to the surface at the end of one point (A). Insert the needle in the center. Let it re-enter the fabric at A, using the same entry point. Then return the needle to the center.

Take the next 2 stitches from B to the center. Continue to work around the design in this manner.

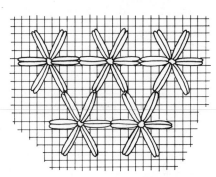

## Openwork Stitch—Four-sided or Square
*See* Four-sided Stitch.

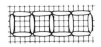

## Oriental Laid Stitch
*See* Couching—Roumanian.

## Oriental Stitch
*See* Roumanian Stitch.

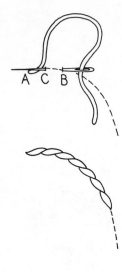

### Outline Stitch

This stitch is often mistaken for Stem Stitch. Actually, the only difference between the two stitches is the placement of the working thread. For Outline Stitch, hold the thread above or to the left of the needle.

Work from left to right, following a straight or curved line. Bring up the needle at the end of the line to be covered (A). Insert it a short distance to the right (B), letting it emerge midway between these 2 points (C).

### Outline Stitch—Kensington
*See* Split Stitch.

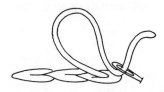

### Outline Stitch—Knotted
*See* Coral Stitch.

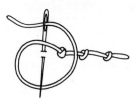

## Overcast Bar
    *See* Bar—Overcast.

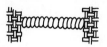

## Overcast Ground—Straight
    *See* Cobbler Filling Stitch.

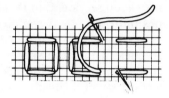

## Overcast Stitch

A firm, raised line can be created by this stitch. Closely placed small stitches are made over a foundation of running stitches.

    Begin with a row of small running stitches. Then bring the needle up at the left-hand end of the line. Take a small satin stitch over the foundation, picking up a tiny amount of the fabric. Continue, placing the stitches close together, until the line is covered.

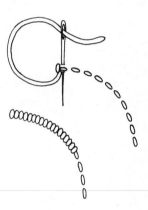

## Palestrina Stitch
    *See* Knot Stitch—Double.

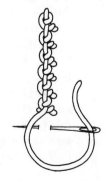

## Parisian Stitch

This canvas work stitch consists of vertical stitches in 2 sizes. The stitches are worked in an alternating pattern. They may be made over a combination of 1 and 3 threads or over 2 and 4 threads.

Begin by making a small stitch, A to B. Follow with a longer one, C to D. This sequence continues until the row is completed.

In the second and succeeding rows, the stitches fit into the spaces left in the previous row. A long stitch is placed below a short one; a short stitch, beneath a long one.

 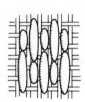

## Pearl Stitch

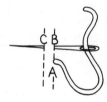

This stitch can produce 2 effects. When the stitches are worked close together, a beaded overcast look results, but when they are made some distance apart, the work resembles Scroll Stitch. The raised effect gives added interest to lines when this stitch is used.

Working upward, bring up the needle at the end of the line to be covered (A). Insert it above this point, taking a small stitch under the fabric, and at a right angle to the design line (B–C). Pull the thread through, leaving a small loop (A–B).

Slip the needle through the loop in an upward direction. Before drawing the thread completely through the loop, take hold of it close to C.

Pull the loop tight so it falls into position. Then draw the working thread through, and the stitch is completed.

The second stitch is worked in the same way. Its position is determined by the effect desired, but in any case place it above the first stitch.

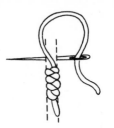

## Pekinese Stitch

This stitch creates a decorative braidlike trim. It is most effective when contrasting threads are used.

Begin with a foundation of backstitches, working from right to left. Keep the stitches even in length. Adjoining stitches should use the same holes for entering and leaving the fabric.

Interlace a second thread into the backstitches. Work from left to right. Bring the needle up at the left-hand end of the line, just below the first stitch (A). Slip the needle upward under the second stitch and then downward under the first. The needle should pass over the working thread as if passing through a loop.

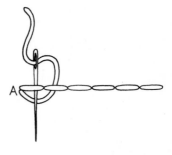

Pull the thread through the first stitch. Keep the thread flat and slightly loose, forming a loop.

Repeat this process for the following looped stitches. Keep them even and quite close to the backstitch foundation along the lower edge. Be sure not to pick up the fabric with the interlacing thread.

## Pessante
*See* Darning Stitch—Double.

## Petal Stitch

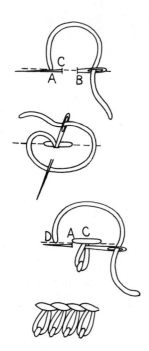

This composite stitch consists of 2 easy-to-make stitches—Daisy and Outline. It is most effective when used for floral motifs.

Begin at the right-hand end of the line to be covered. Make an outline stitch (A–B) with the needle emerging halfway between (C). Keep the working thread above the line.

At the point where the needle emerged, make a daisy stitch. Hold the thread down with the left thumb. Slip the needle under the fabric in a diagonal direction, making a stitch the required length. As the needle emerges, pull it through the loop. Anchor the loop with a short stitch taken over it.

Slip the needle under the fabric, letting it emerge to the left (D). This point should be half the distance of the first stitch. Insert the needle at the top of the previously worked daisy stitch (C), bringing it up at A, ready to make the next daisy stitch. Keep the loops and stitches even.

Continue in this way until the line is covered.

## Picot—Bullion

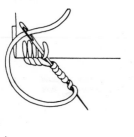

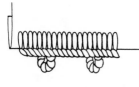

A picot, which is a small loop, adds interest to a buttonholed edge. It is found in various types of embroidery, such as Italian cutwork. The picot can be made in various ways.

For a bullion picot, begin at the left-hand edge. Make several close buttonhole stitches to the point where the first picot is to be made. At that point, slip the needle downward into the upright portion of the last buttonhole stitch.

Hold the needle in this position with the left thumb. Twist the thread 5 or 6 times around the point of the needle to make the bullion.

Put the thumb over the coiled threads. Pull the needle through the coils. Continue to pull the thread to tighten the bullion picot. Straighten it before inserting the needle in the fabric for the next buttonhole stitch. Work this stitch close to the last one. It will hold the picot in place.

## Picot—Buttonhole

In this type of picot, all stitches are worked as close blanket or buttonhole stitches. Instead of working from left to right, reverse the procedure. Although it is a bit awkward to take the buttonhole stitches in this direction, it is easier to make the picot.

After taking several buttonhole stitches, insert a pin at the spot where a picot is needed. Place the pin close to the last stitch.

Put the needle into the fabric as for another buttonhole stitch. Pull the working thread until a loop the size of the required picot is formed under the pin.

Loop the thread under the pin again from right to left. Weave the needle over the right side of the loop and the pin, under the left side of the loop, and over the working thread.

Pull the thread through until the resulting stitch is taut. It forms the base of the picot, holding the loop together at this point.

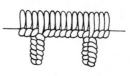

Work buttonhole stitches over the loop until it is completely covered. When the edge is reached, start another group of buttonhole stitches.

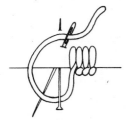

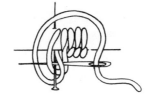

### Picot—Loop

This type of buttonhole is easier to make. It consists of a single loop of thread.

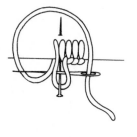

Begin with several buttonhole stitches worked from right to left. Insert a pin in the fabric where the picot is to be placed.

Pass the thread under the pin from right to left. Insert the needle in the fabric in line with the other stitches, and let it emerge below the edge. Carry the thread above the stitches so the needle can enter the loop from right to left. Weave it under the right-hand side of the loop, over the pin, under the left-hand side of the loop and first part of the working thread, but over the second part.

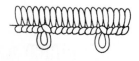

Hold the loop that forms the picot as the working thread is pulled taut. The procedure secures the loop against the edge of the fabric. Continue to make buttonhole stitches until the place for the next picot is reached.

### Picot—Pinned
*See* Picot—Loop.

## Picot—Ring

This type of picot creates a heavier effect but is easier to make. Work buttonhole stitches along the edge until the place for the picot is reached. Insert the needle into the looped edge about 3 or 4 stitches to the right. Pull the thread through, leaving a very small loop. Remember that buttonholing over the thread will increase its size.

When the loop has been covered with buttonhole stitches, make a buttonhole stitch in the fabric. This stitch holds the picot in place.

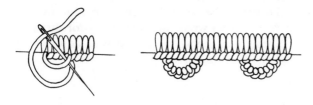

## Picot—Venetian
*See* Picot—Buttonhole.

## Picot Stitch
*See* Chain Stitch—Detached.

### Pin Stitch

This drawn-work stitch resembles a hemstitch. The effect is produced by wrapping groups of threads.

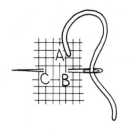

Bring the needle through the fabric 2 threads above the point where the first stitch will be taken (A). Insert it directly below (B), letting it emerge 4 threads to the left (C).

Return the needle to B, coming up again at C. Insert the needle once again at B, but this time slide the needle diagonally under the fabric to a point 2 threads above C (D). Pull the thread taut so that the wrapped threads will be drawn together, leaving a tiny opening.

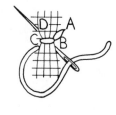

To begin the second stitch, insert the needle at C, ready to wrap the next group of threads.

Sometimes this stitch is used as an edging and called Point de Paris.

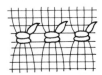

### Plaid Filling Stitch

The use of straight stitches and contrasting colors creates this filling stitch with a plaid effect. Start with a foundation of straight stitches. The vertical and horizontal stitches are equally spaced so a series of squares are produced. The threads should be interlaced as in weaving.

Place 2 horizontal stitches over alternate squares in checkerboard fashion. Cross these with 2 vertical stitches, producing the effect of a double cross.

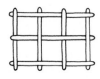
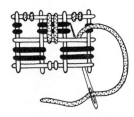

## Plait Stitch

*See* Feather Stitch—Spanish Knotted.

## Plumage Stitch

*See* Long and Short Stitch.

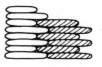

## Plush Stitch

*See* Turkey Work.

## Point de Paris Stitch

This stitch is an attractive way to hold 2 pieces of material together, such as a hem or an appliqué. It creates an openwork effect along the joined edge.

After basting the hem in place, bring the needle through the folded edge of the hem (A). The end of the working thread is concealed within the hem.

Insert the needle in the fabric just below the folded edge (B). Bring it up a short distance to the left (C).

Return the needle to B and come up again at C. Insert the needle again at B, but this time bring the needle up through the hem, emerging above C, ready to begin the next stitch (D).

Openings in the fabric appear when the horizontal stitches are pulled tight. Be sure to use the same holes for these stitches.

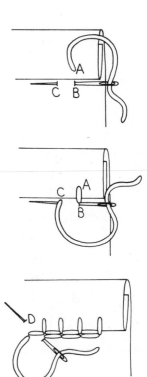

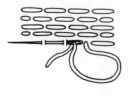

### Point de Reprise
*See* Darning Stitch.

When a darning stitch is used to embroider net, it is given this name.

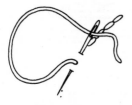

### Point de Sable
*See* Backstitch.

### Point Turc
*See* Three-sided Stitch.

### Porto Rico Rose
*See* Bullion Knot or Stitch.

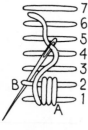

### Portuguese Border Stitch

This attractive border stitch creates a raised effect. The best results will be obtained if a firm thread is used. The stitch pattern is worked over a foundation of horizontal stitches, placed about ⅛ inch (3 mm) apart.

Begin by making a series of horizontal stitches or bars, the required width. Bring up the needle below the base stitch (A). Wrap 3 satin stitches around the first 2 bars. For the fourth stitch, slip the needle under only one bar (B).

Take 2 diagonal stitches over the second and third bars. The second stitch is wrapped around only the third bar, ready to make the next group of stitches over the third and fourth bars.

Repeat this procedure to the end of the band. Insert the needle in the fabric and fasten the thread.

Begin again at the base of the design on the right-hand side. Start the stitches toward the center so they meet those on the left-hand side.

Be sure to avoid tight stitches. The work should lie flat.

## Portuguese Knot Stitch

*See* Portuguese Stem Stitch.

## Portuguese Stem Stitch

The easy-to-make Stem Stitch is given a new look when it is wrapped. A knotted effect results.

Begin by making a stem stitch on the line to be covered. Bring the needle up at the end of the line (A). Insert it to the right (B), bringing it up halfway between these 2 points (C).

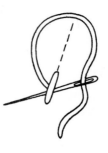

For the wrapped effect, slide the needle under the stitch twice. Do not let the needle enter the fabric. The second stitch should lie below the first. Pull the working thread tight.

Make a second stem stitch. Slip the needle under the section of the first and second stitches that overlap, and wrap them twice.

Continue in this way, alternating a stem stitch with wrapped stitches.

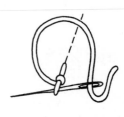

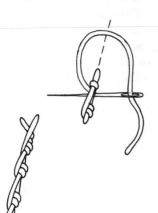

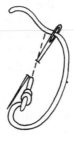

## Post Stitch
*See* Bullion Knot or Stitch.


## Punch Stitch

To decorate an area with this stitch creates an openwork effect. The surface is dotted by holes in a regular design. Remember to pull each stitch taut.

Bring the needle to the right side of the fabric on the right-hand side of the work (A). Insert the needle 4 threads above (B), returning it to A.

Insert the needle again at B, making the second vertical stitch. Slide the needle diagonally under the fabric so that it comes up 4 threads to the left (C), on a line with A.

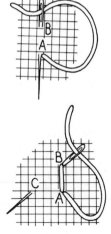

Put the needle in the fabric 4 threads above (D), in a line with point B. Return it to C and then to D. Continue this procedure, making 2 vertical stitches over 4 threads, at 4-thread intervals, until the row is completed. Be sure that each of the 2 stitches is made in the same hole.

Work a second row of stitches from left to right. Let the stitches enter the holes made by the first row. Cover the area in this way.

Then turn the work so that the same type of stitches can be made, filling in the spaces between the stitches to form small squares. Make the stitches through the holes made by the vertical stitches. Be sure each stitch is pulled taut.

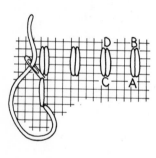

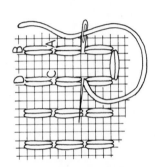

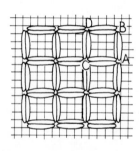

## Raised Band—Diagonal

Crossed stitches, pulled tightly, create an interesting openwork effect. Raised ridges follow a diagonal direction. A series of vertical stitches is crossed by a series of horizontal ones to form this stitch pattern.

Work from the lower right-hand corner to the upper left-hand one. Bring up the needle at the bottom of the first vertical stitch (A). Insert it 6 threads above (B), letting it emerge 3 threads to the left and 3 below (C), halfway between A and B.

For the second vertical stitch, put the needle in the fabric 6 threads above (D). Continue to make vertical stitches until the top left-hand corner of the work is reached.

At this point, bring up the needle as for another vertical stitch (E). However, here the stitch direction changes to horizontal. Crossing the last vertical stitch, insert the needle 6 threads to the right (F).

Slide the needle diagonally under the fabric, coming up at the end of the last vertical stitch (G), 3 threads to the left and 3 below. Continue to make horizontal stitches, using the holes made by preceding stitches. Draw the thread tightly in order to make the holes.

When the first row is completed, make other rows in the same way until the area is filled.

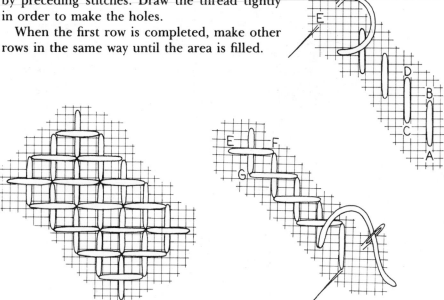

## Rambler Rose Stitch

A series of small stem stitches, worked round and round in spiral fashion, produces a rose effect.

## Renaissance Stitch

This is a canvas stitch in which the stitches are arranged in blocks of 4 with each group placed vertically beneath the preceding one. Two stitches are padded or trammed in one operation before 2 vertical stitches are made.

Start on the right-hand side (A). Carry the working thread horizontally over 2 canvas threads. Slide the needle downward, under 1 thread, coming up at B. Insert the needle 2 threads above, at C. Slip the needle downward, emerging 1 thread to the right and 2 threads below (D). Take a second stitch over the padding thread, entering the canvas 2 threads above this point. Bring the needle up 1 thread to the right and 3 threads below (E) ready to start the next block of stitches.

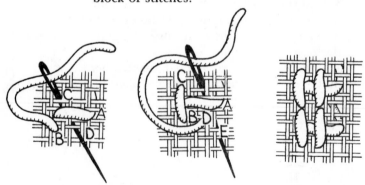

## Rep Stitch
*See* Aubusson Stitch.

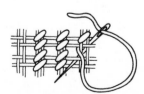

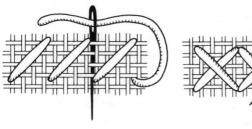

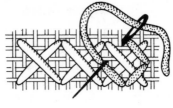

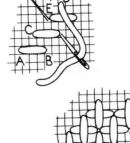

## Rice Stitch

A variation in stitch lengths allows crossed stitches to be superimposed on a foundation of cross stitches. A diagonal stitch crosses the arms of each cross stitch, to create the effect of large and small crosses.

Begin by covering the space with cross stitches made over 4 vertical and 4 horizontal canvas threads. Over each arm, make a small diagonal stitch. Work at right angles so that a small cross is formed. Take the stitch over 2 threads of the canvas, both vertically and horizontally.

## Ridge Filling Stitch

This stitch is similar to the Diagonal Raised Band in appearance. This stitch, however, begins with a foundation of horizontal stitches instead of vertical ones. Remember to pull the stitches tight.

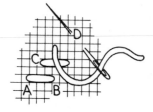

Start the work at the lower left-hand corner and proceed to the upper right-hand one. Bring the needle up at A. Insert the needle 4 threads to the right (B), letting it emerge 2 threads above and 2 to the left (C), ready to make the second stitch.

When the row of horizontal stitches is completed, bring the needle up 2 threads above and 2 to the left (D). Insert the needle at the end of the horizontal stitch 4 threads below, making a vertical stitch. Bring the needle up again 2 threads above and 2 to the left (E), ready to make the next vertical stitch. Continue in this way to the end of the row. Always use the holes made by the previous stitches. Ridges are formed by pulling each stitch tight.

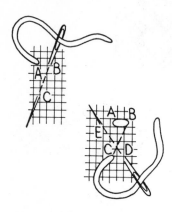

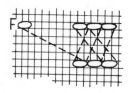

### Ripple Stitch

This drawn-fabric stitch is similar to a Double Backstitch. The backstitches appear on the right side and crossed stitches on the back. When the stitches are pulled taut, a ripply effect results.

Begin by bringing up the needle on the right-hand side (A). Insert it 2 threads to the right (B), letting it emerge 5 threads below and 2 threads to the left (C), under A.

Insert the needle to the right (D), under B. Slip the needle diagonally under the fabric, appearing 2 threads to the left of A, at E. Continue this way until 3 pairs of stitches are made.

Then slip the needle under the fabric, bringing it up 10 vertical threads to the left (F). Make another set of stitches. Alternate the stitches until the row is completed.

For the second row, fill in the spaces left in the lower edge of the first set of stitches. This allows a solid row of backstitches to be made.

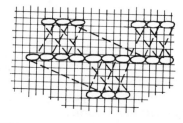

## Rococo Stitch

This complicated canvas stitch creates an attractive effect. Four knotted Roumanian stitches are worked into the same hole. The blocks of stitches are arranged in alternate squares, producing a checkerboard effect. Open squares are left between the stitch blocks. The canvas is, however, completely covered if the yarn is correctly chosen.

Bring the needle to the surface in the upper right-hand corner of the area to be covered (A). Take a stitch up over 2 horizontal threads with the needle inserted at B and emerging 1 thread below and 1 thread to the right (C). Carry the thread across the first stitch with the needle slipped under the canvas, returning to A.

To make the second stitch, insert the needle at B. Keep the working thread to the left so the needle can emerge between the 2 stitches. Carry the thread across the second stitch, bringing the needle up again at A.

The third stitch is made in the same way. The fourth stitch is also made this way. However, when the working thread crosses the vertical stitch, it also passes over a canvas thread, anchoring the block of stitches.

To make the next block of stitches below and to the left of the first, slip the needle under 2 canvas threads, coming up at D. Insert it 2 threads above, ready to make another block of 4 stitches.

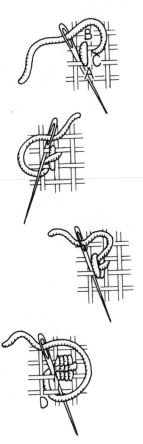

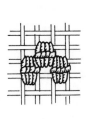

### Roll Stitch

*See* Bullion Knot or Stitch.

### Roman Stitch

*See* Roumanian Stitch.

### Rope Stitch

The width of this stitch can vary, creating different looks. In the wider width, the effect seems to be that of a slanting satin stitch; the narrow width is more ropelike. Both effects are obtained with a small loop which, although invisible, results in a raised effect along one edge.

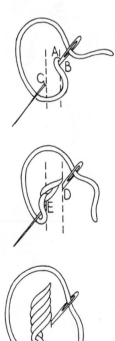

For the **broad version,** work between 2 parallel guidelines. Bring the needle up on the right-hand line (A). With the working thread above, insert the needle just below this point (B). Slip the needle diagonally under the fabric, coming up in the left-hand guideline (C). Loop the thread upward under the needle. Draw the thread through the loop, making a chain stitch. Pull it taut so it lies flat.

Return the needle to the right-hand line, inserting the needle just below the first stitch (D). Bring it up in the left-hand line, just below the first stitch (E). The stitches should be placed close together.

Twist the working thread under the needle in an upward direction. Pull the thread through the fabric and the loop. Draw the thread tight. The tiny loop should disappear under the diagonal stitch. Be sure to pull the thread downward in a diagonal direction.

Repeat this procedure to the end of the row. Be sure to keep the slant of the stitches constant.

The **narrow version** of the Rope Stitch is worked in a similar way. However, the position of the needle is different, and the working thread is moved in the opposite direction.

Bring the needle up at the end of the line to be covered (A). Insert the needle directly below (B) with the working thread to the right of the needle. Let it emerge a stitch length below B (C). Pass the thread over and under the needle. Pull the needle through the loop, forming a chain stitch.

Insert the needle at the narrow end of the chain stitch so that the stitches touch (D). Bring it up below this point in the guideline (E). Pass the working thread under the needle. Pull the needle through the loop. Continue to draw the thread to tighten it so that the stitch lies flat and the loop disappears. Repeat this procedure to the end of the line.

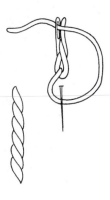

**Rosette Stitch**
*See* Chain Stitch—Rosette.

**Roumanian Stitch**

The effect of this stitch can be varied by the size and direction of a small stitch used to cross a longer line. The stitches can be placed close together or with small spaces between.

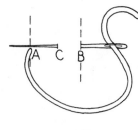

Work the stitches between 2 parallel guidelines. Bring the needle through the fabric on the left-hand line (A). Insert it in the right-hand line (B), directly opposite, letting it emerge slightly to the right of the center point (C), between A and B. The working thread should be below the stitch.

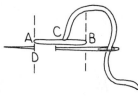

Pull the thread through. Insert the needle just to the left of the center point so that a small stitch is taken over the longer one. Bring the needle up in the left-hand line (D), the required distance below A. Repeat this process. Keep the small stitches even and below each other.

To vary the effect, use a longer crossing stitch, as can be seen in the accompanying diagrams. Bring the needle up at E. Go down at F. Come up at G, about one third of the distance between E and F. Insert the needle again at H, an equal distance from the left-hand line. Come up in the left-hand line, and return the needle to the right-hand line to repeat the procedure.

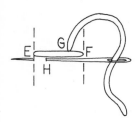

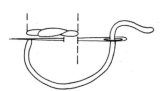

## Running Stitch

This is the simplest of all stitches to construct. It is used for sewing as well as for embroidery. It is used to define an outline or as a foundation for a composite stitch.

The stitches can be made by picking up and passing over an equal number of threads, or by picking up only 1 or 2 threads on the underside. Work from right to left. Several stitches may be picked up on the needle before the thread is drawn through the fabric.

## Running Stitch—Interlaced

The running stitch becomes more decorative when a second thread is laced through the stitches, leaving a looped motif. When this is done in contrasting threads, the effect is most attractive. Using a blunt needle makes the lacing easier to do.

Bring up the needle under the first stitch at the right-hand end. Slip the needle downward under the next stitch, and then upward under the following one. Continue in this way to the end of the line. Be careful not to pick up any of the fabric or split the stitches when passing the needle in and out.

At the end of the line, begin a return trip, filling in the spaces. Keep the loops even and flat.

### Running Stitch—Threaded

When only 1 thread is laced through the running stitches, the stitch is sometimes called Threaded Running Stitch.

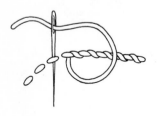

### Running Stitch—Whipped

After the foundation of running stitches is made, place a second thread over each stitch. Slip the needle downward under each stitch. This results in a diagonal stitch falling between the running stitches. Avoid picking up the fabric or entering a stitch.

### Russian Stitch
   *See* Herringbone Stitch.

### Saddle Stitch
   *See* Running Stitch.

### Sampler Stitch
   *See* Cross Stitch.

## Satin Stitch

Although this stitch is easy to make, it requires a great deal of skill and patience to keep the edge of the design even and well defined. The length can vary; however, it is best to avoid long stitches. The stitches can follow a straight or diagonal direction, but they must always be placed close together to create a satiny look. If a raised effect is desired, pad the design with closely placed running or chain stitches before beginning to work the satin stitches. Be sure to work between 2 guidelines.

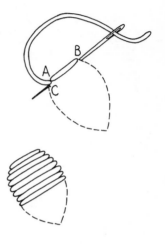

Bring the needle up to the surface in the left-hand guideline (A). Carry the thread across the design, inserting the needle in the right-hand line (B). Slide the needle under the fabric, letting it emerge on the left-hand side (C) just below A.

Continue to make stitches this way until design area is covered. Be sure the stitches are close together and flat.

## Satin Stitch—Encroaching

This stitch is used when a shading effect is needed. A color can change from one tone to another without any definite line of demarcation. To make this blending possible, let the head of each stitch in the second and subsequent rows fall between the base of 2 stitches in the preceding row. Sometimes a split stitch is used to define the design outline.

Begin the work at the top of the design on the left-hand side. Make a row of satin stitches. Start the second row the required distance below the first one. Insert the needle between the first 2 stitches in the first row. Continue to make the stitches in this way until the design is filled.

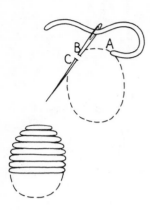

## Satin Stitch—Surface

Although this stitch is sometimes used as a substitute for the satin stitch, it is not as pretty. It does not create a smooth, flat effect because the stitches cannot be placed as close together.

Begin by bringing the needle up in the design outline on the right-hand side (A). Carry the thread across the design. Insert the needle on the opposite design line (B). Pick up a very small amount of material so the needle emerges in the line (C) just below B. Pass the thread to the opposite side of the design and take another tiny stitch. Continue to make stitches in this way.

## Satin Stitch—Whipped

Placing diagonal or whipping stitches over a group of satin stitches produces a raised and corded effect. The satin stitches should slant in one direction; the whipping stitches, in the opposite, crossing the satin stitches at right angles. Make the whipping stitches a small distance apart, with the thread carried over and under the design.

## Scottish Stitch

This canvas stitch forms a series of squares outlined with small diagonal stitches and filled in
with larger ones. Using contrasting colors creates a pleasing effect.

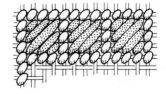

Decide on the size of the square. Work over
2 intersections of the canvas for the small
stitches forming the border. Fill in the square
with diagonal stitches. The size of the stitches
will vary. They can be taken over 2, 4, 6, 4, and
2 intersections in that sequence, or over 1, 2,
3, 2, and 1, as in the accompanying diagram.
Adjoining squares share a common border.

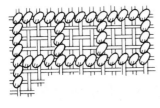

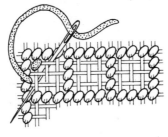

## Scroll Stitch

This stitch creates a wavy effect. It can be used
to cover a single design line or in several rows
for a band. The position of the stitches can be
alternated from row to row.

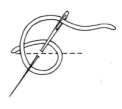

Work from left to right. Bring the needle up
at the end of the line to be covered. In moving
the thread to the right, make a loop below the
line on the surface of the fabric. Place the needle
inside this loop, picking up a small amount of
the fabric. Point the needle in a diagonal, downward position. Pull the loop tight before drawing
the thread through it. Repeat this procedure for
the next stitch.

## Seed or Seeding Stitch

This filling stitch consists of a series of tiny straight stitches, equal in length and scattered irregularly over the surface of the work. Sometimes 2 stitches are used instead of 1. For a raised, bumpy effect, keep the stitches loose.

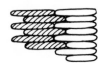

## Serpentine Stitch
    *See* Hemstitch—Serpentine.

## Shading Stitch
    *See* Long and Short Stitch.

## Shadow Stitch
    *See* Backstitch—Crossed or Double.

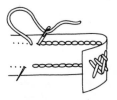

## Sheaf Filling Stitch

Easy-to-make stitches, grouped together, produce a sheaf motif. Scattering them over an area in rows, sometimes in alternating fashion for a checkerboard effect, creates a dainty filling.

Make 3 satin stitches. Then bring the needle up on the left-hand side of the group. Without entering the fabric, slip the needle over and under the satin stitches twice. Keep the 2 stitches close together, pulling the thread tight. This creates the sheaf-like design.

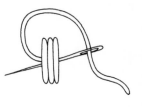

Insert the needle in the fabric. Slip the needle to the place where the next sheaf will be made.

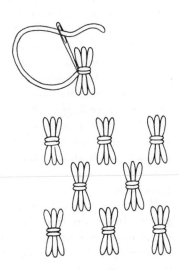

### Sheaf Stitch

This border stitch creates a heavy, raised effect. It is complicated to make and requires careful attention to the placement of each stitch. Tiny knots hold satin stitches in position.

The stitch is worked in 4 steps in an upward, vertical direction. A firm thread will produce the best results.

Begin by laying the foundation stitches. They consist of pairs of horizontal stitches. Three are needed for the first stitch. Place the stitches for each pair close together, forming a bar. Keep the spacing between each pair even; the distance depends on the desired length of the sheaf motif.

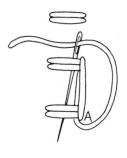

For the second step, work satin stitches over the first and second bars. Begin at the right-hand corner of the lowest bar (A). Do not let the needle enter the fabric or bar. Keep the stitches flat and parallel to each other.

When the bar is filled—usually this takes about 6 stitches—slip the needle under the first bar before proceeding to the second bar. This time make the satin stitches over the second and third bars. Work from left to right (B). The bottom of each stitch should fall between the tops of 2 in the previous group of stitches. This is most important.

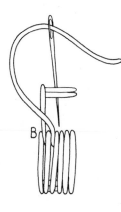

When the second group of stitches is completed, begin the third step, making a series of knots to anchor the satin stitches in place. Slip the needle under the second bar. Pass the needle over the first stitches in the lower and upper groupings, sliding the needle downward under the bar without entering the material.

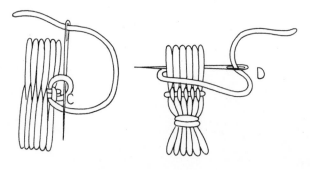

Before pulling the thread completely under the bar, pass the needle over and through the loop (C) that has been formed. Draw the thread taut, forming a knot. Follow this procedure, making knots over each pair of satin stitches. The knots seem to make the stitches fan out along the bar.

The final step in the making of this stitch consists of 2 satin stitches wrapped around the vertical stitches (D). They pull the stitches together, creating the sheaf motif.

## Shell Stitch

The sheaf motif dominates this canvas stitch. The stitches are made on the surface of the canvas.

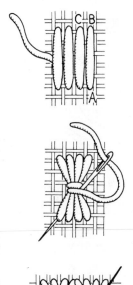

Bring up the needle at the lower right-hand corner of the design (A). Insert it 6 threads above (B). Let it emerge 1 thread to the left (C). Continue this way until 4 stitches have been made.

At the end of the fourth stitch, slip the needle under the canvas, bringing it up in the center of the canvas threads covered by the stitches. Slip the needle under the stitches. Wrap the thread twice around the stitches. Insert the needle in the canvas. The horizontal stitches pull the vertical ones together, forming the sheaf motif.

After making rows of sheaves, link them together with an interlacing thread, passed twice through the horizontal stitches.

To finish the design, place a row of backstitches between the rows. The stitches cover the spaces.

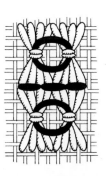

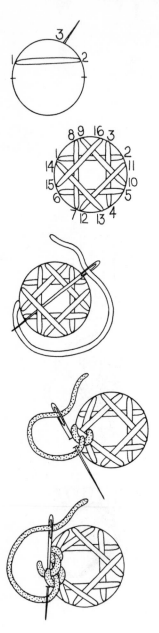

## Shisha Stitch

This stitch is used to hold small disks in place with a decorative framing. The disks can be made of Mylar, foil, fabric, or mirrors. Straight stitches are interlaced to form a foundation for blanket-type stitches.

Begin by anchoring a disk in place with a small stitch on each side. In order to place the foundation stitches in a regular pattern, divide the circle horizontally and vertically into thirds.

Bring up the needle on the left-hand side of circle close to the edge (1). Insert it on the right-hand side directly opposite this point (2). Let it emerge again at 3.

Continue making these long stitches by following the numbers in the sequence shown on the accompanying diagram. Always let the needle enter and emerge close to the edge of the disk.

To make the blanket-type stitch, bring up the needle close to 1. Hold the thread down with the thumb, slip the needle under the crossed foundation threads and through the loop that has been formed. Pull the thread tight.

Loop the thread to the left of the disk. Take a small stitch close to and parallel to the edge of the disk. Draw the needle through the loop, pulling the thread taut.

Repeat these 2 stitches around the disk. Alternate the stitches—first over the foundation stitches, then into the fabric. The blanket stitches should conceal the foundation stitches.

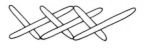

**Slav Stitch—Plaited**

> *See* Cross Stitch—Long-armed or Long-legged.

**Smyrna Stitch**

> *See* Knot Stitch—Double.

**Sorbello Stitch**

This stitch can be scattered over an area for an interesting filling. Care should be taken to keep the loops and stitches even.

Begin a short horizontal stitch with the needle coming up at A and going down at B. It reappears below the starting point (C).

Slip the needle over and under the stitch. As the thread is pulled through the loop, slide the needle over and under the stitch for the second time. Pull the needle through the loop made by the working thread. Arrange the loops carefully. Then insert the needle into the fabric below the right-hand end of the stitch (B) to complete the stitch.

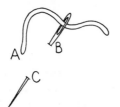

**Spanish Stitch**

> *See* Feather Stitch—Spanish Knotted.

**Speckling Stitch**

> *See* Seed or Seeding Stitch.

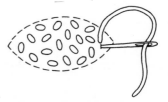

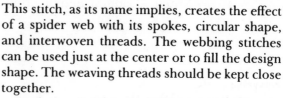

### Spider Web Stitch

This stitch, as its name implies, creates the effect of a spider web with its spokes, circular shape, and interwoven threads. The webbing stitches can be used just at the center or to fill the design shape. The weaving threads should be kept close together.

Begin by dividing a circle into eighths with foundation stitches. Bring up the needle on the left-hand side (A). Insert it on the right-hand side (B), letting it emerge at C. Continue to make a series of straight stitches, crossing each other at the center, as shown in the accompanying diagram.

After making 4 stitches, bring up the needle between H and B (I). Slip the needle under all stitches at the intersection. Pass the thread over and under the needle. Draw the needle through the loop. Pull the thread, forming a knot that ties the stitches together.

With the foundation spokes in place, begin, at the center, to weave the thread over and under the spokes. Continue until the design has been completed.

### Spine Stitch

*See* Loop Stitch.

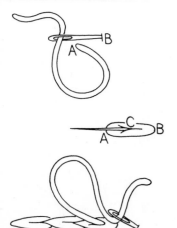

### Split Stitch

The method for making this stitch is similar to that for Stem Stitch but the finished stitch resembles a chain stitch. It creates an interesting effect for outlining designs. It is necessary to use a thread or yarn that will split easily.

Working from left to right, bring up the needle at the end of the line to be covered (A). Insert the needle to the right (B), the required length of the stitch. Make a small stitch under the fabric, letting the needle emerge about halfway between these two points (C), splitting the first stitch. Keep all of the stitches even.

**Square Stitch**
> *See* Holbein Stitch.

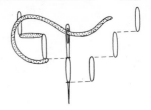

**Square Stitch—Diagonal**
> *See* Faggot Stitch—Single.

**Stalk Stitch**
> *See* Stem Stitch.

**Star Eyelet**
> *See* Algerian Eye Stitch.

**Star Stitch**

This canvas stitch creates a starlike effect. Eight straight stitches radiate from the same central mesh. The outer points of the stitches form a square motif.

Begin the first stitch at an outer point (A). Insert the needle in the canvas at the center, 2 threads to the left and 2 threads below (B). Let it emerge 2 threads above at C. Return to the center before proceeding to D, 2 threads above and 2 threads to the left. The upper edge of the square has been made. Continue in this way until the star motif is completed.

Work the motifs in horizontal rows from left to right, with the adjoining motifs using the same holes. This allows the stitches to cover the canvas completely.

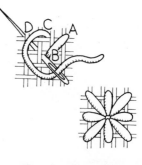

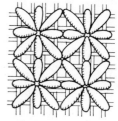

## Stem Stitch

This is an easy-to-make stitch that produces a solid line. It is effective for outlining a design or forming a foundation for other stitches. By a variation in the direction of the stitches, the width can be changed.

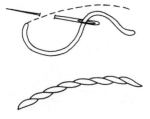

Working from left to right, bring up the needle at the end of the line to be covered. Insert it a short distance to the right, letting it emerge halfway between these 2 points. Usually the needle is taken at a slight angle, with the needle entering the fabric below the line and coming up above it. However, the stitch can be made in a straight line if a narrower effect is desired. Always keep the thread below or to the right of the needle.

## Stem Stitch—Raised

A series of stem stitches worked on a foundation of straight stitches produces a decorative effect. Although usually thought of as a band stitch, it can be used as a filling.

Begin by making a series of horizontal stitches, placed about ¼ inch (6 mm) apart and parallel to each other. If more of a raised effect is required, these stitches can be taken over a band of padding stitches.

Start the stem stitches by bringing up the needle at the left-hand end of the lowest stitch (A). Keep the thread below the needle. Slip the needle under this stitch, encircling it. Do not enter the fabric.

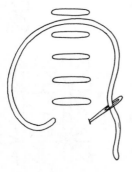
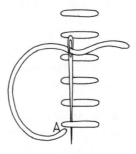

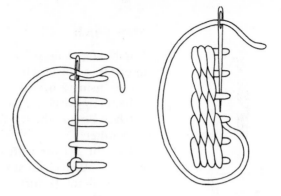

Repeat this procedure, working over the next horizontal stitch. Continue this way to the end of the design. Fasten the thread.

Begin again at the lower end. Make enough rows of stem stitches to cover the foundation stitches.

Sometimes the ends of the design are rounded. This is done by letting each row of stitches begin and end in the same place.

## Stem Stitch—Whipped

Wrapping stem stitches with another thread creates a heavy line with a corded effect. This stitch is often used to embroider stems or outline a design. Contrasting threads add interest.

Start by covering the line with stem stitches. To whip the stitches, bring up the needle at the left-hand end of the line. Carry the thread over the stitches. Slip the needle under a stitch without picking up any of the fabric. Space the whipping stitches evenly so the slant of the stitches remains the same.

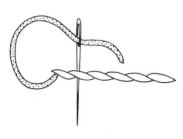

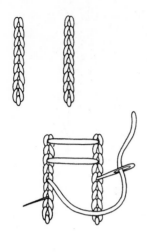

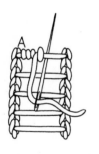

## Step Stitch

Combining chain stitches with bars produces an interesting border effect. It is worked in several stages, using a firm thread.

Begin by working 2 parallel lines of small chain stitches. Be sure the stitches are directly opposite each other.

Join the 2 rows with straight stitches placed in every other chain stitch. This makes a series of bars about ¼ inch (6 mm) apart, linking 2 chain stitches.

Bring up the needle at the left-hand end of the top stitch (A). With the thread to the left of the needle, wrap the thread around the horizontal stitch by passing the needle downward under the bar. Do this until half of the bar is covered.

When the center is reached, insert the needle in the fabric just above the stitch, letting it emerge just below the bar, ready to continue the wrapping process. This procedure makes a small straight stitch that will be used as an anchor for the remaining center stitches.

Continue to wrap the bar stitch. This time slip the needle upward under it.

To work the second bar, slip the needle under the fabric, returning it to the left-hand side. Wrap the bar to the center in the same way as for the first bar. At this point, slip the needle under the center stitch, bringing it back to the bar. The loop that is formed at the center creates a chain stitch effect. Continue to wrap the remainder of the bar.

Work the subsequent rows in the same way.

## Straight Stitch

This is a single, isolated flat or satin stitch. It can vary in length and direction but should not be loose. This stitch is most effective when used for short lines or grouped together to form a design, such as a flower. Do not use a straight stitch for curved lines or to cover a long line.

To make the stitch, bring the needle up at A. Insert it at B, coming up at C for the next stitch.

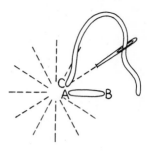

## Stroke Stitch

*See* Straight Stitch.

## Sword Stitch

By linking 2 stitches together, this interesting effect is obtained. Sword Stitch is easy to make and can be used as a filling or line stitch.

Before beginning the stitch, plan the placement of the 4 points that determine the length of the stitches—A, the starting point; B, to the right and above; C, to the right of B and in line with A; D, which marks the end of the stitch, below B. This portion of the stitch should appear longer than the other arms of the stitch.

Bring up the needle at A. Go down at B and up at C. Leave the stitch between A and B slightly loose. Pass the needle over and under this stitch. Insert it at D. Pull the thread slightly so the arms of the "sword" fall in place.

Begin the next stitch to the left of the first one. Continue the work in this way.

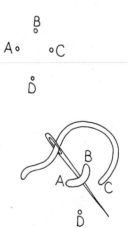

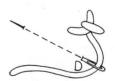

## Tent Stitch

This basic needlepoint stitch can be worked in various ways, moving diagonally, horizontally, or vertically. When the Tent Stitch is worked in a diagonal direction, it is also called Basket Weave Stitch.

**Tent Stitch—Diagonal.** Working in a diagonal direction is most successful. It creates a smooth, firm piece that wears well and seems to prevent the canvas from being pulled out of shape. The stitches are first worked downward with the needle held vertically, and then upward with the needle in a horizontal position.

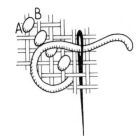

To begin a row of stitches, start at the upper point and work downward. Take a diagonal stitch over 1 intersection of canvas (A–B). Slip the needle vertically under the canvas, coming up 2 threads below.

When the first row is completed, begin the next one, working upward. Place the stitches to the left. Make a small stitch over a single intersection of canvas, placing it in a space left by the first row of stitches. To position the needle ready for the next stitch, slip it horizontally under 2 vertical threads of canvas.

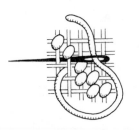

Continue in this way, working the rows alternately from top to bottom, and bottom to top, until area is covered.

**Tent Stitch—Horizontal.** To work the stitch horizontally, begin at the lower right-hand side of the area to be covered. Bring up the needle at A. Go down at B, 1 thread to the right and 1 above. This makes a diagonal stitch.

For the second stitch, come up at C, 2 threads to the left, on a line with A, going down at D. Continue to fill the row, working from right to left.

When the row is complete, turn the canvas. Work an identical row above the previous one. Use the same holes as in the first row. By your turning the canvas, the stitches can always be made from right to left.

**Tent Stitch—Vertical.** Make the stitches from the top of the work to the bottom. Begin at the upper point. Bring the needle up at A. Insert it at B, 1 thread to the right and 1 above. Come up at C, 2 threads below and 1 to the left, and then go down 1 thread to the right of A and below B, at D. Continue to the end of the row.

Turn the work so that the stitches can again be worked from the upper to the lower edge.

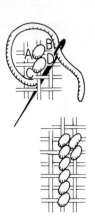

## Tête-de-boeuf Stitch

By combining detached chain and straight stitches, an attractive filling stitch is made. It is most effective when the stitches are arranged in alternating rows to create diagonal lines.

Begin with a detached chain stitch. To make it, bring the needle up at A. Let the thread form a loop. Insert the needle again at A, coming up at B. Pull it through the loop. Take a small stitch over the loop with the needle going down at C, to hold it in place.

Put a diagonal straight stitch on each side of the detached chain stitch.

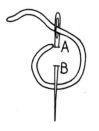

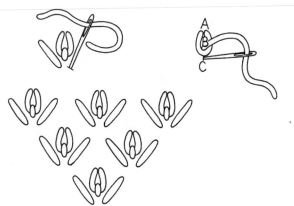

### Thorn Stitch

Straight stitches crossing over a central line seem to look like thorns on a stem.

Bring up the needle at one end of the line to be covered (A). Insert it at the other end (B), making the center line of the design.

Working from this end, let the needle emerge to the right and below (C). Take a diagonal stitch over the long stitch, inserting the needle close to it (D). The length of the stitch and the angle depends on the required effect.

Slip the needle under the fabric, coming up at E, marking the position of the next diagonal stitch. It should be equal in length and direction to the first one. Carry the thread over the center line, inserting the needle close to it (F). Notice that a tiny cross has been made.

The second group of stitches is constructed in the same way. The length and spacing can vary for each group.

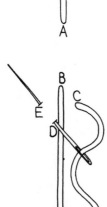

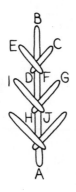

## Three-sided Stitch

This stitch creates an openwork effect. It is easier to work on fabric in which the threads can be counted. The design is comprised of a series of adjoining triangles. Two satin stitches form each side of the triangle. Pulling the stitches tight creates the open effect. Following the accompanying diagram makes the placement of the stitches easier to understand.

Working from right to left, bring up the needle at A. Insert it at B, 4 threads to the right. Return the needle to A. Go down again at B, coming up at A. The first 2 satin stitches have been made.

Begin the triangle by inserting the needle 2 threads to the right and 4 threads above A, at C. Return it to A and go down again at C.

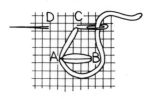

Slide the needle under the fabric, coming up at D, 4 threads to the left. Make 2 stitches between C and D. Follow with 2 stitches between D and A, with the needle emerging at E, 4 threads to the left of A, ready to begin the next group of stitches.

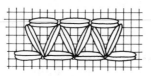

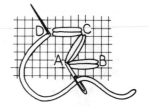

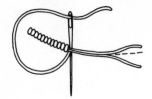

### Trailing Stitch
*See* Couching—Satin.

### Tramé Stitch

This is a long stitch used as a padding or backing in canvas work. A line of yarn is placed over the double threads of the canvas. The yarn should lie flat. If the line to be covered is too long to permit this, insert the needle in the canvas between the double threads. Pass the needle back under the canvas, coming up in the stitch that has been made, splitting it. Continue to the end of the line.

Work stitches over the traméing threads. The stitches should completely cover these threads.

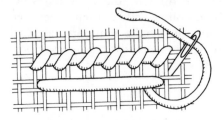

### Trellis Filling Stitch
*See* Couched Filling Stitch.

### Trellis Stitch

Loops, knots, and chain stitches characterize this filling stitch. The lacy effect requires a careful attention to details. The size of the loops must be kept even.

Begin by outlining the area to be covered with chain stitches or backstitches. Then bring the needle up in the center of the chain stitch in the upper left-hand corner (A). This is the last time the needle enters the fabric until the work is completed.

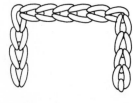

Slip the needle under the first horizontal chain stitch, coming up in the center (B). Leave a small loop between the 2 chain stitches.

Pass the needle under and through the loop from left to right. Pull the working thread tight, making a firm knot.

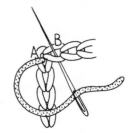

Slip the needle under the next horizontal chain stitch. Repeat the looping and knotting procedure. Continue this way until the right-hand side of the design is reached.

At the right-hand side, insert the needle in the middle of the first vertical chain stitch. Bring it up in the middle of the next vertical stitch.

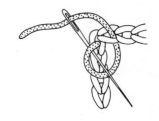

Now work from right to left. Continue to make the knotted stitches. For the first stitch, slip the needle upwards under the loop that falls between the first 2 knots (C). Then pass the needle from right to left under thread and through the loop (D), mirroring the procedure used for the left-hand corner. Notice that the knot slants alternately from right and left as the rows are worked. Continue in this way until the area is completely filled.

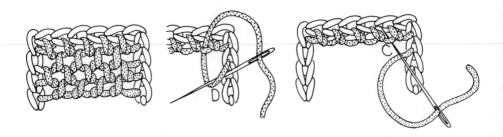

**Trellis Stitch—Cross-stitched**
   *See* Couched Filling Stitch.

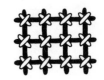

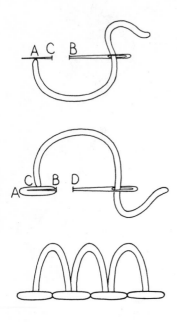

## Turkey Work

A combination of backstitches and loops create this shaggy stitch. The loops can be cut to give a ruglike effect or left uncut. This stitch can be worked on fabric or canvas, using yarn or embroidery floss.

Begin with a backstitch. Bring the needle up at A, down at B, and up at C. The thread should be below the stitch as it is made.

The second stitch is taken with the thread above the needle. Insert it at D, coming up at B. Instead of pulling the thread completely through, leave a loop the required length.

Continue to alternate the first and second stitches until the row is completed. Remember, when the thread is above the stitch a loop should be left, but not when it is below the stitch.

Keep all the stitches and loops even in length. Start each row at the left.

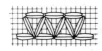

## Turkish Stitch
*See* Three-sided Stitch.

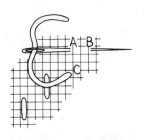
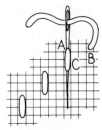
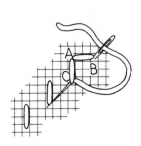

## Turkish Triangular Stitch

It is unusual to find a stitch that appears the same on both sides of the fabric, but this one does. Straight stitches are combined to produce a triangular design moving in a diagonal direction. The stitches can be used in a single row or duplicated for a filling. When the stitches are pulled tightly, an openwork effect is produced.

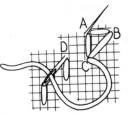

Make the stitches in 2 trips—upward and downward. Begin with a series of evenly spaced vertical stitches, made over 3 threads, with 3 threads separating them.

At the end of the row (A), slip the needle under the fabric, coming up 3 threads to the right (B), ready to start the downward trip. The spaces left by the vertical stitches are now filled in. Return the needle to A, bringing it up at C.

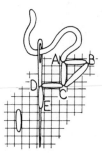

To complete the triangle, insert the needle at B, coming up at C.

Now move horizontally to the left and insert the needle at D. Slide it diagonally upward to A.

Return the needle to D, completing the second triangle. Let the needle emerge at E. Continue this way, alternating from right to left, when filling in the spaces.

Sometimes this stitch is called Triangular Two-sided Turkish Stitch.

## Two-sided Line Stitch
*See* Holbein Stitch.

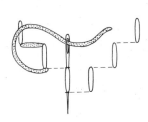

## Two-sided Stroke Stitch
*See* Holbein Stitch.

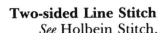

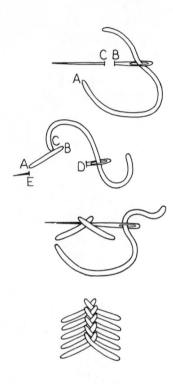

## Vandyke Stitch

A braided effect in the center of the design gives this stitch an interesting look. The crossed stitches at the center should remain even, although the length of the stitches can vary. It may be used for a line or band, and even as a filling for a leaf motif.

Begin at A, bringing the thread up at this point. Carry the thread diagonally upward. Insert the needle at B, slightly to the right of center. Slide the needle under the fabric, coming up at C, a short distance to the left. To complete the stitch, put the needle in the fabric at D, on a line with A. The 2 stitches should be the same length. Notice that a small cross has been made at the center.

To start the next stitch, slide the needle under the fabric to a point (E) below A. Bring up the needle. Slip it under the crossed threads at the center. Carry the thread to the right-hand side. Insert the needle below D. Be sure that the needle does not enter the fabric as it moves under the crossed stitches. Make the subsequent stitches in this way.

## Velvet Stitch

A cross stitch with a loop creates this canvas work stitch. It is most effective when made of a thick yarn on double-thread canvas. In making the stitch, care should be taken to keep all the loops the same length. The use of a knitting needle, pencil, or similar article as a gauge is helpful. Work from the lower edge upward. After the first row has been made, start the second row above it, allowing the loops to overlap the preceding row.

The stitch can be made in 2 ways. The **first method** starts with a diagonal stitch taken over 1 intersection of the canvas—A to B. This process is repeated, making a second diagonal stitch. This time, however, instead of drawing the thread tight, a loop the desired length is left.

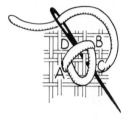

To finish the cross stitch, bring up the needle 1 thread below (C) and insert it diagonally, 1 thread above A, at D. The crossing of the previous stitches holds the loop in place.

Pass the needle under the canvas, emerging at C, ready to start the second cross stitch. When the area is covered, the loops can be cut and trimmed.

The **second method** for making the velvet stitch uses a three-step procedure. Instead of completing a stitch before beginning another, make a row of diagonal stitches over 1 intersection of canvas. Follow this with a second row of diagonal stitches, at which time the loops are made. The third step consists of another series of diagonal stitches that cross the first set, completing the stitch. Always work from left to right.

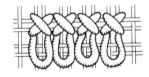

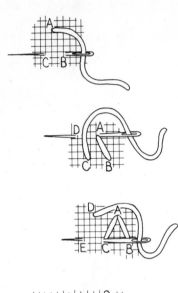

## Wave Filling Stitch

This drawn-fabric stitch creates a pattern of diamonds dotted with tiny eyelets when the stitches are pulled taut. The stitches move in a zigzag direction, with the needle always entering the fabric horizontally.

To establish the pattern, bring up the needle at A. Insert it at B, 4 threads down and 2 threads to the right, bringing it up again at C, 4 threads to the left. Insert the needle at A, letting it emerge 4 threads to the left (D).

Put the needle in the fabric again at C, coming up 4 threads to the left (E). Continue in this way to the end of the row.

At this point, after going down at F, come up 8 threads below, at G. Turn the work upside down. Begin the next row of stitches by inserting the needle at H.

Continue this way, alternating the work procedure for each row.

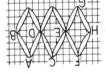

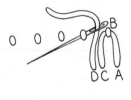

## Wave Stitch—Open

This filling stitch produces a lacy, looped effect. Begin with a row of small straight stitches placed at regular intervals across the top of the area to be covered.

Make the second row of stitches by slipping the needle under each of the straight stitches. To do this, bring the needle up at A. Slide it under the straight stitch at B. Be sure the needle does not enter the fabric as this is done. Insert it in the fabric at C. Let the needle emerge at D, the start of another stitch.

For the third and subsequent rows, slip the needle under adjoining arms of 2 stitches. To do this, bring up the needle at E. Slide it under the stitches in the first row at F. Return it to the fabric at G. Start the next stitch at H.

Continue in this way until the area is covered.

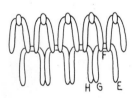

## Web Stitch

This canvas stitch creates a closely woven effect.
Diagonal stitches grow gradually longer, then
shorter, as the work progresses. Slanting stitches
hold them in place by crossing them at regular
intervals. Use double-thread canvas.

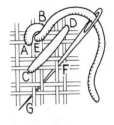

Start at the upper left-hand corner of the area
to be covered. Take a diagonal stitch over 1 intersection of the canvas, A to B. Work another
stitch parallel to and below it, over 2 intersections of the canvas, C to D. Bring the needle
up between these 2 stitches and the double
threads of canvas at the intersection (E). Pass
the thread over the second diagonal stitch at
right angles, inserting the needle in the intersection below (F).

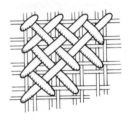

Bring the needle up at G, ready to begin the
next long diagonal stitch.

As the diagonal stitches get longer, alternate
the position of the crossing stitches to produce
the woven effect.

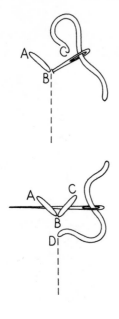

### Wheatear Stitch

This decorative design is worked downward. Start by making 2 diagonal straight stitches, bringing the needle up at A, down at B, up at C, and down close to B. Make the stitches at a right angle to each other.

Pass the needle under the fabric, coming up a little below B on the design line, at D. Carry the thread upward, slipping the needle under the 2 straight stitches from right to left. Return the needle to point D, completing a chainlike loop. Do not let the needle pick up the fabric as it passes under the straight stitches.

Let the needle re-emerge ready to begin the next series of stitches. Continue this way until the design line is covered.

### Wheatear Stitch—Detached

Although the effect is similar to that of the Wheatear Stitch, the construction is different. Make 2 diagonal straight stitches at right angles to each other. Over the base of these place a single daisy stitch. The stitches can be scattered in rows to cover an area.

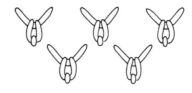

## Worm Stitch
*See* Bullion Knot or Stitch.

## Y Stitch
*See* Fly Stitch.

## Zigzag Stitch

The final effect of this stitch does not seem to relate to its construction. It is made by working first from right to left and then from left to right.

Begin by bringing the needle up at A. Insert it directly above, at B. Return the needle to A by passing it under the fabric, completing the first vertical stitch. Make a diagonal stitch by inserting the needle above and to the left, at C.

To make the next vertical stitch, bring the needle up at point D, below C. Return it to point C, coming up again at D ready to make the next diagonal stitch.

At the end of the row, begin the return trip to the starting point. Make the stitches in the same way, alternating between the vertical and diagonal stitches.

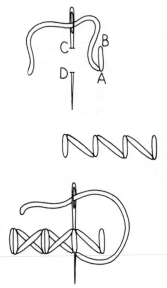

# STYLES AND TYPES OF EMBROIDERY

As the art of embroidery has developed, basic stitches have been employed or combined in special ways to create a characteristic style. Often its distinct look relates to a certain people, place, or area. Some of the most interesting embroidery is developed by adapting these embroidery styles.

## Assisi

In this type of decorative work, the background is embroidered, leaving the design plain. Cross stitches form the background. Sometimes the design is emphasized by defining it with the Holbein Stitch. It is a form of old Italian needlework. Traditionally, bright red or blue stitches were worked on creamy linen.

## Bargello

The word **bargello** is often thought to mean a stitch. Instead it should be identified as a form of design or embroidery. Sometimes it is referred to as Florentine work. Designs found in the Bargello Palace in Florence established the stitch patterns.

Bargello is worked on canvas in vertical stitches, forming peaks or points. By varying the colors, lovely shaded effects can be produced. Also, by using stitches in 2 lengths, long and short, interesting patterns develop. Bargello is sometimes called flame work or Hungarian point.

Begin bargello patterns by working horizontally across the center of the canvas, producing the first zigzag line. This creates a balance to the pattern. In most designs, the remaining rows of stitches follow this design line.

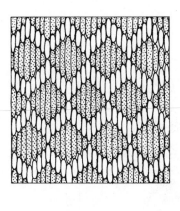

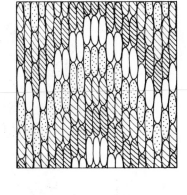

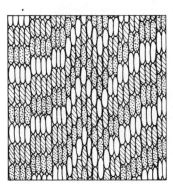

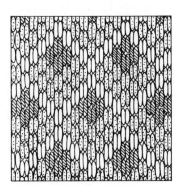

### Beadwork

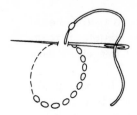

Adding beads to conventional stitches is referred to as beadwork. It is found in examples of Victorian needlework and in American Indian needlework.

Sew each bead on separately, using a beading needle to make the backstitch. This type of work can be used effectively as an outline and filling.

## Berlin Work

This is another type of canvas work embroidery. Cross and Tent stitches are usually employed to interpret the realistic designs. These might be an elaborate floral arrangement, a family pet, or a pictorial scene. Wools in bright colors were used, with the best yarns coming from Berlin. Although identified with Berlin, it was a popular form of embroidery in England and France—especially with the Victorian ladies. The designs were developed on squared paper so they could be worked on canvas.

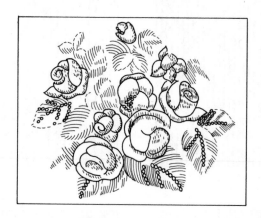

## Black Work

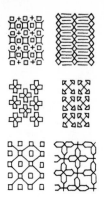

Black silk thread on white or cream linen, defining geometric designs, identifies this form of embroidery. It is probably of Spanish origin, with Arabic and Moorish influences. When Catherine of Aragon arrived in England, black work began to flourish there.

Simple stitches—Back, Cross, and Running— are used most often to develop the designs. Place them on fabric that allows the threads to be easily counted. Work with a blunt needle.

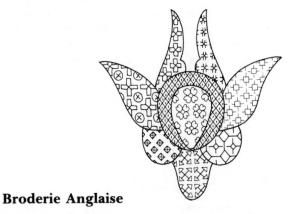

## Broderie Anglaise

Originally, broderie anglaise was a simple type of cutwork. Small round or oval eyelets were characteristic. Today the term is used to describe fine white work, combining eyelets with Buttonhole, Overcasting, Running, and Satin stitches. It is sometimes referred to as Madeira work.

## Candlewicking

This interpretation of the running stitch is associated with early American bedspreads. The running stitches are made of a special thick cotton thread. When the threads are cut, the design becomes a series of tiny tufts.

Usually the work is done on a good-quality muslin that has not been washed. For the running stitches, pick up about ⅛·inch (3 mm) of material on the needle, leaving about ¾ inch (2 cm) between the stitches. Keep the stitches flat and even so the fabric does not pucker. Cut the top stitches in half. In order to hold the stitches in place, put the work in warm water. Let it dry without ironing. Then shake, to fluff up the tiny tufts. The soaking seems to hold the threads in place.

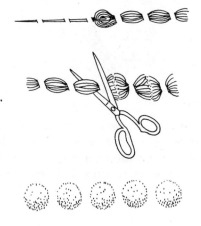

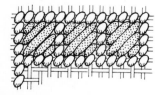

## Canvas Work

This type of embroidery is worked on an open, evenly woven mesh material called canvas. The work is called needlepoint and sometimes erroneously referred to as tapestry.

## Card Embroidery

Instead of fabric being used for the background or foundation, the stitches are worked on perforated paper or cards. This type of embroidery was popular during the nineteenth century. Designs were created by placing the thread through the holes in various ways. It was possible to copy different styles of embroidery.

## Composite Stitches

By combining various stitches, additional stitch patterns are formed. They are called composite stitches and are frequently found in different types of embroidery. They provide an excellent way of introducing metallic or heavy threads that should not be pulled through the material.

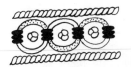

## Counted-thread Embroidery

This type of embroidery requires no design marking on the foundation fabric. The design is produced by counting threads. Each stitch is taken over a definite number of threads. To obtain the correct effect, the fabric and canvas must be woven evenly. Back, Cross, Four-sided, Hem, and Holbein stitches fall into this category.

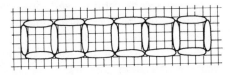

## Crewel Work

Crewel work is sometimes called Jacobean embroidery because it resembles this type of needlework, which was so popular in England during the latter part of the seventeenth century. It is noted for graceful, flowing designs, beautiful color combinations, and interesting use of stitches. The early designs were influenced by the lovely fabrics that Britain imported from China, India, and Persia. Stylized trees, fruits, and flowers were prominent design details. However, the word **crewel** actually refers to the wool yarn used. And so crewel work refers to embroidered stitches in wool.

A wide variety of stitches can be used. Among them are Back, Chain, Chevron, Cross, Fishbone, Long and Short, Satin, and Stem stitches. Linen has always been the traditional fabric for crewel work. However, other firmly woven fabrics, such as twill and ticking, can be used for modern adaptations.

## Cutwork

This style of embroidery creates an openwork effect. Parts of the design are cut away before or after the motif has been embroidered. There are two ways that this can be done.

If the fabric frays easily, the outline should be worked with a buttonhole stitch before cutting. Then, with very sharp scissors, cut away the material close to the looped edge.

If the material is firmly woven, however, the design can be cut out and the buttonhole stitch worked over the raw edges. Sometimes the background material is slashed enough to enable the material to be turned under before the buttonhole stitch is worked. If this method is used, the protruding bits of fabric must be cut away as close to the stitches as possible.

Whichever method is used, place tiny running stitches close to the edge. This gives a raised effect to the buttonhole stitches.

Picots or ornamental loops are an attractive feature of Italian cutwork.

## Drawn-fabric Work

This type of embroidery is sometimes confused with drawn-thread work. **Drawn-fabric** refers to embroidery in which the threads are not removed or fabric cut away. Instead, the threads are pulled together, creating an openwork effect. In fact, this type of work is sometimes referred to as openwork. Stitches such as the Punch and Three-sided create this effect.

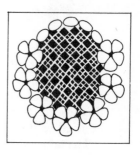

The stitches should be worked on a loosely woven fabric whose threads can be counted accurately. Use a blunt needle that can be slipped between the fabric threads without penetrating them. The thread should be fine and strong. It should not show, but at the same time it must be strong enough to pull the fabric threads apart and hold them in place without any danger of breaking.

## Drawn-thread Work

As its name implies, threads are removed from the embroidery material. This produces a lacy foundation on which to work the stitches. Hem-stitching is a form of drawn-thread work.

## Florentine Work

This style of embroidery is worked in the Florentine stitch—a basic counted-thread stitch moving in a vertical direction. The stitches are arranged to give a pointed effect, with subsequent rows following the design line of the first. It is also called bargello.

## Gros Point

When this term is used, it refers to the size of the stitches and canvas. Tent stitches are worked on a large-mesh canvas—8 to 12 meshes to the inch (2.5 cm).

## Hardanger

This distinctive form of embroidery is of Norwegian origin. It combines satin stitches with drawn- and cutwork. The satin stitches are usually worked in blocks. They can vary in shape, depending on the design. After the stitches are made, the threads are cut and withdrawn, one by one, as the design indicates.

In some of the designs, not all of the threads are removed. These threads are overcast or woven into bars. Various filling stitches can be used to decorate the spaces.

The fabric should have an even weave with the crosswise and lengthwise threads in perfect alignment. There should be the same number of threads to the inch in both the crosswise and the lengthwise direction.

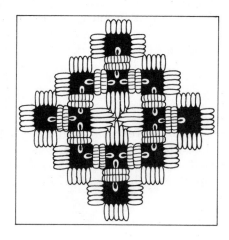

## Hedebo

This type of cutwork is of Danish origin. The openwork parts are cut away and filled in with a variety of lacy stitches. Satin stitches are used for solid areas, with Buttonhole Stitch covering the edges. The open area can vary in shape, depending on the design.

Begin the work by placing buttonhole stitches around the edge of the design. Fill in the opening with various stitches to produce a lacy pattern. Add satin stitches to complete the solid areas.

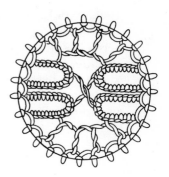

## Huck Embroidery

Huck toweling gives this style of embroidery its name. The textural quality of the fabric, with its pairs of raised threads, makes it possible to pass a thread under the raised threads.

Work on the back of the fabric. Using a blunt needle, slip the needle through a pair of raised threads, following the design. Do not let the needle penetrate the fabric. Six-strand floss or pearl cotton is generally used.

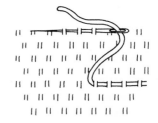

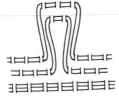

## Insertion Stitches

Sometimes it is necessary to hold 2 finished edges of material together. Certain embroidery stitches, such as Buttonhole Insertion, Faggoting, and Knotted and Twisted Insertion stitches, provide an attractive linking. An openwork effect results.

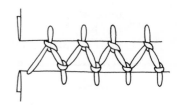

## Laid Work

In this type of embroidery, a large design area is covered with threads placed close together. The long threads are held in place with a second series of stitches made in a diagonal or crisscross direction. Although the threads create the effect of satin stitches, the stitches do not extend across the back of the design. Instead, after the first stitch has been made from A to B, start the second stitch by bringing the needle up close to B, at point C.

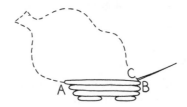

## Machine Embroidery

Although many feel that the beauty of hand embroidery cannot be duplicated by machine, there are times when this type of needlework may seem more appropriate. A decorative touch on jeans and a monogram on a bath towel falls into this category. Those who enjoy sewing by machine more than by hand will probably find it fun to create a decorative trim this way.

The results depend on the skill with which the machine is used. Perfect control is needed. Gaining this skill, just like playing a musical instrument, requires practice. However, when this skill is acquired, machine embroidery offers a quick way to produce a pleasing trim.

It should be remembered that, no matter what type of sewing machine one has, some form of embroidery can be done. A straight-stitch machine allows for a free style of embroidery as well as the decorative use of simple rows of straight stitches. Even a zigzag design can be produced by adding an attachment. And of course the zigzag machine offers both the automatic zigzag stitch patterns and the free-style type of embroidery.

**Designs.** The designs employed for hand embroidery can usually be adapted for machine work. It depends on one's ability to translate the effect of hand stitches into machine stitches.

A continuous line effect that is made by Chain, Back, Outline, Running, and Stem stitches can be simulated with straight stitching or small zigzag stitches. Adding a thicker thread or yarn can give the effect of couching.

For filling in an area, replace Chain or Satin stitches with free-style machine embroidery worked on either the straight or zigzag machine. Spots of Satin stitches can be used in place of detached stitches, such as the French Knot and Seed Stitch.

Today it is easy to find designs appropriate for machine embroidery. Suggestions for hot-iron and pressure transfer designs can be found in pattern catalogues and in some magazines and leaflets. However, if these do not seem appropriate, you can create a personal motif or trace one from a favorite design, perhaps found on fabric.

**Transferring a design** to fabric can be done in several ways. For the hot-iron transfer method, read the directions accompanying the design carefully for correct temperature settings and timing. They vary according to the fabric. Test the directions on a scrap of the same material. Cut out the design. Protect the ironing board with an old piece of fabric such as a sheet. Place the transfer ink side down on the right side of the fabric. Place the heated iron on the transfer for the correct length of time. Raise the iron straight up—never slide it from side to side. Remove the transfer. The design should be clearly defined. Sometimes it is necessary to wash the material first to remove the sizing in order to get a clear outline.

It is possible to produce a hot-iron transfer by using a special pencil made for this purpose. Trace the design onto transparent paper. Remember to trace the wrong side instead of the right if a specific direction in the design, as in a monogram, must be maintained.

If the hot-iron method is not feasible, transfer the design with straight stitching or with dressmaker's carbon paper. On sheer fabrics, the design can be traced with a sharp marking pencil—never a lead pencil. Instead of plain fabric, a patterned one can be employed with the embroidery stitches superimposed.

**Equipment.** It is obvious that a sewing machine is needed with correct needles. In the optional category are the embroidery foot or spring, hoop, and plate for covering the feed dog. Their use depends on the type of embroidery and sewing machine being used.

An **embroidery hoop,** in a 6- or 8-inch (15 cm or 20.5 cm) size, is often used for free-style embroidery. It keeps the fabric taut so puckers will not develop. Although the hoop is the same as that used for hand embroidery, it is employed in a different way. To place

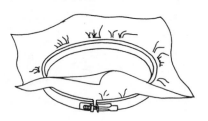

the fabric in it, put the outer ring on the table. Lay the material over it with the right side up. Press the small ring inside the larger one. Be sure the fabric is very taut and that the threads cross each other at right angles. Tighten the screw if necessary. Pushing the small ring about ⅛ inch (3 mm) below the outer edge of the outside ring helps to keep the fabric firm.

A needle in the correct size is a necessity. It should be fine, smooth, and sharp. The number depends on the brand of the sewing machine. Always use the specific one suggested for the machine. Before starting to stitch, make sure that it is correctly set. Change it the minute it becomes slightly blunt.

Sometimes a **special plate** covers the feed dog. This is necessary on some machines in order to control the action of the feed dog.

The **presser foot** is removed for certain types of embroidery. This is done when the operator is controlling the movement of the fabric for free-style embroidery. A darning or embroidery foot or spring can be used in its place. If an attachment is being added, replace the presser foot with it.

Although **sewing machines** bear many different manufacturers' names, they fall into two general types: the straight-stitch and the zigzag-stitch. The straight-stitch machine sews forward and backward in a straight line with the needle moving up and down. An attachment or accessory can be added to the machine to produce a zigzag effect.

The automatic zigzag machine also sews backward and forward, but the needle moves from side to side to form a zigzag pattern. By adjusting the width and length of the stitch, the stitches can be made to appear wide or narrow, apart or close together. The machine is also programmed to make different stitch patterns. By setting a dial or inserting a disk or cam, one of many patterns can be selected and repeated automatically.

Knowing the sewing machine—each part and how it performs—is a must. Carefully study the manual that accompanies the machine. Keep the machine in excellent condition. It should be completely

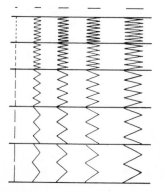

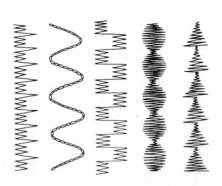

free of lint, oiled, and lubricated so the parts run smoothly and without noise.

Two things that need consideration are the **feed dog** and **tension.**

**Feed dog** may seem like a strange name for the tiny teeth that appear under the presser foot. This part is responsible for moving the fabric. In free-style embroidery, this function is not needed. The feed dog should therefore be lowered or covered with a special plate.

**Tension** plays an important part in machine embroidery. The correct tightness or looseness of the thread is needed for certain effects. The upper tension can be adjusted by turning the screw in the correct direction. To obtain just the proper amount requires a gentle touch.

The adjustment of the bobbin tension demands more skill. The screw on the bobbin case must be turned carefully. In fact, it should be adjusted only when it is impossible to get the proper effect simply by turning the upper tension screw.

Learn to operate the machine at an even speed, guiding the fabric gently and smoothly. Always feel that you are in perfect control of the speed and direction.

**Fabric and thread.** A wide variety of materials can be used for machine embroidery. In fact, there are few limitations except those imposed by the sewing machine. Because of this, always test the stitching on the specific material before starting the embroidery.

Generally, **fabrics** made of natural fibers, such as cotton and linen, seem to produce better results. Puckers tend to develop less frequently. When they do, there is a possibility that they may be removed by pressing.

Backing the fabric helps to prevent puckering. Indeed, the backing is almost a necessity if the fabric is fine or soft. It provides the necessary stability. Organdy is frequently employed, as is a non-woven interfacing. The backing can be cut away after the stitching has been completed. Tissue paper is another backing material; however, its removal does cause a problem. Small pieces must be picked out. Using tweezers may make the job easier. Sometimes placing the work in water will dissolve the tissue. Of course, this should only be done if it seems right for the fabric.

**Thread** depends on the type of embroidery. A fine cotton thread, made especially for machine embroidery, is best. It is smooth and lustrous and less liable to break, fray, or knot.

Thicker threads and yarns can be used for special effects. The type depends on the capabilities of the sewing machine. If the thread will not pass through the needle eye, it may be possible to use it for the bobbin thread or to lay it on the surface, using a couching technique to anchor it in place. Buttonhole twist is among the thicker threads that can be used. When working with a thicker thread, combine it with regular machine embroidery thread.

**Styles and stitches.** Machine embroidery falls into three types: free-style, straight stitching, and zigzag stitching. Each type can be achieved if the capabilities of the machine allow for it. Before starting the work, be sure that the machine is clean and in perfect condition.

Machines vary according to brand and style, so only general guidelines can be given here. Study the directions found in the manual that accompanies the machine. Follow them carefully. Start by working on a practice piece using the same fabric and thread as for the actual embroidery. Record the stitch and tension setting. File this information with the sample swatch for future reference.

**Free-style stitching** allows a certain creativity that cannot be achieved in other types of machine embroidery. Removing the presser foot, lowering or covering the feed dog, and then moving the fabric freely in any direction produces a sense of abandonment that structural types of sewing cannot give. Although this technique can be used for creating definite designs, it is fun just to move the material in random fashion and be surprised with the results. Let the fabric move forward, backward, sideways, and diagonally for curving and geometric patterns. Free-style embroidery can be done by straight and zigzag stitching.

The directions for using the machine will suggest that the presser foot be replaced with a darning or embroidery foot or embroidery spring. Although the work can be done without these pieces of equipment, they do help to protect the fingers—one thing that must be carefully watched. It is so easy to let the fingers slip under the needle when guiding the fabric.

The directions will also mention whether the feed dog can be lowered or whether it must be covered. Since the fabric is being moved by hand, the feed dog is not needed.

Be sure to thread the machine correctly and check tension and stitch length for desired effect. When the machine is ready, put the fabric in a hoop and slip it under the needle and foot.

Select the spot for the first stitch. It is usually best to start at the center of the design. Insert the needle in the fabric by turning the hand wheel. Lower the presser foot lever. This is something that is easy to forget if a foot is not used. The lever controls the tension, and unless it is lowered there will be unwanted loops and tangled threads.

To secure the thread ends, hold the upper thread in the left hand as the needle is lowered and raised. A gentle tug on the thread will bring a loop of bobbin thread to the upper side. Pull the loop through the fabric. Hold the 2 threads together while making 2 or 3 stitches in place. Do this by turning the hand wheel. Then clip the thread ends.

In order to guide the fabric, place the fingers in a position that makes it easy to control and, at the same time to keep the material against the needle plate. Some people like to keep the thumb and little finger outside the hoop to guide it, with the middle fingers inside, holding the material down.

Move the hoop smoothly, working at a moderate speed. Stitching too fast, with jerky motions, will break the thread. Check frequently to be sure that the threads are not bunching on the underside. End by holding the threads together so there will be no strain on the embroidery. This technique keeps the embroidery from puckering.

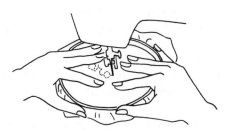

For **free-style zigzag** embroidery, follow the same general techniques. Remember, however, that the needle moves from side to side instead of just up and down. Practice to co-ordinate the movement of the fabric with that of the needle. Work forward, backward, sideways, diagonally, or around curves. When stitching around a curve, it is usually better to slide around it rather than to turn the fabric.

The **satin stitch** is probably the one most frequently used. The stitches can be worked in various directions for a solid effect. Small solid blocks of stitches can produce the effect of French knots.

For outlining a design or constructing design lines, a **side stitch** is useful. The width of the stitch depends on the effect desired. Move the work sideways along the design line. Allow the needle to swing from side to side in the direction of the line. The width of the zigzag stitch decides the thickness of the embroidered stitching line.

A side-type stitch can be used for **filling** in an area. However, do not follow the design line. Instead, work in an irregular, side-to-side motion. Usually it is best to use a narrow stitch for small areas, a wide one for large ones. Sometimes the stitching must fan out to create the desired effect. For this work in a side-to-side motion while rotating the hoop gradually. Design areas can also be filled in by stitching in a random fashion, creating an open or closed effect.

When **shading** is needed, begin the embroidery at the center of the design. Fill in the area as far as necessary, leaving some spaces along the outer edge. This allows a new color to be introduced for a blended effect.

**Straight stitching** can produce decorative effects, although it is usually thought of in its functional capacity. Variations in thread color, type, or weight and in stitch length and tension provide many ways of producing embroidered looks. Combining hand and machine stitches also offers possibilities.

Using a heavier thread, such as buttonhole twist or pearl cotton, gives topstitching a decorative look. Sometimes it is impossible to stitch with a heavier thread as the upper one. In such a case, wind it on the bobbin. Adjust the stitch length and tension to obtain the correct effect. Work on the wrong side so the heavier thread appears on the right side. Check the placement of the stitches frequently.

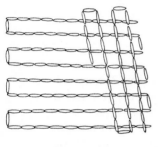

Stitching in parallel rows, crossing at right angles, produces a crosshatched effect. It makes an attractive filling for a design area. Begin with a row of stitches. At the end of the row, raise the presser foot. Leave the needle in the material and turn. Lower the presser foot and take 1 or 2 stitches. The number depends on the spacing desired. Then repeat the turning procedure and stitch another row. Use the presser foot as a guide in keeping the stitching an even distance from the first row.

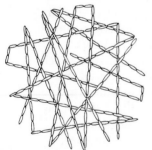

When all of the rows have been made in this direction, turn the material so that crossing lines can be stitched. This forms a checkered pattern of stitches. Diagonal rows of stitches can be added.

For a more informal pattern, the crosshatching can be done by stitching first forward and then backward. This develops an irregular design with a pointed effect at the outer edges.

Attractive embroidered effects result when yarn or cord is laid on the surface and held in place with a row of straight stitching. The task is easier if a special foot is used to hold the yarn or cord in place. This allows the stitches to fall directly in the center.

Rows of straight stitching can also form a base for interlacing threads. After the machine stitching is completed, pass a needle threaded with embroidery thread under the stitches to form a pattern of loops.

Another effect can be achieved by loosening the bobbin tension and tightening the upper one. This allows tiny loops to appear on the right side. The size of the loops depends on the looseness of the tension.

Straight stitching can also be used as an accent. Outline the design details with a row of stitches. Using a contrasting thread makes it most effective.

**Zigzag stitching** offers interesting possibilities for embroidery, although it is usually seen as rows of geometric pattern stitches. Setting a dial or inserting a cam is an easy way to produce embroidery. To do automatic zigzag, consult the manual accompanying the machine for available stitch patterns and machine adjustments to achieve the desired effects. It is usually better to embroider a piece of fabric rather than a finished item. To do this, plan the placement of the embroidery so that it will fall in the correct place when the pattern is cut out.

The most frequent use of automatic zigzag stitches is for borders and bands. The various stitch patterns can be used alone or combined in individual ways. It is also possible to simulate certain hand embroidery effects. By shortening the basic zigzag stitch, a satin-type stitch results. Placing satin stitches over a piece of yarn or cord results in a solid raised effect. When open zigzag stitches are worked over a piece of yarn or cord, the look is similar to couching. A row of zigzag stitches can replace hand overcast stitches to secure the threads at the top of a fringed edge. Using unequal tension and length of the zigzag stitches can produce an effect similar to a feather stitch. By using a special cam or machine setting, an eyelet can be made for an openwork effect. Instead of blanket stitches, a zigzag can be placed over an edge for a decorative effect. Rows of zigzag stitches can be put close together to give the effect of encroaching stitches.

## Metal Thread Work

Examples of ancient embroideries show the use of gold and other metals. Because of the difficulty of manipulating this type of thread, the threads were often couched in place. Today there are metallic threads that can be used to reproduce similar effects.

## Monogramming

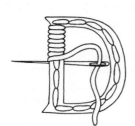

Embroidering one's initials on clothing or household linens adds a personal touch. The initials should be carefully designed and placed. To give the stitches a rounded effect, pad the area to be embroidered. This can be done in various ways. Define the outline with tiny running stitches or cover the area with chain or running stitches. Then cover these stitches with satin stitches.

Instead of using the monogramming technique, fill the area with rows of chain or outline stitches, cross stitches, or French knots. This method is easier.

## Needlepoint

Needlepoint, or needlework tapestry, is the art of putting stitches, made with needle and thread, on openwork mesh canvas so that the canvas is completely covered. This procedure creates the effect of loom tapestry. Various stitches worked on different sizes of canvas produce different results, varying from the very fine to the very coarse.

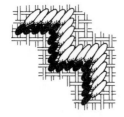

Sometimes needlepoint has been known as Berlin work, canvas work, cushion style, and opus pulvinarium. Today it is a general term that includes gros point, quick point, and petit point.

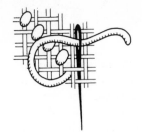

The Tent Stitch is the basic one. It is often referred to in other terms such as Basket Weave, Continental, Gros Point, and Petit Point. **Basket Weave** indicates that the stitch is worked diagonally; **Continental,** horizontally or vertically; **Gros Point,** on large-mesh canvas; **Petit Point,** on very-small-mesh canvas.

## Needleweaving

This is a form of drawn work. Threads are pulled from the fabric and then replaced by weaving a design pattern over and under the remaining threads. It is often referred to as Swedish weaving and can produce colorful borders.

Work with fabric from which threads can be removed easily and on an exact on-grain alignment. Use 6-thread floss or pearl cotton to create the design.

## Net Embroidery

Embroidery stitches can be placed on net or tulle to create the effect of old pillow lace. Some of the stitches that can be used are Blanket, Darning, Running, and Stem.

The hexagonal mesh fabric should be strong enough to resist breaking while being embroidered. The weight of the thread can vary, depending on the effect desired. Never use a knot. Instead, darn in the ends of the thread.

To develop the design, count the meshes or place a stiff paper on which the pattern is marked under the net. Defining the design with running stitches sometimes simplifies the work.

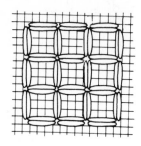

### Openwork

As the name implies, the embroidery creates an open effect. To obtain this look, threads are not removed from the fabric. Instead, the threads are pulled together to produce small holes. It is often referred to as pulled-thread work or drawn-fabric work.

It is impossible to create openwork on all types of fabrics. One that is accurately woven but in a fairly loose fashion, so that the threads can be separated easily, is needed. The thread for the stitches should be strong, so it will not break when the stitches are tightened.

Openwork is used mainly as a filling. Stitches such as the Punch, Three-sided, and Four-sided create the correct effect.

### Petit Point

This term refers to needlepoint worked in fine yarn on very small, single-thread canvas, usually about 20 meshes to the inch (2.5 cm) or smaller.

### Pulled-thread Work

This type of embroidery is often referred to as openwork or drawn-fabric work. As its name implies, fabric threads are not removed but instead are pulled apart and secured by stitches.

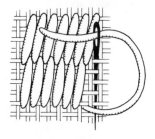

### Quick Point

When needlepoint is worked on a large-mesh canvas, 5 to 7 to the inch (2.5 cm), it is called quick point. Rug or doubled tapestry yarns are needed to cover the canvas.

## Raised Work

This type of embroidery can be worked on canvas or fabric. It is usually done in wool. When the stitch is completed, it stands above the foundation, giving a 3-dimensional realism to a design.

## Reticella Work

This is a form of cutwork. Of all of the cutworks, this is the most open type, creating an elaborate effect.

## Richelieu Work

This is another type of cutwork. Picots and buttonhole bars dominate the work. It is named for a seventeenth-century Venetian lace.

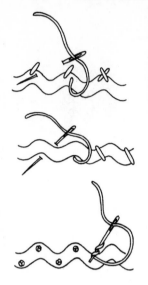

### Rickrack Embroidery

Adding embroidery stitches to rickrack gives a new dimension to needlework. Dainty stitches take on a bold look when combined with rickrack. It is quick and easy to do, allowing for imaginative use of stitches, colors, and textures. The points become the focal point for the stitches.

Begin by planning the placement of the rickrack. Baste it in position. Then, with embroidery floss, thread, or yarn, hold the trim in place with embroidery stitches. There are many that can be used, such as Cross, Diagonal, Fern, French Knot, Herringbone, Detached Chain, and Straight stitches. They can be placed at the points or pass over the braid.

## Sampler

Originally this term referred to a test piece of embroidery. The basic stitches were perfected by working on a bit of fabric before the real needlework began. By the seventeenth century, these practice pieces had taken a definite form and were called samplers.

### Shadow Work

Originally this type of embroidery was worked on sheer fabric with stitches placed on the wrong side so they showed through in shadow effect. The Crossed or Double Backstitch creates the correct illusion.

Today shadow appliqué is also included. Another piece of material is basted to the wrong side of the material. The design is then defined with Three-sided or Point de Paris stitches. The extra fabric surrounding the design is cut away on the wrong side.

## Smocking

Smocking provides a decorative method for gathering a piece of material into regular folds. Lovely effects can be created when it is worked on soft fabrics.

**General directions.** Holding the fullness in place can be done in two ways. In the first, the decorative stitch controls the folds; in the second, small, uneven basting stitches gather the material and the decorative stitches are added.

Certain types of smocking, such as those creating a zigzag or wavy effect, should be placed on gathered fabric. However, either method can be used for cable and outline smocking. Whichever method is employed, the important thing to remember is that the folds or gathers are kept even.

Smocking is worked before the article is constructed. Usually the piece of fabric to be smocked is 3 or 4 times the width of the finished area.

In order to keep the folds even, mark the fabrics with a series of dots to show the placement of the stitches. This can be done by using a commercial transfer pattern or by lightly penciling the dot on the fabric. If the material is to be gathered before the smocking begins, place the dots on the wrong side. Otherwise, the marks will appear on the right side. Usually the dots are ¼ to ½ inch (6 to 13 mm) apart.

If the fabric is to be gathered, work rows of small uneven basting stitches on the wrong side. Start with a strong knot. Sew from right to left, placing a tiny stitch under each dot. At the end of a row, leave the thread unfastened and remove the needle. Repeat this process for each row of dots.

When the rows of basting stitches have been completed, take all of the thread ends in the left hand and gently pull them so that the fabric falls in regular folds. Wrap the threads securely around one or more pins, placed at the end of the gathered rows. Remove the gathering threads after embroidering the decorative stitches.

**Cable Stitch Smocking.** Working from left to right, begin by bringing the needle to the right side of the fabric through the first dot. Put the thread above the needle. Insert the needle in the fabric a short distance to the right of the second dot. Let it reappear at the dot. For the second stitch, hold the thread below the needle. Take another stitch at the third dot. Repeat this procedure, alternating the placement of the thread above and below the stitches until the row is completed.

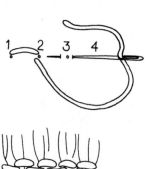

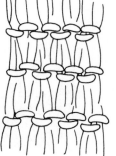

**Chevron or Diamond Smocking.** Work from left to right. Bring the needle to the right side of the material through the first dot in the second row. Holding the thread below the needle, insert the needle to the right of dot 2 in the second row. Bring it up, passing through dot 2. Tighten the thread by pulling it at right angles to the stitch.

The next stitch is made in the first row by taking a stitch through dot 3 in the first row. Then hold the thread above the needle and make a stitch through dot 4. Pull the thread tight so that a small horizontal stitch is made, holding the fabric together in folds. Continue this procedure, working from dot to dot, following the sequence of numbers as shown on the accompanying diagram.

When the stitches have been made in the first and second rows, start to embroider along the third and fourth. Bring up the needle through the dot lettered A, directly below dot 1. Make a stitch through dot B, pulling the thread tight. Take the next stitch in the fourth row through dot C and another one through dot D. Continue this sequence of stitches until the third and fourth rows are completed.

Although the horizontal stitches on the underside of the fabric should be pulled tight in order to create the necessary folds, the thread that lies on the right side should not. The smocking will be drawn out of shape if it is.

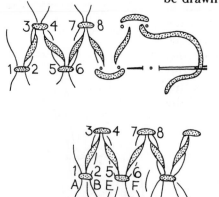

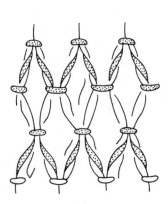

**Honeycomb or Seed Smocking.** Start at the left-hand side of the work. Bring the needle to the right side of the material through the first dot. Take a small stitch under dot 2 and then dot 1 by inserting the needle to the right of dot 2, letting it emerge through dot 2, re-entering the fabric to the right of dot 1, and coming up through dot 1. To tighten the stitches, pull the thread upward at right angles to the stitch.

Insert the needle at dot 2, leaving 2 horizontal stitches on the right side. Come up through dot 3, which is in the second row of dots. Repeat this procedure using dots 3 and 4, with the following 2 stitches taken in the first row between dots 5 and 6. Continue in this way, working from dot to dot in groups of 2 and in the order in which they are numbered.

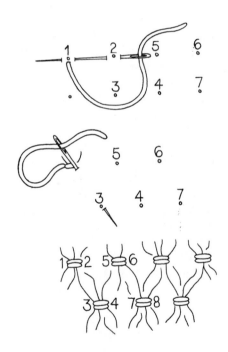

**Lattice Smocking.** This is a different type of smocking. There is no evidence of stitches on the right side, but, instead, deep, soft folds. They are made by taking tiny stitches on the wrong side, following a series of dots. This type of smocking has been most effectively used for decorative pillows. Although various fabrics can be used, velvet seems to create the most beautiful results.

If, however, one is not available, the back of the fabric can be marked with dots in vertical rows with the rows 1 inch (2.5 cm) apart. The number of dots will depend on the size of the article being made. Use an odd number of dots horizontally, an even number vertically. Be sure to place the dots on the straight of the fabric, keeping the rows evenly placed.

Work in vertical rows, progressing from dot to dot in a definite sequence with the stitches following a diagonal direction. Three lines of dots are needed for each smocked row.

Use a strong thread such as buttonhole twist or heavy-duty sewing thread. Put a knot at the end of the thread.

Start the work at the upper left side. Sew on the wrong side. Take a tiny stitch under dot A, passing the needle from right to left. Make another stitch at this same point.

Move the needle to dot B and take a stitch. Then return the needle to dot A and make another stitch. Draw dots A and B together and fasten securely, with several small stitches in place or a knot.

Take the next stitch at dot C. Loop the thread above this point, slipping the needle under the thread connecting dots A and C. Pull the thread tightly at dot C to form a knot, but keep fabric flat between dots A and C.

Slip the needle under dot D, returning to dot C. Pick up dot C again. Pull dots C and D together and fasten thread securely.

Proceed to dot E. Make a stitch. Slip needle under thread connecting dots C and E. Pull thread tightly at dot E to form knot, but remember to keep fabric flat between dots C and E.

Continue to work down row of dots, repeating the above procedure. Follow the lettering, taking the next stitch at dot F.

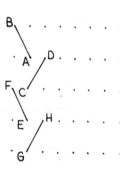

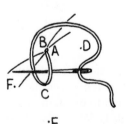

**Outline Stitch Smocking.** Start at the left-hand end of a row of dots placed an equal distance apart. Bring the needle up at the first dot. Hold the thread above the needle. Insert the needle a short distance to the right of the second dot. Slip the needle under the fabric, coming up through the dot. Pull the threads so that the fold is formed. Repeat the procedure until one stitch has been made at each dot in the row.

If the design requires the embroidering of a second row of outline stitches, close to the first, make the stitches in the same way but with this exception: hold the thread under the needle instead of above it.

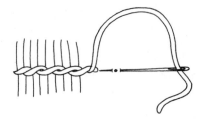

## Stump Work

White satin with fine silken threads was the material traditionally used for stump work. This elaborate form of needlework was popular during the seventeenth century. Garden scenes were favored, with parts of the design raised from the background in high relief. To give this effect, padding was done with wool, horsehair, or wooden molds on the white satin background. The padded areas were then covered with heavy silk upon which stitches were embroidered. Lacy stitches, such as Hollie, were combined with various laid stitches to add to the three-dimensional effect.

Today an adaptation of stump work can be done by combining appliqué and raised wool embroidery. Raise the appliqué with padding. Add to the three-dimensional look with Buttonhole, Trellis, and Turkey Work stitches.

## Swedish Weaving

Needleweaving is sometimes called Swedish weaving.

## Tambour Work

A chain stitch distinguishes this type of embroidery. However, it is not made in the usual way. A special needle similar to a crochet hook is needed. The thread is drawn in and out through the fabric.

This form of embroidery originated in the East. The frame, resembling a drum (tambour) in shape, was held between the knees of the worker as he worked cross-legged on the floor. A lacy effect is obtained when the embroidery is done on fine fabric.

## Teneriffe Embroidery

This type of needlework resembles drawn-thread work or needleweaving in effect. However, the stitches are made on top of the material instead of through it. Bars form a foundation onto which various stitches can be made or woven. Gingham works well when making a square motif.

## Tufted Wool Embroidery

Floral designs can be given a three-dimensional effect by embroidering Turkey Work loops, using wool yarn. Begin by working the stems in Outline or Stem Stitch. Then, starting in the center, embroider the largest flower with Turkey Work stitches. When these are completed, cut the loops. Some areas can be graded to give a rounded feeling to the pile.

## Tufting

This is a term sometimes used in place of **candlewicking.**

## Turkey Work

This style of embroidery tries to duplicate the textures and designs of Turkish rugs. The stitches can be worked on coarse fabric or canvas. The Plush Stitch is another term for the Turkey Work stitch.

## White Work

This is an umbrella term covering all embroidery in which white threads are worked on white fabric. It is usually thought of as being dainty and lacy. Cutwork and drawn threads combine with many stitches to create this look.

## Wool Work

This is a general term that encompasses various embroideries worked in wool.

# Part III
# Knitting

Knitting has an interesting history. When it began no one is quite sure, but knitted articles dating back to A.D. 200 have been found. While the date is indefinite, historians do agree on where it originated. They feel that knitting was first created in Arabia. Apparently Arabian sailors and traders, as they traveled from country to country, taught people the technique. It offered so many possibilities for the construction of attractive as well as utilitarian articles that its use became widespread.

Like other types of needlecraft, knitting has passed through various fluctuations in popularity. Fortunately, that period in knitting history is over, and today knitting is established as a fashion item.

The knitting section is divided into 5 parts. Each is arranged in alphabetical order for easy reference.

## ABBREVIATIONS AND TERMS

Knitting has a language of its own. Unless one understands the meaning of the words and phrases, it is impossible to transform yarn into fabric by using 2 needles. To avoid a confusing situation, one should study the definitions of knitting terms, interpreting them with action. This practice makes it easier to read directions and to avoid mistakes.

Directions for making a knitted article are usually written in abbreviated terms. The abbreviations vary from author to author, country to country. At first they may seem confusing, meaningless, and difficult to remember. However, it is often possible to break the code if one realizes that, in many instances, the first letter of the word becomes the abbreviation.

Always study the meaning of abbreviations before beginning to knit. If the directions contain unfamiliar procedures, mark the pages on which the abbreviations are listed for quick reference. Unusual abbreviations and directions often need frequent checking in order to avoid mistakes. As every one knows, mistakes are time-consuming and annoying to correct. For a quick reference, the most commonly used abbreviations and terms are listed on the facing page. Some of the abbreviations need specific explanation for perfect understanding. This information is given here, as well as an interpretation of terms that are abbreviated but need more defining.

| | |
|---|---|
| b | back |
| BC | back cross |
| beg | beginning |
| dec | decrease |
| dec L | decrease left |
| dec R | decrease right |
| d.p. or dpn | double-pointed |
| FC | front cross |
| in(s) | inch(es) |
| incl | inclusive |
| inc | increase |
| inc L | increase to the left |
| inc R | increase to the right |
| K | knit |
| kb | knit into back of stitch |
| LH | left-hand needle |
| M 1 | make one stitch |
| pnso or p.n.s.o. | pass or pull next stitch over |
| psso or p.s.s.o. | pass or pull slipped stitch over |
| pu 1 | pick up one stitch |
| P | purl |
| Pb | purl into back of stitch |
| rep | repeat |
| * or ** | repeat directions in same order following asterisk |
| * * or ( ) | repeat directions found between asterisks or parentheses |
| RH | right-hand needle |
| rnd | round |
| sp | single-pointed |
| sl, s | slip |
| ssk | slip, slip knit |
| st(s) | stitch(es) |
| tog | together |
| tw | twist |
| yo or o | yarn over |
| yh or wyib | yarn to back of work |
| yf or wyif | yarn to front of work |

### Cross Knit

This is a variation of plain knitting. It is sometimes referred to as Italian or Twist Stitch. Instead of working into the front of the stitch, place the needle in the back. The row of purl stitches is made in the regular way.

### Cross Purl

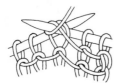

This technique creates a purling variation. Instead of inserting the needle into the front of the stitch, put it into the back. Plain knitting is used for the knit row.

### Decreasing

To shape a knitted piece, the number of stitches can be reduced. This can be done in various ways. The 2 methods most commonly used are mentioned here.

**Method 1.** Two stitches are knitted together for this method of decreasing. It is done on a knit row.

To decrease in knitting, place the right-hand needle through the front of the second stitch and then through the first. Make a regular knit stitch, drawing the yarn through both stitches. Slip the 2 stitches off the needle as 1, decreasing the number of stitches by 1.

This method can also be used for knitting more than 2 stitches together.

To decrease in purling, purl 2 stitches together on a purl row.

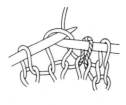

**Method 2.** Another method utilizes a slip stitch. Slip 1 stitch from the left-hand needle to the right-hand one without knitting. Then knit the next stitch.

Using the left-hand needle, bring the slipped stitch over the knitted one and off the tip of the right-hand needle.

An abbreviation seen in directions for this decrease method is "psso."

## Double Throw

This term is found in directions when a lacy or openwork effect is required. Insert the needle into the stitch as for knitting or purling. Wind the yarn around the needle as many times as required. Pull all loops through the stitch.

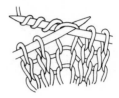

## Increasing

To increase the number of stitches in knitting, knit first into the front of the stitch in the regular way but do not remove the old stitch from the left-hand needle (A). Instead, move the right-hand needle under the left one. Knit into the back of the same stitch to produce the extra stitch (B). Then slip the old stitch off the left-hand needle (C), leaving 2 stitches on the right-hand needle instead of 1.

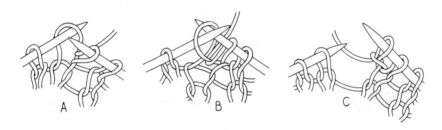

To increase in purling, purl first into the front of the stitch in the regular way but do not remove the stitch from the needle (A). Instead, make the extra stitch by purling into the back of the same stitch (B). Then slip the old stitch off the left-hand needle, leaving 2 stitches on the right-hand needle instead of 1 (C).

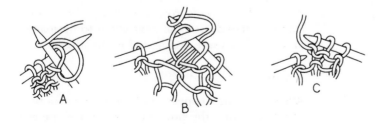

### Knit in Back

When the directions mention knitting in back (or knitting through the back of a stitch), the needle is slipped into the back of the stitch instead of the front. The right-hand needle moves from right to left under the needle in the left hand and to the back of it. The needle is then inserted in the stitch, moving in the same direction, and the stitch knitted in the usual manner.

### Knit the Row Below

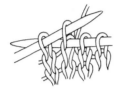

This technique is sometimes used to produce a ribbed effect without purling a stitch. Instead of knitting into the stitch on the needle, insert the needle into the stitch or row below, dropping the stitch down 1 row. On checking the wrong side, 2 loops appear instead of the usual 1. This procedure should never be used for the first or last stitch of a row.

### Knit Two Together

Sometimes it is necessary to knit 2 stitches together. When the directions mention this term, slip the needle through 2 stitches instead of 1 and knit in the usual way. One stitch has been made from 2. The 2 stitches can be seen grouped together under the needle.

### Knitting a Loop from Below

In order to create a decorative effect, this procedure is included in some directions. In the instructions, the stitch in which the right-hand needle is to be inserted will be indicated. Knit through this stitch. Pull up the loop until it reaches the working row of knitting. The loop may be slipped over the next stitch to be made or worked in a way designated in the directions.

### Knitwise

When this term appears in knitting directions, it indicates that the procedure is to be done as though it is to be knitted.

## Multiple Of

This is another term often seen when a pattern stitch is being made that requires a definite number of stitches. When the instructions read "multiple of," it indicates that the number of foundation stitches to be made must be divisible by the stated number. For instance, a multiple of 5 would mean that 10, 15, or 20 stitches would be needed.

If the directions read "multiple of 5 plus 3," then 3 would be added to the total number, making it necessary to use 13, 18, or 23 stitches.

## Pull or Pass Next Stitch Over

This term indicates a way to decrease a stitch while purling. Sometimes it is referred to as *purl reverse.*

Begin by purling the first stitch of decrease. Return it to the left-hand needle.

Insert the right-hand needle in the next stitch to the left. Draw it over the purled stitch. Then return the original purled stitch to the right-hand needle.

## Purling in Back of Stitch

This direction may seem confusing unless the drawing is followed carefully. Instead of inserting the needle into the stitch in front of the needle, put it through the back of the stitch, and at the same time move the right-hand needle in front of the left-hand needle. Then place the yarn around the needle and finish the purl stitch.

## Purlwise

When this term appears in knitting directions, it indicates that the procedure is to be done as though it is to be purled.

### Reverse Stitch

By reversing the position of the yarn, a different effect can be created, although the knit and purl stitches are worked in the usual manner. The yarn is placed over the needle on the knit row and under the needle on the purl row. This stitch is also known as *plaited stockinette stitch.*

### Ridge

A ridge is made by knitting 2 rows of knit stitch, once across in one direction and then once back.

### Row

A row is made when the knitting proceeds once across the needle.

### Slip a Stitch

This is a term indicating that a stitch is to be passed from the left-hand needle to the right-hand needle without knitting. It is sometimes done at the beginning of a row. When following directions for a stitch pattern, however, it may be necessary to slip a stitch some distance from the end.

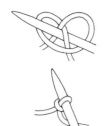

Usually a stitch is slipped purlwise from the left-hand needle to the right-hand needle by inserting the right-hand needle into the front of the stitch. Then transfer the stitch without knitting or purling it. Keep the yarn in back of the work.

### Slip Loop

This is a term used sometimes instead of *slip knot.* To make the loop, hold the yarn a short distance from the end, between the thumb and first (index) finger. Make a small circle of yarn by bringing the ball end of the yarn over the short end. Pull the ball end of the yarn through the circle with the knitting needle. Draw the ends of the yarn in opposite directions to make the loop smaller, so that it fits the needle closely.

## Slip, Slip Knit (ssk)

Sometimes in directions for decreasing the number of stitches, this term is found. Slip, one at a time, the first and second stitches knitwise from the left-hand needle to the right-hand one. Insert the point of the left-hand needle into the front of these stitches, moving from left to right. With the needles in this position, knit the stitches together.

## Work Even

This term means to continue knitting the pattern as previously done, using the same number of stitches without any decreases or increases.

## Yarn Forward

Sometimes this term is used in place of the words *yarn in front.*

## Yarn in Front

It is sometimes necessary to bring the yarn from the back of the work to the front. To do this, slip the yarn between the 2 needles. In this position, the knitting can continue.

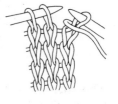

## Yarn Over

The way this procedure is done depends on whether it is on a knit row or a purl row. But in each case a loop is formed on the right-hand needle, adding an extra stitch.

Before a knit stitch, bring yarn to front of the work and place it under and over right-hand needle (A). Then knit the stitch. When the next row is knitted, the stitch will appear as in B.

Before a purl stitch, wrap yarn completely around the right-hand needle. Then purl the stitch (C).

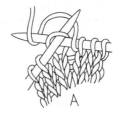

A

C

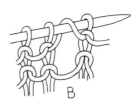

B

## BASIC STITCHES AND TECHNIQUES

All knitting is based on 2 stitches—the knit stitch and the purl stitch. It is possible to use these stitches in such a variety of ways that the patterns and designs seem limitless.

### Garter Stitch

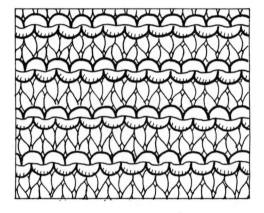

This stitch is made of 2 rows of knit stitches. Knit the first row following the directions for knit stitch. When all of the stitches have been removed from the left-hand needle, exchange needles, transferring the empty one to the right hand. Slip or knit the first stitch. Continue to knit the remaining stitches. The 2 rows of knit stitches make a ridge of garter stitches.

## Knit Stitch

This term refers to the basic stitch in knitting. When it is used for 2 rows, the garter stitch results, and when a row of knit stitches is combined with a row of purl stitches, the stockinette stitch is made.

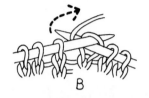

To knit, put the needle with the cast-on stitches in the left hand, the empty one and the yarn in the right hand. Place the point of the needle into the front of the stitch (A).

Bring the yarn under and over the top of the right-hand needle (B). Draw the yarn through the stitch (C), making a new stitch on the right-hand needle.

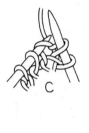

Slip the old stitch from the left-hand needle (D). Continue to make all knit stitches this way.

## Knitting on Circular Needle

After the required number of stitches has been cast on, lay the needle on a flat surface. Make sure that the stitches are not twisted.

Insert the point of the needle in the right hand into the first stitch on the left-hand needle. Begin to knit.

When working with a circular needle, the stitches are always made in the same direction. Instead of making the garter stitch, this type of knitting produces the stockinette stitch.

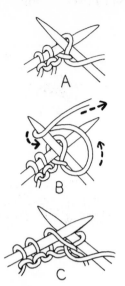

## Purl Stitch

Although this is the second basic stitch used in knitting, it is never used alone. By combining it with the knit stitch in different ways, a variety of stitches can be made.

In purling, the needles are held in the same way as for knitting. However, the yarn is held in front of the work instead of in the back, and the right-hand needle is placed in front of the left-hand needle.

Slip the needle in the stitch from the back (A). Put yarn around the point of the needle (B). Draw yarn through stitch. Slip old stitch off the left-hand needle (C). Continue to make all purl stitches this way.

### Ribbing

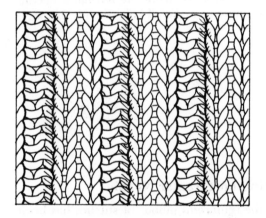

In order to obtain a ribbed effect, make a row of stitches, alternating a certain number of knit stitches with a number of purl stitches. Combinations such as knit 1 and purl 1 or knit 2 and purl 2 are frequently used.

Begin by knitting the required number of stitches in the regular way. Then bring the yarn in front of the needle and purl the necessary stitches. Return the yarn to the back of the work. Then repeat the knit and purl stitches, as previously made, until the required number of stitches are completed.

In making the next row, remember that the stitches that were knitted in the first row will be purled in the second, and the purled stitches will be knitted. In other words, when the stitches with the smooth surface are toward you, knit the stitches, but when the stitches with the bumpy surface are toward you, purl the stitches.

In binding off ribbing, continue as if ribbing is being made. Knit the knit stitches and purl the purl stitches as the process is done.

## Stockinette stitch—Circular Needle

*See* Knitting on Circular Needle for directions.

In this instance, the stockinette stitch results from making knitting stitches.


## Stockinette Stitch—Straight Needle

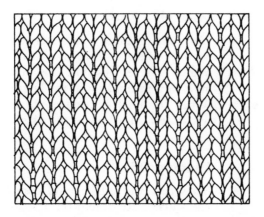

This stitch is made by combining 1 row of knitting with 1 row of purling. After a row of stitches has been knitted, insert the empty needle, in the right hand, into the first stitch on the left-hand needle. Pass it through the front of the stitch from right to left. Slip the stitch to the right-hand needle. Then bring the yarn to the front of the work to begin purling.

Insert the right-hand needle into the first stitch on the left-hand needle. Pass it through the front of the stitch from right to left.

Put the yarn, which is in front of the needle, over and under the right-hand needle. Draw the yarn through the stitch by pulling the needle backward and under the left-hand needle. Then pull the old stitch off the left-hand needle, completing the stitch.

Continue this process until a row of purl stitches has been made. Knit the third row; purl the fourth. Follow this alternating procedure the required number of times.

Remember that when the smooth surface of the stockinette stitch, which resembles vertical rows of chain stitches, is toward you, the row is knitted. When the rough surface of the stockinette stitch, which appears as horizontal rows of garter stitches, is toward you, the row is purled.

## BASIC TECHNIQUES

There are a few basic techniques that are used in all types of knitting. Understanding how to do them contributes to the ease of knitting.

### Attaching Yarn

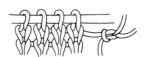

Yarn should always be attached in such a way as to produce a strong and inconspicuous joining. Whenever possible, it is best to attach the new yarn with a knot at the beginning of a row. When the work is completed, weave each end separately into the knitting or seam.

### Binding Off

To secure the stitches and complete an edge, the stitches are bound off. Usually this is done on the wrong side of the work. There is a tendency to make the binding-off stitches too tight. They should be worked loosely enough that the finished edge will have the necessary amount of stretch.

To bind off on the **knit side,** slip or knit loosely the first stitch to be removed from the left-hand needle to the right-hand one. Knit the second stitch loosely, leaving 2 stitches on the right-hand needle.

A

Slip the left-hand needle through the left side of the first stitch on the right-hand needle. Pass the first stitch over the second stitch and the tip of the right-hand needle, dropping it from the needle (A). One stitch remains on the needle.

Knit the next stitch loosely, leaving 2 stitches on the right-hand needle. Again slip the first stitch over the second stitch and tip of needle, leaving 1 stitch on the needle (B).

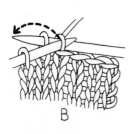

B

Continue the process until only 1 stitch remains on the needle. Clip the yarn about 3 inches (7.5 cm) from the stitch. Pass the end through the remaining stitch. Pull to tighten. The end can be woven into the knitting.

To bind off on the **purl side,** purl 2 stitches. Pass the yarn to the back of the work (C). Then, working as for the knit side, insert the left-hand needle through the left side of the first stitch on the right-hand needle. Pass the first stitch over the second and the tip of the needle. Continue as for the knit side, remembering to bring the yarn to the back after each new stitch has been purled.

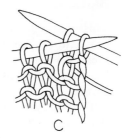

C

To bind off **ribbing,** follow the correct procedure for the knit stitches and the purl stitches, alternating in the proper sequence. This allows the ribbing to retain the close ribbed appearance. If the binding off is not done this way, the edge of the ribbing opens up in a fluted fashion.

## Binding Off Two Pieces Together

Two pieces of work, with the same number of stitches, that have to be joined can be bound off together. This process produces an almost invisible seam.

Hold the 2 parts together with the left hand. Each part is on its needle and the right sides are together. The points of the needles are toward the right.

Insert the right-hand needle into the front of the first stitch on both needles and knit a stitch. Repeat procedure for the second stitches. Then slip the first stitch over the second one, as for the binding-off process. Continue until all the stitches are removed from the needle.

## Blocking

This procedure changes a puckered piece of knitting into a smooth one. Although the yarn may be lovely and the stitches perfect, the finished work may seem amateurish and ill fitting unless it is blocked. For the best results, block individual pieces before sewing them together.

To do this, begin by checking the measurements listed in the direction sheet. Then place the piece to be blocked on a flat, well-padded surface with the wrong side up.

Pin the edges of the knitted piece to the padding, using rustproof pins placed about ¼ inch (6 mm) apart. Measure carefully so that the size of the piece will correspond to the measurements given in the directions. Two identical pieces, such as 2 sleeves, can be blocked together. When working with ribbing, be careful not to stretch it.

When the piece is correctly shaped, put a damp cloth over it. Press lightly with a hot iron so that the steam will pass through the knitting. Be careful not to let the weight of the iron rest on the knitting. When it is thoroughly dry, remove the pins. It can then be removed from the padded board.

### Casting Off

This is a term used instead of **binding off.** The directions are the same.

### Casting On

Putting stitches on a knitting needle is the first step in knitting. There are several ways to do this. Whichever method is used, remember that the stitches should be placed close together and the yarn should wrap the needle closely. However, it must not be so tight that the stitches cannot be moved on the needle—or so loose that the needle falls out.

**Method 1.** This is the easiest method and produces a stretchy, openwork finish. Work with 1 needle and 1 end of yarn.

Start with a slip knot. Place it on the needle held in the right hand. Wrap the yarn around the thumb of the left hand from right to left.

Insert the needle upward through the loop of yarn around your thumb. Transfer loop to needle. Repeat procedure until required number of stitches have been cast on.

**Method 2.** This method uses 2 ends of thread and 1 needle. It creates a firm edge.

Begin with a slip knot placed some distance from the end of the yarn. The length will depend on the number of stitches to be cast on. Usually 1 inch (2.5 cm) of yarn is allowed for each stitch.

Pass the needle through the loop. Gently pull the ends of the yarn to tighten the loop. Arrange the yarn so the shorter end is on the left; ball end, on the right.

Hold the needle in the right hand as you would a pencil. Put the yarn over the first (index) finger, under the middle, and over the middle joint of the ring finger (A). The first finger moves the yarn around the needle, while the middle and ring fingers regulate the flow of the yarn, so that the stitches will not be too tight nor too loose. Hold the yarn loosely so that it will not be stretched.

Pick up the free end of the yarn with the left hand. Hold it lightly against the palm with the middle, ring, and little fingers. Wrap the yarn around the thumb, forming a loop close to the needle (B).

Insert the needle into the loop. Pass the yarn in the right hand under the point of the needle and over it (C).

Draw the needle and yarn through the loop, and slip the loop from the thumb, leaving a stitch on the needle (D). Tighten the loop or stitch by pulling the free end of the yarn with the left hand (E).

Repeat the procedure until the required number of stitches have been cast on.

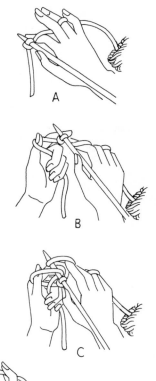

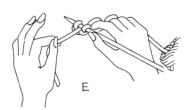

**Method 3.** This method of casting on stitches is referred to as knitting on stitches. It is worked with 2 needles and 1 end of thread. It is used especially when it is necessary to cast on stitches in the middle of a piece and no free end of yarn is available for use.

To begin the process, make a slip knot at the end of the yarn. Put the needle held in the left hand into the loop. Then insert the needle in the right hand into the loop, under the left-hand needle. Put the yarn under and over the right-hand needle (A).

Draw the yarn through the loop, being careful not to pull the stitch off the needle. It should remain on the left-hand needle (B).

Transfer the new loop from the right-hand needle to the left-hand one (C). Notice that the stitch is twisted as it is put on the left-hand needle, and that the right-hand needle is placed on top of the left-hand one in this process.

When the transfer is completed, remove the needle from the upper position and place it under the left-hand needle, ready to make the next stitch.

Continue this procedure until the required number of stitches have been cast on.

### Casting On—Left-handed

All of the methods for casting on stitches can be used by the left-handed knitter by converting the procedure from right to left and left to right. However, if this seems a problem, follow these directions for Method 2.

Make a slip knot the required distance from the end of the thread. Place the loop on the needle. Pull the ends of the thread so that it fits the needle closely. The yarn from the ball will be on the left, and the free end of yarn on the right.

Hold the needle in the left hand between the thumb and first, or index, finger as you would a pencil. With the loop near the tip of the needle, put the ball end of the yarn over the first finger of the left hand, under the middle, and over the ring finger at the middle joint. Hold the yarn firmly, but not tightly, so that the flow of the yarn can be kept even.

The free end of the yarn is held lightly in the right hand by the middle, ring, and little fingers. Place the yarn around and under the thumb, forming a loop. Keep it close to the needle.

With the hands close together, place the needle through the underside of the loop. Slip the yarn in the left hand under and over the needle. Pull the needle and yarn through the loop. Slip the loop from the thumb, leaving a stitch on the needle. Pull the free end of the yarn gently with the right hand to tighten the stitch. Continue this procedure until the required number of stitches have been placed on the needle.

### Casting On, Using Four Needles

When knitting in the round, stitches can be cast on using 4 double-pointed needles. If **Method 2** is employed, cast on ⅓ of the required number of stitches on the first needle.

Then place the second needle below and slightly to the right so the first stitch on the second needle will be close to the last stitch on the first needle. Cast on ⅓ of the required number of stitches.

Then place the third needle below and slightly to the right of the second needle and cast on the remaining ⅓ of the stitches.

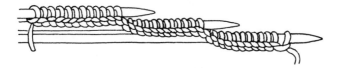

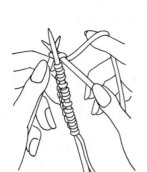

If **Method 3** is used, cast on ⅓ of the required number of stitches. Then make an extra stitch, but leave it on the right-hand needle. Shift this needle to the left hand, picking up a new needle in the right hand. Cast on ⅓ of the required number of stitches. Make the extra stitch, leaving it on the right-hand needle.

Then change the needle to the left hand. Continue casting on the remaining third of the stitches on the third needle, with the fourth needle in the right hand. Often this process seems awkward because of the dangling needles. Be careful to work so that no stitches slip off the needles.

After all of the stitches have been cast on, lay the needles on the table to form a triangle with the first needle forming the left side of the triangle. Be sure that the stitches are not twisted on the needle. The loop edge should be on the outside, with the finished edge on the inside.

## Changing Colors

When one color is to be changed to another, twist one color around the other at the joining. Carry the unused yarn loosely across the knitting on the wrong side. Pick up the new color from under the one that is to be dropped. This procedure prevents holes from appearing.

## Dropped Stitches

When a stitch falls off the needle accidentally, it can be picked up and returned to the needle. Use a crochet hook for best results. Insert the hook in the dropped stitch. Pull the horizontal strand of yarn of the row above through the loop. Continue until the row of stitches on the needle is reached. Slip the picked-up stitch onto the needle. Be careful not to twist it.

If working with Stockinette Stitch, it is best to pick up the dropped stitch with the smooth or right side of the knitting toward you.

For Garter Stitch, turn the work first to one side and then to the other so that the stitch design will be kept.

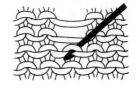

## Grafting

This term indicates a method of joining 2 knitted parts horizontally, with invisible results. Work with a blunt embroidery needle and matching yarn. Lay the pieces flat on a table so that the loops are opposite each other. Withdraw the knitting needles, loop by loop, as the blunt needle passes through the stitches, duplicating knitting (A) and purling (B). Except for the first and last stitch in a row, the needle enters each loop twice. Be sure to keep the tension between the new grafted stitches and the other stitches even.

A

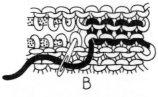

B

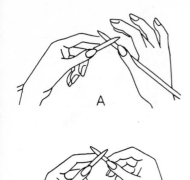

A

B

## Holding Needles

The position of the hands can vary. The choice is a personal matter, depending how natural and comfortable the needles feel in the hands.

**Method 1.** Holding the needle in the right hand, between the thumb and first or index, finger, as if holding a pencil, is referred to as English knitting. The left hand is placed above the left-hand needle (A).

**Method 2.** In this method, both hands are above the needles. It is known as Continental or German knitting (B).

## Holding Yarn

The position of the yarn also varies. Again, it is ease and comfort that control the method. The yarn can be held in either the left or the right hand.

**Left hand.** The Continental method of knitting places the yarn in the left hand. The yarn is wrapped twice around the first finger, with the little finger guiding the yarn by holding it lightly against the palm.

The tension on the yarn is maintained by the first finger. The finger moves downward as each stitch is formed.

The right-hand needle is inserted through the loop from front to back and then twisted around the yarn in order to pull the yarn through the loop, forming a new stitch.

**Right hand.** The English method places the yarn in the right hand. Put the yarn over the first finger, under the middle, and over the middle joint of the ring finger. The first finger moves the yarn around the needle, whereas the middle and ring fingers regulate the flow of yarn, so that the stitches will not be too tight or too loose. Hold the yarn loosely so that it will not be stretched.

## Pick Up One Stitch

This term indicates a type of yarn over. It produces a slightly smaller space in the work.

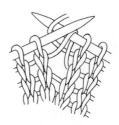

Put the tip of the right-hand needle under the yarn stretching between the 2 needles. Make a knit or purl stitch under this yarn. It is used as a stitch.

## Picking Up Stitches

When one part of an article is to be knit onto another one, such as a band added to a neckline or a sleeve at the armhole, this term is used. Picking up may be done with a knitting needle or crochet hook. If a knitting needle is used, the stitch is placed directly on the needle. If a crochet hook is used, however, the loop must be transferred from the crochet hook to the knitting needle.

Work from right to left with the right side of the knitting toward you. Hold the needle and yarn in the right hand, the knitting in the left.

Insert the needle in the first stitch of the first row below the edge. Bring the yarn around the needle. Draw it through, forming a loop or stitch on the right-hand needle. Repeat this procedure until the required number of stitches have been picked up.

## Placing Marker

It is helpful to place a marker to indicate a special procedure, such as making a decrease or increase. The marker can be a plastic ring or a piece of yarn in a contrasting color. It should be first placed on the right-hand needle at the specified spot, and then slipped from one needle to the other as work progresses.

If yarn is used, select a contrasting color. Use a slip loop to hold the yarn in place. Leave ends of about 2 inches (5 cm) in length.

## Putting Stitches on Needle After Ripping

Sometimes it is necessary to ravel out some of the knitting in order to make a correction. As the stitches are put back on the needle, keep them from twisting. Insert the left-hand needle from front to back through each loop, both for the knit side and the purl side.

## Ripping Back

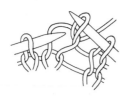

No one likes to rip. However, there are times when it must be done. Mistakes do happen. They should be detected as soon as possible to simplify the ripping process.

If the error appears on the rows being worked on, do not take the knitting off the needles. First retract, returning the stitches to the left-hand needle. Do this by inserting the needle into the loop or stitch through which the yarn is passing. Slip the right-hand needle out of the last stitch that was made, leaving 1 less stitch on this needle. Continue this technique until the point of the mistake is reached. This procedure keeps the stitches from becoming twisted. It can be used for both knit and purl stitches.

If the mistake is not discovered until the knitting has been turned, the work should be ripped back in the same way, row by row. Some persons find this tedious and prefer to ravel out the stitches in order to make a correction. When this is done, the stitches may become twisted unless the task is carefully undertaken. To avoid this, ravel the last row, stitch by stitch, placing each stitch on a fine needle as it is ripped. The stitches can then be knitted onto the regular needle.

## Twisted Stitches

Twisted stitches should be avoided. They upset the regularity of the work, producing a flaw. If the stitches are being made correctly, the yarn passes over the needle always in the same direction with the stitches lined up evenly on the needle. The part of the loop or stitch that is in front of the needle should be closer to the point (A). If it isn't (B), then the stitch is twisted and should be turned on the needle. Learn to recognize twisted stitches quickly so that stitches that have fallen off the needle or been ripped off can be returned to the needle in their proper position.

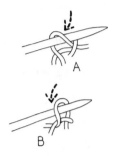

## Winding Yarn

If the yarn needs to be wound into a ball, it can be done this way. Wrap the yarn loosely around 3 fingers about a dozen times. Remove the coils of threads from the fingers. Lay them in the left hand, turning them in the opposite direction. Continue to wrap the yarn around the fingers and bundle of wool. Slip the fingers from the yarn at intervals. As the ball of yarn increases in size, keep turning it so that it becomes perfectly round. Be sure the yarn is always placed over the fingers.

## Working In Ends

Exposed ends of yarn and knots should be avoided. If it is necessary to join 2 pieces of yarn with a knot while knitting, the knot can be eliminated when the article is completed. Untie the knot, which should be on the wrong side of the work. Slip the left-hand yarn into the back of several stitches to the right, the right-hand end in the stitches to the left. When carefully interlocked, they will be invisible. If the ends are too long, they should be clipped. Yarn tied at the edge can be finished by working the threads up and down in the same way.

## MATERIALS AND TOOLS

Although the equipment needs for knitting are simple, it is important to select the correct needles and yarn. A few other devices such as a tape measure, stitch holder, and yarn markers may prove helpful.

### Knitting Accessories

Although needles and yarns are the 2 items necessary for knitting, there are a few accessories that some persons find helpful to use. They include counters, gauges, stitch and yarn holders, and markers.

**Counters** are small devices that keep track of stitches, rows, increases, and decreases when knitting. By placing 1 on each needle, the need to count personally is avoided. This makes knitting less time-consuming, with fewer possibilities for error. There is also a **counter gauge** for determining the gauge of stitches and rows.

A **gauge card** for checking needle sizes is handy to have.

**Stitch holders** are available in 2 types. One resembles a safety pin. It is used to hold stitches that have been set apart for future use. It keeps one section from raveling while another is being knitted.

Then there is the stitch holder used in cable knitting. It looks like a small double-pointed needle with a bend in the middle. There is also a U-shaped type for bulky yarns.

**Yarn holders** or **bobbins** make the work easier to do when knitting with multicolors, as for Argyle and Fair Isle patterns. They should be lightweight and hold the yarn firmly in place.

Yarn **markers** or rings are used to indicate separate sections, the places where patterns begin and end and where increases and decreases are to be made.

There are other items such as a **tape measure, scissors,** and **crochet hook** that should be available. And of course a container for holding the tools is a must.

## Knitting Needles

Knitting needles are usually made of aluminum, bone, plastic, steel, or wood. They are available in various types—straight and circular. The straight needles can be single-pointed or double-pointed. Each of these is available in a variety of sizes, as shown in drawings below. And the sizing can vary, depending on whether it is standard U.S. or English.

Directions for knitting an article suggest the size of needle to use. It is advisable to follow this suggestion. Since foreign books and magazines are available in the United States, always check the general information accompanying the directions to make certain which sizing is being used—U.S. Standard or English. By studying the drawing on this page, it is easy to see that there is quite a difference.

Knitting needles are made in different lengths. Some knitters find it easier to knit with short needles; others, with long. Usually the chosen length depends on the article being constructed. If only a few stitches are required, then a short needle seems more convenient, saving the longer type for a larger item. Crowding stitches onto a needle makes it difficult to watch the stitch pattern as it is being made. Choosing needles that are a contrast in color to the yarn being knitted makes the job easier.

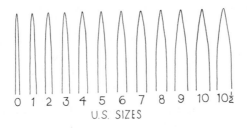

0  1  2  3  4  5  6  7  8  9  10  10½
U.S. SIZES

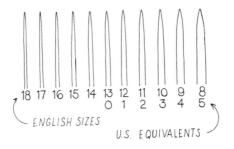

18  17  16  15  14  13  12  11  10  9  8
                    0   1   2   3  4  5
ENGLISH SIZES

U.S. EQUIVALENTS

A **circular needle** is used in constructing a tubular article, such as a seamless skirt. Circular needles are made of metal, nylon, or plastic in varying sizes and lengths. The 9-inch (23 cm) length is available in sizes 0 to 4; 11- to 36-inch (28 to 91.5 cm) length, sizes 0 to 10½. The 36-inch length is also made in sizes 11, 13, and 15.

**Double-pointed straight** needles are sometimes called sock needles because they are used for tubular knitting, such as for socks or mittens. The knitting proceeds round and round. The needles are purchased in sets of 4 or 5. When made of aluminum, nickel-plated steel, or plastic, they come in 5-, 7-, and 10-inch lengths (12.5, 17.5, and 25.5 cm). Aluminum needles are available in sizes 0 to 8; plastic, in 1 to 15; steel in British sizing, 18 for the finest; 8, the largest.

**Jumper needles** are a flexible type that can accommodate large, bulky pieces of knitting. There is a firm section on which the stitches are formed and a flexible one for holding the stitches. This permits the weight of the yarn to be held comfortably in the lap. A cap should be put on one end so the stitches will not slip off the needle. Jumper needles are made of nylon or a combination of aluminum and nylon. They come in a 18-inch (46 cm) length and in sizes 4 to 15.

The **straight needle with a single point** is the one most commonly used. Plastic and colored aluminum needles may be purchased in lengths of 7½, 10, 12, and 14 inches (19, 25.5, 30.5, and 35.5 cm), varying in size from 1 to 5 in the shorter lengths and 1 to 10½, 13, and 15 in the longer lengths. Colored aluminum needles are also available in size 0; steel, in 0 to 3. Wooden needles, which are only available in larger sizes, come in sizes 10½ to 15 in a 14-inch (35.5 cm) length. Two needles are sold together as a pair. They are used for flat work with the knitting progressing back and forth in rows. The knitting is turned at the end of each row.

## Yarns

Yarns for knitting vary widely. They can be made of wool, cotton, silk, linen, and rayon and other synthetics. Sometimes the yarn is made of more than 1 fiber. Size, twist, and color of yarn add other dimensions. Some yarns are heavy and tightly twisted, others fine and loosely twisted; some are smooth, others rough; some are made of 1 color, others are multicolored. The marking 2-ply, 3-ply or 4-ply indicates the number of strands twisted together. For instance, 2 strands are used for 2-ply. Sometimes the word **fold** is used in place of **ply,** but the meaning is the same.

Unless you are an expért knitter with a complete understanding of yarn, always use the yarn suggested in a chosen pattern. The specified material has been carefully selected for the particular design. Any change in the type or size of the yarn will probably result in an unsatisfactory article because the yarn is an integral part of the design.

The thickness of the yarn should relate to the stitch pattern. A thick yarn will be appropriate for one, a lightweight yarn for another. The texture should also be considered. Smooth yarns can be used for more intricate pattern stitches, with the fuzzy looped, slubbed, and tweed yarn being employed for simple pattern stitches.

If it becomes necessary to substitute another yarn for the suggested one, choose something similar. Always make a sample swatch in order to check the gauge before starting the actual knitting. Also note whether the texture is right for the pattern stitch. It may be too soft or too stiff, even though the gauge is the same. Another factor to check is the elasticity of the yarn. Cotton and linen yarns have less elasticity than wool.

## STITCH PATTERNS

By combining the 2 basic knitting stitches—knit and purl—hundreds of stitch patterns can be created. They date back to the earliest days of knitting and may vary from lacy, fragile designs to coarse, bulky ones. As knitting spread from country to country, the stitch patterns took on a national feeling. Directions were handed down from generation to generation and adapted to fit the needs of the knitter. Gradually the stitch patterns were given names in the different countries. This has led to some confusion: one stitch pattern may have several names.

Before using one of the pattern stitches given here, knit a sample. This makes it possible to study the resulting effect. The directions have been written without abbreviations in order to make the knitting easier to do. Concentration can be placed on the stitch construction and not on trying to remember the meaning of the abbreviations.

The stitch patterns are arranged in alphabetical order.

### Acorn Pattern

A bulky raised quality results when this old English pattern is used to create an allover effect.

For the **beginning row,** cast on a multiple of 10 stitches plus 2.

For the **first row,** knit 1, purl 3, knit 4. Repeat the following procedure as many times as required. * Purl 6. Knit 4. * End with purl 3, knit 1.

For the **second row,** knit 4, purl 4. Repeat the following procedure. * Knit 6, purl 4. * End with knit 4.

For the **third row,** knit 1, purl 1. Repeat the following procedure. * Slip next 2 stitches onto a double-pointed needle. Leave in back. Knit 2. Purl the 2 stitches on double-pointed needle, making a back cross. Insert needle under thread connecting 2 stitches of previous row. Knit 1 and purl 1. Then slip next 2 stitches onto double-pointed needle and leave in front. Purl 2. Knit 2 from double-pointed needle for front cross. Purl 2.* End by purling 1, knitting 1.

For the **fourth row,** knit 2. Repeat the following procedure. * Purl 2. Knit 2. *

For the **fifth row,** knit 1, purl 1. Repeat the following procedure. * Knit 2. Purl 2. * End row with knit 2, purl 1, and knit 1.

For the **sixth row,** repeat fourth row.

For the **seventh row,** knit 2. Repeat the following procedure. * Slip 1 stitch. Knit 1. Pass slip stitch over. Purl 6. Knit 2 together. Knit 2. *

For the **eighth row,** knit 1. Purl 2. Knit 6. Repeat the following procedure. * Purl 4. Knit 6. * End row with purl 2, knit 1.

For the **ninth row,** knit 1. Insert needle under thread connecting 2 stitches of previous row and knit it. Repeat the following procedure. * For front cross, leave double-pointed needle in front of work. Purl 2. For back cross, leave double-pointed needle in back. Knit 1 and purl 1 into connecting thread of previous row. * End front cross. Purl 2. For back cross, leave needle in back. Knit once into connecting thread of previous row. Knit 1.

For the **tenth row,** knit 1, purl 1. Repeat the following procedure. * Knit 2. Purl 2. * End row with knit 2, purl 1, knit 1.

For the **eleventh row,** knit 2. Repeat the following procedure. * Purl 2. Knit 2. *

For the **twelfth row,** repeat tenth row.

For the **thirteenth row,** knit 1, purl 3. Repeat the following procedure. * Knit 2 together. Knit 2. Slip 1. Knit 1. Pass slip stitch over. Purl 6. * End row with knit 2 together. Knit 2. Slip 1. Knit 1. Pass slip stitch over. Purl 3. Knit 1.

Repeat the **second through thirteenth rows** as many times as required.

## All Fools' Welt Pattern

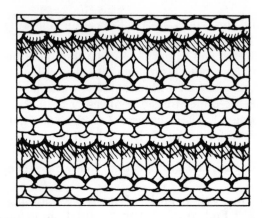

This is an easy-to-make stitch pattern with a striped effect. It is interesting to note that it has many names, such as Dispute, Puzzle, and Wager Welt.

For the **beginning row,** cast on as many stitches as required.
For the **first row,** knit.
For the **second row,** purl.
For the **third row,** knit.
For the **fourth row,** knit.
For the **fifth row,** knit.
For the **sixth row,** knit.
For the **seventh row,** knit.
For the **eighth row,** knit.
Repeat the **eight rows** as many times as required.

Variations of this stitch pattern can be made by changing the number of garter stitch ridges. For instance, this sequence of rows could be used to produce 1 ridge of garter stitches instead of the 3 used in Wager Welt, or All Fools' Welt.

For the **beginning row,** cast on the required number of stitches.
For the **first row,** knit.
For the **second row,** purl.
For the **third row,** knit.
For the **fourth row,** knit.

## Allover Cross Stitch

An unusual arrangement of stitches creates an eyelet effect and at the same time produces a soft, thick feeling.

For the **beginning row,** cast on a multiple of 4 stitches plus 3.

For the **first row,** purl.

For the **second row,** knit 2. In the row below, knit into the next stitch. Then slip that stitch onto the right-hand needle. Knit 2 together. Pass slip stitch over. Repeat the following procedure. * In the row below, knit into the next stitch. Knit that stitch. Knit again into the row below to the left of the stitch. Notice that 1 stitch has produced 3. Slip 1. Knit 2 stitches together. Pass slipped stitch over. * At last 2 stitches on row, knit into the next stitch in the row below. Then knit the stitch itself. Finish by knitting 1.

For the **third row,** purl.

For the **fourth row,** knit 1. Knit 2 together. Repeat the following procedure. * Knit the next stitch 3 times by knitting into the next stitch in the row below, knitting the stitch itself, and knitting again into the row below to the left of the stitch. Then slip 1. Knit 2 together. Pass slipped stitch over. * At the last 4 stitches, knit into the next stitch 3 times, by knitting into the row below, then the stitch itself, and then knitting again into the row below, as in row 2. Slip 1. Knit 1. Pass slipped stitch over. Knit 1.

Repeat the **first through fourth rows,** until work is completed.

## Arabic Cross Pattern

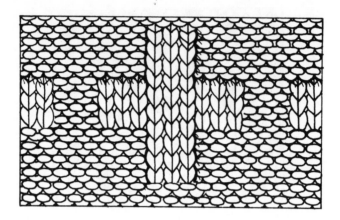

This design resembles those found in very old pieces of knitting.

For the **beginning row,** cast on a multiple of 12 stitches plus 1.

For the **first row,** purl.

For the **second row,** knit.

For the **third row,** purl 5. Repeat the following procedure. * Knit 3 stitches through back loop. Purl 9. * End the last repeat by purling 5 stitches instead of 9.

For the **fourth row,** knit 5. Repeat the following procedure. * Purl 3. Knit 9. * End the last repeat by knitting 5 stitches instead of 9.

For the **fifth row,** repeat the third row.

For the **sixth row,** repeat the fourth row.

For the **seventh row,** purl 2. Repeat the following procedure. * Knit 9 stitches through back loop. Purl 3. * End the last repeat by purling 2 stitches instead of 3.

For the **eighth row,** knit 2. Repeat the following procedure. * Purl 9. Knit 3. * End the last repeat by knitting 2 stitches instead of 3.

For the **ninth row,** repeat the seventh row.

For the **tenth row,** repeat the eighth row.

For the **eleventh row,** repeat the third row.

For the **twelfth row,** repeat the fourth row.

For the **thirteenth row,** repeat the third row.

For the **fourteenth row,** repeat the fourth row.

For the **fifteenth row,** purl.

For the **sixteenth row,** knit.

Repeat the **first through sixteenth rows** as many times as required.

## Baby Fern Pattern

When a delicate, lacy effect is needed for a ribbed effect, this is the pattern to use.

For the **beginning row,** cast on a multiple of 9 stitches plus 4.

For the **first row,** purl.

For the **second row,** knit 2. Repeat the following procedure. * Knit 2 together. Knit 2. Yarn over. Knit 1. Yarn over. Knit 2. Knit 2 together. * End with knit 2.

For the **third row,** knit 1. Then purl across row to last stitch, and knit this.

For the **fourth row,** knit 2. Repeat the following procedure. * Knit 2 together. Knit 1. Yarn over. Knit 3. Yarn over. Knit 1. Knit 2 together. * End with knit 2.

For the **fifth row,** repeat the third row.

For the **sixth row,** knit 2. Repeat the following procedure. * Knit 2 together. Yarn over. Knit 5. Yarn over. Knit 2 together. * End with knit 2.

For the **seventh row,** repeat the third.

Repeat the **second through seventh rows** as many times as required.

## Basket Cable Pattern

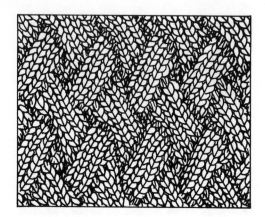

This stitch produces a bulky look that can be effective when worked in panels.

For the **beginning row,** cast on a multiple of 8 stitches plus 4.

For the **first row,** knit 2. Then purl to the last 2 stitches. Knit these.

For the **second row,** knit.

For the **third row,** knit 2. Purl to the last 2 stitches. Knit these.

For the **fourth row,** knit.

For the **fifth row,** knit 2. Purl to the last 2 stitches. Knit these.

For the **sixth row,** knit 2. Repeat the following procedure. * Slip the next 4 stitches onto a double-pointed needle. Hold it in back. Knit 4. Then knit the 4 stitches on the double-pointed needle. * End with knit 2.

For the **seventh row,** knit 2. Purl to the last 2 stitches. Then knit these.

For the **eighth row,** knit.

For the **ninth row,** repeat seventh row.

For the **tenth row,** knit.

For the **eleventh row,** repeat seventh row.

For the **twelfth row,** knit 6. Repeat the following procedure. * Slip the next 4 stitches onto a double-pointed needle. Hold it in front. Knit 4. Then knit the 4 stitches on the double-pointed needle. * End by knitting 6.

Repeat the **first through twelfth rows,** as many times as required.

## Basket Pattern

Stripes of garter stitches can be given added interest by introducing a slip stitch and a second color. The pattern is also effective when worked in 1 color.

For the **beginning row,** cast on multiple of 4 stitches plus 3. Use 1 or 2 colors. If using 2 colors—A and B—follow these directions. Cast on with color A.

For the **first row,** purl.

For the **second row,** attach color B. Knit 3. Repeat the following procedure. * Slip 1 stitch with yarn in back. Knit 3. *

For the **third row,** continue with B, knit 3. Repeat the following procedure. * Slip 1 stitch with yarn in front. Knit 3. *

For the **fourth row,** repeat the second row.

For the **fifth row,** repeat the third row.

For the **sixth row,** change to color A and knit.

For the **seventh row,** purl, continuing with A.

Repeat the **second through seventh rows** as required.

## Basket Pattern—Double

An interesting arrangement of ribs and stripes produces a checkerboard effect. It seems to create a wavy effect when left unpressed.

For the **beginning row,** cast on a multiple of 18 stitches plus 10.

For the **first row,** repeat the following procedure. * Knit 11. Purl 2. Knit 2. Purl 2. Knit 1. * End with knit 10.

For the **second row,** purl 1, knit 8, purl 1. Repeat the following procedure. * Purl 1. Knit 2. Purl 2. Knit 2. Purl 2. Knit 8. Purl 1. *

For the **third row,** repeat the following procedure. * Knit 1. Purl 8. Knit 2. Purl 2. Knit 2. Purl 2. Knit 1. * End with knit 1, purl 8, and knit 1.

For the **fourth row,** purl 10. Repeat the following procedure. * Purl 1. Knit 2. Purl 2. Knit 2. Purl 11. *

For the **fifth row,** repeat the first row.

For the **sixth row,** repeat the second row.

For the **seventh row,** repeat the third row.

For the **eighth row,** repeat the fourth row.

For the **ninth row,** knit.

For the **tenth row,** purl 2. Knit 2. Purl 2. Knit 2. Purl 2. Repeat the following procedure. * Purl 10, knit 2. Purl 2. Knit 2. Purl 2. *

For the **eleventh row,** repeat the following procedure. * Knit 2. Purl 2. Knit 2. Purl 2. Knit 2. Purl 8. * End with knit 2. Purl 2. Knit 2. Purl 2. Knit 2.

For the **twelfth row,** purl 2. Knit 2. Purl 2. Knit 2. Purl 2. Repeat the following procedure. * Knit 8. Purl 2. Knit 2. Purl 2. Knit 2. Purl 2. *

For the **thirteenth row,** repeat the following procedure. * Knit 2. Purl 2. Knit 2. Purl 2. Knit 10. * End with knit 2. Purl 2. Knit 2. Purl 2. Knit 2.

For the **fourteenth row,** repeat the tenth row.

For the **fifteenth row,** repeat the eleventh row.

For the **sixteenth row,** repeat the twelfth row.

For the **seventeenth row,** repeat the thirteenth row.

For the **eighteenth row,** purl.

Repeat the **first through eighteenth rows** as many times as required.

## Basket Weave Pattern

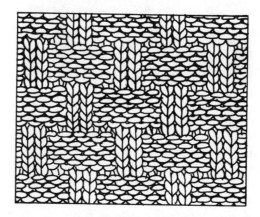

This is a well-known English pattern that is simple to make. The combination of stitches can vary to produce different effects.

For the **beginning row,** cast on a multiple of 8 stitches.

For the **first row,** knit 1. Purl across row. End with knit 1.

For the **second row,** knit 1. Purl 2. Repeat the following procedure. * Knit 2. Purl 6. * End with knit 2, purl 2, knit 1.

For the **third row,** knit 3. Repeat the following procedure. * Purl 2. Knit 6. * End with purl 2, knit 3.

For the **fourth row,** repeat the second row.

For the **fifth row,** repeat the first row.

For the **sixth row,** knit 1. Repeat the following procedure. * Purl 6. Knit 2. * End with purl 6, knit 1.

For the **seventh row,** knit 7. Purl 2. Repeat the following procedure. * Knit 6. Purl 2. * End with knit 7.

For the **eighth row,** repeat the sixth row.

Repeat the **first through eighth rows** as many times as required.

## Beech Leaf Lace Pattern

Solid leaves are outlined with openwork to create lacy columns.

For the **beginning row**, cast a multiple of 14 stitches plus 1.

For the **first row**, repeat the following procedure. * Knit 1. Put yarn over, knit 5. Yarn over, slip 1 stitch. Knit 2 together. Pass slip stitch over. Yarn over. Knit 5. Yarn over. * End with knit 1.

For the **second row**, purl.

For the **third row**, repeat the following procedure. * Knit 1. Put yarn over. Knit 1. Knit 2 together. Purl 1. Slip 1 stitch. Knit 1. Pass slip stitch over. Knit 1. Yarn over. Purl 1. Yarn over. Knit 1. Knit 2 together. Purl 1. Slip 1. Knit 1. Pass slip stitch over. Knit 1. Yarn over. * End with knit 1.

For the **fourth row**, purl 1. Repeat the following procedure. * Purl 3. Knit 1. Purl 3. Knit 1. Purl 3. Knit 1. Purl 4. *

For the **fifth row**, repeat the following procedure. * Knit 1. Put yarn over. Knit 1. Knit 2 together. Purl 1. Slip 1. Knit 1. Pass slip stitch over. Knit 1. Purl 1. Knit 1. Knit 2 together. Purl 1. Slip 1. Knit 1. Pass slip stitch over. Knit 1. Yarn over. * End with knit 1.

For the **sixth row**, purl 1. Repeat the following procedure. * Purl 3. Knit 1. Purl 2. Knit 1. Purl 2. Knit 1. Purl 4. *

For the **seventh row**, repeat the following procedure. * Knit 1. Put yarn over. Knit 1. Yarn over. Knit 2 together. Purl 1. Slip 1 stitch. Knit 1. Pass slip stitch over. Purl 1. Knit 2 together. Purl 1. Slip 1. Knit 1. Pass slip stitch over. Yarn over. Knit 1. Yarn over. * End with knit 1.

For the **eighth row**, purl 1. Repeat the following procedure. * Purl 4. Knit 1. Purl 1. Knit 1. Purl 1. Knit 1. Purl 5. *

For the **ninth row**, repeat the following procedure. * Knit 1. Yarn over. Knit 3. Yarn over. Slip 1 stitch. Knit 2 together. Pass slip stitch over. Purl 1. Knit 3 together. Yarn over. Knit 3. Yarn over. * End with knit 1.

For the **tenth row,** purl.

Repeat the **first through the tenth rows** until work is completed.

## Bell and Rope Pattern

This arrangement of stitches gives the effect of swinging bells.

For the **beginning row,** cast on a multiple of 5 stitches.

For the **first row,** purl 2. Repeat the following procedure. * Knit 1 stitch through the back. Purl 4. * End with knit 1 stitch through the back, purl 2.

For the **second row,** knit 2, purl 1 stitch through the back. Repeat the following procedure. * Knit 4. Purl 1 stitch through the back. * End with knit 2.

For the **third row,** purl 2. Repeat the following procedure. * Knit 1 stitch through the back. Purl 2. Cast on 8 stitches for the bell. Purl 2. * End with knit 1 stitch through the back, purl 2.

For the **fourth row,** knit 2. Purl 1 stitch through the back. Repeat the following procedure. * Knit 2. Purl 8 for the bell. Knit 2. Purl 1 stitch through the back. * End with knit 2.

For the **fifth row,** purl 2. Repeat the following procedure. * Knit 1 stitch through the back. Purl 2. Knit 8 for the bell. Purl 2. * End with knit 1 stitch through the back, purl 2.

For the **sixth row,** repeat the fourth row.

For the **seventh row,** purl 2. Repeat the following procedure. * Knit 1 stitch through the back. Purl 2. In making the bell, slip 1 stitch, knit 1 stitch. Pass slip stitch over knit stitch. Knit 4. Knit 2 together. Then purl 2. * End with knit 1 stitch through the back, and purl 2.

For the **eighth row,** knit 2, purl 1 stitch through the back. Repeat the following procedure. * Knit 2. For the bell, purl 2 together, purl 2, purl 1 decrease in reverse by purling 1 stitch. Return it to the left needle. Insert right needle through the stitch beyond and, lifting it over the stitch just purled, slide it off the needle. Then knit 2. Purl 1 stitch through the back. * End with knit 2.

For the **ninth row,** purl 2. Repeat the following procedure. * Knit 1 stitch through the back. Purl 2. For the bell, slip 1, knit 1, pass slip stitch over knit stitch, knit 2 together. Then purl 2. * End with knit 1 stitch through the back, purl 2.

For the **tenth row,** knit 2. Purl 1 stitch through the back. Repeat the following procedure. * Knit 1. For the top of the bell, knit 2 together, and then knit another 2 together. Knit 1. Purl 1 stitch through the back. * End with knit 2.

Repeat the **first through tenth rows** as many times as required.

## Bell Pattern

A dainty bell-shaped design gives a flowerlike quality to the knitting. Sometimes the pattern is referred to as Blue Bell or Hyacinth.

For the **beginning row,** cast on a multiple of 6 stitches plus 5.

For the **first row,** purl 2. Repeat the following procedure. * Knit 1. Purl 5. * End the row with knit 1, purl 2.

For the **second row,** knit 2. Repeat the following procedure. * Purl 1. Knit 5. * End with purl 1, knit 2.

For the **third row,** purl 5. Repeat the following procedure. * Put yarn over. Knit 1. Yarn over. Purl 5. *

For the **fourth row,** knit 5. Repeat the following procedure. * Purl 3. Knit 5. *

For the **fifth row,** purl 5. Repeat the following procedure. * Knit 3. Purl 5. *

For the **sixth row,** repeat the fourth row.

For the **seventh row,** repeat the fifth row.

For the **eighth row,** repeat the fourth row.

For the **ninth row,** purl 5. Repeat the following procedure. * Slip 1 stitch. Knit 2 together. Pass slip stitch over. Purl 5. *

For the **tenth row,** knit 5. Repeat the following procedure. * Purl 1. Knit 5. *

For the **eleventh row,** purl 5. Repeat the following procedure. * Knit 1. Purl 5. *

For the **twelfth row,** repeat the tenth row.

For the **thirteenth row,** purl 2. Repeat the following procedure. * Put yarn over. Knit 1. Yarn over. Purl 5. * End row with yarn over. Knit 1. Yarn over. Purl 2.

For the **fourteenth row,** knit 2. Repeat the following procedure. * Purl 3. Knit 5. * End the row with purl 3, knit 2.

For the **fifteenth row,** purl 2. Repeat the following procedure. * Knit 3. Purl 5. * End row with knit 3, purl 2.

For the **sixteenth row,** repeat the fourteenth row.

For the **seventeenth row,** repeat the fifteenth row.

For the **eighteenth row,** repeat the fourteenth row.

For the **nineteenth row,** purl 2. Repeat the following procedure. * Slip 1. Knit 2 together. Pass slip stitch over. Purl 5. * End row with slip 1. Knit 2 together. Pass slip stitch over. Purl 2.

For the **twentieth row,** repeat the second row.

Repeat the **first through twentieth rows** as required.

## Bicolor Diagonal Stripe Pattern

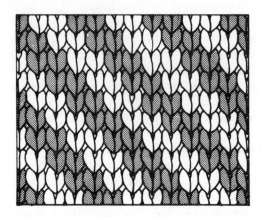

Introducing a second color adds interest to a design, especially when it is worked in a diagonal direction.

For the **beginning row,** cast on a multiple of 4 stitches, using the darker color.

For the **first row,** purl.

For the **second row,** work with the lighter color. Knit 1. Repeat the following procedure. * Slip 2 with yarn in back. Knit 2. * End row with slip 2, knit 1.

For the **third row,** continue to use lighter color. Knit 1. Repeat the following procedure. * Slip 1 with yarn in front. Purl 3. * End with slip 1, purl 1, knit 1.

For the **fourth row,** use darker color. Knit 1. Slip 1 with yarn in back. Repeat the following procedure. * Knit 2. Slip 2 with yarn in back. * End with knit 2.

For the **fifth row,** continue with darker color. Knit 1. Purl 1. Repeat the following procedure. * Slip 1 with yarn in front. Purl 3. * End by slipping 1 stitch and knitting 1.

For the **sixth row,** work with lighter color. Knit 1. Repeat the following procedure. * Knit 2. Slip 2 with yarn in back. * End with knit 3.

For the **seventh row,** continue with lighter color. Knit 1. Purl 2. Repeat the following procedure. * Slip 1 with yarn in front. Purl 3. * End with knit 1.

For the **eighth row,** change to darker color. Repeat the following procedure. * Knit 2. Slip 2 with yarn in back. * End with knit 2. Slip 1. Knit 1.

For the **ninth row,** continue to use darker color. Knit 1. Repeat the following procedure. * Purl 3. Slip 1 stitch with yarn in front. * End by purling 2 and knitting 1.

Repeat the **second through ninth rows** as many times as required.

## Bird's Eye Pattern

Although this pattern can be made in wools of different weights, it is most beautiful when worked in fine yarn as it would be in Shetland-type knitting for a lacy effect.

For the **beginning row,** cast on a multiple of 4 stitches.

For the **first row,** repeat the following procedure. * Knit 2 together. Put yarn over needle twice. Knit 2 together. *

For the **second row,** repeat the following procedure. * Knit 1. Then into the 2 yarn-overs in previous row knit 1 and purl 1. * End with knit 1.

For the **third row,** knit 2. Repeat the following procedure. * Knit 2 together. Put yarn over needle twice. Knit 2 together. * End with knit 2.

For the **fourth row,** knit 2. Repeat the following procedure. * Knit 1. Into the 2 yarn-overs of previous row knit 1 and purl 1. Knit 1. * End by knitting 2.

Repeat the **first through fourth rows** as required.

## Blister Check Pattern

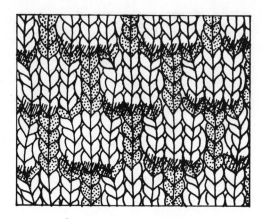

This pattern is sometimes referred to as Coin Stitch. The stitches produce a raised coin-shaped dot. This stitch pattern is most effective when 2 contrasting colors are used—A and B.

For the **beginning row,** cast on a multiple of 4 stitches plus 1, using color A.

For the **first row,** knit, with color A.

For the **second row,** purl, continuing to use color A.

For the **third row,** knit with color B.

For the **fourth row,** purl with color B.

For the **fifth row,** repeat the third row.

For the **sixth row,** repeat the fourth row.

For the **seventh row,** use color A. Knit 2. Repeat the following procedure. * Drop next stitch off needle carefully. Unravel 4 rows down. Pick up color A stitch from the second row below. Insert needle into this stitch and under the 4 connecting threads of color B. Knit, catching the 4 loose strands in back of the stitch. Knit 3. * End with 2 knit stitches.

For the **eighth row,** purl with color A.

For the **ninth row,** knit with color B.

For the **tenth row,** purl with color B.

For the **eleventh row,** knit with color B.

For the **twelfth row,** purl with color B.

For the **thirteenth row,** use color A. Knit 4. Repeat the following procedure. * Drop next stitch. Unravel 4 rows down. Pick up the color A stitch from 5 rows below, in the same way as in the seventh row. Knit 3. * End by knitting 1.

Repeat the **second through thirteenth rows** as required.

## Block Pattern

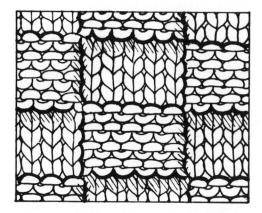

Dice Pattern is the name that is sometimes given this pattern. The easy-to-make check design can be varied in size if different numbers of knit and purl stitches are combined.

For the **beginning row,** cast on a multiple of 10 stitches plus 5.

For the **first row,** knit 5. Repeat the following procedure. * Purl 5. Knit 5. *

For the **second row,** purl 5. Repeat the following procedure. * Knit 5. Purl 5.*

For the **third row,** repeat the first row.

For the **fourth row,** repeat the second row.

For the **fifth row,** repeat the first row.

For the **sixth row,** repeat the first row.

For the **seventh row,** repeat the second row.

For the **eighth row,** repeat the first row.

For the **ninth row,** repeat the second row.

For the **tenth row,** knit 5. Repeat the following procedure. * Purl 5. Knit 5. *

Repeat the **first through tenth rows** as required.

A variation of this pattern can be made by arranging the stitches to appear as oblong blocks.

For the **beginning row,** cast on a multiple of 10 stitches plus 5.

For the **first row,** knit.

For the **second row,** knit 5. Repeat the following procedure. * Purl 5. Knit 5. *

For the **third row,** repeat the first row.

For the **fourth row,** repeat the second row.

For the **fifth row,** repeat the first row.

For the **sixth row,** repeat the second row.

For the **seventh row,** repeat the first row.

For the **eighth row,** purl 5. Repeat the following procedure. * Knit 5. Purl 5. *

For the **ninth row,** repeat the first row.

For the **tenth row,** repeat the eighth row.

For the **eleventh row,** repeat the first row.

For the **twelfth row,** repeat the eighth row.

Repeat the **first through twelfth rows** as many times as required.

## Blue Bell Pattern

*See* Bell Pattern.

## Bobble Stitch

Puffy mounds dot the surface when this pattern stitch is used. They can be arranged singly, as shown here, or grouped together to create motifs.

For the **beginning row,** cast on a multiple of 6 stitches plus 5.

For the **first five rows,** knit.

For the **sixth row,** knit 5. Repeat the following procedure. * To make 6 bobble stitches, do this 3 times in the next stitch—yarn over and knit 1. Turn work around and slip 1 stitch. Purl 5 across the 6 bobble stitches. Turn again and slip 1 stitch. Knit 5. Turn again and purl 2 stitches together 3 times. Turn again and slip 1 stitch, knit 2 together, pass slip stitch over. This sequence of stitches completes the bobble. Knit 5. *

For the **seventh row,** knit 5. Repeat the following procedure. * Purl 1 stitch through its back loop. Knit 5. *

For the **eighth through eleventh rows,** knit.

For the **twelfth row,** knit 8. Repeat the following procedure. * Knit bobble in next stitch as in the sixth row. Knit 5. * End with knit 3.

Repeat the **first through twelfth rows** as required.

## Bowknot Pattern

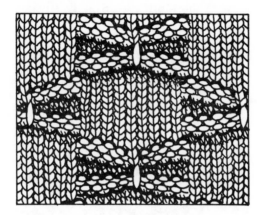

Graceful bows, worked in a block-type design, can produce a dainty effect when knitted in a lightweight yarn.

For the **beginning row,** cast on a multiple of 18 stitches plus 9.

For the **first row,** knit 9. Repeat the following procedure. * Purl 9. Knit 9. *

For the **second row,** purl 9. Repeat the following procedure. * Knit 9. Purl 9. *

For the **third row,** knit.

For the **fourth row,** purl.

For the **fifth row,** knit.

For the **sixth row,** purl.

For the **seventh row,** repeat first row.

For the **eighth row,** repeat second row.

For the **ninth row,** knit 13. Repeat the following procedure. * Insert needle into the front of the next stitch, 9 rows below. Draw up a loop. Slip the loop onto the left-hand needle. Knit the loop and the next stitch together. Knit 17 stitches. * End last repeat with 13 knit stitches.

For the **tenth row,** purl.

For the **eleventh row,** purl 9. Repeat the following procedure. * Knit 9. Purl 9. *

For the **twelfth row,** knit 9. Repeat the following procedure. * Purl 9. Knit 9. *

For the **thirteenth row,** knit.

For the **fourteenth row,** purl.

For the **fifteenth row,** knit.

For the **sixteenth row,** purl.

For the **seventeenth row,** repeat the eleventh row.

For the **eighteenth row,** repeat the twelfth row.

For the **nineteenth row,** knit 4. Repeat the following procedure. * Working in the ninth row below, pull up a loop. Knit it together with next stitch, as in the ninth row. Knit 17 stitches. * End with 4 knit stitches.

For the **twentieth row,** purl.

Repeat the **first through twentieth rows** as required.

## Bramble Stitch

This well-known pattern, which has several names, creates an interesting directional and textural look. It is frequently used for panels in heavy sweaters, but it can also be used for a lacy effect.

For the **beginning row,** cast on a multiple of 4 stitches.

For the **first row,** purl.

For the **second row,** repeat the following procedure. * Working in the same stitch, knit 1, purl 1, knit 1. Then purl 3 stitches together. *

For the **third row,** purl.

For the **fourth row,** repeat the following procedure. * Purl 3 together. Then, working in the same stitch, knit 1, purl 1, and knit 1. *

Repeat the **first through fourth rows** as many times as required.

## Brick Pattern

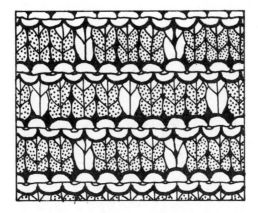

Two colors can be used to create a realistic brick-type design. This stitch is most effective when it is worked in a light and a dark color. Use the dark for the bricks, light for the mortar.

For the **beginning row,** cast on a multiple of 4 stitches plus 3, using the light color.

For the **first row,** knit, using the lighter color.

For the **second row,** repeat the first row.

For the **third row,** change to the darker color. Knit 1. Repeat the following procedure. * Slip 1 stitch with yarn in back. Knit 3. * For the last 2 stitches, slip 1 and knit 1.

For the **fourth row,** use the darker color. Purl 1. Repeat the following procedure. * Slip 1 stitch with yarn in front. Purl 3. * For the last 2 stitches, slip 1 and purl 1.

For the **fifth row,** change to the lighter color. Knit.

For the **sixth row,** repeat the fifth row.

For the **seventh row,** change to the darker color. Knit 3. Repeat the following procedure. * Slip 1 with yarn in back. Knit 3. *

For the **eighth row,** continue to use the darker color. Repeat the following procedure. * Slip 1 with yarn in front. Purl 3. *

Repeat the **first through eighth rows** as many times as required.

## Brioche Stitch

This stitch provides a dainty type of ribbing with a stretchy quality. It has an Eastern origin and is sometimes called Oriental Rib Stitch, Point D'Angleterre, Reverse Lace Stitch, or Shawl Stitch.

For the **beginning row,** cast on an even number of stitches.

For the **first row,** repeat the following procedure. * Put yarn over. Slip 1. Knit 1. *

For the **second row,** repeat the following procedure. * Put yarn over. Slip 1. Knit 2 together. *

Repeat the **second row** as many times as required.

## Brioche Stitch—Double

This pattern is sometimes referred to as Three-dimensional Honeycomb. It is a versatile one, creating different looks when the weight of the yarn and size of the needles are varied.

For the **beginning row,** cast on an even number of stitches.

For the **first row,** knit.

For the **second row,** repeat the following procedure. * Knit 1. To knit the next stitch, insert the needle in the center of stitch in row below and knit through both loops. * End by knitting 2 stitches.

For the **third row,** knit.

For the **fourth row,** knit 1. Repeat the following procedure. * Knit 1. To knit the next stitch, insert the needle in the center of stitch in row below and knit through both loops. * End by knitting 1 stitch.

Repeat the **first through fourth rows** as many times as required.

## Butterfly Pattern

This is a pattern in which slip stitches create the design motif. In fact, this stitch is sometimes called Butterfly Slip Stitch.

For the **beginning row,** cast on a multiple of 10 stitches plus 4.

For the **first row,** knit 2. Repeat the following procedure. * Bring yarn forward. Slip 5. Take yarn back. Knit 5. * End the row with yarn forward. Slip 5. Yarn forward. Slip 5. Yarn back. Knit 2.

For the **second row,** purl.

For the **third row,** repeat the first row.

For the **fourth row,** purl.

For the **fifth row,** repeat the first row.

For the **sixth row,** purl.

For the **seventh row,** repeat the first row.

For the **eighth row,** purl.

For the **ninth row,** repeat the first row.

For the **tenth row,** purl 4. Repeat the following procedure.

* For the next stitch, which falls in the middle of the 5 slipped stitches, insert the right-hand needle upward through the 5 loose strands of yarn. Transfer them to the left-hand needle. Purl this stitch together with the 5 loose strands. Purl 9 stitches. * End row by purling 4 stitches.

For the **eleventh row,** knit 7. Repeat the following procedure. * Yarn forward. Slip 5. Yarn back. Knit five. * End row yarn forward, slip 5. Yarn back. Knit 7.

For the **twelfth row,** purl.

For the **thirteenth row,** repeat the eleventh row.

For the **fourteenth row,** purl.

For the **fifteenth row,** repeat the eleventh row.

For the **sixteenth row,** purl.

For the **seventeenth row,** repeat the eleventh row.

For the **eighteenth row,** purl.

For the **nineteenth row,** repeat the eleventh row.

For the **twentieth row,** purl 9. Repeat the following procedure. **\***
For the next stitch, which falls in the middle of the 5 slipped stitches,
insert the right-hand needle upward through the 5 loose strands of
yarn. Transfer them to the left-hand needle. Purl this stitch together
with the 5 loose strands. Purl 9. **\***

Repeat the **first through twentieth rows** as many times as required.

## Cable Pattern and Stitch

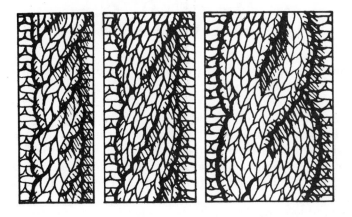

The arrangement of stitches for this type of stitch pattern creates a
ropelike design or cable. They are made by crossing one group of
stitches either in front or in back of a second group of stitches. Usually
a stockinette stitch is used for the cables, with purl stitches defining
them. There are many types of cable pattern, as well as variations
of the basic cable stitch.

## Cable Pattern—Chain

A chainlike wavy effect is created by this cable stitch. Sometimes it is called Double Ribbon Stitch.

For the **beginning row,** cast on 12 stitches for the cable motif.

For the **first row,** knit 2. Purl 8. Knit 2.

For the **second row,** purl 2. Slip next 2 stitches onto a double-pointed needle and leave in back. Knit 2. Then knit the 2 stitches on the double-pointed needle. Slip next 2 stitches onto a double-pointed needle and leave in front. Knit 2. Then knit the 2 stitches on the double-pointed needle. Purl 2.

For the **third row,** repeat the first row.

For the **fourth row,** purl 2. Knit 8. Purl 2.

For the **fifth row,** repeat the first row.

For the **sixth row,** purl 2. Slip next 2 stitches onto a double-pointed needle and leave in front. Knit 2. Then knit the 2 stitches on the double-pointed needle. Slip next 2 stitches onto a double-pointed needle and leave in back. Knit 2. Then knit the 2 stitches on the double-pointed needle. Purl 2.

For the **seventh row,** repeat the first row.

For the **eighth row,** repeat the fourth row.

Repeat the **first through eighth rows** as many times as required.

## Cable Pattern—Clustered

Small blocks of cables create a checkerboard effect. It is a German pattern and sometimes called Checked Cable.

For the **beginning cable,** cast on a multiple of 12 stitches plus 6.

For the **first row,** purl 6. Repeat the following procedure. * Knit 6. Purl 6. *

For the **second row,** knit 6. Repeat the following procedure. * Purl 6. Knit 6. *

For the **third row,** repeat the first row.

For the **fourth row,** repeat the second row.

For the **fifth row,** purl 6. Repeat the following procedure. * Slip next 3 stitches onto a double-pointed needle. Leave in back. Knit 3. Then knit the 3 stitches on the double-pointed needle. Purl 6. *

For the **sixth row,** knit 6. Repeat the following procedure. * Purl 6. Knit 6. *

For the **seventh row,** purl 6. Repeat the following procedure. * Knit 6. Purl 6. *

For the **eighth row,** knit six. Repeat the following procedure. * Purl 6. Knit 6. *

For the **ninth row,** knit 6. Repeat the following procedure. * Purl 6. Knit 6. *

For the **tenth row,** purl 6. Repeat the following procedure. * Knit 6. Purl 6. *

For the **eleventh row,** repeat the ninth row.

For the **twelfth row,** repeat the tenth row.

For the **thirteenth row,** repeat the following procedure. * Slip 3 stitches onto a double-pointed needle. Leave in back. Knit 3. Knit the 3 stitches on the double-pointed needle. Purl 6. * End by slipping 3 stitches onto a double-pointed needle. Leave in back. Knit 3. Knit the 3 stitches on the double-pointed needle.

For the **fourteenth row,** purl 6. Repeat the following procedure. * Knit 6. Purl 6. *

For the **fifteenth row,** knit 6. Repeat the following procedure. * Purl 6. Knit 6. *

For the **sixteenth row,** purl 6. Repeat the following procedure. * Knit 6. Purl 6. *

Repeat the **first through sixteenth rows** as many times as required.

## Cable Pattern—Horseshoe

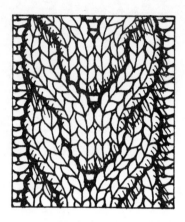

Sometimes this cable pattern is called Double Cable. One design motif seems to melt into the next.

For the **beginning row,** cast on 12 stitches for the cable motif.

For the **first row,** knit 2. Purl 8. Knit 2.

For the **second row,** purl 2. Slip the next 2 stitches onto a double-pointed needle. Leave in back. Knit 2. Then knit the 2 stitches on the double-pointed needle. Slip the next 2 stitches onto a double-pointed needle. Leave in front. Knit 2. Then knit the 2 stitches on the double-pointed needle. Purl 2.

For the **third row,** repeat the first row.

For the **fourth row,** purl 2. Knit 8. Purl 2.

For the **fifth row,** repeat the first row.

For the **sixth row,** repeat the fourth row.

For the **seventh row,** repeat the first row.

For the **eighth row,** repeat the fourth row.

Repeat the **first through eighth rows** as many times as required.

## Cable Pattern—Miniature

This is a dainty version of the Cable Pattern. Only 2 stitches are used to form the design.

For the **beginning row,** cast on a multiple of 4 stitches plus 2.

For the **first row,** knit 2. Repeat the following procedure. * Purl 2. Knit 2. *

For the **second row,** purl 2. Repeat the following procedure. * Knit 2. Purl 2. *

For the **third row,** repeat the first row.

For the **fourth row,** purl 2. Repeat the following procedure. * Knit 2 together but do not remove the needle. Insert right-hand needle between the 2 stitches just knitted together. Knit the first again. Then slip both stitches from needle together. Purl 2. *

Repeat the **first through fourth rows** as many times as required.

## Cable Pattern—Mock

This type of knitting creates a flatter version of a cable pattern.

For the **beginning row,** cast on a multiple of 8 stitches.

For the **first row,** repeat the following procedure. * Purl 5. Knit 3. *

For the **second row,** repeat the following procedure. * Purl 3. Knit 5. *

For the **third row,** repeat the following procedure. * Purl 5. Slip 1. Knit 2. Wrap yarn around needle to make 1 stitch. Then pass the slip stitch over the 2 stitches that were knitted and the 1 that was made. *

For the **fourth row,** repeat the second row.

Repeat the **first through fourth rows** as many times as required.

## Cable Pattern—Plait

This form of cable knitting creates a braided effect that seems to give a smart look and is not complicated to make.

For the **beginning row,** cast on 13 stitches for the cable motif.

For the **first row,** purl 2. Knit 9. Purl 2.

For the **second row,** knit 2. Purl 9. Knit 2.

For the **third row,** purl 2. Slip the next 3 stitches onto a double-pointed needle. Leave in front. Knit 3. Then knit the 3 stitches from the double-pointed needle. Knit 3. Purl 2.

For the **fourth row,** repeat the second row.

For the **fifth row,** repeat the first row.

For the **sixth row,** repeat the second row.

For the **seventh row,** purl 2. Knit 3. Slip next 3 stitches onto a double-pointed needle. Leave in back. Knit 3. Knit the 3 stitches from the double-pointed needle. Purl 2.

For the **eighth row,** repeat the second row.

Repeat the **first through eighth rows** as many times as required.

## Cable—Pattern Slipped

A new twist is given this cable pattern through the use of a slipped stitch.

For the **beginning row,** cast on a multiple of 6 stitches plus 2, and purl a starting row.

For the **first row,** purl 2. Repeat the following procedure. * Skip 1 stitch. Insert right-hand needle from front to back into next stitch and knit the stitch. Do not drop stitch from left-handle needle. Then insert right-hand needle into back loop of skipped stitch and knit the stitch. Drop both stitches from left-hand needle. Skip 1 stitch. Insert right-hand needle into back loop of next stitch and knit the stitch. Do not drop stitch from left-hand needle. Insert right-hand needle into front loop of skipped stitch and knit the stitch. Drop both stitches from left-hand needle. Purl 2. *

For the **second row,** knit 2. Repeat the following procedure. * Purl 4. Knit 2. *

For the **third row,** purl 2. Repeat the following procedure. * Knit 4. Purl 2. *

For the **fourth row,** repeat the second row.

Repeat the **first through fourth rows** as many times as required.

## Cable Stitch Pattern—
### Eight-stitch

For the **beginning row,** cast on 12 stitches for cable.
For the **first row,** knit 2. Purl 8. Knit 2.
For the **second row,** purl 2. Knit 8. Purl 2.
For the **third row,** repeat the first row.
For the **fourth row,** purl 2. Slip the next 4 stitches onto a double-pointed needle. Leave needle in back. Knit 4. Then knit the 4 stitches on the double-pointed needle. Purl 2.
For the **fifth row,** repeat the first row.
For the **sixth row,** repeat the second row.
For the **seventh row,** repeat the first row.
For the **eighth row,** repeat the second row.
For the **ninth row,** repeat the first row.
For the **tenth row,** repeat the second row.
Repeat the **first through tenth rows** as many times as required.

## Cable Stitch Pattern—
### Four-stitch

For the **beginning row,** cast on 12 stitches for cable.
For the **first row,** knit 4. Purl 4. Knit 4.
For the **second row,** purl 4. Knit 4. Purl 4.
For the **third row,** repeat first row.
For the **fourth row,** purl 4. Slip next 2 stitches onto a double-pointed needle. Leave in back. Knit 2. Then knit the 2 stitches on the double-pointed needle. Purl 4.
Repeat the **first through fourth rows** as many times as required.

## Cable Stitch Pattern—
### Six-stitch

For the **beginning row,** cast on 10 stitches for cable.
For the **first row,** knit 2. Purl 6. Knit 2.
For the **second row,** purl 2. Knit 6. Purl 2.
For the **third row,** repeat the first row.
For the **fourth row,** purl 2. Slip the next 3 stitches onto a double-pointed needle. Leave in back. Knit 3. Then knit the 3 stitches on the double-pointed needle. Purl 2.
For the **fifth row,** repeat the first row.
For the **sixth row,** repeat the second row.
Repeat the **first through sixth rows** as many times as required.

## Candle Pattern

A series of eyelets is the central point of each of the candlelike motifs that form this design pattern.

For the **beginning row,** cast on a multiple of 10 plus 1.

For the **first row,** knit 3. Repeat the following procedure. * Knit 2 together. Put yarn over. Knit 1. Yarn over. Then slip 1, knit 1, and pass slip stitch over knit stitch. Knit 5. * End by knitting 3.

For the **second row,** purl.

For the **third row,** knit 2. Repeat the following procedure. * Knit 2 together. Knit 1. Yarn over. Knit 1. Yarn over. Knit 1. Then slip 1, knit 1, and pass slip stitch over knit stitch. Knit 3. * End by knitting 2.

For the **fourth row,** purl.

For the **fifth row,** knit 1. Repeat the following procedure. * Knit 2 together. Knit 2. Yarn over. Knit 1. Yarn over. Knit 2. Then slip 1, knit 1, and pass slip stitch over. Knit 1. *

For the **sixth row,** purl.

For the **seventh row,** knit 2 together. Repeat the following procedure. * Knit 3. Yarn over. Knit 1. Yarn over. Knit 3. Slip 1. Knit 2 together. Pass slip stitch over the 2 stitches that are knit together. * End with slip 1, knit 1, and pass slip stitch over.

For the **eighth row,** purl.

For the **ninth row,** knit 1. Repeat the following procedure. * Yarn over. Then slip 1, knit 1, and pass slip stitch over. Knit 5. Knit 2 together. Yarn over. Knit 1. *

For the **tenth row,** purl.

For the **eleventh row,** knit 1. Repeat the following procedure. * Yarn over. Knit 1. Then slip 1, knit 1, and pass slip stitch over. Knit 3. Knit 2 together. Knit 1. Yarn over. Knit 1. *

For the **twelfth row,** purl.

For the **thirteenth row,** knit 1. Repeat the following procedure. * Yarn over. Knit 2. Then slip 1, knit 1, and pass slip stitch over. Knit 1. Knit 2 together. Knit 2. Yarn over. Knit 1. *

For the **fourteenth row,** purl.

For the **fifteenth row,** knit 1. Repeat the following procedure. * Yarn over. Knit 3. Slip 1. Knit 2 together. Pass slip stitch over the 2 stitches that are knit together. Knit 3. Yarn over. Knit 1. *

For the **sixteenth row,** purl.

Repeat the **first through sixteenth rows** as many times as required.

## Cat's Eye Pattern

This is a Shetland allover lace pattern that is easy to make. By varying the weight of the yarn and size of the needle, the size of the meshes can be changed.

For the **beginning row,** cast on a multiple of 4 stitches.

For the **first row,** purl 2. Repeat the following procedure. * Put yarn around needle to make 1 stitch. Purl 4 together. * End with purl 2.

For the **second row,** knit 2. Repeat the following procedure. * Knit 1. Then knit 1, purl 1, and knit 1 into the stitch that was made in the first row. * End with knit 2.

For the **third row,** knit.

Repeat the **first through third rows** as many times as required.

## Cat's Paw Pattern

This openwork pattern is another of the traditional Shetland designs.

For the **beginning row,** cast on 7 stitches.

For the **first row,** purl.

For the **second row,** knit 1. Knit 2 together. Yarn over. Knit 1. Yarn over. Then slip 1, knit 1, and pass slip stitch over. Knit 1.

For the **third row,** purl.

For the **fourth row,** knit 2 together. Yarn over. Knit 3. Yarn over. Then slip 1, knit 1, and pass slip stitch over.

For the **fifth row,** purl.

For the **sixth row,** knit 2. Yarn over. Then slip 1, knit 2 together, and pass slip stitch over. Yarn over. Knit 2.

Repeat the **first through sixth rows** as many times as required.

## Checked Cable Pattern

*See* Cable Pattern—Clustered.

## Chequered Florette Pattern

This eyelet design is one of the many lacy French patterns that give the look of an insertion.

For the **beginning row,** cast on a multiple of 12 stitches plus 5.

For the **first row,** knit 2. Repeat the following procedure. * Knit 4. Purl 2 together. Yarn over. Knit 1. Put yarn around needle. Purl 2 together. Knit 3. * End with knit 3.

For the **second row,** purl.

For the **third row,** knit 2. Repeat the following procedure. * Knit 4. Put yarn around needle. Purl 2 together. Knit 1. Purl 2 together. Yarn over. Knit 3. * End with knit 3.

For the **fourth row,** purl.

For the **fifth row,** repeat the third row.

For the **sixth row,** purl.

For the **seventh row,** repeat the first row.

For the **eight row,** purl.

For the **ninth row,** knit 2. Repeat the following procedure. * Knit 1. Put yarn around needle. Purl 2 together. Knit 7. Purl 2 together. Put yarn over needle. * End with knit 3.

For the **tenth row,** purl.

For the **eleventh row,** knit 2. Repeat the following procedure. * Knit 1. Purl 2 together. Yarn over. Knit 7. Yarn around needle. Purl 2 together. * End with knit 3.

For the **twelfth row,** purl.

For the **thirteenth row,** repeat the eleventh row.

For the **fourteenth row,** purl.

For the **fifteenth row,** repeat the ninth row.

For the **sixteenth row,** purl.

Repeat the **first through sixteenth rows** as many times as required.

## Chevron Fantastic Pattern

This pattern forms vertical stripes with a rib of eyelets separating each pair of stripes.

For the **beginning row,** cast on a multiple of 8 stitches plus 10.

For the **first row,** knit 1. Then knit 1 stitch and leave it on needle. Insert the needle into the top of the stitch below the one that has just been knitted and make 1 knit stitch. Slip both stitches together from the needle. Knit 2. Repeat the following procedure. * Insert the needle into the back of the next 2 stitches and knit them together. Transfer the resulting stitch to the left-hand needle. Pass the next stitch over it and off the needle. Return the stitch to the right-hand needle. Knit 2. Knit into the top of the stitch below the next stitch. Then knit the next stitch through the back. Follow by knitting again into the top of the stitch already worked in. Knit 2. * End by inserting needle into the back of the next 2 stitches and knitting them together. Pass the next stitch over. Knit 2. Then knit into the stitch below the next stitch. Follow by knitting the next stitch in the regular manner.

For the **second row,** purl.

Repeat the **first and second rows** as many times as required.

## Chevron Pattern

This zigzag design is interesting in that the knitting appears the same on both sides. However, the effect of the stitches is reversed.

For the **beginning row,** cast on a multiple of 8 stitches plus 1.

For the **first row,** knit 1. Repeat the following procedure. * Purl 7. Knit 1. *

For the **second row,** purl 1. Repeat the following procedure. * Knit 7. Purl 1. *

For the **third row,** knit 2. Repeat the following procedure. * Purl 5. Knit 3. * End row with purl 5, knit 2.

For the **fourth row,** purl 2. Repeat the following procedure. * Knit 5. Purl 3. * End row with knit 5, purl 2.

For the **fifth row,** knit 3. Repeat the following procedure. * Purl 3. Knit 5. * End row with purl 3, knit 3.

For the **sixth row,** purl 3. Repeat the following procedure. * Knit 3. Purl 5. * End row with knit 3, purl 3.

For the **seventh row,** knit 4. Repeat the following procedure. * Purl 1. Knit 7. * End row with purl 1, knit 4.

For the **eighth row,** purl 4. Repeat the following procedure. * Knit 1. Purl 7. * End the row with knit 1, purl 4.

For the **ninth row,** repeat the second row.

For the **tenth row,** repeat the first row.

For the **eleventh row,** repeat the fourth row.

For the **twelfth row,** repeat the third row.

For the **thirteenth row,** repeat the sixth row.

For the **fourteenth row,** repeat the fifth row.

For the **fifteenth row,** repeat the eighth row.

For the **sixteenth row,** repeat the seventh row.

Repeat the **first through sixteenth rows** as many times as required.

## Chevron Seed Pattern

Working seed stitches in zigzag fashion creates this pattern with an interesting textural quality.

For the **beginning row,** cast on 22 stitches plus 1.

For the **first row,** knit 1. Repeat the following procedure. * Purl 3. Then knit 1 and purl 1 twice. Knit 1. Purl 5. Knit 1. Then purl 1 and knit 1 twice. Purl 3. Knit 1. *

For the **second row,** purl 1. Repeat the following procedure. * Purl 1. Knit 3. Then purl 1 and knit 1 twice. Purl 1. Knit 3. Purl 1. Then knit 1 and purl 1 twice. Knit 3. Purl 2. *

For the **third row,** knit 1. Repeat the following procedure. * Knit 2. Purl 3. Then knit 1 and purl 1 five times. Knit 1. Purl 3. Knit 3. *

For the **fourth row,** knit 1. Repeat the following procedure. * Purl 3. Knit 3. Then purl 1 and knit 1 four times. Purl 1. Knit 3. Purl 3. Knit one. *

For the **fifth row,** purl 1. Repeat the following procedure. * Purl 1. Knit 3. Purl 3. Then knit 1 and purl 1 three times. Knit 1. Purl 3. Knit 3. Purl 2. *

For the **sixth row,** knit 1. Repeat the following procedure. * Knit 2. Purl 3. Knit 3. Then purl 1 and knit 1 twice. Purl 1. Knit 3. Purl 3. Knit 3. *

For the **seventh row,** knit 1. Repeat the following procedure. * Purl 3. Knit 3. Purl 3. Knit 1. Purl 1. Knit 1. Purl 3. Knit 3. Purl 3. Knit 1. *

For the **eighth row,** knit 1. Repeat the following procedure. * Purl 1. Knit 3, purl 3 and knit 3 twice. Purl 1. Knit 1. *

For the **ninth row,** knit 1. Repeat the following procedure. * Purl 1. Knit 1. Purl 3. Knit 3. Purl 5. Knit 3. Purl 3. Knit 1. Purl 1. Knit 1. *

For the **tenth row,** knit 1. Repeat the following procedure. * Purl 1. Knit 1. Purl 1. Then knit 3 and purl 3 twice. Knit 3. Then purl 1 and knit 1 twice. *

For the **eleventh row,** knit 1. Repeat the following procedure. * Purl 1 and knit 1 twice. Purl 3. Knit 3. Purl 1. Knit 3. Purl 3. Then knit 1 and purl 1 twice. Knit 1. *

For the **twelfth row,** knit 1. Repeat the following procedure. * Purl 1 and knit 1 twice. Purl 1. Knit 3. Purl 5. Knit 3. Then purl 1 and knit 1 three times. *

For the **thirteenth row,** purl 1. Repeat the following procedure. * Purl 1 and knit 1 three times. Purl 3. Knit 3. Purl 3. Then knit 1 and purl 1 twice. Knit 1. Purl 2. *

For the **fourteenth row,** knit 1. Repeat the following procedure. * Knit 2. Then purl 1 and knit 1 twice. Follow by purling 1 and knitting 3 twice; purl 1 and knit 1 three times. Knit 2. *

Repeat the **first through fourteenth rows** as many times as required.

## Close Stitch

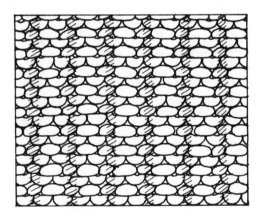

This variation of the Heel Stitch produces a ribbed effect in an interesting texture.

For the **beginning row,** cast on an odd number of stitches.

For the **first row,** knit.

For the **second row,** knit 1. Repeat the following procedure. * Slip 1 with yarn in back. Knit 1. *

Repeat the **first and second rows** as many times as required.

## Coin Stitch
*See* Blister Check Pattern.

## Coral Knot Stitch

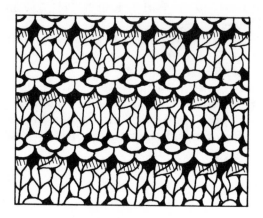

This pattern creates some interesting textural effects with stripes of eyelet and nubby stitches.

For the **beginning row,** cast on a multiple of 2 stitches.

For the **first row,** knit 1. Repeat the following procedure. * Knit 2 together. * End row with knit 1.

For the **second row,** knit 1. Repeat the following procedure. * Knit 1. Insert needle under yarn connecting the next stitch and the one just knitted, and knit a stitch. * End with knit 1.

For the **third row,** knit.

For the **fourth row,** purl.

Repeat the **first through fourth rows** as many times as required.

## Corn-on-the-cob Stitch

Using yarns in 2 colors gives this design pattern a dotted look. Although the colors are worked in stripes, they do not create the usual effect.

For the **beginning row,** cast on a multiple of 2 stitches. Use 2 colors, light and dark.

For the **first row,** knit, using the lighter yarn.

For the **second row,** use the darker yarn. Repeat the following procedure. * Knit 1. Slip 1. * End with knit 1.

For the **third row,** use the darker yarn. Repeat the following procedure. * Bring yarn forward. Slip 1. Put yarn back. Knit 1. * Be sure to slip the light stitches and knit the dark ones, bringing the yarn forward before each slip stitch and back after each.

For the **fourth row,** use the lighter yarn. Repeat the following procedure. * Slip 1. Knit 1 into back of stitch. * Be sure to knit the light stitches into the back of the stitch and slip the dark stitches, keeping yarn in the back.

For the **fifth row,** use the lighter yarn. Repeat the following procedure. * Knit 1. Bring yarn forward. Slip 1. Take yarn to back. * Be sure to knit the light stitches and slip the dark ones, with the yarn brought forward before a slip stitch and back afterward.

Repeat the **second through fifth rows** as many times as required.

## Crest of the Wave Pattern

This is one of the lacy Shetland patterns. Although it appears compli-cated to make, it actually can be knitted without problems.

For the **beginning row,** cast on a multiple of 12 stitches plus 1.

For the **first through fourth rows,** knit.

For the **fifth row,** knit 1. Repeat the following procedure. * Knit 2 together twice. Then put yarn over and knit 1 three times. Yarn over. Then do this twice: slip 1, knit 1, pass slip stitch over. * End with knit 1.

For the **sixth row,** purl.

For the **seventh row,** repeat the fifth row.

For the **eighth row,** repeat the sixth row.

For the **ninth row,** repeat the fifth row.

For the **tenth row,** repeat the sixth row.

For the **eleventh row,** repeat the fifth row.

For the **twelfth row,** purl.

Repeat the **first through twelfth rows** as many times as required.

## Crochet-knit Shell Pattern

By a careful arrangement of stitches, the effect of crocheted shells is produced.

For the **beginning row,** cast on a multiple of 6 stitches plus 3.

For the **first row,** knit 1. Repeat the following procedure. * Yarn over. Knit 1. * End with knit 1.

For the **second row,** knit, dropping off the needle all yarn-overs of previous row.

For the **third row,** knit 1. Knit 3 together. Repeat the following procedure. * Put the yarn over needle twice. Knit 1. Yarn over twice. Then slip 2, knit 3 together, and pass 2 slip stitches over. * End by putting yarn over twice. Knit 1. Yarn over twice. Knit 3 together. Knit 1.

For the **fourth row,** knit 1. Repeat the following procedure. * Knit 1. Knit into front and back of double yarn-over. * End with knit 2.

For the **fifth row,** repeat the first row.

For the **sixth row,** repeat the second row.

For the **seventh row,** knit one. Repeat the following procedure. * Knit one. Yarn over twice. Then do this twice: slip 2, knit 3 together, and pass 2 slip stitches over. * End with knit 2.

For the **eighth row,** repeat the fourth row.

Repeat the **first through eighth rows** as many times as required.

## Crochet-Knit Traveling Eyelet Pattern

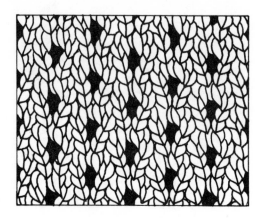

This is a lovely old Italian pattern. It creates a dainty, lacy look.

For the **beginning row,** cast on a multiple of 6 stitches plus 8.

For the **first row,** knit 1. Put yarn over. Then slip 1, knit 1, pass slip stitch over. Knit 2. Repeat the following procedure. * Knit 2 together. Yarn over. Then slip 1, knit 1, and pass slip stitch over. Knit two. * At the last 3 stitches, knit 2 stitches together. Put yarn over. Knit 1.

For the **second row,** knit 1, purl 1. Repeat the following procedure. * Purl 4. Purl into the front and back of the next stitch, which was the yarn-over of previous row. * For the last 6 stitches, purl 5 and knit 1.

For the **third row,** knit 2. Repeat the following procedure. * Knit 2 together. Yarn over. Then slip 1, knit 1, and pass slip stitch over. Knit 2. *

For the **fourth row,** knit 1, purl 2. Repeat the following procedure. * Purl into the front and back of the next stitch. Purl 4. * For the last 4 stitches, purl into the front and back of the next stitch. Purl 2. Knit 1.

Repeat the **first through fourth rows** as many times as required.

**Crown of Glory Pattern**

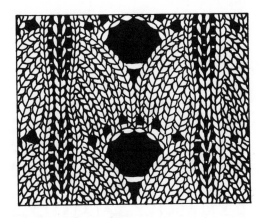

This is a traditional Shetland pattern with a large eyelet at the center of each motif. It probably looks prettiest when worked on small needles in fine yarn.

For the **beginning row,** cast on a multiple of 14 stitches plus 5.

For the **first row,** knit 3. Repeat the following procedure. * Slip 1, knit 1, pass slip stitch over. Knit 9. Knit 2 together. Knit 1. * End row with knit 2.

For the **second row,** purl 2. Repeat the following procedure. * Purl 1. Purl 2 together. Purl 7. Purl 2 together in back. * End row with purl 3.

For the **third row,** knit 3. Repeat the following procedure. * Slip 1, knit 1, pass slip stitch over. Knit 2. Yarn over 3 times. Knit 3. Knit 2 together. Knit 1. * End row with knit 2.

For the **fourth row,** purl 2. Repeat the following procedure. * Purl 1. Purl 2 together. Purl 2. Work 5 stitches—knit 1, purl 1, knit 1, purl 1, knit 1—into the large loop formed by the 3 yarn-overs in the previous row. Then purl 1. Purl 2 together in back. * End row with purl 3.

For the **fifth row,** knit 3. Repeat the following procedure. * Slip 1, knit 1, pass slip stitch over. Knit 6. Knit 2 together. Knit 1. * End by knitting 2.

For the **sixth row,** purl 2. Repeat the following procedure. * Purl 1. Purl 2 together. Purl 6. * End with purl 3.

For the **seventh row,** knit 3. Repeat the following procedure. * Knit 1. Then put yarn over and knit 1 six times. Knit 1. * End with knit 2.

For the **eighth row,** purl.

For the **ninth row,** knit.
For the **tenth row,** purl.
For the **eleventh row,** knit.
For the **twelfth row,** purl.
Repeat the **first through twelfth rows** as many times as required.

## Dewdrop Pattern

This dainty openwork pattern is of English origin. Instead of curling, as so many knitted designs do, this one remains flat.

For the **beginning row,** cast on a multiple of 6 stitches plus 1.

For the **first row,** knit 2. Repeat the following procedure. * Purl 3. Knit 3. * End row with purl 3, knit 2.

For the **second row,** purl 2. Repeat the following procedure. * Knit 3. Purl 3. * End row with knit 3, purl 2.

For the **third row,** repeat the first row.

For the **fourth row,** knit 2. Repeat the following procedure. * Put yarn over. Then slip 1, knit 2 together, and pass slip stitch over. Yarn over. Knit 3. * End with yarn over, slip 1, knit 2 together, and pass slip stitch over. Yarn over. Knit 2.

For the **fifth row,** repeat the second row.

For the **sixth row,** repeat the first row.

For the **seventh row,** repeat the second row.

For the **eighth row,** knit 2 together. Repeat the following procedure. * Yarn over. Knit 3. Yarn over. Then slip 1, knit 2 together, and pass slip stitch over. * End with yarn over. Knit 3. Yarn over. Then slip 1, knit 1, and pass slip stitch over.

Repeat the **first through eighth rows** as many times as required.

## Diagonal Stitch

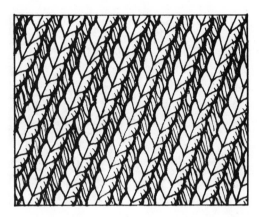

The stitches are worked so that a diagonal striped effect is produced. It can be used for an allover effect as well as for bands and panels.

For the **beginning row,** cast on a multiple of 2 stitches.

For the **first row,** purl.

For the **second row,** repeat the following procedure. * Knit 2 together. Leave them on the left-hand needle. Then insert the right-hand needle between these 2 stitches and knit the first stitch again. Follow by slipping both stitches from the needle at the same time. *

For the **third row,** purl.

For the **fourth row,** knit 1. Repeat the following procedure. * Knit 2 together. Leave them on the left-hand needle. Then insert the right-hand needle between these 2 stitches and knit the first stitch again. Follow by slipping both stitches from the needle at the same time. * End row with knit 1.

Repeat the **first through fourth rows** as many times as required.

## Diamond Brocade Pattern

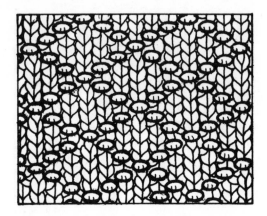

The delicate diamond outline of this well-known old pattern is a favorite. Sometimes it is called the Single Diamond Pattern. It lends itself to variations.

For the **beginning row,** cast on a multiple of 6 stitches plus 1.

For the **first row,** knit 3. Repeat the following procedure. * Purl 1. Knit 5. * End with purl 1, knit 3.

For the **second row,** purl 2. Repeat the following procedure. * Knit 1. Purl 1. Knit 1. Purl 3. * End with knit 1, purl 1, knit 1, purl 2.

For the **third row,** repeat the following procedure. * Knit 1. Purl 1. Knit 3. Purl 1. * End with knit 1.

For the **fourth row,** repeat the following procedure. * Knit 1. Purl 5. * End with knit 1.

For the **fifth row,** repeat the third row.

For the **sixth row,** repeat the second row.

Repeat the **first through sixth rows** as many times as required.

## Diamond Brocade Pattern—Double

The diamond pattern can be given more emphasis by adding another row of stitches.

For the **beginning row,** cast on a multiple of 12 stitches plus 1.

For the **first row,** purl 2. Repeat the following procedure. * Knit 9. Purl 3. * End with knit 9 and purl 2.

For the **second row,** knit 2. Repeat the following procedure. * Purl 9. Knit 3. * End with purl 9 and knit 2.

For the **third row,** repeat the following procedure. * Knit 1. Purl 2. Knit 7. Purl 2. * End with knit 1.

For the **fourth row,** purl 2. Repeat the following procedure. * Knit 2. Purl 5. Knit 10. Purl 3. * End with knit 2. Purl 5. Knit 2. Purl 2.

For the **fifth row,** knit 3. Repeat the following procedure. * Purl 2. Knit 3. Purl 2. Knit 5. * End with purl 2. Knit 3. Purl 2. Knit 3.

For the **sixth row,** purl 4. Repeat the following procedure. * Knit 2. Purl 1. Knit 2. Purl 7. * End with knit 2. Purl 1. Knit 2. Purl 4.

For the **seventh row,** knit 5. Repeat the following procedure. * Purl 3. Knit 9. * End with purl 3, knit 5.

For the **eighth row,** purl 5. Repeat the following procedure. * Knit 3. Purl 9. * End with knit 3, purl 5.

For the **ninth row,** knit 4. Repeat the following procedure. * Purl 2. Knit 1. Purl 2. Knit 7. * End with purl 2. Knit 1. Purl 2. Knit 4.

For the **tenth row,** purl 3. Repeat the following procedure. * Knit 2. Purl 3. Knit 2. Purl 5. * End with knit 2. Purl 3. Knit 2. Purl 3.

For the **eleventh row,** knit 2. Repeat the following procedure. * Purl 2. Knit 5. Purl 2. Knit 3. * End with purl 2. Knit 5. Purl 2. Knit 2.

For the **twelfth row,** purl 1. Repeat the following procedure. * Knit 2. Purl 7. Knit 2. Purl 1. *

Repeat the **first through twelfth rows** as many times as required.

## Diamond Lattice Pattern

Crossed stitches create this raised diamond design, which has an elastic quality.

For the **beginning row,** cast on a multiple of 6 stitches plus 2.

For the **first row,** knit 3. Repeat the following procedure. * Cross right by inserting the right-hand needle into the front of the second stitch on the left-hand needle. Knit but do not slip stitch off the needle. Knit into the front of the first stitch on the needle. Slip both stitches off needle together. Knit 4. * End row by knitting 3.

For the **second row,** purl.

For the **third row,** repeat the following procedure. * Knit 2. Cross right by inserting the right-hand needle into the front of the second stitch on the left-hand needle. Knit but do not remove stitch from needle. Knit into the front of the first stitch on the needle. Slip both stitches off needle together. Then cross left by inserting right-hand needle into the back of the second stitch on the left-hand needle. Knit but do not remove stitch from needle. Bring the right-hand needle with the stitch on it to the front of the work. Knit the first, or skipped, stitch from the front. Slip both stitches off the needle together. * End row with knit 2.

For the **fourth row,** purl.

For the **fifth row,** knit 1. Repeat the following procedure. * Cross right as described in first row. Knit 2. Cross left as described in third row. * End row with knit 1.

For the **sixth row,** purl.

For the **seventh row,** repeat the following procedure. * Cross right as described in first row. Knit 4. * End row with a cross right.

For the **eighth row,** purl.

For the **ninth row,** knit 1. Repeat the following procedure. * Cross left as described in third row. Knit 2. Cross right as described in first row. * End with knit 1.

For the **tenth row,** purl.

For the **eleventh row,** repeat the following procedure. * Knit 2. Cross left as described in the third row. Cross right as described in the first row. * End with knit 2.

For the **twelfth row,** purl.

Repeat the **first through twelfth rows** as many times as required.

## Diamond Pattern

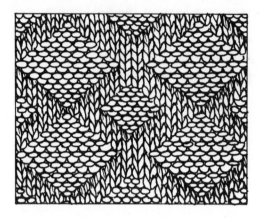

This is another stitch pattern that creates a reversible knitted fabric, although the design does not appear quite the same on both sides.

For the **beginning row,** cast on a multiple of 15 stitches.

For the **first row,** repeat the following procedure. * Knit 1. Purl 13. Knit 1. *

For the **second row,** repeat the following procedure. * Purl 2. Knit 11. Purl 2. *

For the **third row,** repeat the following procedure. * Knit three. Purl 9. Knit 3. *

For the **fourth row,** repeat the following procedure. * Purl 4. Knit 7. Purl 4. *

For the **fifth row,** repeat the following procedure. * Knit 5. Purl 5. Knit 5. *

For the **sixth row,** repeat the following procedure. * Knit 1. Purl 5. Knit 3. Purl 5. Knit 1. *

For the **seventh row,** repeat the following procedure. * Purl 2. Knit 5. Purl 1. Knit 5. Purl 2. *

For the **eighth row,** repeat the following procedure. * Knit 3. Purl 9. Knit 3. *

For the **ninth row,** repeat the seventh row.

For the **tenth row,** repeat the sixth row.

For the **eleventh row,** repeat the fifth row.

For the **twelfth row,** repeat the fourth row.

For the **thirteenth row,** repeat the third row.

For the **fourteenth row,** repeat the second row.

Repeat the **first through fourteenth rows** as many times as required.

**Dice Pattern**
> *See* Block Pattern.


**Dimple Eyelet**

Rows of eyelets give a dainty, striped look to this stitch pattern. Ribbons can be threaded through the eyelets.

For the **beginning row,** cast on a multiple of 2.

For the **first row,** knit.

For the **second row,** purl.

For the **third row,** purl 1. Repeat the following procedure. * Put yarn over needle in reverse by bringing it over the needle from back to front. Purl 2 together. * End by purling 1.

For the **fourth row,** purl. Purl all yarn-over stitches through back loops.

For the **fifth row,** knit.

For the **sixth row,** purl.

For the **seventh row,** purl 2. Repeat the following procedure. * Put yarn over needle in reverse by bringing it over the needle from back to front. Purl 2 together. *

For the **eighth row,** purl. Purl all yarn-over stitches through back loops.

Repeat the **first through eighth rows** as many times as required.


**Dispute Stitch**
> *See* All Fools' Welt Pattern.


**Dot Stitch**
> *See* Sand Stitch.

## Double Hourglass Pattern

This pattern is sometimes called Wavy Ribbing. It can serve as a panel or outline for decorative touches.

For the **beginning row,** cast on a multiple of 14 stitches plus 2.

For the **first row,** knit 1. Repeat the following procedure. * Purl 1. Knit 2. Purl 1. Knit 6. Purl 1. Knit 2. Purl 1. * End with knit 1.

For the **second row,** purl 1. * Then slip 1 stitch onto a double-pointed needle and leave in front, purl 1, and knit the stitch on the double-pointed needle, making a front cross. Purl 1. Make another front cross. Purl 4. Then make a back cross by slipping 1 stitch onto a double-pointed needle and leave in back, purl 1, and knit the stitch on the double-pointed needle. Purl 1. Make another back cross. * End with purl 1.

For the **third row,** knit all the knit stitches and purl all the purl stitches.

For the **fourth row,** purl 1. Repeat the following procedure. * Purl 1. Then make a front cross by slipping 1 stitch onto a double-pointed needle and leave in front, purl 1, and knit the stitch on the double-pointed needle. Purl 1. Make another front cross. Purl 2. Then make a back cross by slipping 1 stitch onto a double-pointed needle and leave in back, purl 1, and knit the stitch on the double-pointed needle. Purl 2. Make another back cross. * End with purl 1.

For the **fifth row,** knit all the knit stitches and purl all the purl stitches.

For the **sixth row,** purl 1. Repeat the following procedure. * Purl 2. Make a front cross by slipping 1 stitch onto a double-pointed needle and leave in front, purl 1, and knit the stitch on the double-pointed needle. Purl 1. Make another front cross. Then make a back cross by slipping 1 stitch onto a double-pointed needle and leave in back, knit 1, and purl the stitch on the double-pointed needle. Purl 1. Then make another back cross. Purl 2. * End with purl 1.

For the **seventh row,** knit all the knit stitches and purl all the purl stitches.

For the **eighth row,** knit all the knit stitches and purl all the purl stitches.

For the **ninth row,** knit all the knit stitches and purl all the purl stitches.

For the **tenth row,** purl 1. Repeat the following procedure. * Purl 2. Make a back cross by slipping 1 stitch onto a double-pointed needle and leave in back, purl 1, and knit the stitch on the double-pointed needle. Purl 1. Make another back cross. Follow with a front cross by slipping 1 stitch onto a double-pointed needle and leave in front, purl 1, and knit the stitch on the double-pointed needle. Purl 1. Make another front cross. Purl 2. * End with purl 1.

For the **eleventh row,** knit all the knit stitches and purl all the purl stitches.

For the **twelfth row,** purl 1. Repeat the following procedure. * Purl 1. Make a back cross by slipping 1 stitch onto a double-pointed needle and leave in back, purl 1, and knit the stitch on the double-pointed needle. Purl 1. Make another back cross. Purl 2. Make a front cross by slipping 1 stitch onto a double-pointed needle and leave in front, purl 1, and knit the stitch on the double-pointed needle. Purl 1. Then make another front cross. Purl 1. * End with purl 1.

For the **thirteenth row,** knit all the knit stitches and purl all the purl stitches.

For the **fourteenth row,** purl 1. Repeat the following procedure. * Make a back cross by slipping 1 stitch onto a double-pointed needle and leave in back, purl 1, and knit the stitch on the double-pointed needle. Purl 1. Make another back cross. Purl 4. Then make a front cross by slipping 1 stitch onto a double-pointed needle and leave in front, purl 1, and knit the stitch on the double-pointed needle. Purl 1. Make another front cross. * End with purl 1.

For the **fifteenth row,** knit all the knit stitches and purl all the purl stitches.

For the **sixteenth row,** knit all the knit stitches and purl all the purl stitches.

Repeat the **first through sixteenth rows** as many times as required.


## Double Ribbon Stitch

*See* Cable Pattern—Chain.

## Drooping Elm Leaf Pattern

This stitch pattern is an adaptation of the Beech Leaf Lace Pattern, using a staggered arrangement of the leaves.

For the **beginning row,** cast on 15 stitches plus 1.

For the **first row,** repeat the following procedure. * Knit 1. Yarn over. Knit 1. Then slip 1, knit 1, and pass slip stitch over. Purl 1. Knit 2 together. Knit 1. Yarn over. Purl 1. Then slip 1, knit 1, and pass slip stitch over. Purl 1. Knit two together. Yarn over. Knit 1. Yarn over. Knit 1. Yarn over. * End with knit 1.

For the **second row,** purl 1. Repeat the following procedure. * Purl 4. Knit 1. Purl 1. Knit 1. Purl 3. Knit 1. Purl 4. *

For the **third row,** repeat the following procedure. * Knit 1. Yarn over. Knit 1. Then slip 1, knit 1, and pass slip stitch over. Purl 1. Knit 2 together. Knit 1. Purl 1. Then slip 1, knit 2 together, and pass slip stitch over. Yarn over. Knit 3. Yarn over. * End with knit 1.

For the **fourth row,** purl 1. Repeat the following procedure. * Purl 6. Knit 1. Purl 2. Knit 1. Purl 4. *

For the **fifth row,** repeat the following procedure. * Knit 1, and yarn over twice. Then slip 1, knit 1, and pass slip stitch over. Purl 1. Knit 2 together twice. Yarn over. Knit 5. Yarn over. * End with knit 1.

For the **sixth row,** purl 1. Repeat the following procedure. * Purl 7. Knit 1. Purl 1. Knit 1. Purl 5. *

For the **seventh row,** repeat the following procedure. * Knit 1. Yarn over. Knit 3. Yarn over. Then slip 1, knit 2 together, and pass slip stitch over. Purl 1. Yarn over. Knit 1. Then slip 1, knit 1, and pass slip stitch over. Purl 1. Knit 2 together. Knit 1. Yarn over. * End with knit 1.

For the **eighth row,** purl 1. Repeat the following procedure. * Purl 3 and knit 1 twice. Purl 7. *

For the **ninth row,** repeat the following procedure. * Knit 1. Yarn over. Knit 5. Yarn over. Then slip 1, knit 1, and pass slip stitch over. Knit 1. Then slip 1, knit 1, and pass slip stitch over. Purl 1. Knit 2 together. Knit 1. Yarn over. * End with knit 1.

For the **tenth row,** purl 1. Repeat the following procedure. * Purl 3. Knit 1. Purl 2. Knit 1. Purl 8. *

Repeat the **first through tenth rows** as many times as required.

## Drop Stitch

Openwork bands dominate this stitch pattern. It is easy and quick to do.

For the **beginning row,** cast on the desired number of stitches.

For the **first row,** insert the needle in the first stitch. Wind the yarn around the needle 3 times before completing the knit stitch. Continue knitting in this way across the row.

For the **second row,** purl, letting the extra 3 loops drop.

Knit and purl the required number of rows before repeating the **first and second rows.**

Repeat the preceding procedure for as many rows as required.

## Eiffel Tower Stitch

The name seems to describe the openwork motifs that dot the surface in alternating rows.

For the **beginning row,** cast on a multiple of 8 stitches plus 1.

For the **first row,** purl 1. Repeat the following procedure. * Yarn over. Purl 2 together. Purl 6. *

For the **second row,** repeat the following procedure. * Knit 7. Purl 1. * End with knit 1.

For the **third row,** purl 1. Repeat the following procedure. * Knit 1. Purl 7. *

For the **fourth row,** repeat the second row.

For the **fifth row,** repeat the third row.

For the **sixth row,** repeat the second row.

For the **seventh row,** repeat the third row.

For the **eighth row,** purl.

For the **ninth row,** purl 5. Repeat the following procedure. * Yarn over. Purl 2 together. Purl 6. * End with purl 2.

For the **tenth row,** knit 3. Repeat the following procedure. * Purl 1. Knit 7. * End with knit 5.

For the **eleventh row,** purl 5. Repeat the following procedure. * Knit 1. Purl 7. * End with purl 3.

For the **twelfth row,** repeat the tenth row.

For the **thirteenth row,** repeat the eleventh row.

For the **fourteenth row,** repeat the tenth row.

For the **fifteenth row,** repeat the eleventh row.

For the **sixteenth row,** purl.

Repeat the **first through sixteenth rows** as many times as required.

**Embossed Check Pattern**

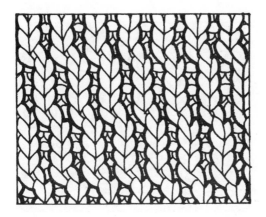

The raised and twisted effect of this Italian pattern gives a smart textural quality to the surface.

For the **beginning row,** cast on an uneven number of stitches.

For the **first row,** knit each stitch through the back.

For the **second row,** repeat the following procedure. * Knit 1. Purl 1 in back. * End with knit 1.

For the **third row,** repeat the following procedure. * Purl 1. Knit 1 in back. * End with purl 1.

For the **fourth row,** repeat the second row.

For the **fifth row,** knit each stitch through the back.

For the **sixth row,** repeat the following procedure. * Purl 1 in back. Knit 1. * End with purl 1 in back.

For the **seventh row,** repeat the following procedure. * Knit 1 in back. Purl 1. * End with knit 1 in back.

For the **eighth row,** repeat the sixth row.

Repeat the **first through eighth rows** as many times as required.

## Embossed Leaf Pattern

The leaves give a 3-dimensional effect to this beautiful old German pattern.

For the **beginning row,** cast on a multiple of 8 stitches plus 7.

For the **first row,** purl 7. Repeat the following procedure. * Knit 1. Purl 7. *

For the **second row,** knit 7. Repeat the following procedure. * Purl 1. Knit 7. *

For the **third row,** purl 7. Repeat the following procedure. * Insert needle between the stitch just knitted and the next, picking up the connecting thread. Then knit into the back of it, making 1 stitch. Knit 1. Again insert the needle between the stitch just knitted and the next, picking up the connecting thread. Then knit into the back of it, making 1 stitch. Purl 7. *

For the **fourth row,** knit 7. Repeat the following procedure. * Purl 3. Knit 7. *

For the **fifth row,** purl 7. Repeat the following procedure. * Knit 1 and put yarn over twice. Knit 1. Purl 7. *

For the **sixth row,** knit 7. Repeat the following procedure. * Purl 5. Knit 7. *

For the **seventh row,** purl 7. Repeat the following procedure. * Knit 2. Yarn over. Knit 1. Yarn over. Knit 2. Purl 7. *

For the **eighth row,** knit 7. Repeat the following procedure. * Purl 7. Knit 7. *

For the **ninth row,** purl 7. Repeat the following procedure. * Knit 2. Then slip 2 knitwise, knit 1, and pass the 2 slip stitches over. Knit 2. Purl 7. *

For the **tenth row,** repeat the sixth row.

For the **eleventh row,** purl 7. Repeat the following procedure. * Knit 1. Then slip 2 knitwise, knit 1, and pass the 2 slip stitches over. Knit 1. Purl 7. *

For the **twelfth row,** repeat the fourth row.

For the **thirteenth row,** purl 7. Repeat the following procedure. * Slip 2 knitwise, knit 1, and pass the 2 slip stitches over. Purl 7. *

For the **fourteenth row,** repeat the second row.

For the **fifteenth row,** purl 3. Repeat the following procedure. * Knit 1. Purl 7. * End with knit 1, purl 3.

For the **sixteenth row,** knit 3. Repeat the following procedure. * Purl 1. Knit 7. * End with purl 1, knit 3.

For the **seventeenth row,** purl 3. Repeat the following procedure. * Insert needle between the stitch just knitted and the next, picking up the connecting thread. Then knit into the back of it, making 1 stitch. Knit 1. Make another stitch. Purl 7. * End by making 1 stitch. Knit 1. Make another stitch. Purl 3.

For the **eighteenth row,** knit 3. Repeat the following procedure. * Purl 3. Knit 7. * End with purl 3, knit 3.

For the **nineteenth row,** purl 3. Repeat the following procedure. * Knit 1 and yarn over twice. Knit 1. Purl 7. * End with knit 1 and yarn over twice. Knit 1. Purl 3.

For the **twentieth row,** knit 3. Repeat the following procedure. * Purl 5. Knit 7. * End with purl 5 and knit 3.

For the **twenty-first row,** purl 3. Repeat the following procedure. * Knit 2. Yarn over. Knit 1. Yarn over. Knit 2. Purl 7. * End with knit 2. Yarn over. Knit 1. Yarn over. Knit 2. Purl 3.

For the **twenty-second row,** knit 3. Repeat the following procedure. * Purl 7. Knit 7. * End with purl 7, knit 3.

For the **twenty-third row,** purl 3. Repeat the following procedure. * Knit 2. Then slip 2 knitwise, knit 1, and pass the 2 slip stitches over. Knit 2. Purl 7. * End with knit 2. Then slip 2 knitwise, knit 1, and pass the 2 slip stitches over. Knit 2. Purl 3.

For the **twenty-fourth row,** repeat the twentieth row.

For the **twenty-fifth row,** purl 3. Repeat the following procedure. * Knit 1. Then slip 2 knitwise, knit 1, and pass the 2 slip stitches over. Knit 1. Purl 7. * End with knit 1. Then slip 2 knitwise, knit 1, and pass the 2 slip stitches over. Knit 1. Purl 3.

For the **twenty-sixth row,** repeat the eighteenth row.

For the **twenty-seventh row,** purl 3. Repeat the following procedure. * Slip 2 knitwise, knit 1, and pass the 2 slip stitches over. Purl 7. * End with slip 2 knitwise, knit 1, and pass the 2 slip stitches over. Purl 3.

For the **twenty-eighth row,** repeat the sixteenth row.

Repeat the **first through twenty-eighth rows** as many times as required.

## Embroidery Eyelet Diamond Pattern

Eyelets are arranged in a diamond design, giving a striped effect to this openwork pattern.

For the **beginning row,** cast on a multiple of 21 stitches plus 3.

For the **first row,** purl.

For the **second row,** knit.

For the **third row,** purl.

For the **fourth row,** knit 10. Repeat the following procedure. * Knit 2 together. Yarn over. Then slip 1, knit 1, and pass slip stitch over. Knit 17. * End with knit 10.

For the **fifth row,** purl, but be sure to purl and knit into each yarn over.

For the **sixth row,** knit 6. Repeat the following procedure. * Knit 2 together. Yarn over. Then slip 1, knit 1, and pass slip stitch over. Knit 4. Knit 2 together. Yarn over. Then slip 1, knit 1, and pass slip stitch over. Knit 9. * End with knit 6.

For the **seventh row,** repeat the fifth row.

For the **eighth row,** knit 3. Repeat the following procedure. * Knit 2 together. Yarn over. Then slip 1, knit 1, and pass slip stitch over. Knit 3. *

For the **ninth row,** repeat the fifth row.

For the **tenth row,** repeat the sixth row.

For the **eleventh row,** repeat the fifth row.

For the **twelfth row,** repeat the fourth row.

Repeat the **first through twelfth rows** as many times as required.

## Escalator Pattern

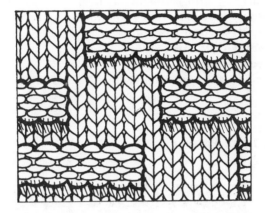

The step formation of purl-stitch bands produces a diagonal movement to this stitch pattern.

For the **beginning row,** cast on a multiple of 32 stitches.

For the **first row,** repeat the following procedure. * Knit 5. Purl 11. *

For the **second row,** repeat the following procedure. * Knit 11. Purl 5. *

For the **third row,** repeat the first row.

For the **fourth row,** purl.

For the **fifth row,** knit.

For the **sixth row,** purl.

For the **seventh row,** purl 4. Repeat the following procedure. * Knit 5. Purl 11. * End with knit 5, purl 7.

For the **eighth row,** knit 7. Repeat the following procedure. * Purl 5. Knit 11. * End with purl 5, knit 4.

For the **ninth row,** repeat the seventh row.

For the **tenth row,** purl.

For the **eleventh row,** knit.

For the **twelfth row,** purl.

For the **thirteenth row,** purl 8. Repeat the following procedure. * Knit 5. Purl 11. * End with knit 5, purl 3.

For the **fourteenth row,** knit 3. Repeat the following procedure. * Purl 5. Knit 11. * End with purl 5, knit 8.

For the **fifteenth row,** repeat the thirteenth row.

For the **sixteenth row,** purl.

For the **seventeenth row,** knit.

For the **eighteenth row,** purl.

For the **nineteenth row,** knit 1, purl 11. Repeat the following procedure. * Knit 5. Purl 11. * End with knit 4.

For the **twentieth row,** purl 4. Repeat the following procedure. * Knit 11. Purl 5. * End with knit 11, purl 1.

For the **twenty-first row,** repeat the nineteenth row.

For the **twenty-second row,** purl.

For the **twenty-third row,** knit.

For the **twenty-fourth row,** purl.

Repeat the **first through twenty-fourth rows** as many times as required.

## Eye of the Lynx Pattern

The arrangement of eyelets gives a honeycomb feeling to this open-work stitch pattern.

For the **beginning row,** cast on a multiple of 8 stitches plus 6.

For the **first row,** purl.

For the **second row,** knit.

For the **third row,** purl.

For the **fourth row,** purl 5. Repeat the following procedure. * Purl 1. Slip 2 purlwise. Purl 5. * End with purl 1.

For the **fifth row,** knit 1. Repeat the following procedure. * Knit 5. Slip 2 purlwise. Knit 1. * End with knit 5.

For the **sixth row,** purl 5. Repeat the following procedure. * Purl 1. Slip 2. Purl 5. * End with purl 1.

For the **seventh row,** knit 1. Repeat the following procedure. * Slip 1, knit 1, and pass slip stitch over. Make 1 stitch by wrapping yarn around needle. Knit 2 together. Knit 1. Slip 2 purlwise. Knit 1. * End with slip 1, knit 1, and pass slip stitch over. Make a stitch by wrapping yarn around needle. Knit 2 together. Knit 1.

For the **eighth row,** purl 2. Then purl into the front and the back of the stitch that was "made" in the previous row. Purl 1. Repeat the following procedure. * Purl 1. Slip 2 purlwise. Purl 2. Purl into the front and the back of the stitch that was made in the previous row and purl 1. * End with purl 1.

For the **ninth row,** knit 1. Repeat the following procedure. * Knit 5. Slip 2 purlwise. Knit 1. * End with knit 5.

For the **tenth row,** knit.

For the **eleventh row,** purl.

For the **twelfth row,** knit.

For the **thirteenth row,** knit 1. Repeat the following procedure. * Knit 1. Slip 2 purlwise. Knit 5. * End with knit 1. Slip 2 purlwise. Knit 2.

For the **fourteenth row,** purl 2. Slip 2 purlwise. Purl 1. Repeat the following procedure. * Purl 5. Slip 2 purlwise. Purl 1. * End with purl 1.

For the **fifteenth row,** knit 1. Repeat the following procedure. * Knit 1. Slip 2 purlwise. Knit 5. * End with knit 1. Slip 2 purlwise. Knit 2.

For the sixteenth row, purl 2. Slip 2 purlwise. Purl 1. Repeat the following procedure. * Purl 2 together. Make 1 stitch by wrapping yarn around needle. Purl next stitch. Return it to left-hand needle. Then pass next stitch on left-hand needle over it and replace it on right-hand needle. Purl 1. Slip 2 purlwise. Purl 1. * End with purl 1.

For the **seventeenth row,** knit 1. Repeat the following procedure. * Knit 1. Slip 2 purlwise. Knit 2. Knit into the front and the back of the stitch that was made in the previous row. Knit 1. * End with knit 1. Slip 2 purlwise. Knit 2.

For the **eighteenth row,** repeat the fourteenth row.

Repeat the **first through eighteenth rows** as many times as required.

## Eyelet Check Pattern

A checkered pattern is given added interest with an eyelet, dotting alternating squares.

For the **beginning row,** cast on a multiple of 8 stitches plus 5.

For the **first row,** repeat the following procedure. * Knit 5. Purl 3. * End with knit 5.

For the **second row,** purl 5. Repeat the following procedure. * Knit 3. Purl 5. *

For the **third row,** repeat the following procedure. * Knit 5. Purl 1. Wrap yarn around needle to make 1 stitch. Purl 2 together. * End with knit 5.

For the **fourth row,** repeat the second row.

For the **fifth row,** repeat the first row.

For the **sixth row,** purl.

For the **seventh row,** repeat the following procedure. * Knit 1. Purl 3. Knit 4. * End with knit 1. Purl 3. Knit 1.

For the **eighth row,** purl 1. Knit 3. Purl 1. Repeat the following procedure. * Purl 4. Knit 3. Purl 1. *

For the **ninth row,** repeat the following procedure. * Knit 1. Purl 1. Wrap yarn around needle to make 1 stitch. Purl 2 together. Knit 4. * End with knit 1. Purl 1. Wrap yarn around needle to make 1 stitch. Purl 2 together. Knit 1.

For the **tenth row,** repeat the eighth row.

For the **eleventh row,** repeat the seventh row.

For the **twelfth row,** purl.

Repeat the **first through the twelfth rows** as many times as required.

## Eyelet Lace Pattern—Grand

Large eyelets dot this lacy stitch pattern, which is sometimes referred to as Reversible Grand Eyelet.

For the **beginning row,** cast on 4 stitches plus 4.

For the **first row,** purl 2. Repeat the following procedure. * Yarn over. Purl 4 together. * End with purl 2.

For the **second row,** knit 2. Repeat the following procedure. * Knit 1. Then, into the yarn-over of the previous row, knit 1, purl 1, and knit 1. * End with knit 2.

For the **third row,** knit.

Repeat the **first through third rows** as many times as required.

## Eyelet Pattern—Diamond

This beautiful lacy pattern seems to develop a diagonal feeling that is most pleasing.

For the **beginning row,** cast on a multiple of 10 stitches plus 4.

For the **first row,** knit 2. Yarn over. Then slip 1, knit 1, and pass slip stitch over. Repeat the following procedure. * Knit 1. Knit 2 together. Put yarn over twice. Then slip 1 stitch, knit 1, and pass slip stitch over. * For the last 5 stitches, knit 1, knit 2 together, yarn over, and knit 2.

For the **second row,** purl. Do this in both the front and the back of each yarn-over.

For the **third row,** knit 2. Repeat the following procedure. * Knit 2 together. Yarn over. Knit 6. Yarn over. Then slip 1, knit 1, and pass slip stitch over. * End with knit 2.

For the **fourth row,** repeat the second row.

For the **fifth row,** knit 3. Repeat the following procedure. * Knit 2 together. Yarn over. Knit 4. Yarn over. Then slip 1, knit 1, and pass slip stitch over. Knit 2. * End with knit 1.

For the **sixth row,** repeat the second row.

For the **seventh row,** knit 4. Repeat the following procedure. * Knit 2 together. Yarn over. Knit 2. Yarn over. Then slip 1, knit 1, and pass slip stitch over. Knit 4. *

For the **eighth row,** repeat the second row.

For the **ninth row,** knit 2. Yarn over. Then slip 1, knit 1, and pass slip stitch over. Repeat the following procedure. * Knit 1. Knit 2 together. Put yarn over twice. Then slip 1, knit 1, and pass slip stitch over. * For the last 5 stitches, knit 1, knit 2 together, yarn over, knit 2.

For the **tenth row,** repeat the second row.

For the **eleventh row,** knit 5. Repeat the following procedure.
* Yarn over. Then slip 1, knit 1, and pass slip stitch over. Knit 2
together. Yarn over. Knit 6. * End with knit 5.

For the **twelfth row,** repeat the second row.

For the **thirteenth row,** knit 4. Repeat the following procedure.
* Yarn over. Then slip 1, knit 1, and pass slip stitch over. Knit 2.
Knit 2 together. Yarn over. Knit four. *

For the **fourteenth row,** repeat the second row.

For the **fifteenth row,** knit 3. Repeat the following procedure.
* Yarn over. Then slip 1, knit 1, and pass slip stitch over. Knit 4.
Knit 2 together. Yarn over. Knit 2. * End with knit 1.

For the **sixteenth row,** purl.

Repeat the **first through sixteenth rows** as many times as required.


## Eyelet Pattern—Ribbon

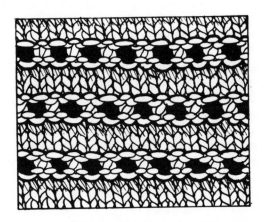

Rows of eyelets seem to give a ridged effect to this stitch pattern.

For the **beginning row,** cast on an odd number of stitches.

For the **first row,** knit.

For the **second row,** purl.

For the **third row,** knit.

For the **fourth row,** knit.

For the **fifth row,** repeat the following procedure. * Knit 2 together.
Yarn over. * End with knit 1.

For the **sixth row,** knit.

Repeat the **first through sixth rows** as many times as required.

## Eyelet Stitch

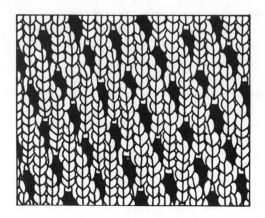

The eyelets seem to be imbedded in the fabric, creating a lovely 3-dimensional effect.

For the **beginning row,** cast on a multiple of 4 stitches.

For the **first row,** repeat the following procedure. * Knit 1. Wind yarn twice around needle, making a double stitch. Knit 2. *

For the **second row,** purl 2 together. Repeat the following procedure. * Knit 1. Purl 1 into the double stitch. Purl 2 together. *

For the **third row,** repeat the following procedure. * Wrap yarn around needle to make 1 stitch. Knit 4. Then wrap yarn around needle to make 1 more stitch. *

For the **fourth row,** repeat the following procedure. * Purl 1. Then purl 2 together twice. Knit 1. *

Repeat the **first through fourth rows** as many times as required.

**Eyelet Zigzag Pattern**

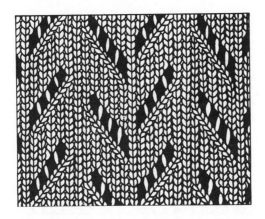

A series of eyelets in the form of a V create a zigzag design.

For the **beginning row,** cast on a multiple of 11 stitches plus 2.

For the **first row,** purl.

For the **second row,** knit 6. Repeat the following procedure. * Yarn over. Then slip 1, knit 1, and pass slip stitch over. Knit 9. * End last repeat with knit 5.

For the **third row,** purl.

For the **fourth row,** knit 7. Repeat the following procedure. * Yarn over. Then slip 1, knit 1, and pass slip stitch over. Knit 9. * End last repeat with knit 4.

For the **fifth row,** purl.

For the **sixth row,** knit 3. Repeat the following procedure. * Knit 2 together. Yarn over. Knit 3. Yarn over. Then slip 1, knit 1, and pass slip stitch over. Knit 4. * End last repeat with knit 3.

For the **seventh row,** purl.

For the **eighth row,** repeat the following procedure. * Knit 2. Knit 2 together. Yarn over. Knit 5. Yarn over. Then slip 1, knit 1, and pass slip stitch over. * End with knit 2.

For the **ninth row,** purl.

For the **tenth row,** knit 1. Repeat the following procedure. * Knit 2 together. Yarn over. Knit 9. * End with knit 1.

For the **eleventh row,** purl.

For the **twelfth row,** repeat the following procedure. * Knit 2 together. Yarn over. Knit 9. * End with knit 2.

Repeat the **first through twelfth rows** as many times as required.

## Fabric Stitch

There is a feeling of homespun to this solid and sturdy stitch pattern, which creates a lovely textured quality.

For the **beginning row,** cast on an uneven number of stitches.

For the **first row,** knit 1. Repeat the following procedure. * Slip 1 stitch with yarn in front. Knit 1. *

For the **second row,** knit 1. Purl 1. Repeat the following procedure. * Slip 1 with the yarn in back. Purl 1. * End with knit 1.

Repeat the **first and second rows** as many times as required.

## Faggot Pattern—Double Herringbone

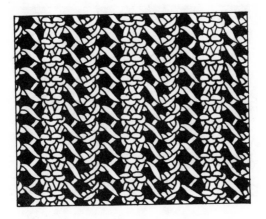

A lovely lacy effect is created when the openwork stitches are defined with ribs moving vertically.

For the **beginning row,** cast on a multiple of 5 stitches.

For the **first row,** repeat the following procedure. * Knit 1. Yarn over. Knit 2 together. Yarn over. Knit 2 together. *

Repeat the **first row** as many times as required.

## Faggot Pattern—Lace Feather

This arrangement of stitches gives a feeling of a lacy insertion.

For the **beginning row,** cast on a multiple of 4 stitches.

For the **first row,** repeat the following procedure. * Knit 1. Yarn over. Purl 2 together. Knit 1. *

Repeat the **first row** as many times as required.

## Faggot Stitch

This is a basic lace stitch that seems to give the feeling of crisscross faggoting stitches in embroidery.

For the **beginning row,** cast on a multiple of 2 stitches.

For the **first row,** knit 1. Repeat the following procedure. * Yarn over. Then slip 1, knit 1, and pass slip stitch over. * End with knit 1.

Repeat the **first row** as many times as required.

## Falling Leaves Pattern

Eyelets in a diamond pattern outline the design motif, giving a lightness to it.

For the **beginning row,** cast on a multiple of 10 stitches plus 6.

For the **first row,** knit 1. Wrap yarn around needle to make 1 stitch. Repeat the following procedure. * Knit 3. Then slip 1, knit 2 together, pass slip stitch over. Knit 3. Wrap yarn around needle to make a stitch. Knit 1. Make another stitch. * End with knit 3. Then slip 1, knit 1, and pass slip stitch over.

For the **second row,** purl.

For the **third row,** knit 2. Wrap yarn around needle to make 1 stitch. Repeat the following procedure. * Knit 2. Then slip 1, knit 2 together, and pass slip stitch over. Knit 2. Wrap yarn around needle to make 1 stitch. * End with knit 3. Wrap yarn around needle to make another stitch. Knit 2. Then slip 1, knit 1, and pass slip stitch over.

For the **fourth row,** purl.

For the **fifth row,** knit 3. Repeat the following procedure. * Wrap yarn around needle to make 1 stitch. Knit 1. Then slip 1, knit 2 together, and pass slip stitch over. Knit 1. Wrap yarn over to make 1 stitch. Knit 5. Wrap yarn over to make another stitch. * Knit 1. Then slip 1, knit 1, and pass slip stitch over.

For the **sixth row,** purl.

For the **seventh row,** knit 4. Wrap yarn around needle to make 1 stitch. Repeat the following procedure. * Slip 1, knit 2 together, and pass slip stitch over. Wrap yarn around needle to make 1 stitch. Knit 7. Wrap yarn around needle to make 1 stitch. * End with slip 1, knit 1, and pass slip stitch over.

For the **eighth row,** purl.

For the **ninth row,** slip 1, knit 1, and pass slip stitch over. Knit 3. Wrap yarn around needle to make 1 stitch. Repeat the following procedure. * Knit 1. Wrap yarn around needle to make 1 stitch. Knit 3. Then slip 1, knit 2 together, and pass slip stitch over. Wrap yarn around needle to make 1 stitch. * End with knit 1.

For the **tenth row,** purl.

For the **eleventh row,** slip 1, knit 1, and pass slip stitch over. Knit 2. Wrap yarn around needle to make 1 stitch. Knit 1. Repeat the following procedure. * Knit 2. Wrap yarn around needle to make 1 stitch. Knit 2. Then slip 1, knit 2 together, and pass slip stitch over. Knit 2. Wrap yarn around needle to make 1 stitch. Knit 1. * End with knit 1.

For the **twelfth row,** purl.

For the **thirteenth row,** slip 1, knit 1, and pass slip stitch over. Knit 1. Wrap yarn around needle to make 1 stitch. Knit 2. Repeat the following procedure. * Knit 3. Wrap yarn around needle to make 1 stitch. Knit 1. Then slip 1, knit 2 together, and pass slip stitch over. Knit 1. Wrap yarn around needle to make 1 stitch. Knit 2. * End with knit 1.

For the **fourteenth row,** purl.

For the **fifteenth row,** slip 1, knit 1, and pass slip stitch over. Wrap yarn around to make 1 stitch. Knit 3. Repeat the following procedure. * Knit 4. Wrap yarn around needle to make 1 stitch. Then slip 1, knit 2 together, and pass slip stitch over. Wrap yarn around needle to make 1 stitch. Knit 3. * End with knit 1.

For the **sixteenth row,** purl.

Repeat the **first through sixteenth rows** as many times as required.


## Feather and Fan Stitch
*See* Old Shale Pattern.


## Fern Pattern

This is a large pattern that forms a deep scallop at the beginning edge. It should be blocked carefully. Ribs appear between the motifs, giving a striped effect.

For the **beginning row,** cast on a multiple of 29 stitches.

For the **first row,** repeat the following procedure. * Knit 1. Then slip 1, knit 2 together, and pass slip stitch over. Knit 9. Wrap yarn around needle to make 1 stitch. Knit 1. Make 1 stitch. Purl 2. Make 1. Knit 1. Make 1. Knit 9. Then slip 1 stitch, knit 2 together, and pass slip stitch over. *

For the **second row,** repeat the following procedure. * Purl 13. Knit 2. Purl 14. *

For the **third row,** repeat the following procedure. * Knit 1. Then slip 1, knit 2 together, and pass slip stitch over. Knit 8. Make 1. Knit 1. Make 1. Knit 1. Purl 2. Knit 1. Make 1. Knit 1. Make 1. Knit 8. Then slip 1, knit 2 together, and pass slip stitch over. *

For the **fourth row,** repeat the second row.

For the **fifth row,** repeat the following procedure. * Knit 1. Then slip 1, knit 2 together, and pass slip stitch over. Knit 7. Wrap yarn around needle to make 1 stitch. Knit 1. Make 1. Knit 2. Purl 2. Knit 2. Make 1. Knit 1. Make 1. Knit 7. Then slip 1, knit 2 together, and pass slip stitch over. *

For the **sixth row,** repeat the second row.

For the **seventh row,** repeat the following procedure. * Knit 1. Then slip 1, knit 2 together, and pass slip stitch over. Knit 6. Make 1. Knit 1. Make 1. Knit 3. Purl 2. Knit 3. Make 1. Knit 1. Make 1. Knit 6. Then slip 1, knit 2 together, and pass slip stitch over. *

For the **eighth row,** repeat the second row.

For the **ninth row,** repeat the following procedure. * Knit 1. Then slip 1, knit 2 together, and pass slip stitch over. Knit 5. Wrap yarn around needle to make 1 stitch. Knit 1. Make 1. Knit 4. Purl 2. Knit 4. Make 1. Knit 1. Make 1. Knit 5. Then slip 1, knit 2 together, and pass slip stitch over. *

For the **tenth row,** repeat the second row.

Repeat the **first through tenth rows** as many times as required.

**Fir Cone Pattern**

This is another Shetland pattern; it creates a lovely, lacy effect.

For the **beginning row,** cast on a multiple of 10 stitches plus 1.

For the **first row,** purl.

For the **second row,** knit 1. Repeat the following procedure.
* Yarn over. Knit 3. Then slip 1, knit 2 together, and pass slip stitch over. Knit 3. Yarn over. Knit 1. *

For the **third row,** purl.

For the **fourth row,** repeat the second row.

For the **fifth row,** purl.

For the **sixth row,** repeat the second row.

For the **seventh row,** purl.

For the **eighth row,** repeat the second row.

For the **ninth row,** purl.

For the **tenth row,** knit 2 together. Repeat the following procedure.
* Knit 3. Yarn over. Knit 1. Yarn over. Knit 3. Then slip 1, knit 2 together, and pass slip stitch over. * End with knit 3. Yarn over. Knit 1. Yarn over. Knit 3. Then slip 1, knit 1, and pass slip stitch over.

For the **eleventh row,** purl.

For the **twelfth row,** repeat the tenth row.

For the **thirteenth row,** purl.

For the **fourteenth row,** repeat the tenth row.

For the **fifteenth row,** purl.

For the **sixteenth row,** repeat the tenth row.

Repeat the **first through sixteenth rows** as many times as required.

## Florette Pattern

This is a beautiful old French pattern that creates a dainty, lacy effect.

For the **beginning row,** cast on a multiple of 6 stitches plus 5.

For the **first row,** purl.

For the **second row,** knit 2. Repeat the following procedure. * Purl 1. Yarn over. Then slip 1, knit 1, and pass slip stitch over. Knit 1. Knit 2 together. Yarn over. * End with knit 3.

For the **third row,** purl.

For the **fourth row,** knit 4. Repeat the following procedure. * Yarn over. Knit 3. * End with knit 1.

For the **fifth row,** purl.

For the **sixth row,** knit 2. Knit 2 together. Repeat the following procedure. * Yarn over. Then slip 1, knit 1, and pass slip stitch over. Knit 1. Knit 2 together. Yarn over. Then slip 2 knitwise, knit 1, and pass the 2 stitches over. * End with yarn over. Then slip 1, knit 1, and pass slip stitch over. Knit 1. Knit 2 together. Yarn over. Then slip 1, knit 1, and pass slip stitch over. Knit 2.

For the **seventh row,** purl.

For the **eighth row,** knit 2. Repeat the following procedure. * Knit 1. Knit 2 together. Yarn over. Knit 1. Yarn over. Then slip 1, knit 1, and pass slip stitch over. * End with knit 3.

For the **ninth row,** purl.

For the **tenth row,** repeat the fourth row.

For the **eleventh row,** purl.

For the **twelfth row,** knit 2. Repeat the following procedure. * Knit 1. Knit 2 together. Yarn over. Then slip 2 knitwise, knit 1, and pass the 2 slip stitches over. Yarn over. Then slip 1, knit 1, and pass slip stitch over. * End with knit 3.

Repeat the **first through twelfth rows** as many times as required.

**Fuchsia Pattern**

This motif creates a raised striped effect with an interesting use of eyelets and is a traditional German stitch pattern.

For the **beginning row,** cast on a multiple of 6 stitches.

For the **first row,** repeat the following procedure. * Purl 2. Knit 2. Yarn over. Purl 2. *

For the **second row,** repeat the following procedure. * Knit 2. Purl 3. Knit 2. *

For the **third row,** repeat the following procedure. * Purl 2. Knit 3. Yarn over. Purl 2. *

For the **fourth row,** repeat the following procedure. * Knit 2. Purl 4. Knit 2. *

For the **fifth row,** repeat the following procedure. * Purl 2. Knit 4. Yarn over. Purl 2. *

For the **sixth row,** repeat the following procedure. * Knit 2. Purl 5. Knit 2. *

For the **seventh row,** repeat the following procedure. * Purl 2. Knit 3. Knit 2 together. Purl 2. *

For the **eighth row,** repeat the fourth row.

For the **ninth row,** repeat the following procedure. * Purl 2. Knit 2. Knit 2 together. Purl 2. *

For the **tenth row,** repeat the second row.

For the **eleventh row,** repeat the following procedure. * Purl 2. Knit 1. Knit 2 together. Purl 2. *

For the **twelfth row,** repeat the following procedure. * Knit 2. Purl 2. Knit 2. *

Repeat the **first through twelfth rows** as many times as required.

## Garter Lace Stitch

Rows of stitches seem to create a lacy insertion.

For the **beginning row,** cast on a multiple of 2.

For the **first six rows,** knit.

For the **seventh row,** repeat the following procedure. * Wrap yarn around the needle to make 1 stitch. Knit 2 together.

For the **eighth row,** repeat the following procedure. * Wrap yarn around needle to make 1 stitch. Purl 2 together. *

For the **ninth row,** repeat the seventh row.

For the **tenth row,** repeat the eighth row.

Repeat the **first through tenth rows** as many times as required.

## Garter Stitch—Bias

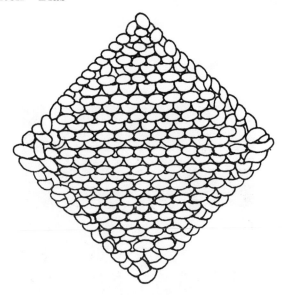

An interesting effect is created when stitches are worked on the bias.

For the **beginning row,** cast on 3 stitches.

For the **first row,** knit 1. Put yarn over from back to front, returning to the back between the needles. Knit 1. Yarn over again. Knit 1.

For the **second row,** knit 5.

For the **third row,** knit 1. Yarn over as in first row. Knit 3. Yarn over. Knit 1.

For the **fourth row,** knit seven.

For the **fifth row,** knit 1. Yarn over as in first row. Knit 5. Yarn over. Knit 1.

For the **sixth row,** knit 9.

Follow the above procedure, increasing the number of stitches, until the required size is reached. Note that each increase follows the first stitch and precedes the last one.

To taper the remaining half of the square, make the decrease on the odd-numbered rows.

For the **odd-numbered rows,** knit 1. Then slip 1, knit 1, and pass slip stitch over. Knit across to last 3 stitches. Then knit 2 together. Knit 1.

For the **even-numbered rows,** knit.

## Garter Stitch—Elongated Crossed
*See* Veil Stitch.

## Garter Stitch—Lace Ladder

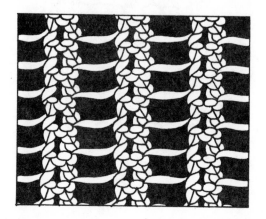

Openwork stripes give this lacy design an interesting look.

For the **beginning row,** cast on a multiple of 4 stitches.

For the **first row,** repeat the following procedure. * Knit 2 together. Put yarn over twice. Then slip 1, knit 1, and pass slip stitch over. *

For the **second row,** repeat the following procedure. * Knit 1. Then, into the double yarn-over, knit 1 and purl 1. Knit 1. *

Repeat the **first and second rows** as many times as required.

## Garter Stitch—Zigzag

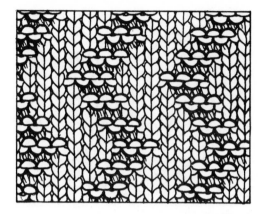

Working in this design pattern gives simple knit and purl stitches an interesting look.

For the **beginning row,** cast on a multiple of 6 stitches plus 2.

For the **first row,** knit 1. Purl across row to last stitch. Knit 1.

For the **second row,** knit 1. Repeat the following procedure. * Knit 3. Purl 3. * Knit 1.

For the **third row,** repeat the first.

For the **fourth row,** knit 1, purl 1. Repeat the following procedure. * Knit 3. Purl 3. * End with knit 3, purl 2, knit 1.

For the **fifth row,** repeat the first.

For the **sixth row,** knit 1, purl 2. Repeat the following procedure. * Knit 3. Purl 3. * End with knit 3, purl 1, knit 1.

For the **seventh row,** repeat the first.

For the **eighth row,** knit 1. Repeat the following procedure. * Purl 3. Knit 3. * End with knit 1.

For the **ninth row,** repeat the first.

For the **tenth row,** knit 1, purl 2. Repeat the following procedure. * Knit 3. Purl 3. * End with knit 3, purl 1, knit 1.

For the **eleventh row,** repeat the first row.

For the **twelfth row,** knit 1, purl 1. Repeat the following procedure. * Knit 3. Purl 3. * End with knit 3, purl 2, knit 1.

Repeat the **first through twelfth rows** as many times as required.

## Gathered Stitch

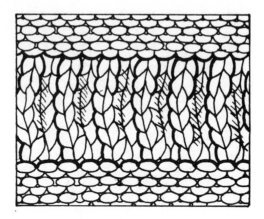

Working with knitting needles in 2 sizes creates rows of stitches with fullness.

For the **beginning row,** cast on the required number of stitches, using fine needles.

For the **first through sixth rows,** knit.

For the **seventh row,** change to larger needles. Knit twice into each stitch.

For the **eighth row,** purl.

For the **ninth row,** knit.

For the **tenth row,** purl.

For the **eleventh row,** knit.

For the **twelfth row,** purl, completing 6 rows of stockinette stitches.

For the **thirteenth row,** return to smaller needles. Knit 2 together across row.

Continue to knit 5 rows, completing 6 rows of garter stitches.

Alternate the rows of stockinette stitches made on the larger needles and garter stitches on the smaller ones as many times as required.

## Grecian Plait Stitch

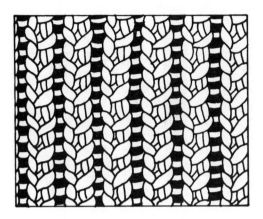

This stitch pattern develops an interesting textural quality, with a small braided effect dotted with open spaces. Work with needles in 2 sizes—one about 4 sizes larger than the other.

For the **beginning row,** cast on a multiple of 2 stitches using larger needle.

For the **first row,** use the smaller needle. Knit.

For the **second row,** use the larger needle. Purl.

For the **third row,** continue with smaller needle. Insert needle in second stitch, lifting it over the first and then knitting it. Then knit the first stitch. Continue this way across row, lifting the even-numbered stitches over the uneven ones before knitting each. End row with knit 1.

For the **fourth row,** return to larger needle. Purl.

Repeat the **third and fourth rows** as many times as required.

## Gull Stitch

The raised effect of this stitch pattern makes a lovely panel motif, which is frequently used for Aran-type knitting.

For the **beginning row,** cast on 10 stitches to make 1 rib or panel.

For the **first row,** knit 2. Purl 6. Knit 2.

For the **second row,** purl 2. Knit 2. With yarn in back, slip 2. Knit 2. Purl 2.

For the **third row,** knit 2. Purl 2. With yarn in front, slip 2. Purl 2. Knit 2.

For the **fourth row,** purl 2. Slip next 2 stitches onto a double-pointed needle. Leave in back. Knit 1. Then knit the 2 stitches on the double-pointed needle. Slip next stitch onto the double-pointed needle. Leave in front. Knit 2. Then knit 1 from the double-pointed needle. Purl 2.

Repeat the **first through fourth rows** as many times as required.

## Harris Tweed Stitch

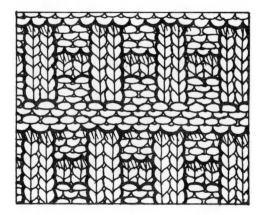

This arrangement of knit and purl stitches gives an interesting raised and somewhat checked effect.

For the **beginning row,** cast on a multiple of 4 stitches.

For the **first row,** repeat the following procedure. * Knit 2. Purl 2. *

For the **second row,** repeat the first row.

For the **third row,** knit.

For the **fourth row,** purl.

For the **fifth row,** repeat the first row.

For the **sixth row,** repeat the first row.

For the **seventh row,** purl.

For the **eighth row,** knit.

Repeat the **first through eighth rows** as many times as required.

## Heel Stitch

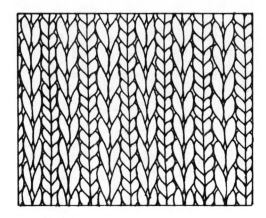

This stitch pattern creates a solid, sturdy fabric with a striped effect.

For the **beginning row,** cast on an uneven number of stitches.

For the **first row,** purl.

For the **second row,** knit 1. Repeat the following procedure. * Slip 1 with yarn in back. Knit 1. *

Repeat the **first and second rows** as many times as required.

**Herringbone Lace Pattern**

Openwork outlines this stitch pattern, giving a zigzag movement to the design.

For the **beginning row,** cast on a multiple of 6 stitches plus 2.

For the **first row,** purl.

For the **second row,** repeat the following procedure. * Slip 1, knit 1, and pass slip stitch over. Knit 2. Yarn over. Knit 2. * End with knit 2.

For the **third row,** purl.

For the **fourth row,** repeat the second row.

For the **fifth row,** purl.

For the **sixth row,** repeat the second row.

For the **seventh row,** purl.

For the **eighth row,** knit 1. Repeat the following procedure. * Knit 2. Yarn over. Knit 2. Knit 2 together. * End with knit 1.

For the **ninth row,** purl.

For the **tenth row,** repeat the eighth row.

For the **eleventh row,** purl.

For the **twelfth row,** repeat the eighth row.

Repeat the **first through twelfth rows** as many times as required.

## Herringbone Pattern

A realistic adaptation of a woven herringbone fabric is produced with this stitch arrangement.

For the **beginning row,** cast on a multiple of 7 stitches plus 1.

For the **first row,** purl.

For the **second row,** repeat the following procedure. * Knit 2 together. Knit 2. Make a 1-stitch increase by inserting tip of right-hand needle downward in back of left-hand needle through the top of the purl stitch below the next stitch, and knit. Then knit the stitch above this. Knit 2. * End row with knit 1.

Repeat **first and second rows** as many times as required.

## Hexagon Pattern

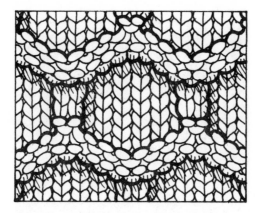

This pattern is most effective when worked in 2 colors—dark and light.

For the **beginning row,** cast on eight stitches plus 6, using the darker yarn.

For the **first row,** knit.

For the **second row,** also knit.

For the **third row,** work with the lighter color. Knit 2. Repeat the following procedure. * Slip 2 with yarn in back. Knit 6. * End by slipping 2 stitches and knitting 2.

For the **fourth row,** purl 2. Repeat the following procedure. * Slip 2 with yarn in front. Purl 6. * End by slipping 2 stitches and purling 2.

For the **fifth row,** repeat the third row.

For the **sixth row,** repeat the fourth row.

For the **seventh row,** repeat the third row.

For the **eighth row,** repeat the fourth row.

For the **ninth row,** change to the darker color. Knit.

For the **tenth, eleventh, and twelfth rows,** knit.

For the **thirteenth row,** change to the lighter color. Knit 6. Repeat the following procedure. * Slip 2 with yarn in back. Knit 6. *

For the **fourteenth row,** purl six. Repeat the following procedure. * Slip 2 with yarn in front. Purl 6. *

For the **fifteenth row,** repeat the thirteenth row.

For the **sixteenth row,** repeat the fourteenth row.

For the **seventeenth row,** repeat the thirteenth row.

For the **eighteenth row,** repeat the fourteenth row.

For the **nineteenth and twentieth rows,** change to darker color. Knit.

Repeat the **first through twentieth rows** as many times as required.

## Honeycomb Tweed Pattern

By using 2 colors, this French pattern is given a solid, tweedy look.

For the **beginning row,** cast on an uneven number of stitches, using the lighter color.

For the **first row,** use the lighter color. Repeat the following procedure. * Knit 1. Slip 1 purlwise. * End with knit 1.

For the **second row,** continue to use lighter color. Purl.

For the **third row,** change to darker color. Knit 2. Repeat the following procedure. * Slip 1 purl stitch. Knit 1. * End with knit 1.

For the **fourth row,** continue with the darker color. Purl.

Repeat the **first through fourth rows** as many times as required.

## Horseshoe Pattern

This stitch pattern is a basic one for lacy Shetland designs.

For the **beginning row,** cast on a multiple of 10 stitches plus 1.

For the **first row,** purl.

For the **second row,** knit 1. Repeat the following procedure. * Yarn over. Knit 3. Then slip 1, knit 2 together, and pass slip stitch over. Knit 3. Yarn over. Knit 1. *

For the **third row,** purl.

For the **fourth row,** purl 1. Repeat the following procedure. * Knit 1. Yarn over. Knit 2. Then slip 1, knit 2 together, and pass slip stitch over. Knit 2. Yarn over. Knit 1. Purl 1. *

For the **fifth row,** knit 1. Repeat the following procedure. * Purl 9. Knit 1. *

For the **sixth row,** purl 1. Repeat the following procedure. * Knit 2. Yarn over. Knit 1. Then slip 1, knit 2 together, and pass slip stitch over. Knit 1. Yarn over. Knit 2. Purl 1. *

For the **seventh row,** repeat the fifth row.

For the **eighth row,** purl 1. Repeat the following procedure. * Knit 3. Yarn over. Then slip 1, knit 2 together, and pass slip stitch over. Yarn over. Knit 3. Purl 1. *

Repeat the **first through eighth rows** as many times as required.

## Hyacinth Pattern
*See* Bell Pattern.

## Imitation Embroidery Pattern

This interesting ribbed effect is dotted with tiny bells and eyelets.

For the **beginning row,** cast on a multiple of 6 stitches plus 3.

For the **first row,** knit 1. Purl 2. Knit 3. Repeat the following procedure. * Purl 3. Knit 3. * End with purl 2, knit 1.

For the **second row,** knit 3. Repeat the following procedure. * Purl 3. Knit 3. *

For the **third row,** knit 1, purl 2. Repeat the following procedure. * Put yarn over right-hand needle. Knit 3 together. Yarn over. Purl 3. * Then end by putting yarn over. Knit 3 together. Yarn over. Purl 2. Knit 1.

For the **fourth row,** repeat the second row.

Repeat the **first through fourth rows** as many times as required.

## Indian Cross Stitch

This arrangement of stitches produces a reversible fabric with many interesting lines.

For the **beginning row,** cast on a multiple of 8 stitches.

For the **first four rows,** knit.

For the **fifth row,** knit 1. Repeat the following procedure. * To start the cross stitches, insert needle into the next stitch. Wind yarn 4 times around tip of needle and knit the stitch, removing all of the wrapped stitches, as well as the needle. *

For the **sixth row,** repeat the following procedure. * To form 8 long stitches on the right-hand needle, slip 8 slip stitches with yarn in back, dropping the extra wrapped stitches. Insert left-hand needle into the first 4 long stitches and slip them over the second 4 stitches. Follow by returning all of the stitches to the left-hand needle in the crossed order. Knit in this order. Note that the first group of 4 stitches is knitted last. * Be careful not to twist stitches when crossing them, and to stretch them upward to keep the lengths the same.

For the **seventh through tenth rows,** knit, making the ridges of garter stitch.

For the **eleventh row,** repeat the fifth row.

For the **twelfth row,** slip 4 stitches, dropping the wrapped stitches. Insert left-hand needle into the first 2 long stitches and slip them over the second 2 stitches, as in sixth row. Knit these 4 stitches. Repeat the following procedure, as for sixth row. * Slip 8 stitches. Cross 4 stitches over 4 and knit as in the sixth row on each group of 8 stitches. * End row by crossing 2 stitches over 2.

Repeat the **first through twelfth rows** as many times as required.

## Knotted Stitch

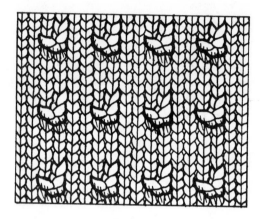

An interesting textural effect results when the surface is dotted with a small grouping of stitches.

For the **beginning row,** cast on a multiple of 4 stitches.

For the **first row,** knit.

For the **second row,** purl.

For the **third row,** knit.

For the **fourth row,** purl.

For the **fifth row,** repeat the following procedure. * Knit 2. To make the knot, wrap yarn around needle, making a stitch. Then pass the second stitch from the point of the right-hand needle over the first stitch and the made stitch. To complete the knot, wrap yarn around needle again and pass the second stitch over the 2 made stitches. *

Repeat **first through fifth rows** as many times as required.

## Laburnum Stitch

Eyelets form part of the ribbed effect of this openwork pattern.

For the **beginning row,** cast on a multiple of 5 stitches plus 2.

For the **first row,** purl 2. Repeat the following procedure. * With yarn in front, slip 1. Then, with yarn in back, knit 2 together and pass slip stitch over. Then wrap yarn over needle twice in reverse, bringing the yarn from the back over the needle and then under and over again. Purl 2. *

For the **second row,** knit 2. Repeat the following procedure. * Purl into the back of the first yarn-over and then into the front of the second yarn-over of the previous row. Purl 1. Knit 2. *

For the **third row,** purl 2. Repeat the following procedure. * Knit 3. Purl 2. *

For the **fourth row,** knit 2. Repeat the following procedure. * Purl 3. Knit 2. *

Repeat the **first through fourth rows** as many times as required.

## Lace Butterfly Pattern

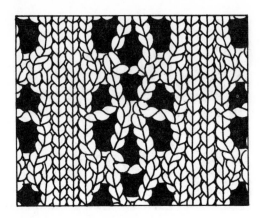

This is a traditional Italian pattern that can be adapted for an allover pattern or for lovely openwork panels.

For the **beginning row,** cast on a multiple of 14 stitches plus 4.

For the **first row,** repeat the following procedure. * Purl 1. Twist 2 by slipping the second stitch on the left-hand needle first, and then the first stitch, sliding both stitches off the needle together. Purl 1. Knit 3. Knit 2 together. Then put yarn over needle twice. Knit 2 together through back of stitch. Knit 3. * End with purl 1, twist 2, purl 1.

For the **second row,** repeat the following procedure. * Knit 1. Purl 2. Knit 1. Purl 4. Then, into the yarn-overs of the previous row, knit 1 in back and knit 1. Purl 4. * End with knit 1, purl 2, knit 1.

For the **third row,** repeat the first row.

For the **fourth row,** repeat the second row.

For the **fifth row,** repeat the following procedure. * Purl 1. Twist 2. Purl 1. Knit 1. Knit 2 together. Put yarn over needle twice. Knit 2 together through back of stitch. Knit 2 together. Put yarn around twice. Knit 2 together in back. Knit 1. * End with purl 1, twist 2, purl 1.

For the **sixth row,** repeat the following procedure. * Knit 1. Purl 2. Knit 1. Purl 2. Then, into the yarn-overs of the previous row, knit 1 in back and knit 1. Purl 2. Then knit 1 in back and knit 1 into the yarn-overs of the previous row. Purl 2. * End with knit 1, purl 2, knit 1.

For the **seventh row,** repeat the fifth row.

For the **eighth row,** repeat the sixth row.

Repeat the **first through eighth rows** as many times as required.

## Lace Cable Pattern

This attractive arrangement of stitches is found among Norwegian patterns.

For the **beginning row,** cast on 19 stitches plus 2.

For the **first row,** repeat the following procedure. * Purl 2. Knit 4 in back. Knit 1. Yarn over. Knit 2 together through back of stitch. Knit 3. Knit 2 together. Yarn over. Knit 1. Knit 4 in back. * End with purl 2.

For the **second row,** repeat the following procedure. * Knit 2. Purl 4 in back. Knit 1. Purl 7. Knit 1. Purl 4 in back. * End with knit 2.

For the **third row,** repeat the following procedure. * Purl 2. Knit 4 in back. Knit 2. Yarn over. Knit 2 together through back of stitch. Knit 1. Knit 2 together. Yarn over. Knit 2. Knit 4 in back. * End with purl 2.

For the **fourth row,** repeat the second row.

For the **fifth row,** repeat the following procedure. * Purl 2. Knit in back of 4 cable stitches. Knit 3. Yarn over. Then slip 1, knit 2 together, and pass slip stitch over. Yarn over. Knit 3. Knit in back of 4 cable stitches. * End with purl 2.

For the **sixth row,** repeat the second row.

For the **seventh row,** repeat the following procedure. * Purl 2. Knit in back of 4 stitches. Knit 9. Knit in back of 4 stitches. * End with purl 2.

For the **eighth row,** repeat the second row.

Repeat **first through eighth rows** as required.

## Lace Chevron Pattern

A series of eyelets seems to be defined in this stitch pattern, giving a zigzag effect.

For the **beginning row,** cast on 10 stitches plus 1.

For the **first row,** purl.

For the **second row,** repeat the following procedure. * Knit 5. Yarn over. Then slip 1, knit 1, and pass slip stitch over. Knit 3. * End with knit 1.

For the **third row,** purl.

For the **fourth row,** repeat the following procedure. * Knit 3. Knit 2 together. Yarn over. Knit 1. Yarn over. Then slip 1, knit 1, and pass slip stitch over. Knit 2. * End with knit 1.

For the **fifth row,** purl.

For the **sixth row,** repeat the following procedure. * Knit 2. Knit 2 together. Yarn over. Knit 3. Yarn over. Then slip 1, knit 1, and pass slip stitch over. Knit 1. * End with knit 1.

For the **seventh row,** purl.

For the **eighth row,** repeat the following procedure. * Knit 1. Knit 2 together. Yarn over. Knit 5. Yarn over. Then slip 1, knit 1, and pass slip stitch over. * End with knit 1.

For the **ninth row,** purl.

For the **tenth row,** knit 2 together. Yarn over. Knit 7. Repeat the following procedure. * Yarn over. Then slip 1, knit 2 together, and pass slip stitch over. Yarn over. Knit 7. * End with yarn over. Then slip 1, knit 1, and pass slip stitch over.

Repeat the **first through tenth rows** as many times as required.

## Lace Leaf Pattern

This graceful motif creates a lovely ribbed effect.

For the **beginning row,** cast on a multiple of 9 stitches plus 4.

For the **first row,** purl.

For the **second row,** knit 3. Repeat the following procedure. * Yarn over. Knit 2. Then slip 1, knit 1, and pass the slipped stitch over the knitted stitch. Knit 2 together. Knit 2. Yarn over. Knit 1. * End with knit 1.

For the **third row,** knit 2. Purl across row to the last 2 stitches. Knit these.

For the **fourth row,** knit 2. Repeat the following procedure. * Yarn over. Knit 2. Then slip 1, knit 1, and pass the slipped stitch over the knitted stitch. Knit 2 together. Knit 2. Yarn over. Knit 1. * End with knit 2.

For the **fifth row,** repeat the second row.

Repeat the **second through fifth rows** as many times as required.

## Lace Medallion Pattern

This is one of the beautiful Italian patterns that create an interesting, lacy effect.

For the **beginning row,** cast on a multiple of 11 stitches plus 4.

For the **first row,** knit 2. Repeat the following procedure. * Knit 3. Knit 2 together. Yarn over. Knit 1. Yarn over. Knit 2 together through back. Knit 3. * End with knit 2.

For the **second row,** knit 2. Repeat the following procedure. * Knit 2. Purl 2 together through back of loop. Wrap yarn around needle. Purl 3. Wrap yarn around needle. Purl 2 together. Knit 2. * End with knit 2.

For the **third row,** knit 2. Repeat the following procedure. * Knit 1. Then knit two together and put yarn over twice. Knit 1. Follow with yarn over, and knit 2 together through back of loop twice. Knit 1. * End with knit 2.

For the **fourth row,** knit 2. Repeat the following procedure. * Purl 2 together through back of loop. Wrap yarn around needle. Purl 2 together through back of loop. Yarn over. Knit 3. Then wrap yarn around needle and purl 2 together twice. * End with knit 2.

For the **fifth row,** knit 2. Repeat the following procedure. * Knit 1. Then put yarn over and knit 2 together through back of loop twice. Knit 1. Follow with knit 2 together and yarn over twice. Knit 1. * End with knit 2.

For the **sixth row,** knit 2. Repeat the following procedure. * Knit 2. Wrap yarn around needle. Purl 2 together. Wrap yarn around needle. Purl 3 together. Wrap yarn around needle. Purl 2 together through back of loop. Yarn over. Knit 2. * End with knit 2.

For the **seventh row,** knit 2. Repeat the following procedure. * Knit 3. Yarn over. Knit 2 together through back of loop. Knit 1. Knit 2 together. Yarn over. Knit 3. * End with knit 2.

For the **eighth row,** knit 2. Repeat the following procedure. * Knit 4. Wrap yarn around needle. Purl 3 together. Yarn over. Knit 4. * End with knit 2.

Repeat the **first through eighth rows** as m/ny times as required.

## Lace Rib Pattern

An interesting arrangement of stitches give the look of linked chains with an eyelet center.

For the **beginning row,** cast on a multiple of 5 stitches plus 2.

For the **first row,** knit 2. Repeat the following procedure. * Purl 3. Knit 2. *

For the **second row,** purl 2. Repeat the following procedure. * Knit 1. Yarn over. Then slip 1, knit 1, and pass slip stitch over. Purl 2. *

For the **third row,** repeat the first row.

For the **fourth row,** purl 2. Repeat the following procedure. * Knit 2 together. Yarn over. Knit 1. Purl 2. *

Repeat the **first through fourth rows** as many times as required.

## Lace Wings Pattern

This airy lace design is found in Dutch stitch patterns.

For the **beginning row,** cast on 7 stitches for a rib or panel of stitches.

For the **first row,** purl.

For the **second row,** knit 1. Knit 2 together. Yarn over. Knit 1. Yarn over. Then slip 1, knit 1, and pass slip stitch over. Knit 1.

For the **third row,** purl.

For the **fourth row,** knit 2 together. Yarn over. Knit 3. Yarn over. Then slip 1, knit 1, and pass slip stitch over.

Repeat the **first through fourth rows** as many times as required.

## Lattice Stitch

This grouping of stitches creates a bold design pattern that gives a basket weave effect.

For the **beginning row,** cast on a multiple of 6 stitches.

For the **first row,** repeat the following procedure. * Knit 4. Purl 2. *

For the **second row,** knit the purl stitches and purl the knit stitches of previous row.

For the **third row,** repeat the following procedure. * Slip 2 stitches onto a double-pointed needle. Leave at back. Knit 2. Knit the 2 stitches on the double-pointed needle. Purl 2. *

For the **fourth row,** repeat the second row.

For the **fifth row,** purl 2. Repeat the following procedure. * Knit 2. Slip 2 onto a double-pointed needle. Leave in back. Knit 2. Purl the 2 stitches on the double-pointed needle. * End with knit 4.

For the **sixth row,** repeat the second row.

For the **seventh row,** repeat the following procedure. * Purl 2. Slip 2 onto a double-pointed needle. Leave in front. Knit 2. Knit the 2 stitches from the double-pointed needle. *

For the **eighth row,** repeat the second row.

For the **ninth row,** knit 4. Repeat the following procedure. * Slip 2 onto a double-pointed needle. Leave in front. Purl 2. Knit the 2 stitches from the double-pointed needle. Knit 2. * End with purl 2.

Repeat the **second through ninth rows** as many times as required.

## Lazy Daisy Stitch

Looped stitches add an embroidered look to an otherwise plain surface.

For the **beginning row,** cast on a multiple of 10 stitches plus 5.

For the **first row,** purl.

For the **second row,** knit.

For the **third row,** purl.

For the **fourth row,** knit.

For the **fifth row,** purl.

For the **sixth row,** knit 5. Repeat the following procedure. * Insert needle into a stitch 5 rows below the third stitch from the tip of the left-hand needle, and pull up a loop. Knit 5. Insert the needle in the same stitch, pulling up a second loop. Knit 5. *

For the **seventh row,** purl 4. Repeat the following procedure. * Purl 2 together in back. Purl 5. Purl 2 together. Purl 3. * End with purl 4.

For the **eighth row,** knit 7. Repeat the following procedure. * Insert needle in the same stitch below in which loops were made in the sixth row, and pull up a loop. Place it on the left-hand needle. Knit through back of loop and front of next stitch together. Knit 9. * End row with knit 7.

For the **ninth row,** purl.

For the **tenth row,** knit.

For the **eleventh row,** purl.

For the **twelfth row,** knit.

For the **thirteenth row,** purl.

For the **fourteenth row,** knit 10. Repeat the following procedure. * Insert needle into a stitch 5 rows below the third stitch from the tip of the left-hand needle, and pull up a loop. Knit 5. Insert the needle in the same stitch, pulling up a second loop. Knit 5. * End row with knit 10.

For the **fifteenth row,** purl 9. Repeat the following procedure. * Purl 2 together in back. Purl 5. Purl 2 together in back. Purl 3. * End with purl 9.

For the **sixteenth row,** knit 12. Repeat the following procedure. * Insert needle in the same stitch below in which loops were made in the fourteenth row, and pull up a loop. Place it on the left-hand needle. Knit through back of loop and front of next stitch together. Knit 9. * End row with knit 12.

For the **seventeenth row,** purl.

Repeat the **second through seventeenth rows** as many times as required.

## Lozenge Pattern

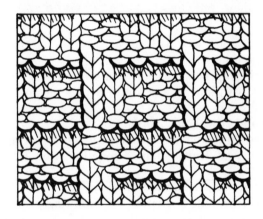

Triangular shapes forming squares give an interesting look to this old Italian stitch pattern.

For the **beginning row,** cast on a multiple of 5 stitches.

For the **first row,** repeat the following procedure. * Purl 1. Knit 4. *

For the **second row,** repeat the following procedure. * Purl 3. Knit 2. *

For the **third row,** repeat the second row.

For the **fourth row,** repeat the following procedure. * Purl 1. Knit 4. *

For the **fifth row,** repeat the fourth row.

For the **sixth row,** repeat the following procedure. * Knit 2. Purl 3. *

For the **seventh row,** repeat the sixth row.

For the **eighth row,** repeat the following procedure. * Knit 4. Purl 1. *

Repeat the **first through eighth rows** as many times as required.

## Madeira Cascade Pattern

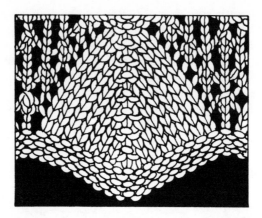

This is an old Spanish lace pattern that uses an interesting arrangement of shapes, both solid and lacy.

For the **beginning row,** cast on a multiple of 20 stitches plus 5.

For the **first row,** knit 2. Then purl across the row to the last 2 stitches. Knit 2.

For the **second row,** knit.

For the **third row,** knit 2. Then repeat the following procedure. * Knit 1. Yarn over. Knit 8. Purl 3 together. Knit 8. Yarn over. * End with knit 3.

For the **fourth row,** repeat the first row.

For the **fifth row,** knit 2. Repeat the following procedure. * Knit 2. Yarn over. Knit 7. Purl 3 together. Knit 7. Yarn over. Knit 1. * End with knit 3.

For the **sixth row,** repeat the first row.

For the **seventh row,** knit 2. Knit 2 together. Repeat the following procedure. * Yarn over. Knit 1. Yarn over. Knit 6. Purl 3 together. Knit 6. Yarn over. Knit 1. * Yarn over. Knit 2 together in back of loop. End with knit 2.

For the **eighth row,** repeat the first row.

For the **ninth row,** knit 2. Repeat the following procedure. * Knit 4. Yarn over. Knit 5. Purl 3 together. Knit 5. Yarn over. Knit 3. * End with knit 3.

For the **tenth row,** repeat the first row.

For the **eleventh row,** knit 2. Repeat the following procedure. * Knit 1. Yarn over. Then slip 1, knit 2 together, and pass slip stitch over. Yarn over. Knit 1. Yarn over. Knit 4. Purl 3 together. Knit 4. Yarn over. Knit 1. Yarn over. Then slip 1, knit 2 together, and pass slip stitch over. Yarn over. * End with knit 3.

For the **twelfth row,** repeat the first row.

For the **thirteenth row,** knit 2. Repeat the following procedure. * Knit 6. Yarn over. Knit 3. Purl 3 together. Knit 3. Yarn over. Knit 5. * End with knit 3.

For the **fourteenth row,** repeat the first row.

For the **fifteenth row,** knit 2. Knit 2 together. Repeat the following procedure. * Yarn over. Knit 1. Yarn over. Then slip 1, knit 2 together, and pass slip stitch over. Yarn over. Knit 1. Yarn over. Knit 2. * End with purl 3 together. Knit 2. Yarn over. Knit 1. Yarn over. Then slip 1, knit 2 together, and pass slip stitch over. Yarn over. Knit 1. Yarn over. Knit 2 together through back of loop. Knit 2.

For the **sixteenth row,** repeat the first row.

For the **seventeenth row,** knit 2. Repeat the following procedure. * Knit 8. Yarn over. Knit 1. Purl 3 together. Knit 1. Yarn over. Knit 7. * End with knit 3.

For the **eighteenth row,** repeat the first row.

For the **nineteenth row,** knit 2. Repeat the following procedure. * Knit 1. Yarn over. Then slip 1, knit 2 together, and pass slip stitch over. Yarn over. Knit 1. Yarn over. Then slip 1, knit 2 together, and pass slip stitch over. Yarn over. Knit 1. Wrap yarn around needle. Purl 3 together. Yarn over. Knit 1. Yarn over. Then slip 1, knit 2 together, and pass slip stitch over. Yarn over. Knit 1. Yarn over. Then slip 1, knit 2 together, and pass slip stitch over. Yarn over. * Knit 3.

For the **twentieth row,** knit.

Repeat the **first through twentieth rows** as many times as required.

## Madeira Mesh Pattern

This is another very old Spanish pattern. It creates a very sheer, lacy effect when worked in fine yarn.

For the **beginning row,** cast on a multiple of 6 stitches plus 7.

For the **first through sixth rows,** knit 2. Repeat the following procedure. * Wrap yarn around needle. Purl 3 together. Yarn over. Knit 3. * End row with wrap yarn around needle. Purl 3 together. Yarn over. Knit 2.

For the **seventh through twelfth rows,** knit 2. Repeat the following procedure. * Knit 3. Wrap yarn around needle. Purl 3 together. Yarn over. * End row with knit 5.

Repeat the **first through twelfth rows** as many times as required.


## Marriage Lines Lace Pattern

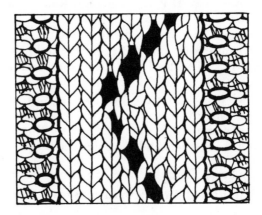

This is an unusual pattern in that it forms distinct panels, one dominated with a zigzag eyelet design and the other with moss or seed type stitches.

For the **beginning row,** cast on a multiple of 14 stitches plus 7.

For the **first row,** repeat the following procedure. * Purl 7. Knit 1. Yarn over. Knit 2 together. Knit 4. * End with purl 7.

For the **second row,** repeat the following procedure. * Knit 1 and purl 1 in back 3 times. Knit 1. Purl 7. * End with knit 1 and purl 1 in back 3 times. Knit 1.

For the **third row,** repeat the following procedure. * Purl 7. Knit 2. Yarn over. Knit 2 together. Knit 3. * End with purl 7.

For the **fourth row,** repeat the second row.

For the **fifth row,** repeat the following procedure. * Purl 7. Knit 3. Yarn over. Knit 2 together. Knit 2. * End with purl 7.

For the **sixth row,** repeat the second row.

For the **seventh row,** repeat the following procedure. * Purl 7. Knit 4. Yarn over. Knit 2 together. Knit 1. * End with purl 7.

For the **eighth row,** repeat the second row.

For the **ninth row,** repeat the following procedure. * Purl 7. Knit 3. Knit 2 together through back of loop. Yarn over. Knit 2. * End with purl 7.

For the **tenth row,** repeat the second row.

For the **eleventh row,** repeat the following procedure. * Purl 7. Knit 2. Knit 2 together through back of loop. Yarn over. Knit 3. * End with purl 7.

For the **twelfth row,** repeat the second row.

For the **thirteenth row,** repeat the following procedure. * Purl 7. Knit 1. Knit 2 together through back of loop. Yarn over. Knit 4. * End with purl 7.

For the **fourteenth row,** repeat the second row.

For the **fifteenth row,** repeat the following procedure. * Purl 7. Knit 2 together through back loops. Yarn over. Knit 5. * End with purl 7.

For the **sixteenth row,** repeat the following procedure. * Knit 1 and purl 1 in back 3 times. Knit 1. Purl 7. * End with knit 1 and purl 1 in back 3 times. Knit 1.

Repeat the **first through sixteenth rows** as often as required.

## Miniature Leaf Pattern

This design pattern creates a tiny diamond motif outlined with eyelets.

For the **beginning row,** cast on a multiple of 6 stitches plus 1.

For the **first row,** purl.

For the **second row,** knit 1. Repeat the following procedure. * Knit 2 together. Yarn over. Knit 1. Yarn over. Then slip 1, knit 1, and pass slip stitch over. Knit 1. *

For the **third row,** purl.

For the **fourth row,** knit 2 together. Repeat the following procedure. * Yarn over. Knit 3. Yarn over. Slip 2 stitches knitwise, knit 1, and pass the 2 slip stitches over. *

For the **fifth row,** purl.

For the **sixth row,** knit 1. Repeat the following procedure. * Yarn over. Then slip 1, knit 1, and pass slip stitch over. Knit 1. Knit 2 together. Yarn over. Knit 1.*

For the **seventh row,** purl.

For the **eighth row,** knit 2. Repeat the following procedure. * Yarn over. Then slip 2 knitwise, knit 1, and pass the 2 slip stitches over. Yarn over. Knit 3. * End with knit 2.

Repeat the **first through eighth rows** as many times as required.

## Mistake Stitch Ribbing

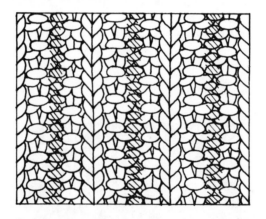

This unusual arrangement of stitches provides a bold ribbing pattern.

For the **beginning row,** cast on a multiple of 4 stitches plus 3.

For the **first row,** repeat the following procedure. * Knit 2. Purl 2. * End with knit 2, purl 1.

Repeat the **first row** as many times as required.

## Mock Kilting Pattern

This is a Scottish pattern that uses an arrangement of triangles for an effective design. If left unpressed, it will roll up, giving a pleated effect.

For the **beginning row,** cast on a multiple of 9 stitches.

For the **first row,** repeat the following procedure. * Knit 8. Purl 1. *

For the **second row,** repeat the following procedure. * Knit 2. Purl 7. *

For the **third row,** repeat the following procedure. * Knit 6. Purl 3. *

For the **fourth row,** repeat the following procedure. * Knit 4. Purl 5. *

For the **fifth row,** repeat the following procedure. * Knit 4. Purl 5. *

For the **sixth row,** repeat the following procedure. * Knit 6. Purl 3. *

For the **seventh row,** repeat the following procedure. * Knit 2. Purl 7. *

For the **eighth row,** repeat the following procedure. * Knit 8. Purl 1. *

Repeat the **first through eighth rows** as many times as required.

## Moss Stitch
*See* Seed Stitch.

## Mrs. Hunter's Pattern

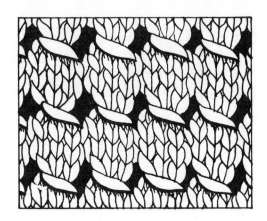

This stitch pattern is named for the woman who designed it, whose family is well known for its development of Shetland lace knitting.

For the **beginning row,** cast on a multiple of 4 stitches plus 2.

For the **first row,** knit.

For the **second row,** purl.

For the **third row,** knit 1. Repeat the following procedure. * Slip 1, knit 3, and pass slip stitch over the 3 knits. * End with knit 1.

For the **fourth row,** purl 1. Repeat the following procedure. * Purl 3. Wrap yarn around needle. * End with purl 1.

Repeat the **first through fourth rows** as many times as required.

## Old Shale Pattern

This pattern is sometimes known as the Feather and Fan Stitch and is among the well-known Shetland lace designs.

For the **beginning row,** cast on a multiple of 18 stitches.

For the **first row,** knit.

For the **second row,** purl.

For the **third row,** repeat the following procedure. * Knit 2 together 3 times. Then put yarn over and knit 1, 6 times. Knit 2 together 3 times. *

For the **fourth row,** knit.

Repeat **first through fourth rows** as required.


## Oriental Rib Stitch
*See* Brioche Stitch.

## Peacock's Tail Pattern

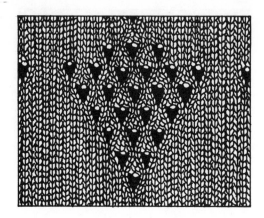

The triangular arrangement of picot eyelets adds interest to a stockinette background.

For the **beginning row,** cast on 28 stitches for each vertical pattern stripe.

For the **first row,** knit.

For the **second row,** purl.

For the **third row,** knit.

For the **fourth row,** purl.

For the **fifth row,** knit 12. Knit 2 together. Put yarn over twice. Then slip 1, knit 1, and pass slip stitch over. Knit 12.

For the **sixth row,** purl, working a purl 1 and knit 1 into each double yarn-over of the preceding row.

For the **seventh row,** knit.

For the **eighth row,** repeat the sixth row.

For the **ninth row,** knit 10. Then work the following sequence of stitches twice: knit 2 together; yarn over twice; and slip 1, knit 1, and pass slip stitch over. Knit 10.

For the **tenth row,** repeat the sixth row.

For the **eleventh row,** knit.

For the **twelfth row,** repeat the sixth row.

For the **thirteenth row,** knit 8. Then work the following sequence of stitches 3 times: knit 2 together; yarn over twice; and slip 1, knit 1, and pass slip stitch over. Follow with knit 8.

For the **fourteenth row,** repeat the sixth row.

For the **fifteenth row,** knit.

For the **sixteenth row,** repeat the sixth row.

For the **seventeenth row,** knit 6. Then work the following sequence of stitches 4 times: knit 2 together; put yarn over twice; and slip 1, knit 1, and pass slip stitch over. Follow with knit 6.

For the **eighteenth row,** repeat the sixth row.

For the **nineteenth row,** knit.

For the **twentieth row,** repeat the sixth row.

For the **twenty-first row,** knit 4. Then work the following sequence of stitches 5 times: knit 2 together; put yarn over twice; and slip 1, knit 1, and pass slip stitch over. Follow with knit 4.

For the **twenty-second row,** repeat the sixth row.

For the **twenty-third row,** knit.

For the **twenty-fourth row,** repeat the sixth row.

For the **twenty-fifth row,** knit 2. Then repeat the following sequence of stitches 6 times: knit 2 together; put yarn over twice; and slip 1, knit 1, and pass slip stitch over. Follow with knit 2.

For the **twenty-sixth row,** repeat the sixth row.

For the **twenty-seventh row,** knit.

For the **twenty-eighth row,** repeat the sixth row.

For the **twenty-ninth row,** repeat the thirteenth row.

For the **thirtieth row,** purl, working 1 purl and 1 knit into each double yarn-over.

Repeat the **first through thirtieth rows** as many times as required.

## Pearl-barred Scallop Pattern

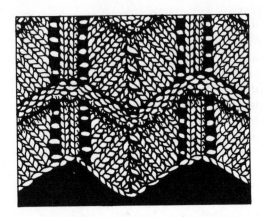

Although the stitch pattern may appear complicated, it is fairly easy to create. It was a favorite of Victorian knitting.

For the **beginning row,** cast on a multiple of 13 stitches plus 2.

For the **first row,** knit 2. Repeat the following procedure. * Yarn over. Knit 4. Then slip 1, knit 2 together, and pass slip stitch over the knit 2 together. Knit 4. Yarn over. Knit 2. *

For the **second row,** purl.

For the **third row,** repeat the first row.

For the **fourth row,** purl.

For the **fifth row,** repeat the first row.

For the **sixth row,** purl.

For the **seventh row,** repeat the first row.

For the **eighth row,** purl.

For the **ninth row,** repeat the first row.

For the **tenth row,** purl.

For the **eleventh row,** purl.

For the **twelfth row,** knit.

Repeat the **first through twelfth rows** as many times as required.

## Pennant Pleating

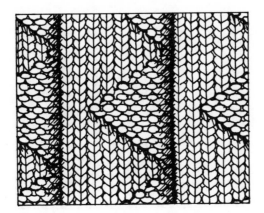

This is another of the triangular patterns that has a tendency to roll, giving a pleated effect.

For the **beginning row,** cast on a multiple of 10 stitches.

For the **first row,** repeat the following procedure. * Knit 2. Purl 2. Knit 6. *

For the **second row,** repeat the following procedure. * Purl 5. Knit 3. Purl 2. *

For the **third row,** repeat the following procedure. * Knit 2. Purl 4. Knit 4. *

For the **fourth row,** repeat the following procedure. * Purl 3. Knit 5. Purl 2. *

For the **fifth row,** repeat the following procedure. * Knit 2. Purl 6. Knit 2. *

For the **sixth row,** repeat the following procedure. * Purl 1. Knit 7. Purl 2. *

For the **seventh row,** repeat the following procedure. * Knit 2. Purl 8. *

For the **eighth row,** repeat the following procedure. * Purl 1. Knit 7. Purl 2. *

For the **ninth row,** repeat the following procedure. * Knit 2. Purl 6. Knit 2. *

For the **tenth row,** repeat the following procedure. * Purl 3. Knit 5. Purl 2. *

For the **eleventh row,** repeat the following procedure. * Knit 2. Purl 4. Knit 4. *

For the **twelfth row,** repeat the following procedure. * Purl 5. Knit 3. Purl 2. *

Repeat the **first through twelfth rows** as many times as required.

## Peppercorn stitch

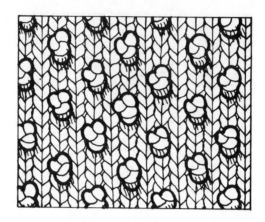

A pebbly, textural quality is given this stitch pattern for an interesting 3-dimensional effect.

For the **beginning row,** cast on a multiple of 4 stitches plus 3.

For the **first row,** purl.

For the **second row,** knit 3. Repeat the following procedure. * Knit next stitch. Then slide this stitch onto the left-hand needle without removing the right-hand needle, and with the left-hand needle in the front of the stitch. With the needles in this position, knit 3 times into the back. Knit 3. *

For the **third row,** purl.

For the **fourth row,** knit 1. Repeat the following procedure. * Knit next stitch. Then slide this stitch onto the left-hand needle without removing the right-hand needle, and with the left-hand needle in the front of the stitch. With the needles in this position, knit 3 times into the back. Knit 3. * End with knit 1.

Repeat the **first through fourth rows** as many times as required.

## Pine Trees Pattern

An effective arrangement of stitches, moving in different directions, creates an unusual design pattern.

For the **beginning row,** cast on a multiple of 14 stitches plus 1.

For the **first row,** knit 1. Repeat the following procedure. * Yarn over. Knit 2. Purl 3. Purl 3 together. Purl 3. Knit 2. Yarn over. Knit 1. *

For the **second row,** repeat the following procedure. * Purl 4. Knit 7. Purl 3. * End with purl 1.

For the **third row,** knit 1. Repeat the following procedure. * Knit 1. Yarn over. Knit 2. Purl 2. Purl 3 together. Purl 2. Knit 2. Yarn over. Knit 2. *

For the **fourth row,** repeat the following procedure. * Purl 5. Knit 5. Purl 4. * End with purl 1.

For the **fifth row,** knit 1. Repeat the following procedure. * Knit 2. Yarn over. Knit 2. Purl 1. Purl 3 together. Purl 1. Knit 2. Yarn over. Knit 3. *

For the **sixth row,** repeat the following procedure. * Purl 6. Knit 3. Purl 5. * End with purl 1.

For the **seventh row,** knit 1. Repeat the following procedure. * Knit 3. Yarn over. Knit 2. Purl 3 together. Knit 2. Yarn over. Knit 4. *

For the **eighth row,** repeat the following procedure. * Purl 7. Knit 1. Purl 6. * End with purl 1.

For the **ninth row,** knit 1. Repeat the following procedure. * Knit 4. Yarn over. Knit 1. Then slip 1, knit 2 together, and pass slip stitch over. Knit 1. Yarn over. Knit 5. *

For the **tenth row,** purl.

For the **eleventh row,** knit 1. Repeat the following procedure. * Knit 5. Yarn over. Then slip 1, knit 2 together, and pass slip stitch over. Yarn over. Knit 6. *

For the **twelfth row,** purl.

Repeat the **first through twelfth rows** as many times as required.

## Pinnacle Crepe Pattern

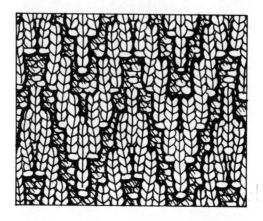

This easy-to-make pattern results in a lovely textural effect with an interesting design that seems to close up in twisted fashion when left unpressed.

For the **beginning row,** cast on a multiple of 18 stitches.

For the **first row,** repeat the following procedure. * Knit 1. Then purl 2 and knit 2 twice. Purl 1. Follow with knit 2 and purl 2 twice. *

For the **second row,** repeat the following procedure. * Knit 2 and purl 2 twice. Then knit 1. Follow with purl 2 and knit 2 twice. Purl 1. *

For the **third row,** repeat the first row.

For the **fourth row,** repeat the second row.

For the **fifth row,** repeat the following procedure. * Purl 2 and knit 2 twice. Then purl 3. Knit 2. Purl 2. Knit 2. Purl 1. *

For the **sixth row,** repeat the following procedure. * Knit 1. Purl 2. Knit 2. Purl 2. Knit 3. Then purl 2 and knit 2 twice. *

For the **seventh row,** repeat the fifth row.

For the **eighth row,** repeat the sixth row.

For the **ninth row,** repeat the following procedure. * Purl 1. Then knit 2 and purl 2 twice. Knit 1. Follow with purl 2 and knit 2 twice. *

For the **tenth row,** repeat the following procedure. * Purl 2 and knit 2 twice. Then purl 1. Follow by knit 2 and purl 2 twice. Knit 1. *

For the **eleventh row,** repeat the ninth row.

For the **twelfth row,** repeat the tenth row.

For the **thirteenth row,** repeat the following procedure. * Knit 2 and purl 2 twice. Knit 3. Purl 2. Knit 2. Purl 2. Knit 1. *

For the **fourteenth row,** repeat the following procedure. * Purl 1. Knit 2. Purl 2. Knit 2. Purl 3. Then knit 2 and purl 2 twice. *

For the **fifteenth row,** repeat the thirteenth row.

For the **sixteenth row,** repeat the fourteenth row.

Repeat the **first through sixteenth rows** as many times as required.

## Point D'Angleterre Stitch
*See* Brioche Stitch.

## Purse Stitch

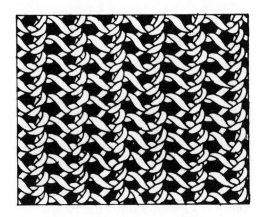

This easy-to-do stitch adds a yarn-over to the basic knit and purl stitches to create a slightly openwork pattern.

For the **beginning row,** cast on a multiple of 2 stitches.

For the **first row,** knit 1. Repeat the following procedure. * Yarn over. Purl 2 together. * End with knit 1.

Repeat the **first row** as many times as required.

## Puzzle Stitch
*See* All Fools' Welt Pattern.

## Quilting Pattern—Diamond

Diagonally placed loops give this English pattern a soft but definite line.

For the **beginning row**, cast on 6 stitches plus 4.

For the **first row**, purl.

For the **second row**, knit 4. Repeat the following procedure. * Knit the next 2 stitches, wrapping yarn twice around needle. Knit 4. *

For the **third row**, purl 4. Repeat the following procedure. * With yarn in front, slip next 2 stitches purlwise, dropping the extra wrapped stitches. Purl 4. *

For the **fourth row**, knit 4. Repeat the following procedure. * With yarn in back, slip next 2 stitches purlwise. Knit 4. *

For the **fifth row**, purl 4. Repeat the following procedure. * With yarn in front, slip next 2 stitches purlwise. Purl 4. *

For the **sixth row**, knit 2. Repeat the following procedure. * Skip next 2 stitches. Knit the next stitch, inserting needle through front. Leave on needle. Then knit the first and second stitches on left needle. Drop the third stitch from needle. Slip the next stitch onto a double-pointed needle and leave in front. Knit 2. Knit the stitch from the double-pointed needle. * End with knit 2.

For the **seventh row**, purl.

For the **eighth row**, knit 2. Then knit 1, wrapping yarn twice around needle. Knit 4. Repeat the following procedure. * Knit next 2 stitches, wrapping yarn around twice. Knit 4. * End with knit 1, wrapping yarn around twice. Knit 2.

For the **ninth row**, purl 2. With yarn in front, slip 1 stitch, dropping the wrapped stitches. Purl 4. Repeat the following procedure. * With yarn in front, slip 2 stitches, dropping the wrapped stitches. Purl 4. * End with yarn in front. Slip 1 stitch, dropping the wrapped stitches. Purl 2.

For the **tenth row,** knit 2. Slip next stitch purlwise with yarn in back. Repeat the following procedure. * Knit 4. With yarn in back, slip next 2 stitches purlwise. * End with knit 4. Then, with yarn in back, slip next stitch purlwise. Knit 2.

For the **eleventh row,** purl 2. With yarn in front, slip 1 stitch purlwise. Repeat the following procedure. * Purl 4. With yarn in front, slip next 2 stitches. * End with purl 4. With yarn in front, slip 1 stitch. Purl 2.

For the **twelfth row,** knit 2. Repeat the following procedure. * Slip next stitch onto a double-pointed needle, leaving it in front. Knit 2. Knit the stitch from the double-pointed needle. Skip next 2 stitches. Knit next stitch, inserting needle in front of stitch. Leave on needle. Knit first and second stitches on left-hand needle. Drop third stitch from needle. * End with knit 2.

Repeat the **first through twelfth rows** as many times as required.

## Raised Diamond Pattern

An interesting 3-dimensional effect results when this design pattern is used.

For the **beginning row,** cast on a multiple of 7 stitches.

For the **first row,** knit.

For the **second row,** purl.

For the **third row,** knit.

For the **fourth row,** purl 3. Knit 1. Purl 3.

For the **fifth row,** knit 3. Then purl the next stitch, first into the front, then into the back, and finally into the front again. Knit 3.

For the **sixth row,** purl 3. Knit 3. Purl 3.

For the **seventh row,** knit 3. Then purl into the front and back of next stitch. Purl 1. Then purl into front and back of next stitch. Knit 3.

For the **eighth row,** purl 3. Knit 5. Purl 3.

For the **ninth row,** knit 3. Purl into the front and back of next stitch. Purl 3. Again purl into the front and back of next stitch. Knit 3.

For the **tenth row,** purl 3. Knit 7. Purl 3.

For the **eleventh row,** knit 3. Purl into the front and back of the next stitch. Purl 5. Then purl into front and back of the next stitch. Knit 3.

For the **twelfth row,** purl 3. Knit 9. Purl 3.

For the **thirteenth row,** knit 3. Purl 2 together. Purl 5. Purl 2 together in back. Knit 3.

For the **fourteenth row,** purl 3. Knit 7. Purl 3.

For the **fifteenth row,** knit 3. Purl 2 together. Purl 3. Purl 2 together in back. Knit 3.

For the **sixteenth row,** purl 3. Knit 5. Purl 3.

For the **seventeenth row,** knit 3. Purl 2 together. Purl 1. Purl 2 together in back. Knit 3.

For the **eighteenth row,** purl 3. Knit 3. Purl 3.

For the **nineteenth row,** knit 3. Purl 3 together. Knit 3.

For the **twentieth row,** purl 3. Knit 1. Purl 3.

Repeat the **first through twentieth rows** as many times as required.

## Reverse Lace stitch

*See* Brioche Stitch.

## Reversible Grand Eyelet

*See* Eyelet Lace Pattern—Grand.

## Rib Pattern—Braided

Ribbing can be given a new look by using this stitch pattern.

For the **beginning row,** cast on a multiple of 5 stitches plus 2.

For the **first row,** purl 2. Repeat the following procedure. * Insert needle between first and second stitches on the left-hand needle, moving from back to front. Then knit the second stitch. Follow by knitting the first stitch. Slip both stitches from needle at the same time. Knit 1. Purl 2. *

For the **second row,** knit 2. Repeat the following procedure. * Purl the second stitch before purling the first stitch. Slip both stitches from needle together. Purl 1. Knit 2. *

Repeat the **first and second rows** as many times as required.

## Rib Pattern—Broken Diagonal

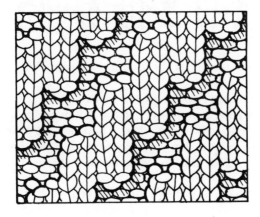

This stitch pattern creates a step effect as bands of ribbing are placed side by side.

For the **beginning row,** cast on a multiple of 8 stitches.

For the **first through fourth rows,** repeat the following procedure. * Purl 4. Knit 4. *

For the **fifth row,** knit 2. Repeat the following procedure. * Purl 4. Knit 2. *

For the **sixth row,** purl 2. Repeat the following procedure. * Knit 4. Purl 2. *

For the **seventh row,** repeat the fifth row.

For the **eighth row,** repeat the sixth row.

For the **ninth through twelfth rows,** repeat the following procedure. * Knit 4. Purl 4. *

For the **thirteenth row,** repeat the sixth row.

For the **fourteenth row,** repeat the fifth row.

For the **fifteenth row,** repeat the thirteenth row.

For the **sixteenth row,** repeat the fourteenth row.

Repeat the **first through sixteenth rows** as many times as required.

## Rib Pattern—Corded

A smart textural quality is the dominant feature of this old Italian pattern.

For the **beginning row,** cast on a multiple of 4 stitches plus 2.

For the **first row,** knit 1. Repeat the following procedure. * Slip 1, knit 1, and pass slip stitch over. Then make 1 stitch by picking up the connecting yarn that runs between the stitch just worked and the next stitch, and knit in back of this stitch. Then purl 2. * Knit 1.

Repeat the **first row** as many times as required.

## Rib Pattern—Cross Cord

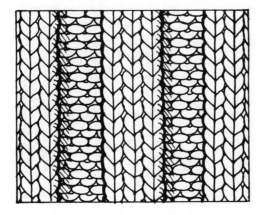

This is another old Italian pattern that has an interesting textural quality.

For the **beginning row,** cast on a multiple of 6 stitches plus 3.

For the **first row,** repeat the following procedure. * Knit 3 stitches in back. Purl 3. * End row by knitting 3 stitches in back.

For the **second row,** purl 3 in back. Repeat the following procedure. * Knit 3. Purl 3 in back. *

Repeat the **first and second rows** as many times as required.

## Rib Pattern—Cross Stitch

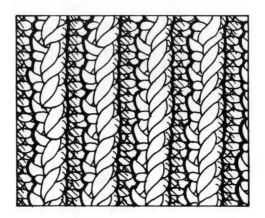

Plain ribbing can be given a different look when it is twisted on both sides of the knitting.

For the **beginning row,** cast on a multiple of 3 stitches plus 1.

For the **first row,** purl 1. Repeat the following procedure. * Knit in back of second stitch. Leave it on the left-hand needle. Then knit in front of the first stitch, and slip both off together. Purl 1. *

For the **second row,** knit 1. Repeat the following procedure. * Purl 2. Knit 1. *

Repeat the **first and second rows** as many times as required.

## Rib Pattern—Diagonal

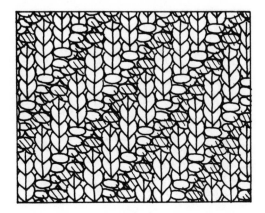

A subtle diagonal effect is achieved by using this arrangement of stitches.

For the **beginning row,** cast on a multiple of 4 stitches.

For the **first row,** repeat the following procedure. * Knit 2. Purl 2. *

For the **second row,** knit the purl stitches and purl the knit stitches of the previous row.

For the **third row,** repeat the following procedure. * Knit 1. Purl 2. Knit 1. *

For the **fourth row,** repeat the second row.

For the **fifth row,** repeat the following procedure. * Purl 2. Knit 2. *

For the **sixth row,** repeat the second row.

For the **seventh row,** repeat the following procedure. * Purl 1. Knit 2. Purl 1. *

Repeat the **second through seventh rows** as many times as required.

## Rib Pattern—Herringbone

When this stitch pattern is left unpressed, the diagonal lines in the rib produce a herringbone effect.

For the **beginning row,** cast on 9 stitches plus 3.

For the **first row,** repeat the following procedure. * Purl 3. Knit 2 together, but do not slip from left-hand needle. Knit the first of these 2 stitches again, slip both stitches off needle. Do this 2 more times. * End with purl 3.

For the **second row,** repeat the following procedure. * Knit 3, purl 6. * End with knit 3.

For the **third row,** repeat the following procedure. * Purl 3, knit 1. Knit 2 together, but do not slip from left-hand needle. Knit the first stitch again, slip both stitches off needle. Do this once more. Knit 1. * End with purl 3.

For the **fourth row,** repeat the second row.

Repeat **first through fourth rows** as required.


## Rice Stitch

*See* Seed Stitch.

## Sand Stitch

This stitch pattern creates a reversible fabric but with different textural effects. The reverse side is sometimes referred to as Dot or Spot Stitch.

For the **beginning row,** cast on a multiple of 2 stitches.

For the **first row,** knit.

For the **second row,** repeat the following procedure. * Knit 1. Purl 1. *

For the **third row,** knit.

For the **fourth row,** repeat the following procedure. * Purl 1. Knit 1. *

Repeat the **first through fourth rows** as many times as required.

## Scattered Oats Pattern

The alternating direction of small looped stitches gives the surface an embroidered look.

For the **beginning row,** cast on a multiple of 4 stitches plus 1.

For the **first row,** repeat the following procedure. * Knit 2. Slip 1 purlwise. Knit one. * End with knit 1.

For the **second row,** purl 1. Repeat the following procedure. * Purl 1. Slip 1 purlwise. Purl 2. *

For the **third row,** repeat the following procedure. * Slip 2 stitches onto a double-pointed needle, leaving needle in back. Knit the slip stitch that was slipped in the second row. Knit the 2 stitches on the double-pointed needle. Knit 1. * End with knit 1.

For the **fourth row,** purl.

For the **fifth row,** repeat the first row.

For the **sixth row,** repeat the second row.

For the **seventh row,** knit 1. Repeat the following procedure. * Knit 1. Place the slip stitch of the previous row on a double-pointed needle and leave in front. Knit 2. Knit the stitch from the double-pointed needle. *

Repeat the **first through seventh rows** as many times as required.

## Scroll Pattern

The lines of this stitch pattern seem to wander, with openwork emphasizing their direction.

For the **beginning row,** cast on a multiple of 2 stitches.

For the **first row,** knit 1. Repeat the following procedure. * Yarn over. Knit 8. Knit 2 together. * End with knit 1.

For the **second row,** purl 1. Repeat the following procedure. * Purl 2 together. Purl 7. Yarn over. Purl 1. * End with purl 1.

For the **third row,** knit 1. Repeat the following procedure. * Knit 2. Yarn over. Knit 6. Knit 2 together. * End with knit 1.

For the **fourth row,** purl 1. Repeat the following procedure. * Purl 2 together. Purl 5. Yarn over. Purl 3. * End with purl 1.

For the **fifth row,** knit 1. Repeat the following procedure. * Knit 4. Yarn over. Knit 4. Knit 2 together. * End with knit 1.

For the **sixth row,** purl 1. Repeat the following procedure. * Purl 2 together. Purl 3. Yarn over. Purl 5. * End with purl 1.

For the **seventh row,** knit 1. Repeat the following procedure. * Knit 6. Yarn over. Knit 2. Knit 2 together. * End with knit 1.

For the **eighth row,** purl 1. Repeat the following procedure. * Purl 2 together. Purl 1. Yarn over. Purl 7. * End with purl 1.

For the **ninth row,** knit 1. Repeat the following procedure. * Knit 8. Yarn over. Knit 2 together. * End with knit 1.

For the **tenth row,** purl 1. Repeat the following procedure. * Yarn over. Purl 8. Purl 2 together from back by inserting needle into back of stitches from left to right. * End with purl 1.

For the **eleventh row,** knit 1. Repeat the following procedure. * Slip 1, knit 1, and pass slip stitch over. Knit 7. Yarn over. Knit 1. * End with knit 1.

For the **twelfth row,** purl 1. Repeat the following procedure. * Purl 2. Yarn over. Purl 6. Purl 2 together from back by inserting needle into back of stitches from left to right. * End with purl 1.

For the **thirteenth row,** knit 1. Repeat the following procedure. * Slip 1, knit 1, and pass slip stitch over. Knit 5. Yarn over. Knit 3. * End with knit 1.

For the **fourteenth row,** purl 1. Repeat the following procedure. * Purl 4. Yarn over. Purl 4. Purl 2 together from back by inserting needle into back of stitches from left to right. * End with purl 1.

For the **fifteenth row,** knit 1. Repeat the following procedure. * Slip 1, knit 1, and pass slip stitch over. Knit 3. Yarn over. Knit 5. * End with knit 1.

For the **sixteenth row,** purl 1. Repeat the following procedure. * Purl 6. Yarn over. Purl 2. Purl 2 together from back, by inserting needle into back of stitches from left to right. * End with purl 1.

For the **seventeenth row,** knit 1. Repeat the following procedure. * Slip 1, knit 1, and pass slip stitch over. Knit 1. Yarn over. Knit 7. * End with knit 1.

For the **eighteenth row,** purl 1. Repeat the following procedure. * Purl 8. Yarn over. Purl 2 together from back, by inserting needle into back of stitches from left to right. * End with purl 1.

Repeat the **first through eighteenth rows** as many times as required.

## Seed Block Pattern

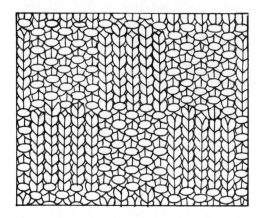

Interesting designs may be made by using Seed Stitch. Here it is used for a checkerboard effect.

For the **beginning row,** cast on a multiple of 10 stitches plus 2.

For the **first row,** knit 1. Repeat the following procedure. * Purl 1. Knit 1. Purl 1. Knit 1. Purl 6. * End with knit 1.

For the **second row,** knit 1. Repeat the following procedure. * Knit 5. Purl 1. Knit 1. Purl 1. Knit 1. Purl 1. * End with knit 1.

For the **third row,** repeat the first row.

For the **fourth row,** repeat the second row.

For the **fifth row,** repeat the first row.

For the **sixth row,** repeat the second row.

For the **seventh row,** repeat the first row.

For the **eighth row,** repeat the second row.

For the **ninth row,** knit 1. Repeat the following procedure. * Purl 6. Knit 1. Purl 1. Knit 1. Purl 1. * End with knit 1.

For the **tenth row,** knit 1. Repeat the following procedure. * Purl 1. Knit 1. Purl 1. Knit 1. Purl 1. Knit 5. * End with knit 1.

For the **eleventh row,** repeat the ninth row.

For the **twelfth row,** repeat the tenth row.

For the **thirteenth row,** repeat the ninth row.

For the **fourteenth row,** repeat the tenth row.

For the **fifteenth row,** repeat the ninth row.

For the **sixteenth row,** repeat the tenth row.

Repeat the **tenth through sixteenth rows** as many times as required.

## Seed Stitch

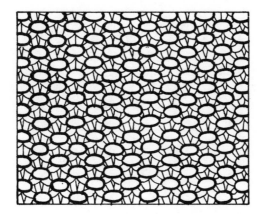

This stitch pattern creates the same pebbled effect on both sides and makes a fabric that lies flat. It is sometimes called Moss or Rice Stitch.

For the **beginning row,** cast on a multiple of 2 stitches.

For the **first row,** repeat the following procedure. * Knit 1. Purl 1. *

For the **second row,** repeat the following procedure. * Purl 1. Knit 1. *

Repeat the **first and second rows** as many times as required.

## Seed Stitch—Double

Double Moss Stitch is probably a better name for this stitch because the sequence of stitches changes after 2 rows.

For the **beginning row,** cast on a multiple of 4 stitches.

For the **first and second rows,** repeat the following procedure. * Knit 2. Purl 2. *

For the **third and fourth rows,** repeat the following procedure. * Purl 2. Knit 2. *

Repeat the **first through fourth rows** as many times as required.

## Shawl Stitch

*See* Brioche Stitch.

## Slip Stitch Mesh

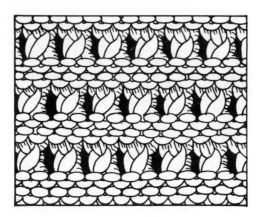

The openwork stripes and the 3-dimensional effect that the stitch creates make this an interesting stitch pattern.

For the **beginning row,** cast on a multiple of 2 stitches.

For the **first row,** purl.

For the **second row,** knit.

For the **third row,** knit 2. Repeat the following procedure. * Slip 1 with yarn in back. Knit 1. *

For the **fourth row,** repeat the following procedure. * Knit 1. Slip 1 with yarn in front. * End with knit 2.

For the **fifth row,** knit 1. Repeat the following procedure. * Yarn over. Knit 2 together. * End with knit 1.

For the **sixth row,** purl.

Repeat the **first through sixth rows** as many times as required.

## Spot Stitch

*See* Sand Stitch.

## Square Pattern

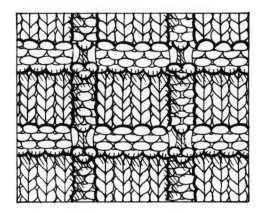

This stitch pattern is frequently used for Swedish designs.

For the **beginning row,** cast on a multiple of 6 stitches plus 2.

For the **first row,** knit 2. Repeat the following procedure. * Purl 4. Knit 2. *

For the **second row,** purl 2. Repeat the following procedure. * Knit 4. Purl 2. *

For the **third row,** repeat the second row.

For the **fourth row,** repeat the first row.

For the **fifth row,** repeat the second row.

For the **sixth row,** repeat the first row.

For the **seventh row,** repeat the second row.

For the **eighth row,** repeat the first row.

Repeat the **first through eighth rows** as many times as required.

## Star Stitch

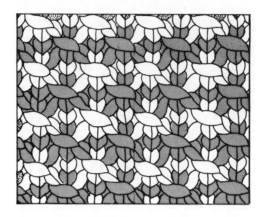

Although this stitch pattern could be made of a single color, the design is more effective when 2 are used.

For the **beginning row,** cast on a multiple of 4 stitches plus 1, using the darker color.

For the **first row,** purl.

For the **second row,** change to the lighter color. Knit 1. Repeat the following procedure. * Slip 1 with yarn in back. Insert needle under the connecting thread between the stitch just slipped and the next one, and knit 1. Slip 1 with yarn in back. Knit 1. Then pass the first slipped stitch over 3 stitches. Knit 1. *

For the **third row,** purl.

For the **fourth row,** use the darker yarn. Knit 3. Repeat the following procedure. * Slip 1 with yarn in back. Insert needle under the connecting thread between the stitch just slipped and the next one, and knit 1. Slip 1 with yarn in back. Knit 1. Then pass the first slipped stitch over 3 stitches. Knit 1. * End with knit 2.

For the **fifth row,** purl.

Repeat the **second through fifth rows** as many times as required.

## Syncopated Brioche Stitch

Broken ribs give a checked effect to this variation of the Brioche Stitch.

For the **beginning row,** cast on an even number of stitches.

For the **first row,** repeat the following procedure. * Put yarn over. Slip 1 stitch purlwise. Knit 1. *

For the **second row,** repeat the following procedure. * Put yarn over. Slip 1 stitch purlwise. Knit 2 together. *

For the **third through seventh rows,** repeat the second row.

For the **eighth row,** put yarn in front. Repeat the following procedure. * Slip 1 stitch purlwise. Put yarn over. Purl 2 together. *

For the **ninth through thirteenth rows,** repeat the eighth row.

Repeat the **second through thirteenth rows** as many times as required.

## Threaded Cross Stitch

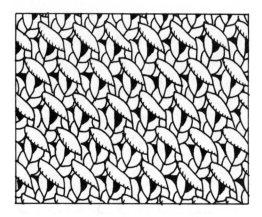

This stitch pattern creates a diagonal direction to the design but adds small crossing stitches for added interest. Needles of 2 sizes are used for this type of knitting. One needle should be about 4 sizes larger than the other one.

For the **beginning row,** cast on a multiple of 2 stitches, using the larger needle.

For the **first row,** knit, using the smaller needle.

For the **second row,** purl with the larger needle.

For the **third row,** use the smaller needle. Repeat the following procedure. * Insert point of right-hand needle through first stitch as if to purl. Knit the second stitch, leaving it on the left-hand needle. Then knit the first stitch through the back loop. Slide both stitches together from the left-hand needle. *

For the **fourth row,** purl, using the larger needle.

For the **fifth row,** use the smaller needle. Knit 1. Repeat the following procedure. * Insert the needle through the second stitch as if to purl. Knit the next stitch, leaving it on the left-hand needle. Knit the previous, or second, stitch through the back loop, as previously done. Slide both stitches together from the left-hand needle. * End by knitting 1.

Repeat the **second through fifth rows** as many times as required.


## Three-dimensional Honeycomb Pattern
*See* Brioche Stitch—Double.

## Traveling Vine Pattern

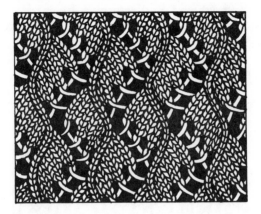

This is a lovely old French design that moves in graceful curves for a lacy effect.

For the **beginning row,** cast on a multiple of 8 stitches plus 4.

For the **first row,** knit 2. Repeat the following procedure. * Yarn over. Knit 1 in back. Yarn over. Then slip 1, knit 1, and pass slip stitch over. Knit 5. * End with knit 2.

For the **second row,** purl 6. Repeat the following procedure. * Purl 2 together in back. Purl 7. * End last repeat with purl 5.

For the **third row,** knit 2. Repeat the following procedure. * Yarn over. Knit 1 in back. Yarn over. Knit 2. Then slip 1, knit 1, and pass slip stitch over. Knit 3. * End with knit 2.

For the **fourth row,** purl 4. Repeat the following procedure. * Purl 2 together in back. Purl 7. *

For the **fifth row,** knit 2. Repeat the following procedure. * Knit 1 in back. Yarn over. Knit 4. Then slip 1, knit 1, and pass slip stitch over. Knit 1. Yarn over. * End with knit 2.

For the **sixth row,** purl 3. Repeat the following procedure. * Purl 2 together in back. Purl 7. * End with purl 1.

For the **seventh row,** knit 2. Repeat the following procedure. * Knit 5. Knit 2 together. Yarn over. Knit 1 in back. Yarn over. * End with knit 2.

For the **eighth row,** purl 5. Repeat the following procedure. * Purl 2 together. Purl 7. * End last repeat with purl 6.

For the **ninth row,** knit 2. Repeat the following procedure. * Knit 3. Knit 2 together. Knit 2. Yarn over. Knit 1 in back. Yarn over. * End with knit 2.

For the **tenth row,** repeat the following procedure. * Purl 7. Purl 2 together. * End with purl 4.

For the **eleventh row,** knit 2. Repeat the following procedure.

* Yarn over. Knit 1. Knit 2 together. Knit 4. Yarn over. Knit 1 in back. * End with knit 2.

For the **twelfth row,** purl 1. Repeat the following procedure. * Purl 7. Purl 2 together. * End with purl 3.

Repeat **first through twelfth rows** as required.

## Tulip Pattern

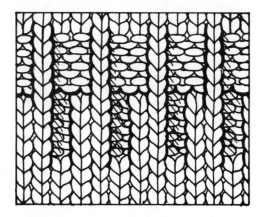

This is another stitch pattern with a French origin. The stitch arrangement creates an unusual textural effect.

For the **beginning row,** cast on a multiple of 3.

For the **first row,** repeat the following procedure. * Knit 1 in back. Knit 2. *

For the **second row,** repeat the following procedure. * Purl 2. Purl 1 in back. *

For the **third row,** repeat the first row.

For the **fourth row,** repeat the second row.

For the **fifth row,** repeat the following procedure. * Knit 1 in back. Purl 1. Knit 1 in back. *

For the **sixth row,** repeat the following procedure. * Purl 1 in back. Knit 1. Purl 1 in back. *

For the **seventh row,** repeat the fifth row.

For the **eighth row,** repeat the sixth row.

For the **ninth row,** repeat the following procedure. * Purl 2. Knit 1 in back. *

For the **tenth row,** repeat the following procedure. * Purl 1 in back. Knit 2. *

For the **eleventh row,** repeat the ninth row.

For the **twelfth row,** repeat the tenth row.

Repeat the **first through twelfth rows** as many times as required.

## Tunisian Stitch

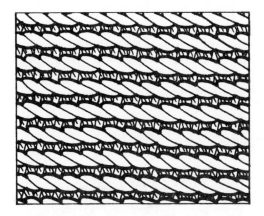

This stich pattern creates a look similar to the Afghan Stitch found in crocheting. It produces a sturdy fabric.

For the **beginning row,** cast on the required number of stitches.

For the **first row,** slip 1 stitch. Then bring yarn forward between the needles. Slip the next stitch. Wrap yarn around needle, leaving yarn in front. Slip the next stitch. Continue this way across row. End the row with a yarn-over. Hold it in position with left thumb as needle is turned.

For the **second row,** knit 2 together through the back across the row. Do this by putting the needle through the back of the last yarn-over stitch and the last slipped stitch and knit them together. Continue this way, knitting each stitch with the correct yarn-over stitch.

Repeat the **first and second rows** as many times as required.

## Twisted Rib Pattern

This is a simple variation of the usual knit-1, purl-1 type of ribbing.

For the **beginning row,** cast on a multiple of 2.

For the **first row,** repeat the following procedure. * Knit 1 with needle in back. Purl 1. *

For the **second row,** repeat the following procedure. * Knit the purl stitches and purl the knit stitches of the previous row. * Remember to work into the back of each knit stitch.

Repeat the **first and second rows** as many times as required.

## Twisted Zigzag Pattern

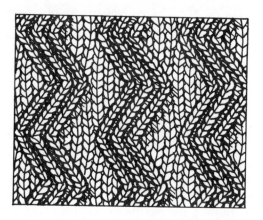

Added interest can be given a zigzag design by using twisted stitches.

For the **beginning row,** cast on a multiple of 9 stitches plus 2.

For the **first row,** purl.

For the **second row,** knit 1. Repeat the following procedure. * Work this sequence of stitches 3 times: insert right-hand needle between first and second stitches on left-hand needle from back to front, and knit the second stitch before knitting the first. Then slip both stitches from needle. Follow by knitting 3 stitches. * End with knit 1.

For the **third row,** purl.

For the **fourth row,** knit 2. Repeat the following procedure. * Work this sequence of stitches 3 times: insert right-hand needle between first and second stitches on left-hand needle from back to front, and knit the second stitch before knitting the first. Then slip both stitches from needle. Follow by knitting 3 stitches. *

For the **fifth row,** purl.

For the **sixth row,** knit 3. Repeat the following procedure. * Work this sequence of stitches 3 times, inserting right-hand needle between first and second stitches on left-hand needle from back to front, and knitting the second stitch before knitting the first. Then slip both stitches from needle. Follow by knitting 3 stitches. * End last repeat by knitting 2 instead of 3.

For the **seventh row,** purl.

For the **eighth row,** knit 4. Repeat the following procedure. * Work this sequence of stitches 3 times: insert right-hand needle between first and second stitches on left-hand needle from back to front, and knit the second stitch before knitting the first. Then slip both stitches from needle. Follow by knitting 3 stitches. * End last repeat with knit 1 instead of knit 3.

For the **ninth row,** purl.

For the **tenth row,** knit 4. Repeat the following procedure. * Work this sequence of stitches 3 times: skip first stitch on left-hand needle and insert needle into second stitch from the front, knitting this stitch before knitting the skipped stitch, and slipping both stitches from needle. Follow by knitting 3. * End last repeat by knitting 1 instead of 3.

For the **eleventh row,** purl.

For the **twelfth row,** knit 3. Repeat the following procedure. * Work this sequence of stitches 3 times: skip first stitch on left-hand needle and insert needle into second stitch from the front, knitting this stitch before knitting the skipped stitch, and slipping both stitches from needle. Follow by knitting 3. * End last repeat by knitting 2 instead of 3.

For the **thirteenth row,** purl.

For the **fourteenth row,** knit 2. Repeat the following procedure. * Work this sequence of stitches 3 times: skip first stitch on left-hand needle and insert needle into second stitch from the front, knitting this stitch before knitting the skipped stitch, and slipping both stitches from needle. Follow by knitting 3. *

For the **fifteenth row,** purl.

For the **sixteenth row,** knit 1. Repeat the following procedure. * Work this sequence of stitches 3 times: skip first stitch on left-hand needle and insert needle into second stitch from the front, knitting this stitch before knitting the skipped stitch, and slipping both stitches from needle. Follow by knitting 3. * Knit last stitch.

Repeat the **first through sixteenth rows** as many times as required.

## Umbrella Pattern

This unusual design is of German origin. It can be used for an allover pattern or as a panel.

For the **beginning row,** cast on a multiple of 18 stitches plus 1.

For the **first row,** repeat the following procedure. * Purl 1. Follow with this sequence of stitches, repeating it 4 times: purl 1 in back of stitch and knit 3. Then purl 1 in back. * End with purl 1.

For the **second row,** repeat the following procedure. * Knit 1. Yarn over. Knit 1 in back. Purl 2 together. Purl 1. Then knit 1 in back and purl 3 twice. Knit 1 in back. Purl 1. Purl 2 together. Knit 1 in back. Yarn over. * End with knit 1.

For the **third row,** repeat the following procedure. * Purl 2. Purl 1 in back. Knit 2. Then purl 1 in back and knit 3 twice. Purl 1 in back. Knit 2. Purl 1 in back. Purl 1. * End with purl 1.

For the **fourth row,** repeat the following procedure. * Knit 2. Yarn over. Knit 1 in back. Purl 2. Then knit 1 in back, purl 1, and purl 2 together twice. Knit 1 in back. Purl 2. Knit 1 in back. Yarn over. Knit 1. * End with knit 1.

For the **fifth row,** repeat the following procedure. * Purl 3. Then do this 4 times: purl 1 in back and knit 2. Then purl 1 in back. Purl 2. * End with purl 1.

For the **sixth row,** repeat the following procedure. * Knit 3. Yarn over. Knit 1 in back. Purl 2 together. Then knit 1 in back and purl 2 twice. Knit 1 in back. Purl 2 together. Knit 1 in back. Yarn over. Knit 2. * End with knit 1.

For the **seventh row,** repeat the following procedure. * Purl 4. Purl 1 in back. Knit 1. Then purl 1 in back and knit 2 twice. Purl 1 in back. Knit 1. Purl 1 in back. Purl 3. * End with purl 1.

For the **eighth row,** repeat the following procedure. * Knit 4. Yarn over. Knit 1 in back. Purl 1. Then knit 1 in back and purl 2 together

twice. Knit 1 in back. Purl 1. Knit 1 in back. Yarn over. Knit 3. *
End with knit 1.

For the **ninth row,** repeat the following procedure. * Purl 5. Then
do this 4 times: purl 1 in back and knit 1. Then purl 1 in back.
Purl 4. * End with purl 1.

For the **tenth row,** repeat the following procedure. * Knit 5. Yarn
over. Knit 2 together through back of loop. Then knit 1 in back
and purl 1 twice. Knit 1 in back. Knit 2 together. Yarn over. Knit
4. * End with knit 1.

For the **eleventh row,** repeat the following procedure. * Purl 6.
Purl 2 in back. Knit 1. Purl 1 in back. Knit 1. Purl 2 in back. Purl
5. * End with purl 1.

For the **twelfth row,** repeat the following procedure. * Knit 6.
Knit 2 in back. Purl 1. Knit 1 in back. Purl 1. Knit 2 in back. Knit
5. * End with knit 1.

Repeat the **first through twelfth rows** as many times as required.

## Veil Stitch

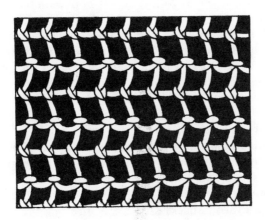

This stitch pattern is sometimes called Elongated Crossed Garter
Stitch, which seems to explain how it is made.

For the **beginning row,** cast on the required number of stitches.

For the **first row,** insert the needle knitwise. Then bring the yarn
over to the right-hand needle as for regular knitting, and continue
to place it under and over the left-hand needle, and finally under
and over the right-hand needle again. Spread the needles slightly.
Then draw the last yarn-over through the first yarn-over and the
stitch. This procedure makes 1 stitch on the right-hand needle. Slip
the stitch off the left-hand needle together with the yarn-over. This
results in a long crossed stitch. Repeat the procedure for each stitch
as row is knitted.

Repeat the **first row** as many times as required.

## Waffle Brioche Pattern

This stitch pattern seems to give a soft honeycomb effect.

For the **beginning row,** cast on a multiple of 3 stitches plus 2.

For the **first row,** knit 1. Repeat the following procedure. * Put yarn over. Slip 1 knitwise with yarn in back. Insert needle into the back of 2 stitches and knit them together. * End with knit 1.

For the **second row,** knit 3. Repeat the following procedure. * Slip 1 knitwise with yarn in back. Knit 2. * End with slip 1 knitwise with yarn in back. Knit 1. Notice that the slipped stitches are the yarn-overs of the previous row.

For the **third row,** knit 1. Repeat the following procedure. * Knit 2 together by inserting needle through back of loops. Yarn over. Slip 1 knitwise with yarn in back. * End with knit 1.

For the **fourth row,** knit 2. Repeat the following procedure. * Slip 1 knitwise with yarn in back. Knit 2. * Notice that the slipped stitches are the yarn-overs of the third row.

Repeat the **first through fourth rows** as many times as required.

## Waffle Stitch

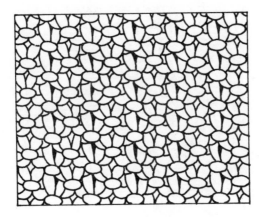

This is another stitch that has an interesting textural quality.

For the **beginning row,** cast on a multiple of 2 stitches.

For the **first row,** repeat the following procedure. * Knit 1 in back. Purl 1. *

For the **second row,** repeat the following procedure. * Purl 1 in back. Knit 1. *

Repeat the **first and second rows** as many times as required.


## Wager Welt Pattern
*See* All Fool's Welt Pattern.

## Wavy Rib Pattern

The slight change in line direction gives a curving effect to this broken diagonal.

For the **beginning row,** cast on a multiple of 6 stitches.

For the **first row,** repeat the following procedure. * Purl 4. Knit 2. *

For the **second row,** repeat the following procedure. * Purl 2. Knit 4. *

For the **third row,** repeat the first row.

For the **fourth row,** repeat the second row.

For the **fifth row,** repeat the first row.

For the **sixth row,** repeat the second row.

For the **seventh row,** repeat the following procedure. * Purl 2. Slip 2 onto a double-pointed needle. Leave in back. Knit 2. Purl the 2 from the double-pointed needle. *

For the **eighth row,** repeat the following procedure. * Knit 2. Purl 2. Knit 2. *

For the **ninth row,** repeat the following procedure. * Purl 2. Knit 2. Purl 2. *

For the **tenth row,** repeat the eighth row.

For the **eleventh row,** repeat the ninth row.

For the **twelfth row,** repeat the eighth row.

For the **thirteenth row,** repeat the following procedure. * Slip 2 onto a double-pointed needle and leave in back. Knit 2. Purl the 2 from the double-pointed needle. Purl 2. *

For the **fourteenth row,** repeat the following procedure. * Knit 4. Purl 2. *

For the **fifteenth row,** repeat the following procedure. * Knit 2. Purl 4. *

For the **sixteenth row,** repeat the fourteenth row.

For the **seventeenth row,** repeat the fifteenth row.

For the **eighteenth row,** repeat the fourteenth row.

Repeat the **second through eighteenth rows** as many times as required.

## Wheat Ear Rib Pattern

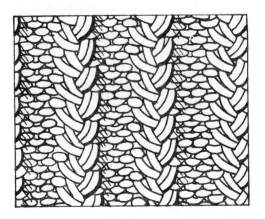

An interesting textural look is created by working ribs in this fashion.

For the **beginning row,** cast on a multiple of 5 stitches plus 2.

For the **first row,** repeat the following procedure. * Purl 3. Put right-hand needle between the first and second stitches on the left-hand needle, moving from the back to the front. Knit the second stitch. Then knit the first stitch and slide both stitches together from the needle. * End with purl 2.

For the **second row,** repeat the following procedure. * Knit 3. Skip the next stitch, purling the second stitch. Then purl the skipped stitch. Slide both stitches together off the needle. * End with knit 2.

Repeat the **first and second rows** as many times as required.

## Woven Check Pattern

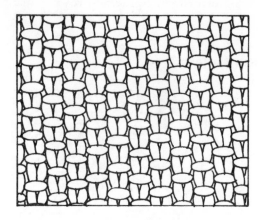

A feeling of woven fabric results when the stitches are worked this way.

For the **beginning row,** cast on an uneven number of stitches.

For the **first row,** knit 1. Repeat the following procedure. * Yarn forward. Slip 1. Yarn back. Knit 1. *

For the **second row,** purl 2. Repeat the following procedure. * Yarn back. Slip 1. Yarn forward. Purl 1. *

Repeat the **first and second rows** as many times as required.

## Zigzag Lace Trellis Pattern

This pattern creates the look of faggot stitches, moving first in one direction and then in the other.

For the **beginning row,** cast on a multiple of 2 stitches.

For the **first row,** purl.

For the **second row,** knit 1. Repeat the following procedure. * Yarn over. Knit 2 together. * End with knit 1.

For the **third row,** purl.

For the **fourth row,** repeat the second row.

For the **fifth row,** purl.

For the **sixth row,** repeat the second row.

For the **seventh row,** purl.

For the **eighth row,** knit 1. Repeat the following procedure. * Slip 1, knit 1, and pass slip stitch over. Yarn over. * End with knit 1.

For the **ninth row,** purl.

For the **tenth row,** repeat the eighth row.

For the **eleventh row,** purl.

For the **twelfth row,** repeat the eighth row.

Repeat the **first through twelfth rows** as many times as required.

## STYLES AND TYPES OF KNITTING

Just like other forms of handwork, knitting has some distinguishing characteristics that provide variety and interest. Sometimes they relate to the country in which the stitch pattern was first made, and sometimes to the way the stitches are formed or to the material used. Some of these special features are mentioned here.

### Aran Knitting

The Aran Isles in Ireland have lent their name to a specific type of knitting that is marked by vertical panels of varying raised designs, placed side by side and usually worked in unbleached wool. Fisherman Sweaters utilize these stitch patterns, such as various cables, diamonds, and ribbings.

**Seed Stitch**                                              **Plaid Cable**

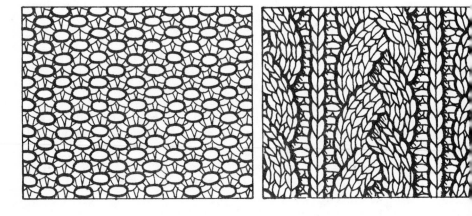

**Diamond Stitch**          **Old Shale**          **Slipped Cable**

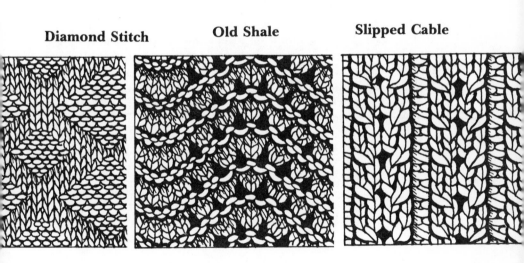

## Argyle Pattern

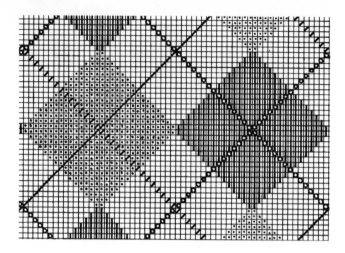

This distinctive design pattern is an adaptation of a Scottish Campbell clan tartan, using diamond-shaped blocks in different colors. They are crossed by lines for a plaid effect.

Usually each color is wound on a separate bobbin. By following a chart, changes in color can easily be made. It is important that the colors be twisted together as the change is made so that no unsightly spaces appear in the finished work. The knit side should be smooth and even. The work is always knitted flat, using a knit row followed by a purl row.

## Design Knitting

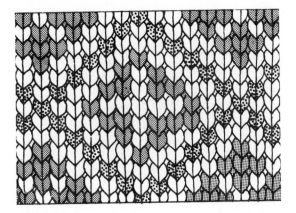

Plain knitting can be given a decorative effect by introducing geometric shapes and lines through the use of a second color. The designs can take on an abstract form or a more realistic representation. Scandinavian-type knitting is often given this distinctive treatment. Fir trees and reindeers mingle with diamond shapes. In creating designs, cross stitch patterns can be copied or an imaginative one can be plotted on graph paper.

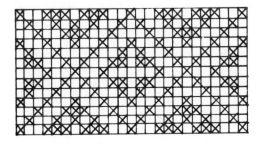

## Duplicate Stitch

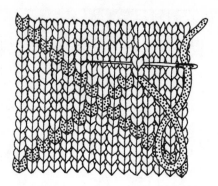

Plain knitting can take on a more interesting look by the use of this stitch, a form of embroidery. Yarn is worked over a knitted stitch, tracing the outline of a stitch. Sometimes this is called Swiss Darning.

Work with a darning or tapestry needle, using yarn of the same weight as the knitting or a heavier one. Usually the Duplicate Stitch is made over a Stockinette Stitch. Bring the needle from the wrong to the right side, passing through the center of the stitch. Follow the outline of the stitch above, inserting the needle so it passes under the 2 strands of this stitch. Draw the yarn through, returning the needle to the point where the yarn first emerged from the fabric.

## Fair Isle Knitting

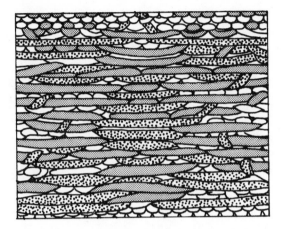

Although Fair Isle and Shetland knitting are sometimes mentioned together, it should be remembered that the real Fair Isle patterns are of Spanish origin. No one knows how they reached Fair Isle, but it is thought that sailors of the Spanish Armada were the carriers.

Today the term Fair Isle is often used to designate multicolor knitting. It really should not be. There are other forms, such as Argyle knitting. A true Fair Isle pattern is marked with an adaptation of the Armada cross and forms a striped motif, moving horizontally.

In this type of knitting, the yarn is manipulated in a distinctive way when changing from one color to another. The out-of-use strand is carried lightly across the back of the work. It can be held in place with the working yarn or left loose if the distance is not too great. When the design requires that it be picked up, it is brought up from under the one that is being dropped. This eliminates the possibility of leaving holes in the work. The stockinette stitch is used, with the rows on the right side knitted, on the wrong side purled (as above drawing illustrates).

## Ribbon Knitting

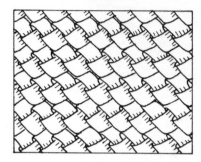 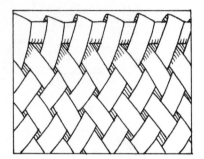

Although this type of knitting is worked on knitting needles using the techniques of regular knitting, it does not give the same effect. A crisp, flat ribbon, about ¼ inch (6 mm) wide is used in place of yarn. The ribbon is woven especially for this purpose.

In working with ribbon, it should be remembered that it does not have the elasticity of yarn. At first it seems awkward to work with. Great care must be taken to keep the ribbon flat when wrapping it around the needle. It should not be allowed to twist. Always keep the same side of the ribbon against the needle. Some persons like to mark one side to be sure that the ribbon will not get twisted as the knitting progresses. Keeping the spool on a spindle or in a small box helps. Keep tension loose by unwinding enough ribbon to work with. Drop the ribbon after each stitch and readjust its position. Do not wind the ribbon around the fingers.

By changing the position of the ribbon, different effects can be created. For instance, when the ribbon is placed over the needle from front to back for a garter stitch, the ribbon seems to form peaked loops before the knitting is blocked or pressed. Afterward it creates a zigzag textured look. For ribbon knitting, this is called a Peak Stitch (illustration above left).

It is also possible to produce a woven effect in which the ribbons seem to move in a diagonal direction. For the knit rows, insert the needle through the back of the stitch. Put ribbon over needle from front to back. For the purl rows, insert needle through front of stitch from right to left and place ribbon over needle from back to front (illustration above right).

## Scandinavian Knitting

Although there are many beautiful Scandinavian stitch patterns, such as the Lace Cable, that are worked in 1 color, it is the colorful patterned knitting that is most often thought of as being from this part of the world. A color used for figures or geometric designs against a white background adds a certain gaiety to plain knitting.

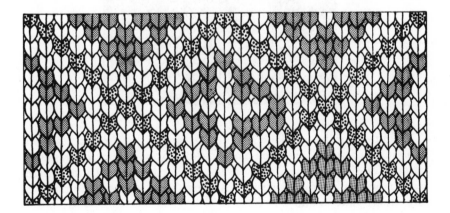

## Shetland Knitting

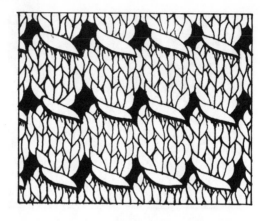

The knitters of the Shetland Islands are famous for their lace shawls. The stitch patterns have been handed down from generation to generation. The simple lace stitches are used to form diamond and hexagonal shapes for openwork stripes. Among their famous stitch patterns are Mrs. Hunter's and Old Shale.

## Slip Stitch Patterns

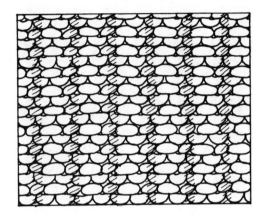

This technique usually produces a closely knitted texture because the slipped stitches bring the other stitches together. It can, however, be used in a variety of ways. It allows yarn to be drawn upward, across, or in a diagonal direction, producing interesting effects, varying from the Close Stitch to the Butterfly Pattern.

## Twist Stitch Patterns

Interesting textural effects can be created by using twisted stitches. This can be done in 2 ways. Two or more stitches can be twisted around each other in cable fashion, but without the use of a cable needle. Or the effect can be obtained by skipping a stitch or stitches, then knitting the next stitch, leaving it on the needle. Follow this by knitting the slipped stitches and slipping this group of stitches off the needle. The effect can vary from the Mock Cable Pattern to the Diagonal Stitch.

## Yarn-over Stitch Patterns

Yarn-over is a simple operation that produces varying results. Lovely openwork designs as well as solid ones can be made.

The yarn is placed over the right-hand needle before taking the next stitch. This procedure adds 1 strand of yarn between 2 stitches. On the return row, the yarn-over is knitted as a separate stitch. Because an extra stitch has been made, it is necessary to remove it at some stage. The time and place to make the decrease will depend on the stitch pattern being made.

Usually a yarn-over is taken in order to leave an opening in the fabric. The Dewdrop Pattern and Laburnum Stitch show that the effects of this technique can vary.

# Part IV

# Macramé

Macramé is another of the handcrafts whose origin is unknown. There is some evidence that it dates back to Assyrian and Babylonian times. However, some people feel that the earliest form of square knot work began in Arabia in the thirteenth century, with the name derived from an Arabic word meaning "fringed shawl." This art of interlocking yarns seems to have spread to Spain and France, where it became a refined art form in the fourteenth century. Sailors used their knowledge of knot tying to develop and spread the making of macramé designs. In fact, it is thought that, by the fifteenth century, the sailors were bartering their work in India and China.

Macramé, like so many needle arts, has been in and out of fashion. It had become almost a lost art until it reappeared at the end of the nineteenth century, becoming popular with Victorian ladies. Recently it has known another resurgence of popularity.

One of the important characteristics of macramé is its versatility, not only in function but also in material. The work can serve in a purely functional or fanciful capacity, or the two characteristics can be combined for a practical and decorative item. The cord that interprets the design pattern can add another dimension because of the wide variety of materials available.

Although many of the designs appear complicated, macramé is actually quite easy to do. Once the 2 basic knots are mastered, it becomes a matter of skill coupled with a creative spirit and attention to detail. To assist you in developing this proficiency, some suggestions are listed on the following pages:

# GLOSSARY OF TERMS

Understanding the meaning of certain words employed in macramé simplifies the construction process. Some of them have a nautical connotation that may seem foreign to those accustomed to needlework terms. In some instances, words are used interchangeably. An attempt has been made here to describe the terms most commonly found in macramé directions.

**Bar.** A row of knots made over a knot bearer or holding cord is referred to as a bar. It can follow a horizontal, vertical, or diagonal direction, with the work progressing from right to left or left to right. Sometimes this knotting procedure is called cording.

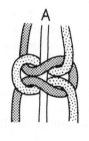

**Cord.** Although the word indicates the material used for making macramé, it also refers to different parts of the knot pattern. For instance, the **filler cord** (A) is one that is not used for the actual knot but is instead the center or core around which the knot is made. The **holding cord** (B) is sometimes called the knot bearer, carrier, or anchor cord. As the name implies, it is the cord around which the knotting cord is looped. The holding cord is sometimes referred to as the mounting cord when the strands of working or knotting cord are fastened to it. The **knotting or working cord** (C) is the one that makes the knot. The **mounting cord** (D) is used at the beginning of a piece of macramé to hold the knotting or working cord. Sometimes it is known as the foundation cord, anchor line, or holding line.

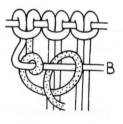

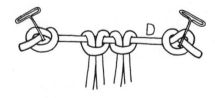

**Core.** The cord around which the knot is tied, which is also sometimes called the filler cord.

**Ends.** This term is sometimes used to indicate the number of cords or strands in use.

**Filler.** Another term used in place of **core.**

**Hitch.** The nautical term indicating a knot.

**Knot.** The raised effect in a cord produced by passing 1 free end through a loop and then drawing it tight.

**Knot bearer.** The cord around which knots are made, sometimes referred to as the carrier strand, filler cord, holding cord, or leader.

**Mounting.** Macramé is started by placing strands of cord around a mounting or holding cord. The process is called **mounting.** The mounting cord is sometimes referred to as the anchor line, foundation cord, holding line, or knot bearer.

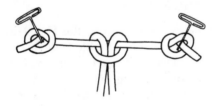

**Row.** Another term used for the word **bar.**

**Sinnet.** When a series of knots is tied along a cord, forming a long line, the resulting braid or chain is called a sinnet, or sennit. A series of square knots produces a flat, solid braid. However, when only half knots are used, the chain twists, creating a spiral effect. A sinnet of half hitches can be kept flat or allowed to spiral.

**Twist.** A chain, or sinnet, or half knots.

**Working strand.** As its name implies, it is used to tie the knots. It is sometimes known as the knotting cord or warp.

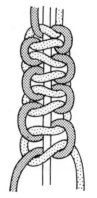

## BASIC KNOTS AND VARIATIONS

An interlocking of knots produces macramé. Although 2 basic knots, the Square and Half Hitch, form the foundation, there are hundreds of knots available for creative combinations. Some people prefer to refer to the basic knots as the Half Knot and the Half Hitch because the Half Knot is used to make the Square Knot. It is interesting to note that the combination of the simplest knots produces fascinating results that appear complicated.

Macramé offers a great chance for individual creativity by coupling imagination and the skill of nimble fingers. By following the diagrams shown here, the knots can be learned quickly.

In some cases a knot is given more than 1 name. Knowing the variations will make the directions for constructing an article easier to understand.

### Clove Hitch

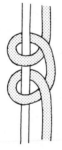

This knot is a variation of the Half Hitch. It is sometimes called the Double Half Hitch or Double Knot. Two half hitches are tied, with the knotting cord passing over and under the holding cord and then over itself to form a loop. When this procedure is done twice, the Clove Hitch has been made.

The Clove Hitch can be made vertically and horizontally. In a vertical direction, use 1 knotting cord to make knots over the other knotting cord. When tied in a horizontal direction, each of the knotting cords is used for that purpose.

### Double Half Hitch
*See* Clove Hitch.

### Double Knot
*See* Clove Hitch.

## Half Hitch

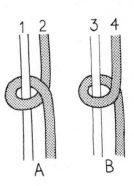

A          B

This is one of the basic knots used in Macramé. It requires 2 cords. The knotting or working cord (2) is looped around the holding or knot bearing cord (1). It is sometimes called the Blanket Stitch, Buttonhole, or Tatting Knot.

The tying can be done in 2 ways. The cord can pass over and under the holding cord and finally back over itself, as shown in diagram A. Or the direction can be reversed with the knotting cord (4) first passing over, then under the holding cord (3) and finally moving under itself, as shown in diagram B.

The Half Hitch can be made with more than 1 cord. For instance, 2 cords can be used in place of 1 for both the holding and knotting cords.

Bars or rows of half hitch knots add an attractive effect to a piece of macramé.

## Half Hitch Chain or Sinnet

Making a series of half hitches along the holding cord produces a chain, or sinnet.

## Half Hitch Chain—Alternating

An interesting variation of the Half Hitch Chain can be made by alternating the cords used for the knotting procedure. Begin by making a half hitch with the knotting cord (1) around the holding cord (2). Then change and make a half hitch with the holding cord around the knotting cord. Continue to alternate the cords. This treatment gives the chain a slightly scalloped edge with a diagonal feeling.

## Half Knot

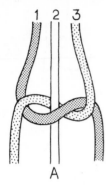

This knot helps to form the Square Knot. It actually is half of a square knot. Sometimes it is referred to as the Macramé, Spiral, or Waved Knot. It can be made in 2 ways, as shown in diagrams A and B. Notice that in A the knotting cord (1) passes over the filler cord (2) but under the knotting cord (3), whereas the knotting cord (3) reverses the direction, moving under the filler cord and over the knotting cord (1). The cords seem to make a figure 8.

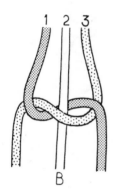

The second version (B) of the Half Knot reverses the position of the knotting cords. The knotting cord (1) passes under the filler cord (2) and then over the knotting cord (3), with the other knotting cord (3) passing over the filler cord (2) and under the knotting cord (1).

The Half Knot can be made over more than 1 filler cord, as shown in diagram C. The filler cords are treated as if they were 1.

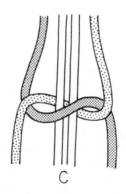

## Half Knot Sinnet

When a series of half knots is made around the filler cord, a twisted chain results. It is often used for a decorative effect.

## Lark's-head Braid—Alternating

A series of half hitches can be given a looped-edge treatment when lark's-head knots are used. Work over the filler cords (2) and (3). Begin with knotting cord (4). Make a lark's-head knot by passing the cord over and under the filler cords (2) and (3). Continue by passing the cord through the loop and over itself before moving under and over the filler cords. Finish by putting the cord through the loop.

Make the second lark's-head knot with the other knotting cord (1). The procedure is the same except the work is done on the left-hand side of the braid.

Alternate the making of the lark's-head knots from one side to the other until the braid is completed.

## Lark's-head Braid—Double Alternating

A more lacy braid can be made by using 6 cords. Two braids are joined by crossing 2 of the knotting cords, creating an open fagoted effect.

In making the braid, cords (2) and (5) act as the filler cords around which the lark's-head knots are made. Cords (3) and (4) are knotting cords that alternate from side to side in constructing the knots. Knotting cord (1) remains on the left-hand side; cord (6), on the right-hand side. Study the accompanying diagram to follow the movement of the different cords.

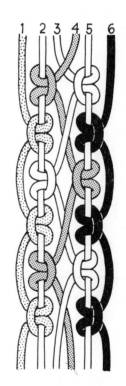

## Lark's-head Knot

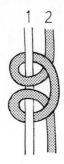

This is another term used to designate a Reversed Double Half Hitch. The knot is made by passing the knotting cord (2) around the holding cord (1) in one direction and then reversing the direction. Notice that the knotting cord slips over the holding cord and then under it before it passes through the loop it made. The knotting cord then passes under and over the holding cord before moving through the loop.

## Lark's-head Sinnet

The Lark's-head Knot can be used to make a chain or sinnet. Make a series of knots along the holding cord. The effect is similar to a blanket stitch.

## Overhand Knot

This is probably the knot that is most familiar. It can be formed by using 1 (A) or more cords (B), tying them together. The Overhand Knot is most helpful in keeping cords from raveling and together (A). It is sometimes referred to as a Bead, Shell, or Thumb Knot.

Before tightening the knot, be sure it is in the correct place. It is difficult to move once it has been tightened. If more than 1 cord is used, pull each cord separately to tighten the knot.

The Overhead Knot can also be made over a filler cord (C).

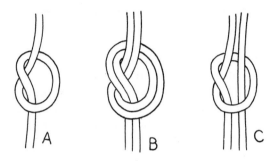

## Reversed Double Half Hitch
*See* Lark's-head Knot.

## Reversed Double Half Hitch Sinnet
*See* Lark's-head Sinnet.

## Square Knot

This, 1 of the 2 basic knots, is the most commonly used in macramé. The 2 versions of the half knot are interlocked, with 1 going to the left, the other to the right. In macramé this knot is always tied around a filler cord. Be sure to hold the filler cord taut. (Sometimes when a square knot is made without a filler cord, it is known as the Granny Knot in macramé terms.) The Square Knot can also be referred to as the Flat, Reef, or Solomon's Knot.

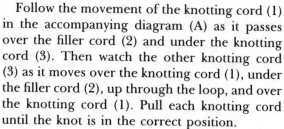

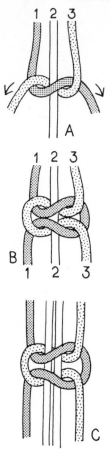

Follow the movement of the knotting cord (1) in the accompanying diagram (A) as it passes over the filler cord (2) and under the knotting cord (3). Then watch the other knotting cord (3) as it moves over the knotting cord (1), under the filler cord (2), up through the loop, and over the knotting cord (1). Pull each knotting cord until the knot is in the correct position.

The second part of the knot (B) is made by bringing the knotting cord (3) under the filler cord (2) and over the knotting cord (1) as this moves over the filler cord (2), down through the loop, and under the knotting cord (3). Both knotting cords are back in their original positions: knotting cord (1) on the left-hand side of the filler cord (2) and knotting cord (3) on the right-hand side. Again the 2 knotting cords are pulled to tighten the knot, bringing it close to the first half of the square knot.

By increasing the number of cords, the square knot can be given different looks. In the accompanying diagram, 1 filler cord has been added (C). However, any number can be added to both filler and knotting cords. Remember the additions to each of the 3 basic cords are tied as if only 1 cord were being used. The method of tying remains the same.

## Square Knot—Reverse

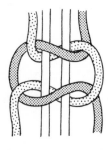

A variation of the Square Knot can be made by reversing the sequence of half knots. Instead of beginning with the first version of the Half Knot, the procedure starts with the second version and ends with the first version. Notice that the cord is positioned differently at the ends. For a regular Square Knot, the cord is uppermost on the left-hand side, but for the Reverse Square Knot, it is under the knotting. When the Square Knot is tied in the regular way, it is sometimes referred to as a Left-hand Square Knot; the Reverse Square Knot is then called the Right-hand Square Knot.

## Square Knot Braid—
### with Alternating Knots

Work with 8 cords. Mount them on a holding
cord with lark's-head knots. Two lark's-head
knots are grouped together, making a grouping
of 4 cords or ends. Secure with pins to a working
surface. Follow the movement of each cord on
the accompanying diagram. Notice that cords
(2) and (7) are used only as filler cords, but cords
(3) and (6) become filler as well as knotting
cords. In the first row of square knots, cords
(2) and (3) are the filler cords for one knot; cords
(6) and (7), for the other. In the second row,
however, the knotting cords (4) and (5) become
the filler cords. The third row repeats the knotting procedure of the first row. The knotting
can result in an openwork design pattern or a
solid one, with knots close together.

If a wider braid is needed, add more cords.

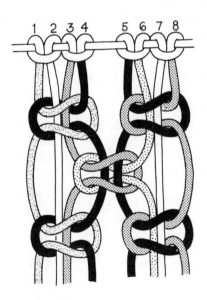

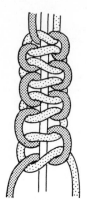

## Square Knot Sinnet

When a series of square knots is made around a filler cord, a flat, solid braid is produced.

## Square Knot Sinnet—
### with Alternating Knots

Use 4 cords for this knotting. The filler cords are sometimes used as fillers and at other times as knotting cords. Notice how the filler cord (3) becomes part of the first square knot but a filler for the second knot, and that the knotting cord (4) does not participate in the first knot. The third knot is made like the first one, using cords (1), (2), and (3). Continue this procedure for the length required.

## Square Knot Sinnet—
### with Interchanging Holding and
### Knotting Cords

Work with 4 cords. Begin with a square knot, using cords (1) and (4) as knotting cords and (2) and (3) as filler cords. However, for the second square knot, reverse the positions of the cords. Use cords (2) and (3) for making the knots and (1) and (4) as filler cords. Continue to alternate the cords as the knots are made, for the required length (A).

A different effect can be achieved by using a reversed square knot (B). The cords are interchanged as for design A.

A square knot sinnet can be used to create a knobby design detail, sometimes called a bobble. After several square knots have been made, take 2 filler cords to the top of the sinnet, bringing them to the front through the space between the second and third cords. A crochet hook can be used if necessary. Then pull the cords down firmly to complete the bobble.

## Square Knot Sinnet— with Picots

An attractive looped effect can be given a sinnet of square knots by allowing an extra bit of cord to protrude between the knots. Carefully regulate the amount of cord so the loops remain even. Secure the loop as the knot is tightened around the filler cord.

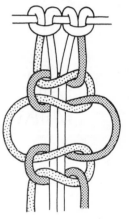

## Square Knot Twist
*See* Half Knot Sinnet.

## GENERAL DIRECTIONS

Learning macramé requires practice, with special attention to details. Until a certain proficiency is achieved, do not start an actual piece of macramé. Practice with a piece of cord, making the basic knots. Gradually you will develop a feel for knotting. One has to learn how tight to pull the cords, and how to keep the knots even. Certain guidelines are helpful in perfecting the work. They are used repeatedly whether the project is simple or complicated.

### Beginning Point

Before the knot tying can start, the cords must be anchored. This can be done in several ways.

When a few cords are being used for a narrow piece of macramé, they may be gathered together and tied with an overhand knot (A). The knot is then pinned to a working surface. Sometimes the cords are fastened to a doorknob.

For a wider piece of macramé, it is best to mount the working cords on a holding or mounting cord that is pinned to a firm working surface (B).

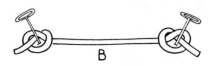

In beltmaking, the cords may be mounted on a buckle or ring (C). For wall hangings, a wooden dowel, a curtain rod, a smooth stick, or even a piece of driftwood could be used in place of the mounting cord.

### Circular Macramé

Macramé can be worked in the round as well as on the flat. There are several ways to begin this type of work. Specific directions will be given for the project being made, such as a hat or bag. This is one way to begin a circular piece of macramé.

Start by cutting the cords. The number of knotting cords depends on the design pattern. However, remember to cut only half of the required number of needed ends. Hold the knotting cords together in the center with a knot made by a cord about 4 inches (10 cm) long. This forms the center of the design. With the knot down, pin the center point to the working surface. Spread the cords in an orderly fashion, radiating from the center. Each of these cords is used for knotting.

Add another cord for holding the knots in order to make a circular bar. Pin 1 end of the holding cord to the working surface. This makes it possible to keep the cord taut as the knots are made. With each knotting cord, tie a clove or double half hitch over the holding cord. Be careful to keep the holding cord the same distance from the center as each knot is made, to ensure a perfect circle. When the circle of knots is completed, tie the ends of the holding cord together and clip. Using groups of 4 cords, start to make a series of square knots around the circular bar.

As the circle increases in size, add knotting cords between the groups. To add 2 knotting cords, fold a length of cord in half. Pin the loop end between each pair of groups. Work with these cords when making the next round of knots.

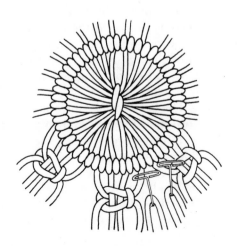

### Color Contrasts

Interesting effects can be created by introducing a variation of color. A simple knotting pattern takes on new importance when contrasts in color are employed. Probably the easiest way to do this is to intermingle the colored cords at the beginning, whether they are knotted or mounted on a holding cord.

A solid checkerboard pattern can be produced by using cords in 2 colors for a series of clove or double half hitches. Before starting, work out the design pattern on graph paper. Begin with a double mounting cord in 2 colors. One should be the usual length; the other longer, so it can be used as a holding cord. Mount the knotting cords.

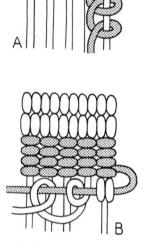

Pass the longer mounting cord across the knotting cords horizontally. Make a series of clove or double half hitches on the holding cord (A). To introduce the second color, use the holding cord to make a vertical double half hitch on each knotting cord (B). This sequence of stitches and rows can be repeated as the design pattern requires.

### Decorative Touches

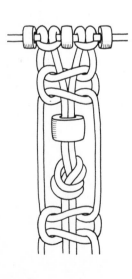

A simple piece of macramé can take on a more important look by introducing ornamental items, such as beads, to the design pattern. Any type of bead can be used as long as the hole is large enough to allow the cords to pass through. The size and shape depend on the proportions of the macramé piece.

The beads can be introduced on the mounting cord, spaced between the knotting cords, as well as interspersed between the knots. This can be done in innumerable ways. One is shown here.

Other decorative items can be used in place of beads as long as they can be slipped over the cords. Other possibilities are buttons with shanks, pierced coins, and shells.

## Ends

If the ends or cords are too long to work with conveniently, wind each separately into a circle or figure 8. Use a rubber band to hold them together. Usually a length of cord about 15 inches (38 cm) long is convenient to work with. As the work progresses, unwind the cord as needed.

## Estimating Cutting Length

To estimate the length of each cord, one must first decide how the macramé piece is to begin. If the cords are gathered together and held with an overhand knot, cut each cord about 4 times as long as the finished item. However, if the cord is to be folded in half and knotted over a mounting cord, then cut it about 8 times the finished length.

To determine the length of the mounting cord, add about 6 inches (15 cm) to the width of the macramé piece.

If one of the knotting cords is also to be used as a holding cord in the making of bars or rows, then cut it longer.

## Finishing

A piece of macramé can be finished off in various ways. One is to gather groups of ends together to form fringe or tassels. Tie groups of cords together with an overhand knot close to the lower edge. Additional rows of knots can be made to create a diamond pattern if a wider fringe is desired.

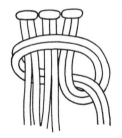

A macramé piece can also be finished with a bar. Then turn the work over. Using a crochet hook, draw each cord through the back of the bar. Cut off the ends, leaving about 1 inch (2.5 cm). Secure the ends by tacking them to the back of the macramé.

The edge can also be given a picot finish. After making a bar across the end of the macramé, turn it over. Working from left to right, pull the first cord end through the back of the second knot and draw it down firmly. Then take the second cord through the back of the first knot. Draw it down, allowing the cord to lie loosely over the first strand, leaving a loop or picot. Work this way with each pair of cords.

## Mounting

After the holding or mounting cord is in place, tie the working or knotting strands of cord onto it. To do this, fold each strand in half. Slip the loop end under the mounting cord (A). Place ends through loop (B). Pull ends to tighten knot. This procedure creates a reversed double half hitch, or lark's-head knot.

Add additional cords in the same manner (C). They can be placed close together or spaced according to the design pattern. If necessary, place pins along the mounting cord to keep it taut and straight.

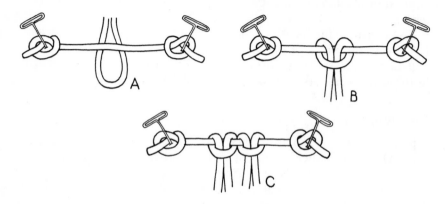

## Mounting Cord

Some macramé pieces begin with a mounting cord. Strands of cord are knotted around it. To do this, cut a piece of cord or yarn about 6 inches (15 cm) longer than the width of the finished macramé design. Make an overhand knot at both ends. Pin the knots to the working surface, keeping the cord taut. It should always be kept in a stable position.

In case it would be better to mount the cords on something other than a cord, a chopstick, dowel, ring, or buckle could be used.

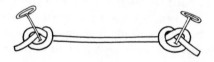

## Mounting—Picot

The mounting edge can take on a more decorative finish through the addition of loops or picots. Instead of mounting the cords with a lark's-head knot, use a clove or double half hitch. The picot appears between 2 clove or double half hitches, employing the same cord.

Begin with a clove or double half hitch. Let one end hang down. With the other end, make a second double half hitch, allowing the cord to loop up between the knots the correct amount. Tighten the knot, bringing it close to the preceding knot, to secure the loop or picot. Sometimes it is easier to pin the loop in position before tying the second knot. Repeat this procedure with the remaining cords.

## Pinning

Pins are used to keep the cords taut and the macramé straight and even. Use them at the ends of the mounting cord and bars when needed. Place the pins on the slant, away from the edge of the macramé. Secure them firmly in the working surface. Move the pins down as the work progresses.

## Position

It is important to find a comfortable working position. In some instances, this will depend on the size and shape of the macramé piece being made. When knotting on a working surface, it can be placed on a table or held in the lap. Sometimes it is easier to have the macramé hanging from a hook or doorknob.

## Regularity

Check the macramé frequently for the regularity of the design. If it seems uneven, note the pinning and the tightness of the knots. Insufficient pinning and a knot tied too tightly can cause an irregular effect.

## Rows

A line of solidly placed half hitches or of clove or double half hitches is called a bar or row. It is used to create design lines moving in a horizontal, vertical, or diagonal direction. After the cords are mounted on the holding cords, a row of knots can be started.

**Diagonal rows.** Clove or double half hitches are tied in a diagonal direction. The procedure is the same as that used for a horizontal row except that the holding cord is held in a diagonal direction. The angle depends on the design pattern.

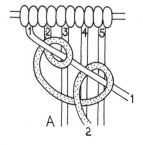

Make the **first diagonal row** (A) by placing clove or double half hitches over cord (1), which becomes the holding cord. Pick up knotting cord (2), and tie a clove or double half hitch. Continue to make a knot with each of the knotting cords. Watch carefully to keep the direction of the diagonal precise.

For the **second row** (B), use cord (2) as the holding cord.

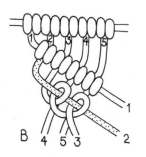

If the design requires a diagonal in the opposite direction, the knots are tied in the same way, beginning at the outside and working toward the center of the design (C). To cross the ends when the diagonal rows meet, allow the cord that has been used to hold the knots on the right-hand side to make the knots over the holding cord on the left-hand side.

Sometimes a design requires an open space. In this case, the diagonal rows are not crossed (D). The rows on the left-hand and right-hand sides are made in the same way, proceeding from the outside toward the center. The outside cords (1) and (8) are used as the holding cords; (2) and (7) are the holding cords for the second row.

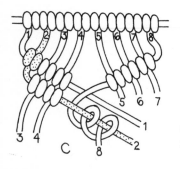

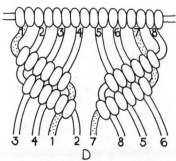

**Horizontal row.** Begin by mounting the cords in the usual manner. Be sure the mounting cord is taut. Use extra pins if necessary to keep the row straight. Then take the first cord, as shown in the accompanying drawing (A), and pass it over the other cords. Arrange it in a horizontal line, holding it in place with pins. This cord becomes the holding or knot bearing cord.

Pick up cord (2) and tie a clove or double half hitch around the holding cord (A). Continue to do this with each of the other cords across the row (B). This procedure should result in a firm, straight bar if the holding cord is kept straight and the knots are tied tightly.

If the design requires another bar, bring the holding cord (1) across the knotting cords again, returning it to its original position (C). To make the knots for this row, start with cord (6), continue across the holding cord. Since it is most important that the macramé be kept even, use pins at the end of a row to keep the holding cord in place.

In planning this type of macramé, remember that more of the holding cord than of the knotting cords is consumed. Therefore, cut this cord longer.

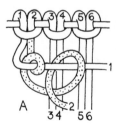
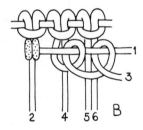
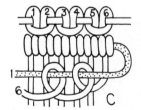

**Vertical row.** In making this type of row, the function of the cords is reversed. The knotting cords become the holding cords, whereas the one that has been used as a holding cord makes the knots.

Begin with the required number of horizontal rows. Then make a clove or double half hitch vertically over the knotting cord (2), using cord (1) (A). Still using cord (1), make the second vertical half hitch over cord (3). Continue this way across the row (B).

To make a second vertical row, tie the first clove or double half hitch over cord (6) (C). Continue across the work in this manner.

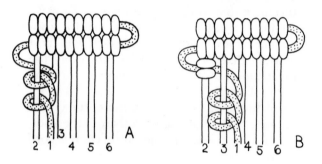

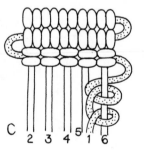

## Splicing

Sometimes the length of the cord has not been cut the correct size, or the cord may break. In such a case, splice the cord. Do this by overlapping the ends if making a row of clove or double half hitches (A), or insert the new end as a holding cord when making a square knot (B).

A

B

## Tension

Tension plays an important part in producing attractive macramé. Developing a certain feel in the fingertips for the correct amount of tautness helps. Balancing the pull between the cords in order to produce a tidy knot can only be accomplished through practice. But even when the skill has been developed, it will need to be adjusted as the type of cord changes. Each requires its own amount of stress.

Try to keep the work taut, with each knot tied close to the preceding one, unless the design dictates otherwise. Do not allow the holding or knot bearing cord to move. It should remain taut and motionless. Keep the cords or strands straight and in precise order. Watch that they do not twist, especially when the knots are being made on them.

## MATERIALS AND TOOLS

The requirements for doing macramé are simple. The hands are the basic tools. They loop a cord or yarn into an interlocking form to create a design pattern. Your hands and the yarn are all that is really needed for simple macramé. There are, however, some accessories and equipment that will help to make the results more pleasing.

### Materials

Cord and yarn of various types, weights, and thickness offer many possibilities. Cord should be pliable enough to knot nicely but firm enough to hold its shape. Too much give or elasticity should be avoided; this eliminates many knitting yarns. Also, the cord should have the strength to resist the abrasion that knotting produces. A tightly twisted cord or yarn with a smooth surface seems to produce the most effective designs, seeming to enhance the textural interest of the knots. Avoid cords that are slippery, fuzzy, or stretchy.

Although many materials are made especially for macramé, it is also possible to use such items as butcher's twine, cable cord, clothesline, and string. The main thing to remember is that the thickness or size of the cord should be appropriate for the article being made. Decorative touches can be added to the basic macramé through the use of such items as beads, buttons, coins, feathers, rings, and shells.

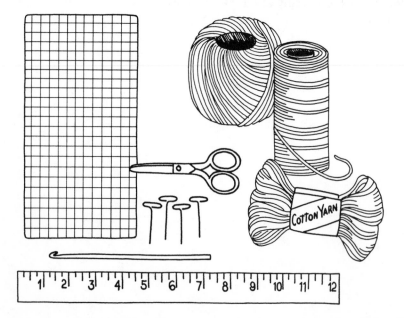

## Tools

A few items are needed to aid the work or hold it in place as the knots are being made. They include pins, scissors, tape measure, and a working surface.

**Crochet hook.** It is not actually used for the knotting, but when the article is completed, the crochet hook helps to weave the ends through the macramé to make a neat finish.

**Pins.** T pins or glass-headed ones are the best to use. They secure the macramé to a working surface to maintain its shape. This procedure makes macramé easier to do, keeping the knots evenly placed.

**Rubber bands.** When working on certain designs, the knotting is less complicated if the excess strands are gathered together and banded. This keeps them out of the way.

**Scissors.** These should be sturdy enough to cut the cord or yarn.

**Tape measure or ruler.** Needed for measuring the strands of cord and for maintaining the correct width.

**Working surface.** There are several types to use. The choice is a matter of personal preference. Some people like to work on a knotting board; others, on a polyurethane-foam pillow form. The knotting board can be a simple piece of plywood, a clipboard, cork board, insulation board, a padded piece of thick corrugated cardboard, or a rectangle of rigid plastic foam. The main qualification is that the working surface be lightweight and rigid, but at the same time soft enough to allow the surface to be pierced easily but securely by pins. It is sometimes helpful to have the board marked with lines, to act as a guide for even knotting. Also, it is easier to work if the color of the board is a contrast to the color of the cord.

The size of the board can vary. Some popular sizes are:

| | |
|---|---|
| 12" by 24" | (30.5 by 61 cm) |
| 20" by 36" | (51 by 91.5 cm) |
| 24" by 48" | (61 by 122 cm) |

**White Glue.** If the cord or yarn is the type that frays, dabbing the ends with white glue is helpful.

# Part V

# Rugmaking

Handmade floor coverings can be made in a variety of ways, such as braiding, crocheting, embroidering, hooking, knitting, and knotting. Although the techniques are different, the results are equally effective and easy to do. The various methods discussed in this book require a small amount of equipment and, at the same time, utilize many different materials. They enable one to make rugs that are appropriate for a wide range of decorative and functional purposes.

## BRAIDED RUGS

This type of rugmaking is often thought to be an American craft, although the use of rushes for plaiting mats is mentioned in the history of the ancient world. Braiding can be done in a simple 3-strand pattern or in more complicated designs, using more strands. It offers a method for making rugs in various shapes and sizes.

### Glossary of Terms

**Butting.** Instead of using a continuous braiding strip in spiral fashion, a strip forms a single ring—a perfect circle, oval, or oblong—with the ends joined or butted together. Join braid to rug within 6 inches (15 cm) of butting point. Cut unfinished ends of all the strips diagonally, tapering to a point. Continue to braid to butting point. Fold back the ends and tuck into braid, pulling through with crochet hook. Keep end square. Sew finished edges together. Butting the strips together eliminates the penetrating of one color into another.

**Interbraiding.** This method of forming a rug eliminates the need for sewing or lacing the braided strips together. As the braiding proceeds, the inside strand of the braid being made is pulled through the finished loop of the previous row. Do this with a large crochet hook.

**Lacing.** This method of joining braids creates an interwoven effect. It forms a stronger bond than sewing.

Work on a flat surface with a blunt needle or lacer and with heavy carpet thread. Lace on the side on which the braiding was done, with the side being laced toward you. When correctly done, the thread is completely hidden.

For lacing straight braids, slide the needle through a loop on one braid and then one on the adjoining braid. Continue in this way, alternating from one braid to the other. Pull the thread tight.

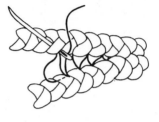

For lacing curved braids, continue as for straight braids except at the rounded areas. Ease the inside of the strip at these points. Sometimes this requires that a loop be skipped. Be sure to keep the rug flat. If it puckers, remove the stitches and redo the lacing. Work with a continuous thread, joining the ends of the thread together with a square knot.

**Splicing.** It provides a quick and easy method for joining braiding strips, eliminating the sewing process. However, the resulting strip is not as smooth and flat.

Cut a 1-inch (2.5 cm) lengthwise slit in the end of each strip. Slip strips through slits as shown in A. Pull ends to flatten strip.

A

## Materials and Tools

A braided rug can be made using only fabric and a needle. However, a few other tools may simplify the procedure.

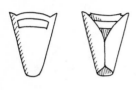

**Braid-aids or cone.** This device folds the strips as the braiding is done.

**Clamp.** This is used to hold or anchor the ends of the braiding strips to a firm surface.

**Clipboard.** Some people find a clipboard a satisfactory method of anchoring braiding strips.

**Fabric.** One of the advantages of braiding is its thrifty possibilities. Pieces of fabric remaining after a sewing project and the good parts of discarded clothing can be used. It is best, however, if old and new fabrics are not used together. Be sure the fabrics are clean and colorfast. Although cotton and silk fabrics are suitable, wool gives the best results. It should be soft, firm, and closely woven. Wool flannel and felt give pleasing results. Usually about ¾ pound (0.3 kg) of fabric is needed for each square foot (930 square cm) of rug.

**Needle.** The type of needle depends on the method used for joining the braids. For lacing, a blunt one or lacer is needed. For sewing, a curved upholstery needle can be used. Sometimes a sacking or packing needle proves handy.

## Preparing Strips

Strips of fabric can be purchased for rugmaking, or the strips can be cut from a piece of material. This can be done on the lengthwise or crosswise grain of the fabric, carefully following the grain. The crosswise strips seem to have more give but require more piecing than those cut on the lengthwise grain. However, those cut lengthwise seem to wrinkle more. Cut the strips evenly. Roll into balls or rolls. A string can be passed through the coil and tied, or the roll can be placed on a special holder (right).

To determine the width of the strip, consider the weight of the fabric in relation to thickness of the braid. In medium wool, a strip cut 1½ to 2 inches (3.8 to 5 cm) wide will yield a finished braid ¾ to 1 inch (2 to 2.5 cm) wide.

To determine the length of the needed strip, estimate the required length of the finished braid. By multiplying this figure by 1½, an estimate can be obtained. Braiding usually takes up about ⅓ to ½ the length of the strip.

For a continuous strip, the pieces should be joined on the bias. This can be done by hand or by machine. After the seam is made, it should be pressed.

Before cutting all the strips, it is best to check the finished results. Usually a narrow braid is used for mats and small rugs; a wider and plumper braid, for larger ones. Planning the color scheme is most important.

## Techniques of Braiding

By varying the number of strips and the sequence of interlacing, the braided design can be changed. Three, 4, 5, or more strands can be used. But whichever number is used, practice before beginning the finished rug in order to make a firm, uniform braid. Pulling each strand after each motion helps to keep the tension even. Keep the folded edges from showing. Avoid having the placement of the joining seams in the same spot. When this happens, a bump results.

**Beginning.** The strips must first be folded. If Braid-aids are being used, slip them into position. If they are not, fold the strip so the raw edges nearly meet at the center. Then fold the strip in half, enclosing the raw edges.

There are 2 ways to start the braiding process. One is referred to as the T method; the other, as the closed-end.

In using the T method, 2 strips are sewed together on the bias. Tack the third strip inside the folded strips, forming a T.

For the closed-end method, turn in the raw edges and slip-stitch the edges together.

**Three-strand braiding.** This is the easiest type of braiding to do. Anchor the ends securely. Start with the second strand. Move it over the third, or middle, strand. Twist the first strand once before crossing it over the second, which is now the middle strand. Keep the open, folded edges to the right as the braiding procedure continues.

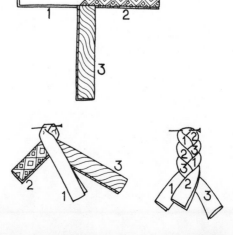

**Four-strand braiding.** Pass the fourth strand over the third, under the second, and over the first. The third strand has now become the fourth, and it repeats the same over-and-under sequence.

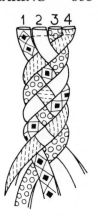

**Five-strand braiding (1).** Slip the fifth strand over the fourth strand and under the third, with the first strand passing over the second strand and under the fifth strand. This procedure continues, working from the outside toward the center.

**Five-strand braiding (2).** This braiding technique creates a heavier braid. Begin by bringing the fifth braid over the fourth and third strands. Then pass the first strand over the second and fifth strands. Continue in this way, working the outside strands toward the center.

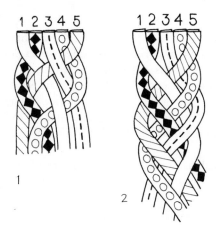

**Finishing off.** About 6 inches (15 cm) from the finishing point, cut the end of each strip into a long point. Continue to braid strands to the end. Work the end slightly under the previous row as the braid is laced into position.

## CROCHET RUGS

Crocheting offers an easy way to create rugs of various types, shapes, patterns, and colors. Basic crocheting techniques are used. Usually the simplest stitches, worked in coarse material, produce interesting results. The materials can vary widely from rags to luxury yarns; those used in a rug should, however, be of good quality and comparable weight. This contributes to an even wearability.

A few of the stitch and pattern possibilities are suggested here. Many more can be found in the crochet section. Single, double, and treble crochet are the basic stitches. Check Part I, "Crocheting," for directions. That section also includes instructions for making many stitches and stitch patterns that are suitable for rugmaking, such as the Popcorn Stitch and Granny Square.

### Filet Mesh—Woven

This openwork stitch pattern is used for a backing, through which strands of different types of materials are pulled to create a woven effect. They can vary from strips of leather and jute to those made from nylon stockings. The pattern also allows for interesting effects.

Use double crochet stitches and a specific number of chain stitches to work the large mesh. Plan the crocheting so that an even number of open spaces are produced. More detailed directions are found in Part I, "Crocheting."

After the backing mesh is completed, lace a strand of interesting material through it. By weaving in and out, the backing can become a colorful rug.

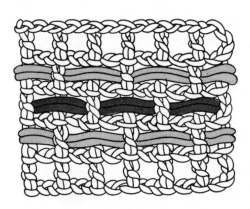

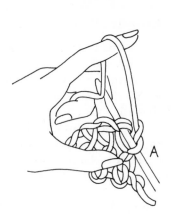

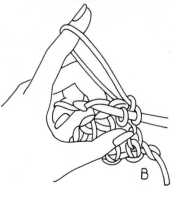

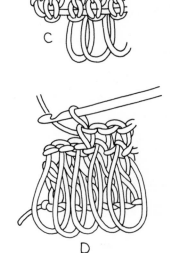

## Looped Pile

For the foundation row, make a chain the required length.

For the **first row,** double-crochet into each chain stitch. Then chain 1 and turn.

For the **second row,** arrange the yarn so the loops can be made with the loops falling on the side turned away from the crocheter. Put the yarn around the ring finger of the left hand and over the raised first, or index, finger. Insert the hook in the space below the top chain of the first double crochet. Catch the yarn close to the ring finger, ready to make a loop (A). Hold the yarn taut. The length of the loop can vary, depending on the effect desired.

Pull the yarn just through the stitch. Make a single crochet, but do not pull through the long loop (B).

Drop the loop from the first finger. Put the yarn over the first finger to make another loop and a second stitch. Continue across row in this way (C). End the row with a turning chain. The type depends on whether the next row will be made of single or double crochet stitches. For a single crochet row, end with 1 chain; for a double crochet, with 3 chains. Turn.

For the **third row,** make single or double crochet stitches, depending on the required spacing between loops (D).

The finished pattern is shown in drawing E.

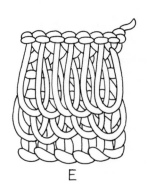

## Tambour Chain Crochet

The chain stitch seems to take on an added dimension when it is used for rugmaking. It has the appearance of embroidery but is made with a crochet hook. Needlepoint canvas or an open-weave fabric that allows a crochet hook to pass through it forms the background. When working on fabric, keep it taut. The stitches can vary in size from very small to larger, bold ones. The yarn should be appropriate to the size of the hook.

Begin by holding the yarn under the backing material. Slip the hook through the fabric. Catch the yarn with the hook. Pull a loop through to the top. Insert the hook a little to the right (A).

Draw a loop through the material and through the first loop, completing a chain stitch (B). Continue this way across the row.

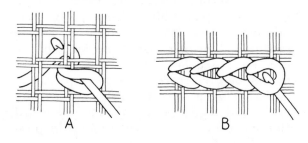

A                    B

# EMBROIDERED RUGS

Although the majority of embroidery stitches are not practical for rugmaking, a few can be used effectively. The Chain, Cross, Knotted, and some needlepoint stitches can be adapted for this purpose when worked on a durable foundation. The stitches should be placed close together and worked in sturdy yarn or other suitable materials.

## Materials and Tools

The selection of an appropriate foundation is important. Canvas or fabric can be used. Select one suitable for the stitch being employed.

**Canvas.** Rugs are usually made on a 3- to 5-mesh canvas that has a twist in the lengthwise threads. Sometimes a double-thread canvas with a coarse mesh is used. There is also a special rya knot canvas that has large mesh spaces between twisted rows.

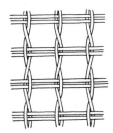  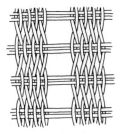

**Fabric.** Burlap and monk's cloth are often used, because the intersections of the lengthwise and crosswise threads can be counted easily.

**Needle.** The only tool that is actually needed is the needle, although scissors and embroidery equipment should be kept handy. The size of the needle depends on the weight of the yarn. Select one that has a blunt point, is long and wide-eyed, and is heavy enough to carry the yarn.

**Yarn.** Rug yarn comes in various weights—light, medium, and heavy. Usually the weights are not mixed unless a special effect is desired. Although synthetic and blended yarns can be used, wool seems to create the most pleasing results.

## Stitch Patterns

Some of the stitch patterns that can be adapted for rugmaking are mentioned here. Other ideas will be found in Part II, "Embroidering."

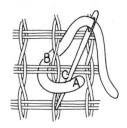

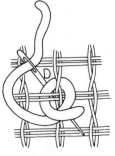

**Asian Cross Stitch.** This stitch produces a bumpy effect on the front and a cross stitch on the back. It creates a durable rug when worked in heavy 3-ply rug yarn on 4-mesh canvas.

Begin by bringing the yarn up in a space (A). Pass the yarn over vertical thread before slipping the needle under the intersection to the left and above (B). Carry the yarn around the intersection, sliding the needle under the yarn (C). Do not let the needle pass through the mesh. With the yarn to the left, insert the needle diagonally downward under the intersection (D). Then slip the needle upward under the loop that has just been made, ready to start the next stitch in the mesh to the left. Continue this way across the row.

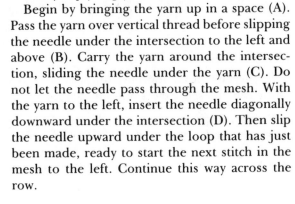

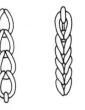

**Chain Stitch.** This easy-to-make embroidery stitch can be worked on a sturdy backing to make an attractive rug. Early American carpets were often constructed this way. Make the rows of stitches close together so the backing fabric is covered. Detailed directions for making this stitch are found in Part II, "Embroidering."

A Heavy Chain Stitch can also be used in rugmaking. It produces a thick, durable foundation and is often used as a background and filling stitch. In order to avoid pulling the stitch too tight, it is best to work with the fabric on a frame. Detailed directions for making this stitch are found in Part II, "Embroidering." Sometimes this stitch is called Braided Chain Stitch in rugmaking.

**Cross Stitch.** Cross stitches worked in heavy yarn on a foundation of burlap or canvas make an effective rug. The easy-to-make stitches should always cross in the same direction.

When working on a **burlap backing:** use the diagonal method for the first part of the cross stitch. (This procedure is used for needlepoint.) It produces a durable backing with its interwoven texture.

The stitches should be kept even. To ensure this, rule lines on the burlap to form squares the correct size. Usually about 3 cross stitches are used to an inch (2.5 cm).

To make the first part of the cross stitch (A), start in the upper right-hand corner. Follow the diagram numbering shown here for correct placement. Hold the needle horizontal when working the upward diagonal rows; vertical, pointing downward, for the downward ones. To begin a new row, slide the needle diagonally under the material.

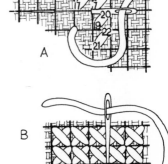

A

B

To make the second part of the stitch (B), work across the complete row. Always cross the stitches in the same direction with the needle in a vertical, downward direction. Always keep the rug in the same position.

On a **canvas backing,** the cross stitches can be made in 2 different ways. A complete row of diagonal stitches can be constructed and then crossed by another row of stitches (A), or a single stitch can be completed before another is started (B). However, the stitches must always be crossed in the same direction.

Make the stitches over 1 or 2 intersections of the canvas, depending on the size of the canvas and the yarn. It is important that the canvas be entirely covered.

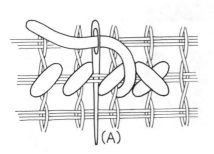

(A)

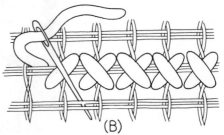

(B)

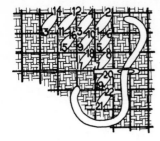

**Diagonal Stitch.** This needlepoint stitch creates a basket weave effect on the underside. Begin the stitch in the upper right-hand corner. Follow the diagram numbering shown here for the correct placement of stitches. Hold the needle horizontal when working upward, vertical when working downward. To begin a new row, slide the needle diagonally under the canvas.

**Half Cross Stitch.** This easy-to-do stitch can be worked effectively on double-thread or twisted double-thread canvas, using a heavy yarn. If a lighter-weight yarn is used, it should be doubled so that the canvas is completely covered.

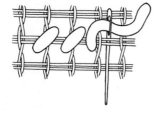

Work from left to right. Bring the needle up at the lower end of the stitch. Pass the yarn over an intersection diagonally above and to the right. Insert the needle in the opening and then bring it up directly below. At the end of the row, turn the rug so the work can continue in a left-to-right direction.

**Jacquard Stitch.** This is a variation of the Half Cross Stitch. Longer diagonal stitches are used for alternating rows. By combining stitches in 2 lengths, a textural quality results.

Work the stitches in a step design with the same number of stitches used horizontally as vertically. After making a row of the shorter stitches, add a row of the longer stitches. Then follow with a row of the shorter ones. Changing the color for various rows gives added interest to the zigzag pattern.

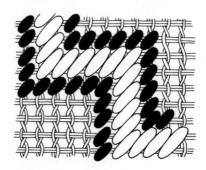

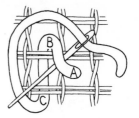

**Loop Stitch.** This stitch can be worked in various materials, such as jute and yarn, using a canvas backing. Work in rows from left to right, starting each new row from the same side.

Begin by bringing the needle up at A. Insert the needle diagonally above and to the left (B) so the yarn crosses 1 intersection. Slide the needle under the canvas, bringing it up 2 spaces below (C). Draw the yarn through the canvas before bringing it over the half cross stitch. Slide the needle under the stitch but not under the canvas. When the yarn is pulled through, a looped effect results and the next stitch can be started.

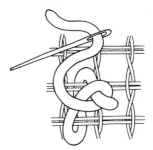

**Turkey Work.** This embroidery stitch can be used on a fabric or canvas backing to make a looped or shaggy rug. The stitch seems to form a lark's-head knot. The stitches can be left looped or the loops can be cut, depending on the look desired. Also, the stitch can be made with more than 1 thread when a multicolor effect is needed. Just thread the needle with the extra yarns and work as with 1.

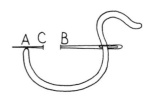

When **working on fabric,** begin with a backstitch. Bring the needle up at A, down at B, and up at C, with the yarn below the needle.

For the second stitch, hold the yarn above the needle. Insert the needle to the right (D). Bring it up close to B, leaving a loop of yarn the correct length.

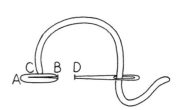

For the third stitch, repeat the first, with the yarn below the needle.

Repeat the procedure, alternating the placement of the yarn until the row is completed.

The loops can be left uncut for a looped effect or cut for a shaggy look. If the loops are to be cut, do it as soon as the row is completed.

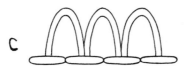

When **working on canvas,** the procedure remains the same generally. Insert the needle in a mesh (A). Slip the needle under the vertical canvas threads to the left, coming up in the adjoining mesh (B). Then carry the yarn to the right, over 2 vertical threads, inserting the needle at C. Slip the needle under the vertical thread, coming up in the first mesh (A). Be sure to keep yarn below stitch.

For the second stitch, carry the yarn to the right over 2 vertical threads. Keep the yarn above the needle, inserting the needle at D. Bring it up at C. Instead of pulling the yarn completely through, leave a loop the required length. Hold it in place with the thumb.

Continue to alternate the first and second stitches until the row is completed.

Double-thread canvas can also be used for rugmaking. When it is, the stitch is sometimes called Smyrna Rug Stitch or Pile Stitch.

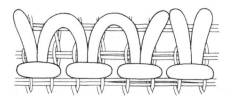

# HOOKED RUGS

Although hooking is a very old art, it seems to be identified closely with the colonial period. It was at this time that the hooking of rugs began. Before this, the technique was employed to make warm clothing and bedcovers. This is one craft that allows the use of leftovers.

Hooking can be done in 2 ways. It can be worked on the right or wrong side of the foundation fabric. If the hooking is done on the right side, the loops of fabric or yarn are pulled up from the wrong side. But if it is worked on the wrong side, the yarn is pushed through the foundation, forming the loops. The effect is the same. It is just a matter of personal preference.

## Materials and Tools

Equipment requirements for hooking are few. Material, a simple tool, and sometimes a frame are all that is necessary.

**Fabric—foundation.** An even and firmly woven material is needed for the rug backing. The threads should be definite so that they can be easily followed. A good-quality burlap is probably the most commonly used. Other fabrics include monk's cloth, canvas, and heavy linen.

**Fabric—strips.** Some hooked rugs are made of fabric strips. The fabric should be clean and of good quality. The same type of material, fiber, weight, and thickness should be used in one rug. Wool provides the most satisfactory results, although washable rugs are often made of cotton.

The strips should be cut on the lengthwise grain of the material. The cutting can be done with shears or a strip-cutting mechanism. It is best not to tear the strips. If the fabric is firmly woven, cut the strips about $\frac{1}{4}$ inch (6 mm) wide; if more loosely woven, slightly wider—$\frac{3}{16}$ to $\frac{5}{16}$ inch (5 to 8 mm) wide.

**Frame.** Although some hooked rugs can be made without a frame, it is usually thought that hooking is easier to do with one. The fabric can be held taut, allowing the loops to be made uniform.

The easel-type frame, which can tilt, seems the most convenient. Some are equipped with rollers at top and bottom, which allow the foundation fabric to be turned so that a certain area can be worked on more easily. The sides of the fabric are laced to the frame. Other types allow the foundation fabric to be tacked to the frame.

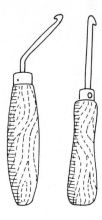

**Hook.** There are 2 types of hooks: with a straight shaft or with a bent one. The hook itself is similar to the one used for crocheting and is available in various sizes. Each performs equally well—it is just a matter of personal preference. Both types pull the material loops to the right side of the rug.

**Punch needle.** This device has a point that carries the yarn through the foundation fabric from the wrong side to the right. When the needle is withdrawn, a loop remains. The needle is equipped with a tubelike part through which the yarn passes. These needles are made in various sizes to accommodate yarn of various weights. The punch needle makes hooking easier to do because it produces the same looped texture automatically.

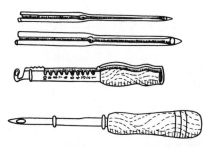

**Shuttle hooker.** To speed up the hooking process, a shuttle hooker can be used. It is often employed for hooking large areas. It seems to make the looping process more automatic.

**Yarn.** If the loops are to be made of yarn, select a good-quality rug yarn. Wool offers the most satisfactory results, although synthetic yarns can be used.

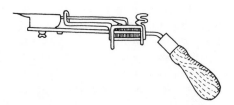

## Methods

The method depends on the tool—the hook, the punch needle, or the shuttle hooker. Working with a hook requires more skill and time.

**Hooking with a hook.** This type of hooking is worked from the right side. Hold the strip of fabric or yarn under and close to the foundation fabric. Push the hook through the material. Let it pick up the end of the strip. Pull a loop to the right side. Decide how long the loop should be. Put the hook in the fabric again. Draw up another loop the same length. Usually the loops are about ¼ inch (6 mm) high, but this is decided by the fabric and the width of the strip. The material also determines the distance between the loops. They should be close enough together to stay in place, usually about 1 or 2 threads apart. The hooking can be done in rows or by design motif.

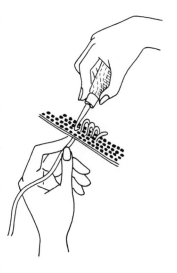

Giving the loop a slight clockwise twist as the loop is pulled through seems to produce a firmer pile. Always draw the ends of a strip through to the right side.

**Hooking with a punch needle.** When using a punch needle, the work is done on the wrong side of the foundation fabric, which is mounted on a frame. The design is marked on the wrong side. Be sure to keep the fabric taut and on grain: the key to even hooking.

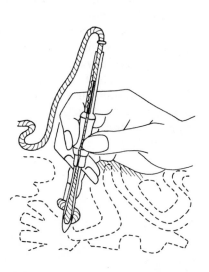

Place the yarn through the needle according to the directions accompanying this tool. The yarn should slide freely through the tube. In working, let about 1 inch (2.5 cm) of yarn hang from the eye of the needle. Hold the punch needle with the open part of the tube upward, in a vertical position.

To begin, push the point of the needle through the fabric between the lengthwise and crosswise threads. Pull the end of the yarn through to the right side of rug. Remember that all ends must be drawn to the right side.

Bring the point of the needle to the surface. Slide it along the fabric for about 2 threads and reinsert it in the fabric as far as is necessary to make the loop. Continue in this way, making evenly spaced loops. Check the right side from time to time to be sure the loops are even.

When a point is reached at which the hooking must be stopped, the needle can be below or above the fabric. In whichever position, cut the yarn about 2 inches (5 cm) from the point. If the end is on the upper surface, it should be pushed through to the under, or right, side.

Begin the second row of loops 1 or 2 threads from the first. Keep the loops of the completed row away from the needle point by holding them with the fingertips.

**Hooking with a shuttle hooker.** This type of hooking device creates the same looped effect. It is usually employed for doing large areas quickly. Two hands are required to hold it. The shuttle hooker works automatically, allowing the needle to move itself ahead to make the next loop. The large frame on which the foundation fabric is stretched can stand upright. Hold the shuttle perpendicular to the surface. Follow the manufacturer's directions for threading and use. In general, the work proceeds as for punch needle hooking.

## KNITTED RUGS

Although knitting is not very popular, the techniques of regular knitting can be employed in making small rugs. Care should be taken to select stitches that are reversible, creating a firm, thick texture with a raised surface.

### Materials and Tools

Yarn and knitting needles form the basic equipment. However, if the rug is knitted in sections, a crochet hook is needed for joining the pieces.

**Knitting needles.** Regular needles, long and large in size, produce the correct effect.

**Materials.** Work with rug yarns of cotton, polyester, or wool. Be sure that the yarn does not stretch. Cords, such as jute welting cord, can be used effectively. Sometimes narrow strips of fabric are knitted.

### Stitch Patterns

The Garter and Seed stitches are frequently used. They produce an interesting textural quality, and at the same time, are easy to make.

**Garter Stitch.** This easy-to-make stitch is produced by knitting each row. Its definite ridges seem to give the work a striped effect. Directions for making the garter stitch are found in Part III, "Knitting."

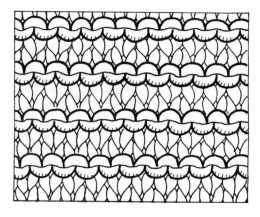

**Seed Stitch.** This stitch creates a uniform pebbled effect. An uneven number of stitches must be cast on, to give an irregular texture. For the first row, start with knit 1 and follow with purl 1. Continue across the row, ending with knit 1. The second row is made in the same way, knit 1 and purl 1. However, because an uneven number of stitches were cast on, a purl stitch falls above a knit one and a knit stitch above a purl one. It is this alternating sequence of stitches that produces the seeded effect. More complete directions are found in Part III, "Knitting."

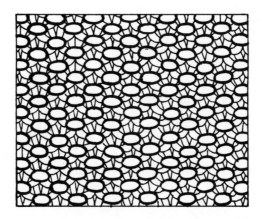

**Seed Stitch—Double.** When the Seed Stitch is worked this way, it creates a more textural effect. Instead of alternating 1 knit stitch with 1 purl stitch, use 2 knit stitches with 2 purl ones.

For the **first row,** knit 2, purl 2, ending with knit 2.

For the **second and third rows,** purl 2, knit 2.

For the **fourth row,** repeat the first row, ending with knit 2.

Repeat these four rows until work is completed.

An interesting effect can be produced by working blocks of Seed and Double Seed stitches, forming a checkerboard look.

## KNOTTED RUGS

The easiest way to make a knotted rug is with a latchet hook. Pieces of yarn are secured automatically to a canvas backing, creating a rug with a uniform pile. Once a rhythm is established for the movement of the hand, the work progresses with great speed.

Working on large pieces of canvas can be awkward. Because of this, smaller pieces are worked and then whipped together, using a curved upholstery needle and carpet thread.

### Materials and Tools

**Canvas.** A course double-thread canvas forms the backing for the knots. Canvas constructed with twisted lengthwise threads is preferable. The spacing for the meshes should be about 4 to the inch (2.5 cm).

**Yarn.** Rug yarn is cut into short pieces before beginning to work. It can be purchased precut. The minimum length is 2½ inches (6.5 cm). A shorter length is difficult to hold. The finished pile is about 1 inch (2.5 cm) high.

### Method

In the beginning, it may seem difficult to hold yarn, hook, and canvas at the same time. Try various ways of doing each process until one feels comfortable and the work can be done automatically.

**Holding the yarn.** Take 1 strand of yarn and loop it under the shank of the hook. Hold it in place with the finger of the hand holding the hook (A). Or the yarn can be placed around the shank of the hook. Fold it so the ends meet. Hold it with the thumb and first (index) finger of the hand not holding the hook (B).

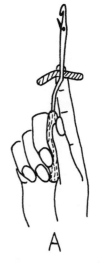

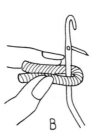

B

A

**Holding the canvas.** The canvas can be left flat or can be folded so that the hook can pass through 2 meshes in 1 motion.

**Inserting the hook.** If the canvas is flat, insert the hook with the lachet in a down position, under a crosswise thread, bringing it up in the space above (C). Continue to push the hook until the latchet is completely through the mesh.

If the canvas is folded, pass the hook through 2 meshes at the same time (D).

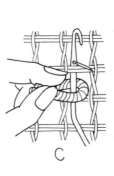

C

D

**Inserting the yarn.** With the ends of the yarn together, begin to pull the hook backward until the latchet is in an up position but not closed. Place the ends of the yarn between the latchet and the hook. Be sure the yarn is completely inside the hook.

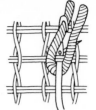

**Completing the knot.** Pull hook back until latchet is closed. Release the ends of the yarn. Continue to draw the hook back, pulling the loose ends through the loop. Tug at the ends to tighten the loop.

Continue to make the knots in this way, working row by row.

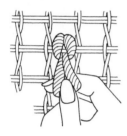

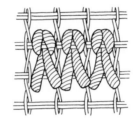

# Part VI

# Sewing

The most versatile type of needlework is sewing. Its function is both useful and decorative. Beautiful, practical articles result by combining the stitches. Some of the sewing stitches are considered in the embroidery category. And, on a more useful note, they can be employed for mending and rejuvenating items. It is this versatility that makes sewing so fascinating.

In recent years, sewing has become associated with machine work. The loveliest examples of sewing are, however, usually made by hand. The hand touch, beautifully executed, contributes an elegant look that the machine is powerless to do.

Hand sewing is not difficult. It does, however, require an interest in detail and a patience for precision, in order to develop the skill. On the following pages, basic information about sewing stitches is found. It includes:

# BASIC TECHNIQUES

Knowing how to handle sewing equipment and materials correctly makes it easier to create perfect stitches. Although some of the details may seem unnecessary, they really aren't. Even little things, such as the position of the needle, may affect the results.

## Hand Sewing

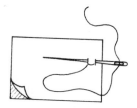

**Beginning.** Sewing starts by threading a needle. Select needle and thread in the size that is correct for the fabric.

Cut the thread diagonally about 20 inches (51 cm) from the spool. Place this end through the eye of the needle. Usually the stitches are made of a single thread.

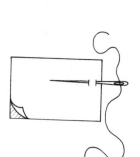

Since sewing stitches are usually made from right to left—unless one is left-handed—start the work on the right-hand side close to the edge. Anchor the thread in one of two ways. For the first, take 2 or 3 tiny stitches, one on top of the other. For the second, make a knot at the end of the thread. When a knot is used for permanent stitches, hide it under a hem or seam allowance.

**Ending.** Be sure to fasten the thread securely but inconspicuously at the end of the row. When making permanent stitches, take 2 or 3 small stitches in the same place. These can be followed by 2 or 3 running stitches. For temporary stitches, such as basting, take 2 or 3 separate backstitches in a diagonal position. Always take the last stitch close to the edge.

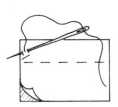

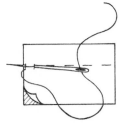

**Holding.** Usually it is better to hold the bulk of the material or article toward you: this seems to make it easier to guide the placement and size of the stitches. Work on a table or lap board if possible. Hold the fabric with the left hand, between the thumb and first (index) finger with the thumb on top, and the needle with the right hand. In this way, the left hand regulates the fabric and the right hand guides the needle.

To hold the needle correctly, place it between the thumb and the first finger so that it touches the side of the thimble near the tip. This allows the middle finger to push the needle through the fabric. Although some people sew without a thimble, it is a technique to be avoided. A thimble protects the finger, allowing one to work faster and with greater precision.

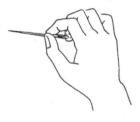 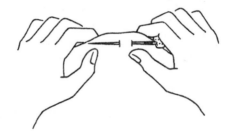

## Machine Sewing

The skillful manipulation of the sewing machine requires practice and a thorough knowledge of the machine. Take time to study the instruction manual. Learn all about the machine before beginning to stitch. Then practice starting and stopping, turning corners, sweeping around curves, and stitching in a perfectly straight line. Unless one has control of the machine, it is impossible to sew successfully.

**Beginning.** Be sure to thread the machine correctly. Bring the bobbin thread to the top by lowering and raising the needle just once. Give the upper thread a little jerk so that a loop of the bobbin thread appears. Place a pin or pair of scissors through the loop and pull up the end.

Bring the take-up lever to its highest position so the needle will not become unthreaded when the first stitch is made. Put the thread ends under the presser foot and back.

Slip the material under the presser foot, with the bulk of it to the left. Be sure that it does not hang down.

Lower the needle with the hand wheel so that it passes through the fabric at the correct point. If it is necessary to secure the stitches, put the needle in the fabric so that a few stitches can be taken in reverse. This procedure is sometimes referred to as back-tacking. Otherwise, insert the needle so that the first stitch falls close to the edge. Lower the presser foot. Hold the 2 threads in back while making the first 2 stitches. This keeps the threads from being caught in the seam or tangled in the bobbin case.

Stitch slowly. Guide the fabric with a light pressure of the fingers. Do not pull or push the material.

**Ending.** The threads can be secured by tying or back-tacking. To tie the threads, stop the machine at the end of the row so the last stitch comes at the edge of the fabric. Raise the take-up lever to its highest point to release the tension. Follow by raising the presser foot. Pull the fabric to the back, far enough to allow the threads to be cut. Bring 1 end through the fabric. Tie both thread ends together securely. Clip the ends.

To back-tack, reverse the direction of the stitching for a few stitches at the end of the row. Then raise the take-up lever to the highest point and raise the presser foot. Pull the fabric back, under the presser foot. Clip the threads close to the stitching.

**Guiding.** Place the hands lightly on the fabric. Fingertips will be sufficient. Let the right hand guide the work and the left hand hold it in place.

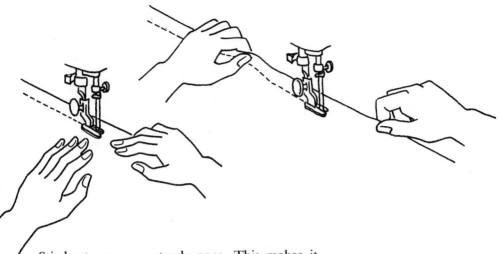

Stitch at an even, steady pace. This makes it easier to guide the work, keeping the stitching line straight.

If the fabric needs to be stretched slightly, place the fingers over the edge of the material and pull gently. The right hand should be in front; left hand, at back.

**Tension.** Before starting to work, test the stitching on a double thickness of material. Check for correctness of threading, balance of stitches, and pressure.

If the stitches appear loose or the thread is drawn tight on one side, then the tension is too loose or too tight and needs to be adjusted. The stitches should appear the same on both sides.

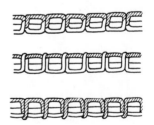

If the needle thread lies along the upper surface in a straight line, the upper tension is too tight or the bobbin tension is too loose. If the bobbin thread lies along the undersurface in a straight line, the bobbin tension is too tight or the upper tension is too loose.

Holding the material in place between the presser foot and feed dog requires a certain amount of pressure. If the pressure is correctly adjusted, the 2 edges match at the end of the stitching. But if a ripple forms on the upper layer so it extends beyond the lower edge, then the pressure is too heavy. If the material does not move through steadily, then the pressure may be too light.

# EQUIPMENT

Sewing requires a certain amount of equipment. Some tools are essential, whereas others are helpful to have but not absolutely necessary. This depends on the type and amount of sewing being done. It is important, however, to select equipment correct for the purpose for which it is being used, and to keep it in good condition.

## Cutting

Good cutting equipment contributes more to sewing accuracy than one realizes. Crooked stitching often results from uneven cutting. Buy good scissors and shears. Always keep them sharp.

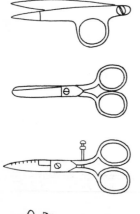

**Scissors.** A pair of scissors should have sharp points and narrow blades that fit together tightly. Use them to clip fabric, to cut buttonholes, and for other exact work. Scissors are available in various lengths but seem to be the most useful in the 3- to 5-inch (7.5 to 12.5 cm) variety.

**Scissors—electric.** Some persons find that electric scissors make it easier to cut fabrics. They are available in various models.

**Shears.** For general sewing, such as clipping and trimming seams, select a pair of shears, 6 or 7 inches (15 or 18 cm) long. Sometimes they are called light trimmers.

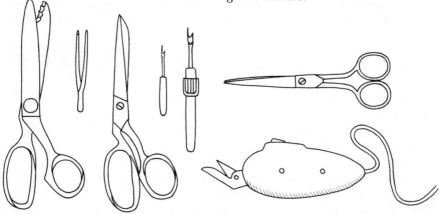

**Shears—dressmaker.** Select a model with bent handles, about 7 or 8 inches (18 or 20.5 cm) long. The blades may be smooth or serrated. Serrated blades can be used effectively when cutting synthetic materials. There are special shears for left-handed people.

**Special.** A seam ripper is a small gadget used to rip stitching that must be removed. It can also cut machine-worked buttonholes.

## Marking

Transferring pattern symbols from pattern to fabric can be done in several ways. Some people prefer to use dressmaker's tracing paper and tracing wheel; others, tailor's chalk or chalk pencil; still others, pins or tailor's tacks. Whichever method is selected, be sure that it produces a clear, accurate marking.

**Chalk pencil.** Comes in several colors. Can be sharpened to a sharp point for marking precise lines. The markings disappear when material is dry-cleaned or washed.

**Dressmaker's tracing paper.** Available in several colors. Choose one in a color that contrasts with the fabric.

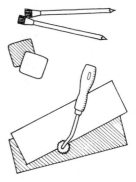

**Tailor's chalk.** This is a square-shaped clay chalk that is available in several colors.

**Tracing wheel.** This device is used with dressmaker's tracing paper. It is made with a small wheel, with or without teeth. Generally one with teeth is employed. The smooth wheel works well on delicate or difficult-to-mark materials.

## Measuring

A variety of measuring tools makes it easier to measure accurately. When purchasing a new item, select one marked in both inches and centimeters.

**French curve.** This device simplifies working with curved lines.

**Hem marker.** An even hemline is a must. Accurate marking can be done more easily by using this device. It is available in a pin type that requires the services of a helper and a chalk type that one can use alone.

**Metal gauge.** A sliding marker is the outstanding feature of this 6-inch (15 cm) ruler. It seems to make for accurate measuring.

**Rulers.** It is handy to have more than 1 ruler. Select a 6-inch (15 cm) and a 12-inch (30.5 cm) ruler that are transparent and flexible, with ⅛ inch (3 mm) markings.

**Tape measure.** This measuring tool is probably used most often. It should be made of firm, nonstretchable flexible material with metal ends. The numbers, marked from 1 to 60, should be placed on both sides, beginning at opposite ends so it is reversible. Some tape measures also have metric markings.

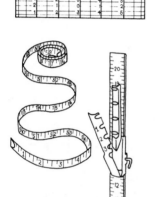

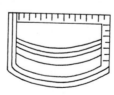

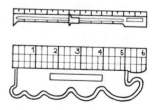

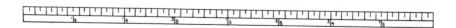

## Pressing

Pressing plays an important part in sewing. It is impossible to produce professional-looking garments without the frequent use of the iron.

**Iron.** Select a good one with an accurate temperature control. The combination steam/dry iron gives the most satisfactory results.

**Ironing board.** It should be firm and well padded, with a removable outer cover to ensure that it is always clean. An adjustable board allows the height to be changed.

**Press cloth.** It is a protection as well as a useful aid. Although specially treated ones can be purchased, a piece of thoroughly washed, unbleached muslin or closely woven cheesecloth can be used with great success. A wool press cloth for woolens gives satisfactory results. Sometimes a slip cover for the iron is used instead of a press cloth.

**Special aids.** There are several devices that aid in the pressing of certain areas:

- dressmaker's or tailor's ham for curving areas
- needle board for velvets and pile fabrics
- point presser for opening pointed seams
- pounding block or clapper to flatten edges and seams on heavy fabrics or when tailoring
- pressing mitt for small details for which the ham cannot be used

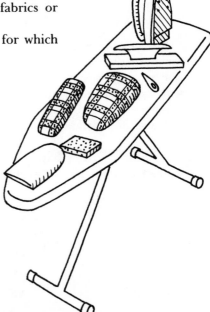

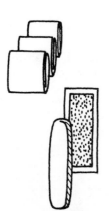

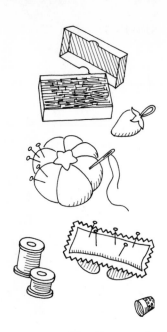

## Sewing

A few small items are needed. Some are required for the actual sewing; others, to aid the process. The most important, needle and thread, vary in type and size. Always select the one most appropriate for the work.

**Emery bag.** This handy cushionlike article contains a dust-removing powder. By moving a needle in and out of it, it is possible to clean the needle and keep it sharp.

**Needle threader.** This is a handy aid for anyone who has trouble threading a needle.

**Needles.** For hand sewing, select a package of needles in assorted sizes. Number 1 denotes a coarse needle; number 10, fine. Sizes 1 to 5 can be used for heavy material; 6 to 8, for medium-weight; 9 to 10, for sheers.

Needles are also available in a variety of types and shapes. Although one usually thinks of needles having a pointed end, some feature a rounded end for sewing on knits.

- Betweens are short and used for fine sewing.
- Embroidery needles are also used for sewing. They resemble sharps but have a longer eye. This feature makes them easier to thread. They are sometimes called crewel needles.
- Milliner's are longer than sharps. They are sometimes used for basting as well as millinery.
- Quilting needles are betweens in size 7.
- Sharps are of medium length and most frequently used for general sewing. Some of them are made with an open end for easy threading and are known as calyx-eyed sharps.

**Needles for machine sewing.** Although some needles can be used on more than one type of machine, it is always best to select the one recommended for the machine being used. Most machines work with only 1 needle, but there are some that require twin or triple needles.

There are certain standard needles that vary mostly in the type of point.

Ballpoint needles have a rounded point that separates the yarns instead of piercing them. They are designed for sewing on knits.

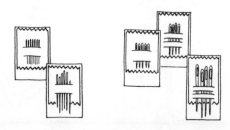

There is also a universal ballpoint needle that has a special taper and can be used on both knits and woven material.

Sharp pointed needles are made for sewing on woven materials.

Wedge needles have a wedge-shaped point, making them excellent for working on leather and leatherlike fabrics.

**Pincushion.** This sewing aid helps to keep the sewing surface neat. The type depends on personal preference. Some people feel that one worn on the wrist is the handiest.

**Pins.** Be sure to select good-quality pins that are smooth, thin, rustproof and with sharp points. They are sometimes called dressmaker or silk pins. For general use, size 17 is satisfactory.

**Thimble.** This is an essential piece of equipment. It makes sewing easier and faster and the results more professional. The thimble should be lightweight and fit the middle finger of the hand holding the needle.

**Thread.** Thread is available in a wide range of colors, fibers, types, and weight. The fabric and its use influence the selection.

**Cotton thread** has less strength and stretch than a synthetic thread. It is available as mercerized thread, button and carpet thread, quilting thread, and basting thread.

- Basting thread is available only in white. It is fine and soft and breaks easily.
- Button and carpet thread has a glacé finish and is extra strong and heavy. It can be used only for hand sewing.
- Mercerized thread has a special finish that adds smoothness and luster. It can be used for all types of light- and medium-weight fabrics. It is available in size 50 in colors; 40, 50, and 60, in white; 60, in black.
  Another type of mercerized cotton thread is available in black and white and in 6 sizes. Size 8 is the coarsest; size 60, the finest.
- Quilting thread has a glacé finish but is fine and strong. It is used for hand and machine quilting.

**Silk thread:** sewing thread and buttonhole twist are made of silk. The thread works well on silk and lighter-weight wool fabrics. It may be purchased in 1 size—A.

The twist is strong. It is designed for making hand-worked buttonholes but can also be used for decorative stitching by hand or machine.

**Synthetic thread** may be cotton-covered polyester, spun polyester, or nylon. It is strong and elastic—characteristics needed for working on knits and permanent press and stretch fabrics. Synthetic thread is available in various weights from the very fine to the heavier, such as a buttonhole twist.

Whichever type of thread is being used, select it in a color slightly darker than the fabric.

## STITCHES—HAND AND MACHINE

Although a large amount of sewing is done by machine, there are certain details that require a hand stitch. In fact, it is the hand touch that contributes the special look to custom-made clothes. Learning to select the appropriate stitch is important. It takes a thorough knowledge of the stitches and where to use them to make the right choice.

### Backstitch

This is the strongest hand stitch. It resembles machine stitching on the upper side.

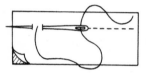

Bring the needle up on the stitching line In- sert the needle 1/16 inch (1.5 mm) to the right. Slip the needle under the fabric, coming up 1/8 inch (3 mm) to the left.

Put the needle in the fabric at the beginning of the first stitch, making another stitch 1/16 inch (1.5 mm) long. Continue this procedure, moving backward and then forward, forming a continuous row of stitches.

### Backstitch—Half

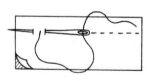

This stitch is both functional and decorative. It is used for the hand finishing of a zipper insertion. When the stitches are very small and placed farther apart, as in tailoring a lapel, it is known as the Pick Stitch.

Bring the needle to the right side. Take a stitch to the right about 1/16 inch (1.5 mm) long, coming up 3/16 inch (5 mm) to the left. Take another stitch 1/16 inch (1.5 mm) long to the right. Tiny spaces remain between the stitches, as in the Running Stitch.

## Basting

Basting is a temporary stitch. The stitches can be even or uneven in length. Work with thread in a contrasting color.

**Even basting.** Use when there is strain on the area to be sewn. Start with a knot at the end of the thread. Make stitches ¼ inch (6 mm) long and ¼ inch (6 mm) apart. End with 2 or 3 back-stitches. To remove, snip the thread at frequent intervals.

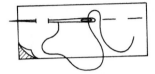

**Uneven basting.** Use this type of basting for marking, as a guideline, and for holding layers of fabric together when there is little strain. Take a long stitch on the upper side and a short stitch underneath.

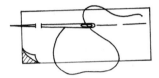

## Basting—Diagonal

When it is necessary to hold layers of material together, use this stitch. Sew at right angles to the fabric edge. This results in a diagonal stitch on the upper side, a vertical one on the under-side.

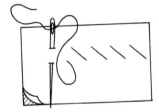

## Basting—Machine

The longest stitch made by the sewing machine is used for this type of basting. It holds the layers of fabric together more firmly than hand basting can. Be sure to work carefully because machine basting is not as easy to remove as hand basting. Work with thread that matches the material.

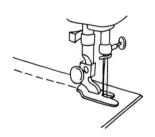

## Basting—Slip
*See* Slip Stitch.

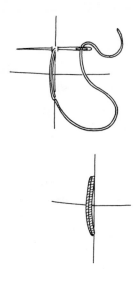

## Blanket Stitch Carriers or Loops

Although the stitch resembles the one used in embroidery, the needle never enters the fabric as the stitches are made. Instead, the stitch is taken over several threads to form a loose carrier or loop, used for fastening and tacking.

Begin with 3 or 4 stitches to form the foundation. To do this, take small stitches at the ends so all threads fall on top of the fabric. Cover the longer stitches, extending between the ends, with blanket stitches, placed close together. It is easier to work if the needle is held eye first. Fasten the thread securely on the wrong side.

## Blind Stitch

This stitch is often referred to as Blind Hemming. The stitches should be so small that they are almost invisible on the right side. Never pull the thread tight.

When the stitches are taken over a folded or finished edge, work with the material flat. Secure the thread in the hem fold. Pick up only 1 or 2 threads with the needle. Slip the needle through the hem about ¼ inch (6 mm) to the left. Then pull the thread through. For the next stitch, pick up the thread directly below this point.

When working inside the hem, fold back the hem. Anchor the thread at the stitching line of hem. Pick up on 1 or 2 threads in the garment and then in the hem, producing a zigzag effect inside the hem.

Sometimes this stitch is called Invisible or French Hemming.

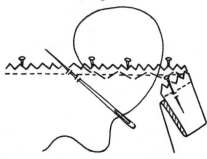

## Buttonhole Stitch

Although this stitch resembles Blanket Stitch in the making, it has a special loop or purl edge that produces a firm finish. It is sometimes referred to as Tailor's Buttonhole Stitch, for it is used most often in working thread buttonholes.

**Work from right to left.** After securing the thread so the ends will be invisible, put the needle in the fabric from the underside about $\frac{1}{16}$ inch (1.5 mm) below the cut edge. Hold the 2 threads near the eye of the needle. Slip them under the needle from right to left. As the needle is pulled through, an extra loop or purl is formed. Draw the thread away from you so the purl will fall exactly on the edge. Do not pull the thread too tight.

For the second stitch, insert the needle from the underside, close to the first stitch. Repeat the technique used in making the first stitch for the remaining stitches.

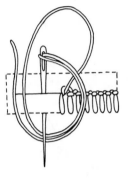

## Catch Stitch

This stitch is also listed as an embroidery stitch. In sewing, it is associated most often with hems and facings when raw edges must be held in place.

Work the row of stitches from left to right. After anchoring the thread in the hem or facing, take a small stitch—1 or 2 threads—in the under fabric. Do this with the needle pointing from right to left. Then take a stitch a short distance to the right in the upper section, again from right to left. This allows the threads to cross each other at the ends of the stitches and to be put over a raw edge, holding it in place. Do not pull the stitches tight.

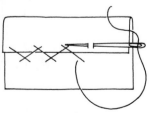

## Chain Stitch Carriers and Tacks

A form of crochet stitch can be used to make a cord for a thread loop, French tack, or belt carrier. Instead of using a crochet hook, work with the fingers and a needle.

Bring the needle to the right side at the point where one end of the loop will be fastened. Take a small stitch at this point.

Begin to make another stitch, but do not pull the thread completely through. Instead, leave a loop. Pick up the thread with the thumb and first (index) finger. Pull the thread through the loop, making another. Draw each stitch tight as the new loop is pulled through the preceding one.

When the cord or chain is the correct length, put the needle through the last loop. Draw the thread tight. Insert the needle in the fabric at the correct point and fasten the thread securely with several backstitches.

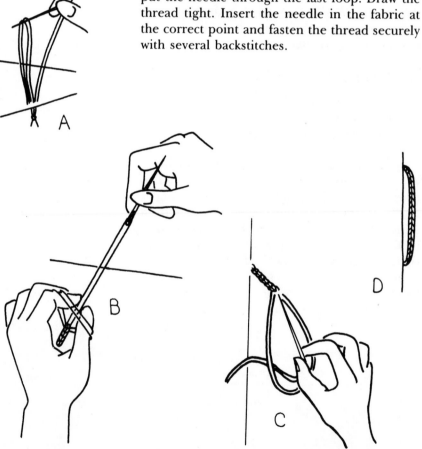

## Darning Stitch

This stitch is actually the Running Stitch. It is used to strengthen worn areas and repair tears and small holes. The stitches should always be tiny and as invisible as possible.

Work with a fine needle and a short thread in a matching color. A thread drawn from the fabric gives satisfactory results. Start without a knot, leaving an end of thread on the wrong side. Clip the end when the work is completed.

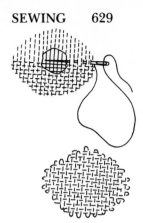

## Fishbone Stitch

This is a diagonal stitch used to hold 2 raw edges together, such as at a slash or a tear. Make the stitch from left to right, with stitches alternating from one side to the other. Pass the needle through the slit each time. Keep the stitches even in length.

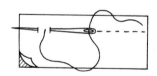

## French Hemming Stitch
*See* Blind Stitch.

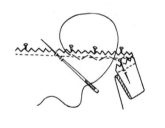

## Half Backstitch
*See* Backstitch—Half.

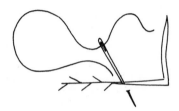

## Handpicked Stitch

This variation of the Half Backstitch is used on a finished part of a garment, such as a lapel. The stitches do not show on the underside. Work through the top layer of fabric and interfacing.

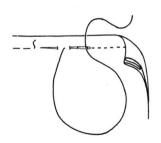

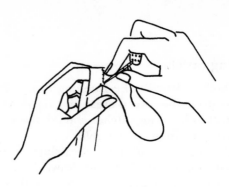

### Hemming Stitch

A folded edge can be held in place with this stitch. It appears slanting on the wrong side but not on the right.

After securing the thread end in the folded edge, place the folded edge in the left hand over the first (index) finger, with the bulk of the fabric in the lap. Point the needle toward the left shoulder, picking up 1 or 2 threads in the single thickness of material under the fold. Pass the needle through the edge of the fold. Take the next stitch a little to the left.

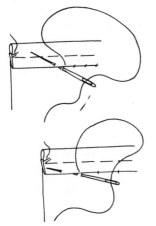

**Vertical hemming.** For an inconspicuous type of hemming, this is the one to use. The needle enters the single thickness of material directly below the point where it emerged from the fold, making a short vertical stitch on the wrong side. Pick up 1 or 2 threads. Slip the needle into the fold some distance from the first stitch.

### Invisible Stitch
*See* Blind Stitch.

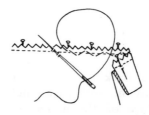

## Overcast Stitch

Edges on fabrics that ravel can be finished with overcast stitches. Work in either direction, left to right or right to left. Point the needle toward the left shoulder. Take a diagonal stitch over the raw edge.

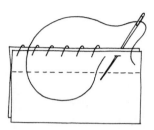

The stitches should be evenly spaced and slant in the same direction. Make the stitches ⅛ to ¼ inch (3 to 6 mm) deep and ¼ inch (6 mm) apart. The depth depends on the type of fabric— shorter for fine materials.

## Overhand Stitch

This stitch is used to hold 2 finished edges of fabric together. The stitches appear straight on the upper side, slanting on the under. It produces a strong, invisible seam that can be opened out flat.

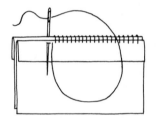

Turn under the edges the required distance. Put the sections right sides together, with finished edges matching. Pass the needle straight through the back fold and then the front fold with the needle pointing toward you. Pick up only 1 or 2 threads in the folds. Continue this way, placing the stitches close together.

## Padding Stitch

In tailoring, the Padding Stitch attaches the interfacing to the undercollar when making lapels. The stitches are almost invisible on the outer fabric.

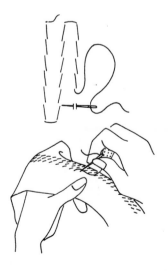

Work on the interfacing side. Use thread matching the garment fabric and a short needle. Start with a backstitch. Sew through the thickness of fabric at right angles to the edge so that a diagonal stitch appears on the interfacing side and a small horizontal one on the fabric side, catching only 1 or 2 threads. The stitches can be ¼ to ½ inch (6 mm to 1.3 cm) long, depending on where they are placed. Work rows of parallel stitches about ⅜ inch (1 cm) apart.

### Pick Stitch

This is a variation of the Half Backstitch and is sometimes referred to as Prick Stitch. It is used for the hand application of a zipper, attaching a facing to the interfacing, and finishing a lapel.

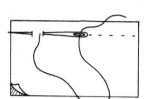

Start by bringing the needle to the right side of the fabric. Insert the needle to the right, picking up 1 or 2 threads. Slide the needle diagonally through the fabric, letting it emerge ¼ inch (6 mm) to the left. Continue this way. Pull each stitch tight.

When finishing a lapel, use a basted line as a guide. Remove these stitches as you work. Notice that the stitches do not show on the underside. Do not pull the stitches tight here.

### Rantering Stitch

Tailors use this stitch to make a seam line less obvious on tweeds and men's-wear materials. Fold the fabric edge to the wrong side along the seam line. Hold it between the thumb and first or index, finger. Take a stitch over the folded seam line and through both folds. Pull the thread. Then repeat the process, picking up 1 thread a short distance away and crossing the folded edge in the opposite direction. Take the stitches close to the seam line. They should be invisible.

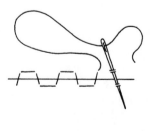
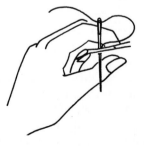

## Running Stitch

This stitch is used for gathering, mending, quilting, shirring, and making tucks. It is a tiny, even stitch that is easy to do.

Pick up a small amount of fabric with the needle. Continue to work the needle in and out of the fabric until there are several stitches on it. Then pull the needle through the material ready to start the second series of stitches. Make the stitches $\frac{1}{16}$ to $\frac{1}{8}$ inch (1.5 to 3 mm) long.

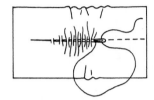

## Saddle Stitch

For decorative hand top-stitching, use this stitch. It is usually worked with buttonhole twist or embroidery floss in a matching or contrasting color. The stitches should be placed an even distance from the edge through all thicknesses of fabric. They can be even in length and spacing, or the stitches on the upper side can be longer than the stitches on the underside. When the stitches are even, the stitch is sometimes called Glove Stitching. Stitches in $\frac{1}{4}$-inch (6 mm) length are generally used.

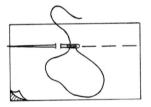

## Slip Stitch

This stitch is useful for basting alterations and for matching patterned fabrics. It is worked on the right side but with no sign of the stitch on the right side. However, on the underside regular basting stitches appear.

Fold under seam allowance on one side. Press or baste. Place this section over the other one, right sides up. Match seam line and design accurately. Pin in position.

Anchor the thread at the right-hand side with a stitch on the seam line of the lower section. Slip the needle into the upper section in the seam line fold, coming out again on the fold line about $\frac{1}{4}$ inch (6 mm) away. Insert the needle in the lower seam line directly below the point from which it emerged. Continue this way until the row is completed.

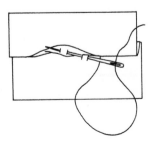

### Sloating Stitch

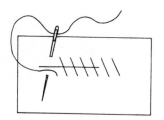

A cut or tear in heavy fabrics, such as felt and firmly woven tweeds, can be mended with this stitch. The stitch should be invisible on the right side but appear as a small slanting stitch on the wrong side.

Take the stitch through the fabric so that it does not appear on the right side. Insert the needle about $\frac{1}{16}$ inch (1.5 mm) from the torn edge. Work it through the fabric to the opposite side, coming out $\frac{1}{16}$ inch (1.5 mm) from the opening. Make the next stitch $\frac{1}{16}$ inch (1.5 mm) from the first. Work with the needle straight. Never allow it to pierce the right side of the fabric.

### Stitching

The term **stitching** is usually mentioned in connection with machine stitches. There are 2 basic types of machine stitches. The **straight stitch** is the one most commonly used. The needle is held in the same place as it goes up and down while the feed dog moves the fabric backward or forward. The stitches can vary in length.

For **zigzag stitches,** the needle moves from side to side while the feed dog moves the fabric backward or forward. The appearance of the stitches can be varied depending on the distance between them, the width, and the stitch pattern selected.

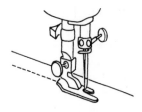

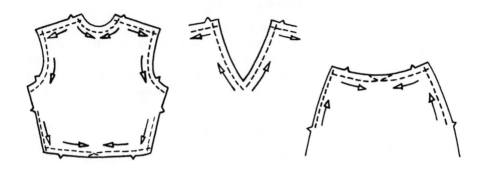

## Stitching—Directional

Usually stitching results are more satisfactory if the construction of the fabric is considered. Stitching woven fabrics with the grain helps to keep edges from stretching. The accompanying diagrams indicate the direction the stitching lines should take. The grain can be checked by moving the fingers along the cut edge. If the edge remains smooth, the fingers are moving with the grain, but if edge becomes frayed, the fingers are moving against it.

Since knits do not have a grain to follow, it is wise to stitch all corresponding seams in the same direction.

## Stitching—Edge

Edgestitching is a form of topstitching with the row of stitches placed close to a finished or folded edge. Seam edges are sometimes edgestitched, as are pleats and the crease in pants. Guide the stitching carefully so the stitches are an even distance from the edge.

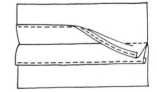

For finishing a seam edge on non-bulky fabrics, turn under the raw edge ¼ inch (6 mm) and machine-stitch ⅛ inch (3 mm) from the edge.

### Stitching—Stay

If a fabric is loosely woven, it is sometimes best to place a row of stitches an even distance from the cut edge in order to control the fabric threads. This type of stitching is called stay stitching. Always stitch in the correct direction.

### Stitching—Top

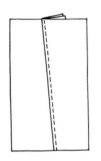

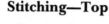

When stitching appears on the outside of an article, it is called topstitching. It can be decorative or functional. The work is generally done on the right side, except when it is necessary to wind a heavier thread, such as buttonhole twist, on the bobbin.

The length of the stitches can vary, depending on the effect desired. Usually the thread is the same as that used for making the article. Be sure to keep the stitching lines an even distance from the edge.

### Stitching—Under

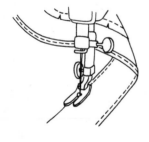

This line of stitching holds a facing securely to the seam allowance, preventing it from rolling to the right side. Slip the work under the presser foot, right side up. The facing should be opened out flat, with the seam allowance lying flat under the facing. Stitch on the facing side close to the seam line. Of course, the stitches do not show on the right side of the garment.

## Tack and Tacking

These terms can vary in meaning. Sometimes directions use the word **tack** to indicate a technique for holding 2 parts of a garment together at a given point. At other times, **tack** refers to a decorative arrangement of stitches to reinforce the end or ends of various construction details where there is strain.

In tacking, a certain amount of freedom is given the fastened part. An otherwise free edge, such as a facing, is attached at a seam line with a hand stitch. Small back, catch, or cross stitches can be used. The stitches never show on the right side of the garment.

**Arrowhead tack.** This is a decorative motif placed at the ends of a slit pocket, pleats, or slits. It is most effective when worked in buttonhole twist or embroidery floss.

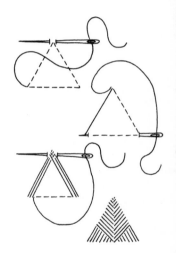

Begin by marking the triangular outline of the tack with basting stitches. The sides should be equal in length, ranging from ⅜ inch to ¾ inch (1 to 2 cm). Bring up the needle at the lower left-hand corner. Carry the thread to the upper point, taking a small stitch under it from right to left.

Insert the needle at the lower right corner, coming up just inside the first stitch. Continue this procedure until the triangle is filled. Be sure to place stitches close together.

**Bar tack.** This tack is less conspicuous than the arrowhead or crow's-foot tack. It can be worked on the right or wrong side of the garment. When made on the right side, take several stitches through the fabric at the required point. Cover these threads with overhand stitches. As this is done, pick up a few fabric threads with each overhand stitch. Sometimes the ends of the bar are finished with small threads.

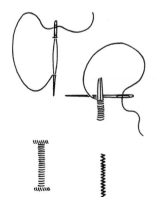

It is also possible to cover the loose threads with overhand stitches without entering the fabric.

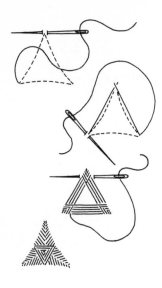

**Crow's-foot tack.** This decorative arrangement of stitches creates an attractive reinforcement at the end of a pleat, pocket, or seam. Buttonhole twist or embroidery floss can be used.

Begin by marking the triangular outline of the tack on the right side of the fabric with chalk pencil or basting stitches. Bring up the needle at the lower left-hand corner. Make a small horizontal stitch under the upper corner from right to left.

Insert the needle at the lower right-hand corner. Take a small diagonal stitch under the point from left to right. Make the next stitch under the lower left-hand corner by slipping the needle under it from left to right. Continue to place stitches close together in this way around the triangle until the space is filled in.

**French tack.** Another method of tacking that allows the sections more freedom employs the French tack. A lining and the outer part of a coat can be held together loosely at the hemline with this type of tack.

Begin by taking a small stitch in one section to fasten the thread. Then make a small stitch in the other section. Make several stitches between the 2 parts, holding them apart the required distance. Hold the threads together with blanket stitches. Keep them even and close together.

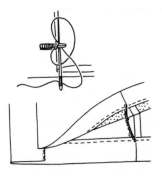

**Tailor's tack.** This type of tack is used for marking. Work with a long double thread that is soft, such as basting thread, darning cotton, or embroidery floss. Because of the thread's softness, the stitches do not slip out of the fabric so easily. A thread in a contrasting color is best.

Take a small stitch through both pattern marking and fabric at the spot to be marked. Leave an end of thread about 1½ inches (3.8 cm) long. Then take a second stitch in the same place, leaving a loop of about 1 inch (2.5 cm). If only 1 point is to be marked, clip the thread 1½ inches (3.8 cm) from the stitch. A tailor's tack has been made.

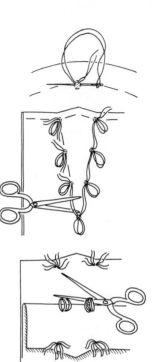

If, however, a series of stitches is to be made, make another tailor's tack where the next marking is needed. Leave the thread slack between the 2 markings.

When the markings are completed, cut the threads between the looped stitches. Remove the pattern carefully. Gently separate the 2 layers of fabric. Cut the threads between the layers. Tiny tufts of thread remain in each piece of material.

## Whip Stitch

This stitch is sometimes used instead of the Overhand Stitch. It forms a tiny, firm seam as 2 finished or folded edges are sewn together.

Place the right sides of the 2 sections together. Take a small stitch over the edges, picking up 1 or 2 threads of the material. Slip the needle through in a slanting position.

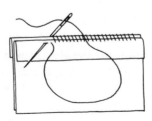

# DECORATIVE SEWING

Many decorative patterns are produced by using easy-to-make sewing stitches, both hand and machine. Lovely appliqués and colorful patchwork and quilting in various forms result. Small stitches, made with precision, are the dominating factor.

## Appliqué

Appliqué is a decorative method for applying a design in one fabric to a background of another. The sewing can be done by hand or machine, with the design taking many forms. For the creative person, appliqué work allows for great freedom of expression. If one desires, however, the motif can be cut from a patterned fabric.

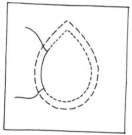

A closely woven fabric with a soft texture, colorfast and preshrunk, is best to use. Calico, muslin, and percale are examples. Interesting effects can be created by using felt.

**Design.** If the design is to be cut from patterned fabric, machine-stitch around the outline of the design. Cut out, leaving a ⅛- to ¼-inch (3 to 6 mm) seam allowance around it.

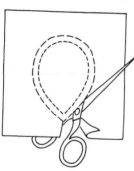

If an original design is being used, make a cardboard pattern as a guide for tracing. Then mark the design on the right side of the fabric the required number of times. Space the designs at least ½ inch (1.3 cm) apart. Machine-stitch around the outline of the design. Cut around the design, leaving a ¼-inch (6 mm) seam allowance.

**Hand appliqué.** Clip the curved edges or corners so the design will lie flat. Turn under the raw edges along stitching line, and press. Some people like to press the fabric over the pattern piece.

To ensure the accurate placement of the motif on the background material, trace the design on it. Then pin the appliqué in position. For an intricate design, baste it in place.

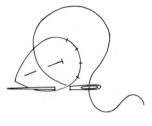
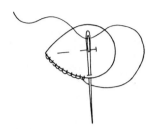

Various stitches can be used to sew the appliqué. The most commonly employed are the Hemming and Slip stitches. They should be kept invisible. For a more decorative effect, try Blanket Stitch.

If a non-ravel fabric such as felt is being used, it is not necessary to leave a seam allowance around the design.

**Machine appliqué.** After the design has been basted in position, place a row of straight machine stitches around the design. The edge may then be finished in one of two ways. A line of straight machine stitches may be covered with small zigzag stitches and the fabric trimmed close to the stitches, or the seam allowance can be trimmed away close to the stitching line before the zigzag stitches are made.

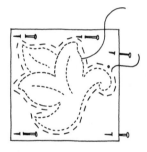

Cover the raw edge and stitching line in either method with closely placed zigzag or satin stitches. Test the stitches for correct length and width. Stitch slowly for best results. Other stitch patterns can be substituted.

Be sure that the ends of the stitching do not overlap. Bring the threads to the underside and tie. Remove the basting stitches.

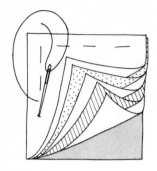

### San Blas Appliqué

This is a unique type of appliqué. In fact, it prob-ably should not be called an appliqué, for instead a layer of fabric being added to create a design, layers of material are cut away, revealing a design in different colors. It is a reverse appliqué, which the Indian women on the San Blas Islands do beautifully.

Before starting the work, plan the design and color combination carefully. Several layers of fabric can be used, sometimes as many as 5 or 6.

After these details have been decided, baste the layers of fabric together around the edges. Cut out the design on the top layer. Use a pair of small, sharp scissors, keeping the cut edge even. This procedure reveals the color of the layer beneath. Clip the corners and curves on the cut edge so they may be turned under. Fold in the edges ⅛ inch (3 mm). Slip-stitch the folded edge to the layer below, using matching thread.

The other layers are finished in the same way, 1 layer at a time, always allowing a bit of the under color to show. An interesting color pat-tern develops.

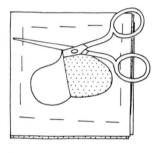

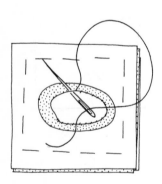

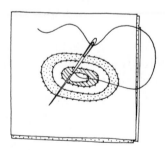

## Patchwork

Although patchwork is generally thought of in connection with quilts, the technique is sometimes used to prepare fabric for other decorative articles, as well as clothing. Pieces of fabric are sewn together to form a geometric design, usually in block form because the work seems easier to handle. Sometimes squares of fabric are sewn together to produce the desired size and shape. Although patchwork is easy to do, it does require a preciseness of detail.

**Design.** There are hundreds of old designs from which to select a patchwork pattern. A few are shown here. By varying fabric and color combinations, the patchwork can be given an individual touch. Of course, original designs can be created.

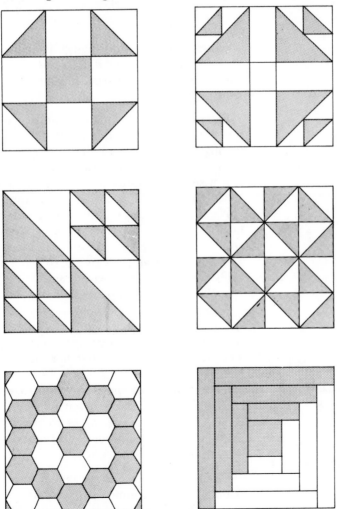

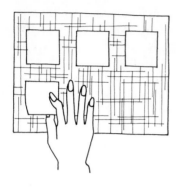

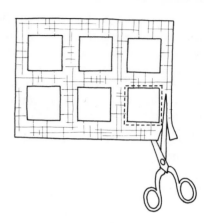

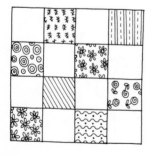

**Fabric.** The material should be firmly woven but soft. Be sure that it is colorfast and pre-shrunk. Broadcloth, calico, muslin, and percale work well.

**Pattern.** After selecting the motifs, trace each piece onto paper. Use this as a pattern for transferring the design to a more durable substance such as cardboard, fine sandpaper, or blotter. It is wise to cut out more than 1 pattern so that it can be replaced as the edges become worn.

Place the pattern on the wrong side of the fabric. Observe the grain lines carefully. The edges of a square should fall on the lengthwise and crosswise grain; a diamond, so that 2 parallel sides are on the lengthwise grain.

Trace around each pattern. Be careful not to pull or stretch the fabric out of position.

Cut out the patch, leaving a ¼-inch (6 mm) seam allowance. Exact cutting is most important. The patches will not fit together unless each is cut accurately.

Keep patches of the same type together in groups. An old-fashioned but efficient way to keep them from scattering is to run a thread through the center of each. This produces stacks of identical patches.

**Piecing.** The patches are joined with a plain seam, using tiny running stitches. An occasional backstitch will strengthen the seam. Place the right sides of the patches together and sew on the marked line. Use a short thread. Watch the corners carefully, especially where more than 2 pieces meet. Be careful not to stretch the edges. Generally, in making a block, the pieces for the design motif are joined from the center to the outside.

The patches can also be sewn together by machine.

**Pressing.** Press each seam on both sides before opening it. This procedure smooths out the stitches. Press each seam open first on the wrong side and then on the right side. This simplifies the sewing, making it easier to match seams. Pressing as each seam is made produces a better result.

**Setting.** This term refers to the assembling of the blocks to form a quilt top. After deciding the position of each block, sew them together in strips. Press seams open. Then join the strips together and press. Be sure the seams match perfectly.

## Quilting—Hand and Machine

Bed coverings seem to be immediately thought of when quilting is mentioned. However, from time to time quilting becomes a fashion feature. Garments and household articles can be made of quilted fabrics.

When several layers of material are held together with stitches in an allover design, the procedure is called quilting. It can be done by hand or machine and with or without a frame.

**Frames and hoops.** For quilting large pieces, such as a quilt, by hand, a frame is a requirement. It holds the material taut and on grain. This makes it possible to take tiny, even stitches more easily.

Frames can be purchased in different sizes. Four strips of wood are held together with clamps. Care should be taken that each corner forms a perfect right angle. Set the frame on sawhorses or 4 straight-back chairs when quilting.

**Materials.** Layers of material form the foundation for quilting stitches. First there is the backing, which will vary, depending on how the quilting is to be used. For a quilt, the top fabric can also be used for the backing. Sheeting or muslin in a good quality are possibilities.

For a garment in which the quilting is not to be used for a reversible effect, a firmly woven cheesecloth makes a good backing.

On the backing is placed an interlining or filler, sometimes referred to as padding. It can be made of cotton or polyester batting or wadding, polyester fleece, or even a lightweight blanket.

The top, or outside, fabric can vary from calico to velvet. It depends on the effect desired. But whatever type is chosen, it should be of good quality, firmly woven, and soft.

**Preparation.** Assembling the 3 layers should be done carefully. Place the backing fabric, wrong side up, on the floor or a large smooth surface. On this lay the filler or interlining. Keep it free from wrinkles or lumps. Over this lay the outside material, right side up.

To hold the layers together evenly, begin by basting diagonally from corner to corner, starting in the center. Work to the outer edge. Add other rows of basting stitches, evenly spaced. Then baste around the outer edges.

**Hand quilting.** Work with a short quilting needle, threaded with a short length of quilting thread, which is strong and smooth, with less possibility of knotting. Conceal the knot in the filler. Then bring the needle through the top layer.

There are 2 ways to make the stitches. Tiny running stitches can be used if the material is thin enough to allow the needle to pick up several stitches before drawing the thread through the material. However, for thicker material move the needle up and down in 2 motions. Although this method takes longer, it is easier to make even stitches with it.

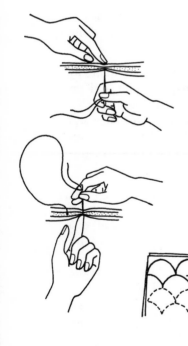

To work this way, put the first, or index, finger of the left hand over the point through which the needle should appear. Insert the needle from below, pushing it upward through the material with the right hand. When it touches the left finger on the top side, reverse the position of the hands. Pull the needle through with the right hand. With the left hand below the material, push the needle down through the 3 layers with the right hand. When the needle touches the first finger, reverse the position of the hands so the needle can be pulled through. Continue to make the stitches in this stabbing fashion until the quilting design is completed.

**Machine quilting.** Although quilting is considered a hand art, simple designs and parallel lines can be stitched by machine. Be sure the layers are securely basted together before beginning to stitch.

For stitching straight lines, draw a line along 1 edge of the piece to be quilted. Stitch with a long stitch on the marked line. To regulate and guide the placement of the stitching lines, use a quilting bar or quilter. It can be adjusted so the distance between the rows can be controlled. Let the bar ride along the stitched line as the second row is stitched. Continue this way across the fabric, always stitching in the same direction. Turn the fabric. Repeat the procedure, crossing the rows of stitching. This creates a design pattern, which might be a series of squares or diamonds.

For quilting a patterned design in fabric or one that has been marked on the top fabric, start stitching in the center of the work, continuing to the outer edge. Do not stitch over a stitched line twice. Fasten the thread ends on the wrong side by tying them.

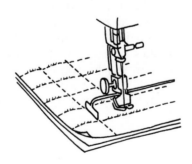

## Special Types of Quilting

**Corded Quilting.** In this form of quilting the outline of the design is given more prominence through the use of cord. The technique is most effective when used for parts of a design such as a stem or vine.

Before starting to quilt, mark the design on a lightweight backing. Baste the piece to the wrong side of the top piece. Firmly woven cheesecloth or fine muslin work well.

Begin with 2 parallel lines of quilting stitches to form a casing. Then run a blunt needle threaded with upholstery cord or soft rug yarn through the casing. The strands should fill the space between the stitches.

Never allow the needle to penetrate the top of the quilting pieces. To create the most pleasing effect, bring the needle through the backing material at a curve or turn. Then insert the needle again at this point, leaving a small loop if necessary, to keep the shape of the design.

**English Quilting.** This type of quilting produces an embroidered effect. Backstitches made with a thick mercerized cotton create a solid line.

Select a simple design. Transfer it to the right side of the top material. Attach this material to the filler or interlining with rows of basting stitches placed 2 inches (5 cm) apart. Do this in both the horizontal and vertical directions.

With the material properly prepared, backstitch firmly along the design lines.

**Trapunto Quilting.** This type of quilting is sometimes referred to as Italian quilting. Small design areas are stuffed to give a puffed or raised effect. Flower petals, leaves, and such design areas are given a 3-dimensional effect when this quilting technique is used.

Transfer the design to lightweight muslin. Double lines are needed to mark the parts of the design to be padded. Baste the designs to the wrong side of the material to be decorated.

Take small, even running stitches along the design lines. Make the stitches through both thicknesses of fabric. Be sure they appear even on the right side. After quilting the entire design with running stitches, begin the stuffing.

For areas that are formed by 2 parallel rows of stitching, thread a blunt-end needle with soft, heavy cotton rug yarn, wool, or cord. Gently spread the fabric threads on the backing so the needle can be inserted between the rows of stitches. To turn a definite curve, bring the needle to the surface. Then insert it again in the same place. To turn a sharp angle, bring the needle out. Leave the yarn slack and insert the needle again close to where it emerged.

For small areas, poke small bits of batting between the 2 layers of fabric. Stuff each motif evenly and firmly so it is raised in relief along the surface.

When the complete design has been padded, tuck any protruding ends into the holes made by the needle. If this is impossible, clip the ends close to the backing.

## Tying a Quilt

This is another method for holding layers of fabric together. Make a straight ¼-inch (6 mm) stitch through the material. On the right side, tie the ends of the heavy yarn or thread in a firm double knot. Cut the yarn, leaving a ½-inch (1.3 cm) end. Continue to scatter the knots over the surface of the quilt. Be sure the ends are trimmed to the same length. If wool yarn is used, the ends can be steamed to produce a tufted effect.

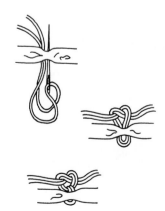

# Part VII

# Tatting

Tatting is a form of lace made with a shuttle and thread. The knots and loops that are formed are drawn into circles and semicircles, creating a fragile effect. Although its origin is in doubt, tatting might be traced back to the oldest of all kinds of lace, known as macramé. Examples of this type of lace were found in the tombs of Egypt. However, tatting as we know it probably came from Italy in the sixteenth century. As in all other types of needlework, tatting has passed through various phases of popularity.

On the next few pages some suggestions for perfecting the art of tatting are given. Although it seems difficult to do, it can be executed by those with nimble fingers and the patience to practice.

## ABBREVIATIONS AND TERMS

An understanding of the abbreviations and terms makes the reading of directions easier. The ones most commonly found are listed here:

| | |
|---|---|
| Beginning | beg |
| Chain | ch |
| Close | cl |
| Double stitch or knot | d or ds |
| Join | j |
| Picot | p |
| Picot chain | p ch |
| Picot—long | lp |
| Picot—small | sm p |
| Reverse work | rw |
| Ring | r |
| Ring—large | lr |
| Ring—small | sr or sm r |
| Separated | sep |
| Skip | sk |
| Space | sp |
| Repeat instructions following asterisks as many times as specified | * |

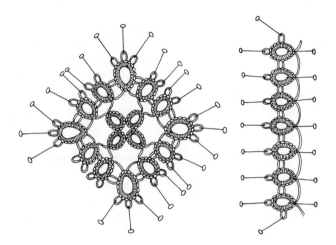

## Blocking

To give a finished look to a completed article, it should be shaped and pressed. Before starting the process, launder the article if necessary. Place the article on a well-padded board with the right side down. Gently smooth it out until its shape and measurements are correct. Pin each picot along the outer edge. If the article has been laundered, cover with a dry cloth before pressing. If the article is dry, use a damp cloth.

Do not remove the pins until the article is thoroughly dry.

## Pressing

Some tatters find that, when making such things as doilies and motifs, it is easier to work if the article is pressed after every 2 or 3 rows. This also seems to make the tatting appear prettier.

Put the work on a thick pad. Arrange in the correct shape. Cover with a dry cloth and a damp one. Press until the article is dry.

## Right Side

In determining the right side of the article, use these factors:

• If the design has more rings than chains, the right side of the stitches or rings becomes the right side of the finished article.

• If the design has more chains than rings, the right side of the stitches or chains becomes the right side of the finished article.

# BASIC STITCHES AND TECHNIQUES

Tatting is often thought to be difficult. However, once the technique for making the basic stitch is learned, the procedure becomes automatic. The shuttle seems to fly in graceful movements.

The basic stitch is used to form rings, picots, and chains for a variety of lacy designs. It should be remembered that all stitches are made on the shuttle thread. This makes it possible for the stitches to slide along this thread. Unless they do, the tatting cannot proceed.

## Chain—Working with Two Threads

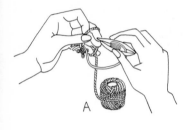

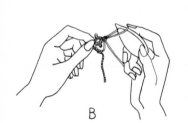

Some tatting designs are made with chains, as well as with rings and picots. Rings are made with the shuttle thread placed completely around the left hand. Chains, however, cannot be made with the thread held in this position. They are made when the thread is placed halfway around the hand. Therefore, in order to make both rings and chains, 2 threads must be used. By using 2 threads, more tatting designs can be made.

The 2 threads can be wound in different ways—on 2 shuttles, or on a ball and a shuttle. It seems easier to differentiate between the 2 threads when a ball and a shuttle are used. But whichever method is employed, tie the 2 ends of thread together.

When making a ring, hold and manipulate the shuttle thread in the regular manner. When the ring is finished, begin to make the chain.

Reverse the tatting so that the base of the ring is held between the thumb and first (index) finger. Then place the ball thread over the back of the fingers in the same way as for the shuttle thread, but wind it twice around the little finger instead of carrying it around the hand (A).

Use the shuttle to make the stitches over the ball thread in the same way as for making rings. They create the chain. When the chain is completed, draw the stitches close together.

Put the ball thread down. Reverse work, turning it so that the shuttle thread is at top.

Start to make the next ring with the shuttle thread (B).

## Double Stitch

This is the basic stitch or knot used in tatting. It slides smoothly along the thread and is made in 2 parts. It is a form of a clove hitch knot.

For the first half of the stitch, pull the shuttle thread out the correct amount, about 12 inches (30.5 cm). Keep the left and right hands on an equal level (A).

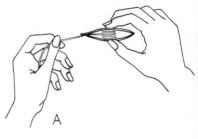

A

Wrap the thread around the left hand in the correct position. Place the shuttle thread over the back of the right hand. The little finger may be extended slightly to support the thread. Some tatters prefer to pass the shuttle thread across the palm and around the back of the little finger.

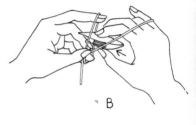

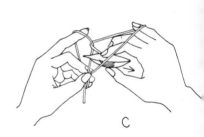

B

With the hands and thread in the proper position, bring the right hand toward the left hand. Pass the flat top of the shuttle under the ring thread that extends between the first or index, and middle fingers (B). Be sure to hold on to the shuttle. The ring thread will slide between the shuttle and the fingers. Then slide it back over the ring thread and under the shuttle thread (C).

C

In doing this, lower the middle finger of the left hand so that the ring thread falls slack. Notice that the shuttle thread is encircled by a loose loop that is made by the ring of thread in the left hand. It is most important that the shuttle thread be kept taut until this loop is in position. So, after the middle finger has been dropped, pull the shuttle thread taut. The thread slips off the right hand. The relaxation of the thread in the left hand and the tautness of the shuttle thread allow the loop to turn over.

Then slowly raise the middle finger of the left hand so that the loop slides into position between the thumb and the first finger (D).

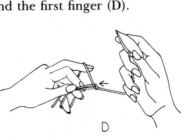

D

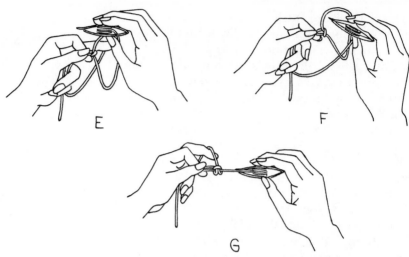

E

F

G

For the second half of the double stitch, the procedure is reversed. Let the shuttle thread fall slack. It is not necessary to wrap it around the right hand.

Bring the shuttle over the thread that is held in the left hand between the thumb and first finger (E). Then slip it under the ring thread and over the shuttle thread (F).

Lower the middle finger of the left hand. Draw the shuttle thread taut. Hold it this way until the second half of the stitch is completed.

Slowly raise the middle finger of the left hand, allowing the loop to fall into position between the thumb and first finger (G). This completes the second half of the double stitch.

The movements of the fingers that have been mentioned should be so thoroughly learned that they can be done automatically and at just the right moment. Unless they are, problems will develop. If the shuttle thread does not slide easily when it is pulled, one of the steps has been neglected. The stitch must be made again.

### Double Stitch—Left-handed

For a left-handed tatter, the directions remain the same. By placing a mirror to the left of each drawing, it is possible to check the position of the fingers and thread.

## Finishing Thread Ends

To give the work a finished look, whip-stitch
the ends to the wrong side. Make the stitches
over a cut end, until it is completely covered.
Work through the tatting with a slanting stitch.
Use a sewing thread in a matching color.

### Holding the Shuttle—Left-handed

For the left-handed person, the shuttle is held in the left hand, in the same position as that used by the right-handed person, except that the point of the shuttle faces the right hand.

### Holding the Shuttle—Right-handed

For the right-handed person, the shuttle is held in the right hand. After unwinding about 12 inches (30.5 cm) of thread, pick up the shuttle so that it can be held in a horizontal position between the thumb and first or index, finger. The thread should come from the back of the bobbin with the pointed end of the shuttle facing the left hand. The other fingers should be kept on a level with the first finger.

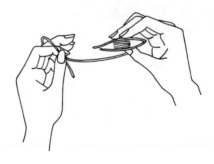

## Holding Thread—Left-handed

For the left-handed person, hold the thread with the right hand. Follow the directions given for the right-handed person.

## Holding Thread—Right-handed

For the right-handed person, the thread is held with the left hand. Place the end of the thread between thumb and first (index) finger. Then spread the middle, ring, and little fingers. Bring the thread around these fingers. Place it between the thumb and first finger, forming a circle. Hold it securely (A).

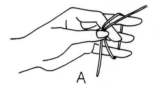

Then bend the little finger and ring finger in order to hold the thread against the palm of the hand. Stretch the middle finger so that it catches the loose part of the circle (B). At first the fingers will feel strained, but keep adjusting the thread until their position seems natural.

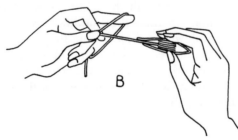

## Joining Threads

When it is necessary to attach a new thread, fasten it close to the base of the last ring or chain, using a square knot. Be sure not to join a new thread in a ring, as the knot will not pass through the double stitch.

## Joining Two Rings

After 1 ring has been completed, put the thread around the left hand, ready to make the second ring.

Start the second ring a short distance from the first ring. Usually this distance is about ¼ of the circumference of the finished ring. Make the desired number of double stitches to the point of the picot.

Insert the pointed end of the shuttle through the last picot of the first ring. Catch the thread that is around the left hand.

Draw the thread through the picot until a loop is formed large enough to allow the shuttle to be inserted (A). Then draw the shuttle through the loop and pull the shuttle thread tight. Remember to raise the middle finger of the left hand slowly to draw up the loop.

This procedure joins the rings. The first half of a double stitch is made. The second half of the stitch can now be made. Continue to make the ring (B).

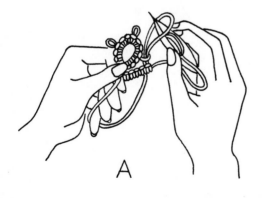

A

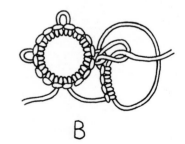

B

## Josephine Knot

This small ornamental ring is formed by using stitches made of only the first half of the double stitch.

## Knot

A knot is formed when a stitch is made with the shuttle thread instead of onto it. No longer will the stitch slide. The work is at a standstill until the knot is unpicked with a pin or point of shuttle.

## Leaving a Space

The distance between rings depends on the thread being used. For fine thread, the distance is usually about ¼ inch (6 mm); for coarse thread, such as pearl cotton, about ½ inch (1.3 mm).

## Picot

A picot is a loop of thread placed between 2 double stitches. It is used as a decorative touch and a joining device. When reading directions, remember that the term **picot** refers only to the loop. The double stitch that secures the loop is not included.

Begin with several double stitches. At the point where the picot is to the placed, make the first half of a double stitch. Then, as it is being slipped into place, stop about ¼ inch (6 mm) from the last completed double stitch, leaving a small amount of thread between the last stitch and the one being constructed.

Continue, making the second half of the double stitch. When it is completed, draw the stitch close to the other stitches. The loop that is formed becomes the picot.

## Reverse Stitch

Turn the tatting so the base of the ring that
has just been completed is at the top of the work.
Make the next ring in the usual way.

Make one half of ring. Remove work from
hand. Turn over and put on hand so that the
thread that was under the hand is now over it.
Make the other half of the ring with second shuttle. Take work from hand and turn over. Close
ring, using first shuttle.

It is possible to make an edging by reversing
the work.

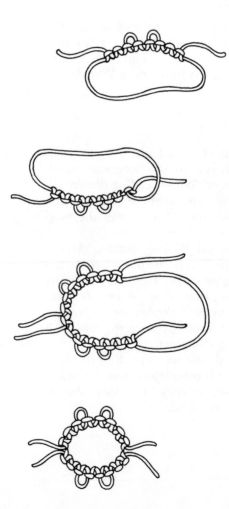

## Ring

All tatting designs contain rings. They form the basis for the pattern.

Make the desired number of double stitches. Hold the stitches firmly between the thumb and first, or index, finger of the left hand. Pull the shuttle thread so that the first and last stitches meet, forming a ring.

## Twisted Thread

Sometimes the shuttle thread becomes twisted. When this happens, let the shuttle dangle a moment, untwisting the thread.

## Winding Thread on Bobbin

This is the first step in tatting. Fasten the thread with a knot to the bar or bobbin inside the shuttle. If there is a hole in the bobbin center, put the thread through it and then tie the knot. If the bobbin is removable, wind it before replacing it in the shuttle. Always wind the thread evenly, layer upon layer, around the bobbin. Never let the thread extend beyond the edge.

## Working with Two Colors

To make rings in 2 different colors, wind the thread on separate shuttles. When working, alternate the shuttles, using first one and then the other. The shuttle that is not in use can just hang down.

The second color can also be used for a chain. In this case, the second color can be worked over the first, following the directions described in making a chain with a shuttle and a ball.

## MATERIALS AND TOOLS

Tatting requires very little equipment: only a shuttle and thread are needed.

### Shuttle

The shuttle is made of various materials, such as bone, plastic, and metal. It has 2 blades that are held together by a bar or bobbin in the center. The blades are elongated ovals with pointed ends. The blades should be close enough together at the ends so that the thread does not slip out of the shuttle too easily.

Some shuttles are made with a hook in one end. This type seems more difficult to use.

The shuttle is available in various sizes. Usually one about 2½ to 3 inches (6.5 to 7.5 cm) in length and ¾ to 1 inch (2 to 2.5 cm) in width is best for fine work. A longer and broader one can be used for coarse work, but it is more clumsy to use, making the work slower to do.

### Thread

Usually a fine thread specially made for tatting is used for a lacy effect. Coarser threads may, however, be employed if they have an adequate amount of twist. Always purchase the type of thread suggested in the directions.

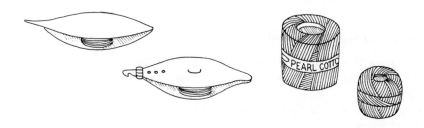

## STITCH PATTERNS

By using rings and picots in various sizes plus chains in different lengths, innumerable designs can be created for edgings, insertions, and motifs. Lacy items can be made for the home as well as for personal use. Doilies, tablecloths, collars, and baby bonnets are a few of them. Once simple designs are mastered, more ambitious projects can be undertaken.

A few design suggestions are shown on the following pages. They begin with the simple, proceeding to the more complicated.

### Edging (A)

This is one of the easiest trims to make. A series of small rings are joined and spiked with dainty picots.

For the **first ring,** make 4 double stitches. Follow with 1 picot, 4 double stitches, 1 picot, 4 double stitches, 1 picot. End with 4 double stitches. Close the ring.

For the **second ring,** start ¼ inch (6 mm) from the first, thus leaving a space. Make 4 double stitches. Then join the first and second rings as a picot is made. This will link the last picot of the first ring to the first picot of the second ring. Follow with 4 double stitches, 1 picot, 4 double stitches, 1 picot, ending with 4 double stitches.

For the **third ring,** repeat the procedure for making the second. Continue in this manner for the desired length.

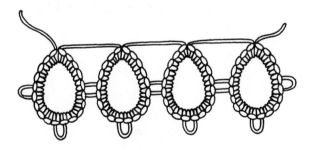

## Edging (B)

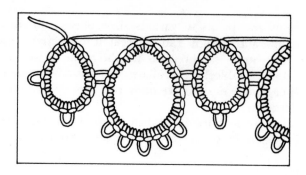

Rings in 2 sizes give importance to this edging. By adding extra picots, it seems to have a more decorative look.

For the **first small ring,** begin with 5 double stitches. Follow with 1 picot, 5 double stitches, 1 picot, 5 double stitches, 1 picot, ending with 5 double stitches.

For the **second ring,** which is larger, begin with 5 double stitches, leaving an appropriate space between rings. At the first picot, join the ring to the last picot of the previous ring. Follow with 5 double stitches. For the arch of picots, take 1 picot, 2 double stitches, 1 picot, 2 double stitches, 1 picot, 2 double stitches, 1 picot, 2 double stitches, 1 picot. Then make 5 double stitches, 1 picot, and 5 double stitches.

For the **third ring,** use the directions for the first ring. Join it to the second ring at the first picot.

Alternate the making of the large and small rings for the required length, ending with a small ring.

## Edging (C)

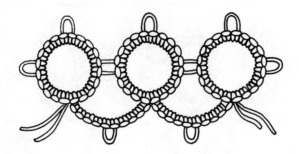

A scalloped effect has been added to this tatting design, which can be used as an edging or an insertion. To create this look, a chain is looped between 2 rings. The rings are made with the shuttle thread; the chain, with a second thread.

For the **first ring,** use 5 double stitches, 1 picot, 5 double stitches, 1 picot, 5 double stitches, 1 picot, ending with 5 double stitches.

For the **chain,** make 5 double stitches, 1 picot, and 5 double stitches.

For the **second ring,** begin with 5 double stitches. Make 1 picot, joining the first and second rings. Follow with 5 double stitches, 1 picot, 5 double stitches, 1 picot, ending with 5 double stitches.

Continue this sequence of stitches, alternating the rings and chains until the edging is the required length.

## Edging (D)

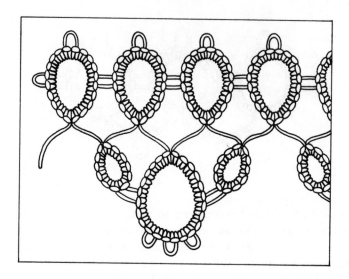

This arrangement of rings provides a wider, more elaborate edging. All of the tatting is done with the shuttle thread.

For the **first ring,** start with 5 double stitches. Follow with 1 picot, 5 double stitches, 1 picot, 5 double stitches, 1 picot, ending with 5 double stitches.

For the **second ring,** which is a small one, make 6 double stitches, 1 picot, and 6 double stitches.

For the **third ring,** make 5 double stitches and 1 picot, joining the first and third rings. Follow with 5 double stitches, 1 picot, 5 double stitches, 1 picot, ending with 5 double stitches.

For the **fourth ring,** which is a large one, make 6 double stitches and 1 picot, joining the second and fourth rings. Follow with 4 double stitches, 1 picot, 2 double stitches, 1 picot, 2 double stitches, 1 picot, 4 double stitches, 1 picot, ending with 6 double stitches.

For the **fifth ring,** repeat the directions for the third ring.

For the **sixth ring,** make 6 double stitches. Then join rings, ending with 6 double stitches.

Repeat until the edging is the required length.

**Edging (E)**

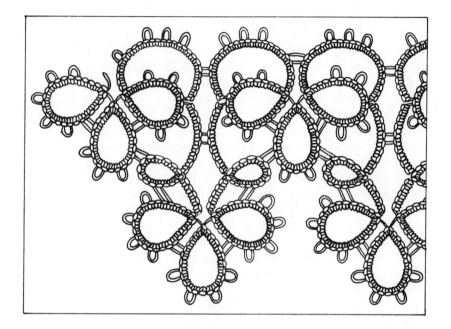

This beautiful edging is made with a shuttle thread plus a second one.

For the **first ring,** which is part of a 3-leaf group, begin with 5 double stitches. Follow with 1 picot, 3 double stitches, 1 picot, 3 double stitches, 1 picot, 3 double stitches, 1 picot, 3 double stitches, 1 picot, 3 double stitches, 1 picot, ending with 5 double stitches.

For the **second leaf ring,** start with 5 double stitches. At the first picot, join the 2 rings. Follow with 3 double stitches, 1 picot, 3 double stitches, 1 picot, 3 double stitches, 1 picot, 3 double stitches, 1 picot, 3 double stitches, 1 picot, ending with 5 double stitches.

For the **third leaf ring,** start with 5 double stitches. At the first picot, join to preceding ring. Follow with 3 double stitches, 1 picot, 3 double stitches, 1 picot, 3 double stitches, 1 picot, 3 double stitches, 1 picot, 3 double stitches, 1 picot, ending with 5 double stitches.

For the **chain,** begin with 5 double stitches, follow with 1 picot, 5 double stitches, 1 picot, 3 double stitches, 1 picot, 3 double stitches, 1 picot, 5 double stitches, 1 picot, 5 double stitches, and then join to center of unattached picots of preceding leaf ring.

For the **next chain,** make 5 double stitches, 1 picot, and 5 double stitches.

For the **fourth ring,** make 5 double stitches, then join to second picot of second or center leaf ring. Follow with 5 double stitches, 1 picot, and 5 double stitches.

For a **chain,** make 5 double stitches.

For the **fifth ring,** which is the first of the second grouping of 3 leaves, start with 5 double stitches. At the first picot, join this and the fourth ring. Follow with 3 double stitches, 1 picot, 3 double stitches, 1 picot, 3 double stitches, 1 picot, 3 double stitches, 1 picot, 3 double stitches, 1 picot, ending with 5 double stitches.

For the **sixth ring,** start with 5 double stitches. At the first picot, join this and the fifth ring. Follow with 3 double stitches, 1 picot, 3 double stitches, 1 picot, 3 double stitches, 1 picot, 3 double stitches, 1 picot, 3 double stitches, 1 picot, ending with 5 double stitches.

For the **seventh ring,** begin with 5 double stitches. At the first picot, join this and the sixth ring. Follow with 3 double stitches, 1 picot, 3 double stitches, 1 picot, 3 double stitches, 1 picot, 3 double stitches, 1 picot, 3 double stitches, 1 picot, ending with 5 double stitches.

For the **next chain,** take 5 double stitches.

For the **eighth ring,** start with 5 double stitches. At the first picot, join this and the seventh ring. Follow with 5 double stitches, 1 picot, and 5 double stitches.

For the **next chain,** make 5 double stitches. Join at the first picot. Then make 5 double stitches and another picot.

For the **next chain,** start with 5 double stitches. Join at the first picot. Follow with 5 double stitches, 1 picot, 3 double stitches, 1 picot, 3 double stitches, 1 picot, 5 double stitches, 1 picot, ending with 5 double stitches.

Repeat this sequence of stitches as many times as required.

## Edging or Insertion

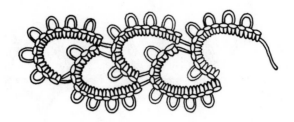

Picots and chains dominate this type of tatting, creating a lacy, scroll-like effect. Work with a shuttle and a second thread.

For the **first chain,** begin by making 2 double stitches. Follow with 1 picot, 2 double stitches, 1 picot, 2 double stitches, 1 picot, 2 double stitches, 1 picot, 2 double stitches, 1 picot, 2 double stitches, 1 picot, ending with 2 double stitches.

Reverse work.

For the **second chain,** begin by making 2 double stitches. Follow with 1 picot, 2 double stitches, 1 picot, 2 double stitches, 1 picot, 2 double stitches, 1 picot, 2 double stitches, 1 picot, 2 double stitches, 1 picot, ending with 2 double stitches.

Join this chain to the first chain at the second picot.

Repeat this procedure until the tatting is the required length.

## Edging and Insertion (A)

These directions are for a delicate edging and matching insertion.

**Edging.** For the **first ring,** which is the larger, begin with 3 double stitches. Follow with a series of 9 picots, made with this sequence of stitches: 1 picot, 3 double stitches, 1 picot, 3 double stitches, 1 picot, 3 double stitches, 1 picot, 3 double stitches, 1 picot, 3 double stitches, 1 picot, 3 double stitches, 1 picot, 3 double stitches, 1 picot, 3 double stitches, 1 picot, ending with 3 double stitches.

Repeat the following procedure as many times as needed for required length.

* For the **chain,** make 5 double stitches, 1 picot, 2 double stitches, 1 picot, 2 double stitches, 1 picot, ending with 5 double stitches.

For the **second ring,** which is the smaller one, begin with 5 double stitches. Join in the eighth picot of the large ring. End with 5 double stitches.

For the **third ring,** which is the second small one, make 5 double stitches, 1 picot, and 5 double stitches.

For the **next chain,** make 5 double stitches, 1 picot, 2 double stitches, 1 picot, 2 double stitches, 1 picot, ending with 5 double stitches.

For the **next large ring,** make 3 double stitches, 1 picot, 3 double stitches, join in picot of small ring, 3 double stitches, 1 picot, 3 double stitches, 1 picot, 3 double stitches, 1 picot, 3 double stitches, 1 picot, 3 double stitches, 1 picot, 3 double stitches, 1 picot, 3 double stitches, 1 picot, ending with 3 double stitches. *

**Insertion.** A band of insertion follows the same sequence of stitches and picots for the first row.

For the **second row,** begin by making a **large ring,** using 3 double stitches, 1 picot, 3 double stitches, 1 picot, 3 double stitches, 1 picot, 3 double stitches, 1 picot, 3 double stitches. Then join in fifth picot of large ring of previous row, and continue with 3 double stitches, 1 picot, 3 double stitches, 1 picot, 3 double stitches, 1 picot, 3 double stitches, 1 picot, ending with 3 double stitches.

Repeat the following procedure as many times as required.

* For the **chain,** make 5 double stitches, 1 picot, 2 double stitches, 1 picot, 2 double stitches, 1 picot, ending with 5 double stitches.

For the **small ring,** start with 5 double stitches. Join in eighth picot of large ring. End with 5 double stitches.

For the **next small ring,** make 5 double stitches, 1 picot, ending with 5 double stitches.

For the **next chain,** start with 5 double stitches. Follow with 1 picot, 2 double stitches, 1 picot, 2 double stitches, 1 picot, ending with 5 double stitches.

For the **large ring,** begin with 3 double stitches, 1 picot, 3 double stitches. Then join in picot of small ring, 3 double stitches, 1 picot, 3 double stitches, 1 picot, 3 double stitches. Then join in center picot of next large ring of last row. Follow with 3 double stitches, 1 picot, 3 double stitches, 1 picot, 3 double stitches, 1 picot, 3 double stitches, 1 picot, ending with 3 double stitches. *

# Edging and Insertion (B)

A scalloped edge gives this matching edging and insertion added interest. Chains create the scallops. It is worked with a shuttle and second thread.

**Edging.** Repeat the following procedure for the required length of the edging.

* For the **first ring,** begin with 3 double stitches. Follow with 1 picot, 3 double stitches, 1 picot, 3 double stitches, 1 picot, ending with 3 double stitches.

For the **chain,** begin with 9 double stitches. Follow with 1 picot, 2 double stitches, 1 picot, 2 double stitches, 1 picot, ending with 9 double stitches.

For the **next ring,** start with 3 double stitches, 1 picot, 3 double stitches. Then join in center picot of preceding ring. Continue with 3 double stitches, 1 picot, ending with 3 double stitches. *

**Insertion.** Follow the same sequence of rings and chains as used for the edging for the first row of the insertion.

For the **second row,** start with a **ring,** beginning with 3 double stitches. Then join in first picot of ring in preceding row. Follow with 3 double stitches, 1 picot, 3 double stitches, 1 picot, ending with 3 double stitches.

Repeat the following sequence of stitches and picots for the required length.

For the **chain,** begin with 9 double stitches. Follow with 1 picot, 2 double stitches, 1 picot, 2 double stitches, 1 picot, ending with 9 double stitches.

For the **next ring,** make 3 double stitches, 1 picot, 3 double stitches. Then join in center picot of last ring, 3 double stitches, join in picot of next ring of preceding row, ending with 3 double stitches.

For the **next ring,** start with 3 double stitches. Then join in picot of ring in preceding row. Follow with 3 double stitches, 1 picot, 3 double stitches, 1 picot, ending with 3 double stitches.

## Medallion (A)

This motif can be used to add a decorative touch or be joined with other medallions to produce an article such as a place mat. It is versatile in that it looks equally attractive as a square or a diamond.

For the **first ring,** which forms the middle of the motif, begin with 6 double stitches. Follow with 1 picot and 6 double stitches.

For the **second ring,** start with 3 double stitches. Follow with 1 picot, 3 double stitches, 1 picot, 2 double stitches, 1 picot, 2 double stitches, 1 picot, and 4 double stitches.

Follow with a **Josephine knot** made with 6 half stitches.

For the **third ring,** begin with 2 double stitches. Join picot with the last picot of the previous ring. Follow with 4 double stitches, 1 picot, 2 double stitches, 1 picot, 2 double stitches, 1 picot, 2 double stitches, 1 picot, 4 double stitches, 1 picot, ending with 2 double stitches.

Follow with a **Josephine knot** made with 6 half stitches.

For the **fourth ring,** begin with 4 double stitches. Join rings with this picot. Follow with 2 double stitches, 1 picot, 2 double stitches, 1 picot, 3 double stitches, 1 picot, ending with 3 double stitches.

Repeat the preceding sequence a total of 4 times.

## Medallion (B)

This motif is made with rings of different sizes and shapes. It can be used alone or in combination with other medallions.

For the **inner ring,** start with 4 double stitches. Follow with 1 picot, 4 double stitches, 1 picot, 4 double stitches, 1 picot, 4 double stitches, 1 picot, 4 double stitches, 1 picot, four double stitches, 1 picot, 4 double stitches, 1 picot, 4 double stitches, 1 picot. Tie together for eighth picot but do not cut thread.

For the **second ring,** begin with 8 double stitches. Follow with 1 picot, 3 double stitches, 1 picot, 3 double stitches, 1 picot, 3 double stitches, 1 picot, 3 double stitches, 1 picot, 3 double stitches, 1 picot, 3 double stitches, 1 picot, three double stitches, 1 picot, 3 double stitches, 1 picot, 3 double stitches, 1 picot, 8 double stitches. Then join rings.

For the **third ring,** begin with 8 double stitches. Join to third picot on previous ring. Follow with 3 double stitches, 1 picot, 3 double stitches, 1 picot, 3 double stitches, 1 picot, 8 double stitches. Then join rings.

For the **fourth ring,** start with 8 double stitches. Join rings. Follow with 3 double stitches, 1 picot, 3 double stitches, 1 picot, 3 double stitches, 1 picot, 3 double stitches, 1 picot, 3 double stitches, 1 picot, 3 double stitches, 1 picot, 3 double stitches, 1 picot, 3 double stitches, 1 picot, 3 double stitches, 1 picot, 8 double stitches. Join rings.

Repeat the last 2 rings 4 times in all, alternating one with the other to complete medallion.


**Medallion (C)**

This starlike motif is made with 5 rounded points.

For the **inner ring,** begin with 5 double stitches. Follow with 1 picot, 5 double stitches, 1 picot, 5 double stitches, 1 picot, 5 double stitches, 1 picot, 5 double stitches, 1 picot. Tie ends for fifth picot and cut.

For the **next ring,** start with 2 double stitches, 1 picot, 2 double stitches, 1 picot, 2 double stitches. Join to center ring. Then make 2 double stitches, 1 picot, 2 double stitches, 1 picot, ending with 2 double stitches.

For the **chain,** make 5 double stitches.

For the **third ring,** begin with 2 double stitches. Follow with 1 picot, 2 double stitches, 1 picot, 2 double stitches, 1 picot, 2 double stitches, 1 picot, 2 double stitches, 1 picot, 2 double stitches, 1 picot, 2 double stitches, 1 picot, 2 double stitches, 1 picot, 2 double stitches, 1 picot, 2 double stitches, 1 picot, 2 double stitches, 1 picot, 2 double stitches. Eleven picots have just been made.

For the **chain,** make 3 double stitches. Follow with 1 picot, 3 double stitches, 1 picot, 3 double stitches, 1 picot, 3 double stitches, 1 picot, 3 double stitches.

For the **fourth ring,** start with 4 double stitches. Join with second picot of large ring. Then make 4 double stitches.

For the **chain,** make 3 double stitches. Follow with 1 picot, 3 double stitches, 1 picot, 3 double stitches, 1 picot, 3 double stitches, 1 picot, 3 double stitches, 1 picot, 3 double stitches, 1 picot, and 3 double stitches.

For the **fifth ring,** start with 4 double stitches. Join to fifth picot of larger ring. End with 4 double stitches.

For the **chain,** make 3 double stitches. Then follow with 1 picot, 3 double stitches, 1 picot, 3 double stitches, 1 picot, 3 double stitches, 1 picot, 3 double stitches. Join to ring at this point, and then make 5 double stitches.

For the **chain,** make 5 double stitches.

Repeat this procedure 5 times in all to complete motif.

## Medallion (D)

Two shuttles are used to make this beautiful motif.

For the **large inner ring,** start with 4 double stitches. Follow with 1 picot, 4 double stitches, 1 picot, 4 double stitches, 1 picot, 4 double stitches, 1 picot, 4 double stitches, 1 picot, 4 double stitches, 1 picot, 4 double stitches, 1 picot, 4 double stitches. Tie together for eighth picot and cut.

With the first shuttle, start the **first 3-leaved clover design.** For the first ring, begin with 5 double stitches. Follow with 1 picot, 3 double stitches, 1 picot, 3 double stitches, 1 picot, 3 double stitches, 1 picot, 5 double stitches.

For the **second ring,** start with 5 double stitches. Join first picot to the picot on the first ring. Follow with 3 double stitches, 1 picot, 3 double stitches, 1 picot, 3 double stitches, 1 picot, 3 double stitches, 1 picot, 3 double stitches, 1 picot, ending with 5 double stitches.

For the **third ring,** start with 5 double stitches. Join the first picot to the picot on the second ring. Follow with 3 double stitches, 1 picot, 3 double stitches, 1 picot, 3 double stitches, 1 picot, ending with 5 double stitches.

For the **chain,** make 10 double stitches. Then, with second shuttle, make a ring of 6 double stitches, 1 picot, 6 double stitches, joining before making another 10 double stitches.

Repeat the 3-leaved clover design 8 times in all to complete medallion.

**Medallion (E)**

This circular motif features a series of picots. It is worked with 1 shuttle and a second thread.

For the **inner large ring,** begin with 4 double stitches. Follow with 1 picot, 4 double stitches, 1 picot, 4 double stitches, 1 picot, 4 double stitches, 1 picot, 4 double stitches, 1 picot, 4 double stitches, 1 picot, 4 double stitches, 1 picot, 4 double stitches. Tie together for eighth picot and cut.

For the **second ring,** begin with 2 double stitches. Follow with 1 picot, 2 double stitches, 1 picot, 2 double stitches, 1 picot, 2 double stitches. Then join to inner ring. Follow with 2 double stitches, 1 picot, 2 double stitches, 1 picot, 2 double stitches, 1 picot, 2 double stitches.

For the **chain,** make 2 double stitches, 1 picot, 2 double stitches, 1 picot, 2 double stitches, 1 picot, 2 double stitches, 1 picot, 2 double stitches, 1 picot, 2 double stitches, 1 picot, 2 double stitches, 1 picot, 2 double stitches, 1 picot, 2 double stitches, 1 picot, 2 double stitches, 1 picot, 2 double stitches, 1 picot, 2 double stitches, 1 picot, 2 double stitches, 1 picot, 2 double stitches, 1 picot, 2 double stitches.

For the **third ring,** begin with 2 double stitches. Follow with 1 picot, 2 double stitches, 1 picot, 2 double stitches. Join second picot to the fifth picot in previous ring. Make 2 double stitches. Join at this point. Follow with 2 double stitches, 1 picot, 2 double stitches, 1 picot, 2 double stitches, 1 picot, 2 double stitches.

For the **chain,** start with 2 double stitches. Join picot. Make 2 double stitches. Join picot. Follow with 2 double stitches, 1 picot, 2 double stitches, 1 picot, 2 double stitches, 1 picot, 2 double stitches, 1 picot, 2 double stitches, 1 picot, 2 double stitches, 1 picot, 2 double stitches, 1 picot, 2 double stitches, 1 picot, 2 double stitches, 1 picot, 2 double stitches, 1 picot, 2 double stitches, 1 picot, 2 double stitches, 1 picot, 2 double stitches, 1 picot, 2 double stitches.

Repeat the preceding procedure until 8 outside rings and chains have been made.

## Medallion (F)

This circular motif has a scalloped edge, outlined with picots. Work with a shuttle and a second thread.

For the **first ring,** start with 2 double stitches. Follow with 1 picot, 2 double stitches, 1 picot, 2 double stitches, 1 picot, 2 double stitches, 1 picot, 2 double stitches, 1 picot, 2 double stitches, 1 picot, 2 double stitches, 1 picot, 2 double stitches, 1 picot, 2 double stitches, 1 picot, 2 double stitches, 1 picot, 2 double stitches, 1 picot, 2 double stitches, 1 picot, 2 double stitches.

For the **chain,** make 2 double stitches. Follow with 1 picot, 2 double stitches, 1 picot, 2 double stitches, 1 picot, 2 double stitches, 1 picot, 2 double stitches, 1 picot, 2 double stitches, 1 picot, 2 double stitches, 1 picot, 2 double stitches, 1 picot, 2 double stitches, 1 picot, 2 double stitches, 1 picot, 2 double stitches.

For the **second ring,** start with 2 double stitches. Follow with 1 picot, 2 double stitches, 1 picot, 2 double stitches, 1 picot, 2 double stitches. Then join ring to tenth ring of preceding ring. Follow with 2 double stitches, 1 picot, 2 double stitches, 1 picot, 2 double stitches, 1 picot, 2 double stitches, 1 picot, 2 double stitches, 1 picot, 2 double stitches, 1 picot, 2 double stitches, 1 picot, 2 double stitches, 1 picot, 2 double stitches.

For the **chain,** make 2 double stitches. Follow with 1 picot, 2 double stitches, 1 picot, 2 double stitches, 1 picot, 2 double stitches, 1 picot, 2 double stitches, 1 picot, 2 double stitches, 1 picot, 2 double stitches, 1 picot, 2 double stitches, 1 picot, 2 double stitches, 1 picot, 2 double stitches, 1 picot, 2 double stitches.

Repeat the preceding procedure until 9 rings and 9 chains have been made.

# Bibliography

In preparing a book, one always peruses the works of other authors. I found the books and booklets listed here filled with information and inspiration. I am sure you will also.

**General**
Clabburn, Pamela. *The Needleworker's Dictionary.* William Morrow and Company, 1976.
Coats & Clark. *Learn How Book—No. 170-C.* Coats & Clark, 1975.
Guild, Vera P. *Good Housekeeping New Complete Book of Needlecraft.* Hearst Corporation, 1971.
Editors of McCall's Needlework and Crafts Magazine. *McCall's Needlework Treasury.* Random House/McCall's, 1964.
Th. de Dillmont. *The Complete Encyclopedia of Needlework.* Running Press, 1972.


**Crocheting**
Aytes, Barbara. *Adventures in Crocheting.* Doubleday & Company, 1972.
Blackwell, Liz. *A Treasury of Crochet Patterns.* Charles Scribner's Sons, 1971.
Coats & Clark. *Learn to Crochet—No. 210 A.* Coats & Clark. 1974.
———. *Hairpin Lace—No. 235.* Coats & Clark, 1974.
Dawson, Mary M. *Crochet Stitches.* Crown Publishers, 1972.
Feldman, Annette. *Crochet and Creative Design.* Harper and Row, 1973.
Mon Tricot. *Knitting Dictionary, Stitches, Patterns.* Crown Publishers.
Star Book. No. 209. *Let's Crochet.* American Thread Company.
Taylor, Gertrude. *America's Crochet Book.* Charles Scribner's Sons, 1972.


**Embroidering**
Ambuter, Carolyn. *Needlepoint Celebrations.* Workman Publishing Company, 1976.
Bucher, Jo. *Complete Guide to Creative Needlepoint.* Meredith Corporation, 1973.

Coats & Clark. *Needlepoint Stitches—No. 226-A.* Coats & Clark, 1974.
_____. *One Hundred Embroidery Stitches.* Coats and Clark, 1975.
Coats, J. & P. *100 Embroidery Stitches.* Charles Scribner's Sons, 1967.
Dawson, Barbara. *Metal Thread Embroidery.* Watson Guptill Publications, 1976.
D.M.C. Corporation. *Machine Embroidery.* Distributed by William E. Wright Company, 1976.
Donnelly, B. H., and Gullers, K. W. *The Crewel Needlepoint World.* Morgan and Morgan, 1973.
Fanning, Robbie. *Decorative Machine Stitchery.* Butterick Publishing, 1976.
Gostelow, Mary. *A World of Embroidery.* Charles Scribner's Sons, 1975.
Gray, Jennifer. *Machine Embroidery.* Van Nostrand Reinhold Company, 1973.
Hanley, Hope. *The ABC's of Needlepoint.* Charles Scribner's Sons, 1973.
_____. *Patterns for Needlepoint.* Charles Scribner's Sons, 1976.
Kaestner, Dorothy. *Four Way Bargello.* Charles Scribner's Sons, 1974.
McNeill, Moyra. *Pulled Thread Embroidery.* Taplinger Publishing Co., 1972.
Myers, Carole Robbins. *A Primer of Left-handed Embroidery.* Charles Scribner's Sons, 1974.
Nordfors, Jill Denny. *Needle Lace and Needleweaving.* Van Nostrand Reinhold Company, 1974.
Perrone, Lisbeth. *The New World of Crewel.* Random House, 1975.
Rush, Beverly. *The Stitchery Idea Book.* Van Nostrand Reinhold Company, 1974.
Slater, Elaine. *The New York Times Book of Needlepoint for Left-Handers.* Quadrangle/New York Times, 1974.
Thomas, Mary. *Dictionary of Embroidery Stitches.* William Morrow and Company, 1935.
Editors of Time-Life Books. *Decorative Techniques.* Time-Life Books, 1975.
Wilson, Erica. *Embroidery.* Charles Scribner's Sons, 1973.

## Knitting
Abbey, Barbara. *The Complete Book of Knitting.* The Viking Press, 1974.
Aytes, Barbara. *Adventures in Knitting.* Doubleday & Company, 1968.
Coats & Clark. *Learn to Knit—No. 190-A.* Coats and Clark, 1975.
Mon Tricot. *Knit and Crochet.* Crown Publishers.
_____. *Knitting Dictionary, Stitches, Patterns.* Crown Publishers.
Norbury, James. *Traditional Knitting Patterns.* Dover Publications, 1973.
Thomas, Mary. *Book of Knitting Patterns.* Dover Publications, 1972. This Dover edition is an unabridged republication of the work originally published in 1943 by Hodder and Stoughton, London.
_____. *Knitting Book.* Dover Publications, 1972. This Dover edition is an unabridged republication of the work orginally published in 1938 by Hodder and Stoughton, London.
Taylor, Gertrude. *America's Knitting Book.* Charles Scribner's Sons, 1974.

**Macramé**

Andes, Eugene. *Practical Macramé.* Van Nostrand, Reinhold Co., 1971.

Brass, Helene. *The Macramé Book.* Charles Scribner's Sons, 1972.

Editors of McCall's Needlework and Crafts Magazine. *McCall's Macramé.* The McCall Pattern Company, 1972.

Meilach, Dona Z. *Macramé: Creative Design in Knotting.* Crown Publishers, 1971.

Phillips, Mary Walker. *Step-by-Step Macramé.* Golden Press, 1970.
*Vogue Guide to Macramé.* Stein and Day Publishers in Association with the Condé Nast Publications, 1973.

Walker, Louisa. *Graded Lessons in Macramé, Knotting and Netting.* Dover Publications, 1971.

Weber, Betty, and Singleton, Mary. *Simply Macramé.* Printed in the United States, 1971.

**Rug Making**

Marein, Shirley. *Creating Rugs and Wall Hangings.* Viking Press, 1975.

Editors of McCall's Needlework and Crafts. *McCall's Rugmaking.* The McCall Pattern Co., 1974.

**Sewing**

*Coats & Clark's Sewing Book.* Coats & Clark, printed in U.S.A. by Western Publishing Company, 1976.

Echols, Margit. *The New American Quilt.* Doubleday & Company, 1976.

Hutton, Jessie, and Cunningham, Gladys. *Singer Sewing Book.* The Singer Company, 1972.

Editors of the McCall's Needlework and Crafts Publication. *The McCall's Book of Quilts.* Simon & Schuster/The McCall Pattern Company, 1975.

*McCall's Sewing Book.* Random House/McCall's, 1968.

Newman, Thelma R. *Quilting, Patchwork, Appliqué and Trapunto* Crown Publishers, 1974.

**Tatting**

Auld, Rhoda L. *Tatting.* Van Nostrand, Reinhold Company, 1974.

Coats & Clark. *Learn to Tat—No. 240.* Coats & Clark, 1974.